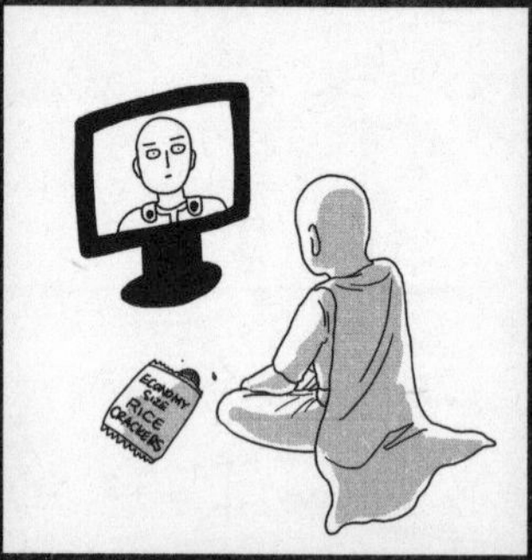
ECONOMY SIZE RICE CRACKERS

O N E

Thanks to everyone, this is going to be an anime. Isn't that great, Mr. Saitama?

—ONE

Manga creator ONE began *One-Punch Man* as a webcomic, which quickly went viral, garnering over 10 million hits. In addition to *One-Punch Man*, ONE writes and draws the series *Mob Psycho 100* and *Makai no Ossan*.

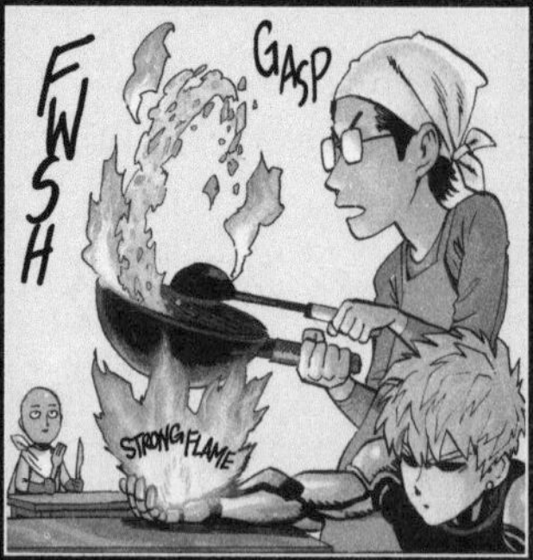
FWSH
GASP
STRONG FLAME

Y U S U K E M U R A T A

I wanna write a cookbook.

—Yusuke Murata

A highly decorated and skilled artist best known for his work on *Eyeshield 21*, Yusuke Murata won the 122nd Hop Step Award (1995) for *Partner* and placed second in the 51st Akatsuka Award (1998) for *Samui Hanashi*.

ONE-PUNCH MAN 08

ONE + YUSUKE MURATA

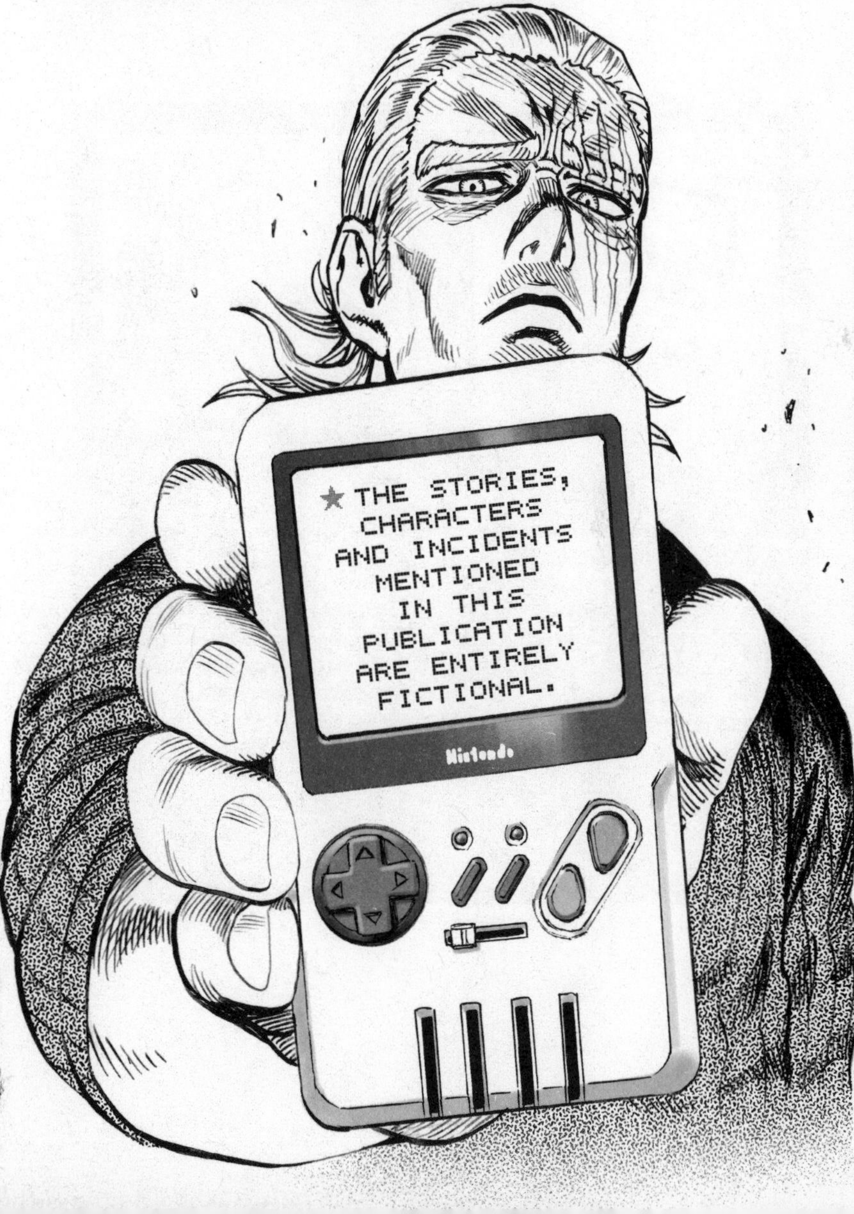
★ THE STORIES, CHARACTERS AND INCIDENTS MENTIONED IN THIS PUBLICATION ARE ENTIRELY FICTIONAL.

ONE-PUNCH MAN 08

STORY BY
ONE

ART BY
YUSUKE MURATA

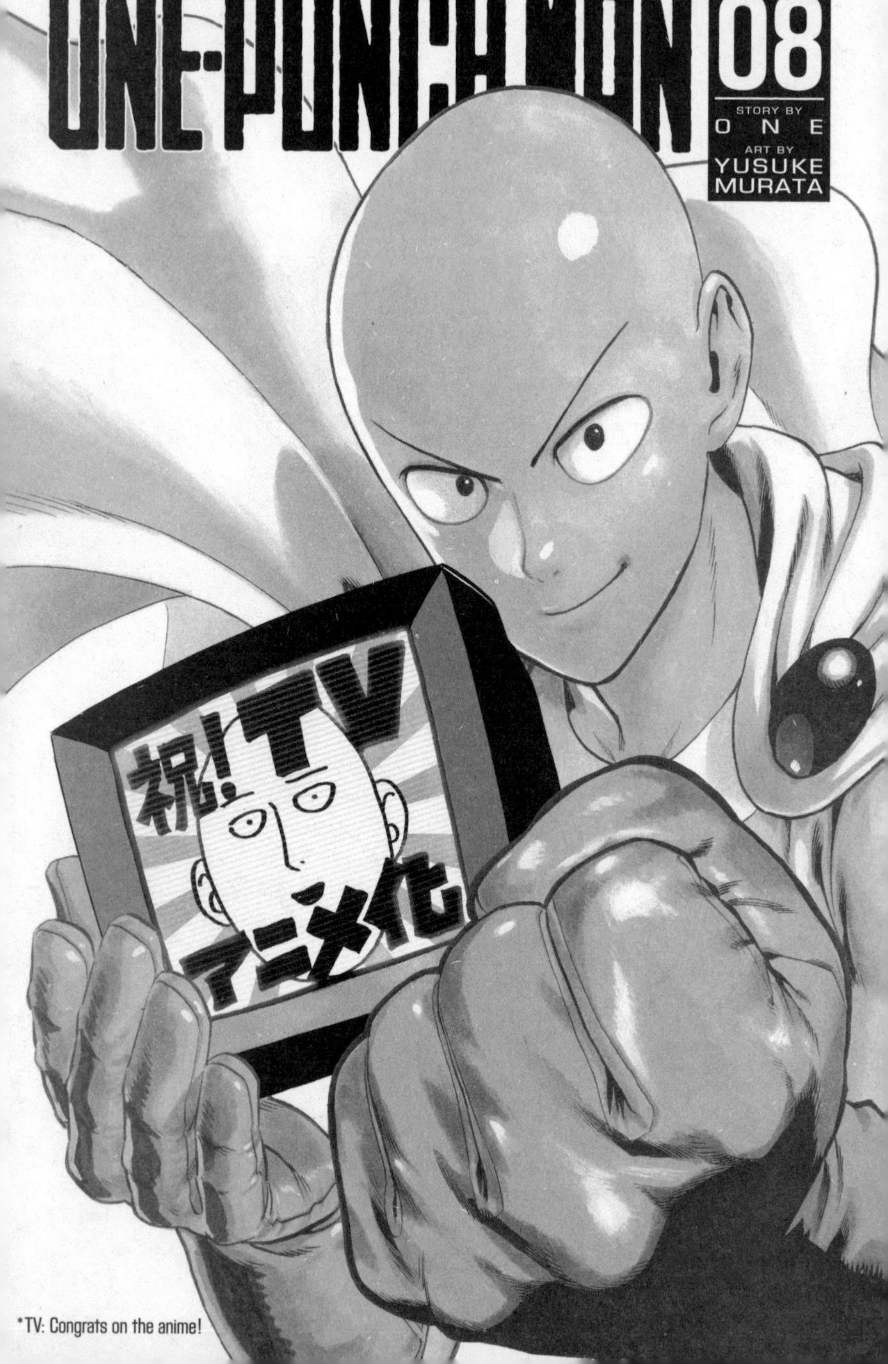
祝！TV
アニメ化

*TV: Congrats on the anime!

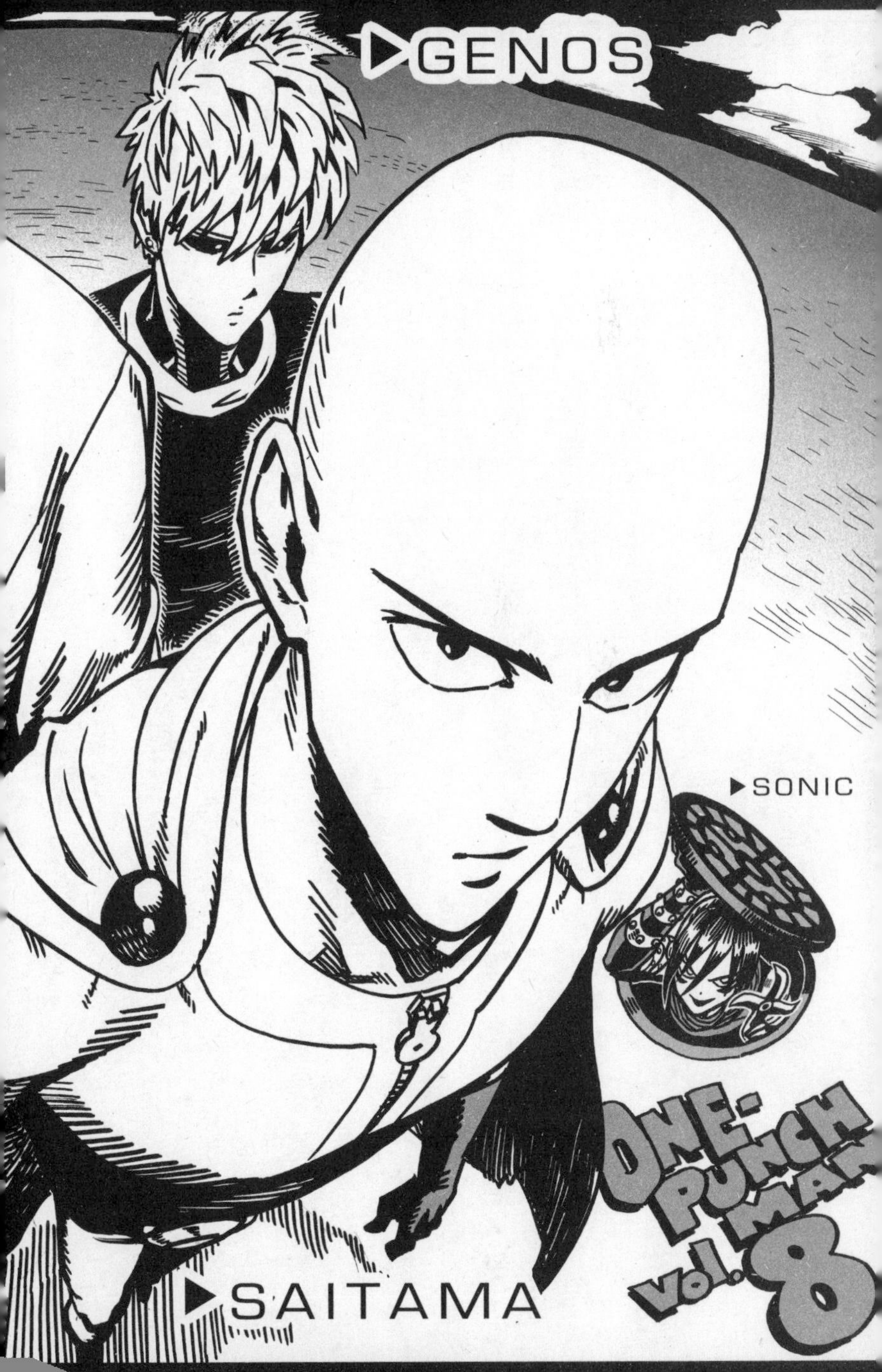
GENOS
SONIC
SAITAMA
ONE-PUNCH MAN
vol. 8

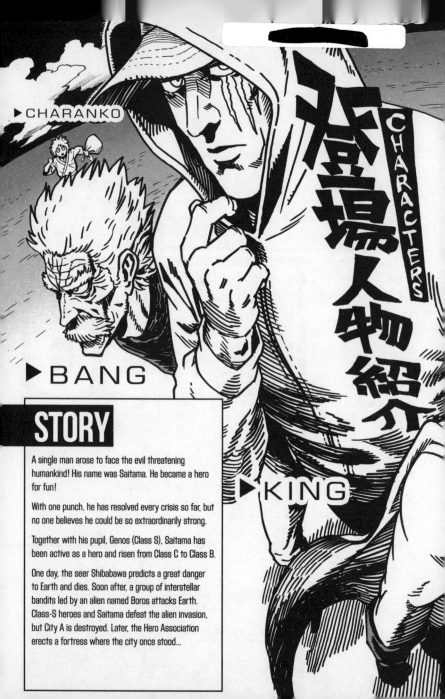

[redacted]

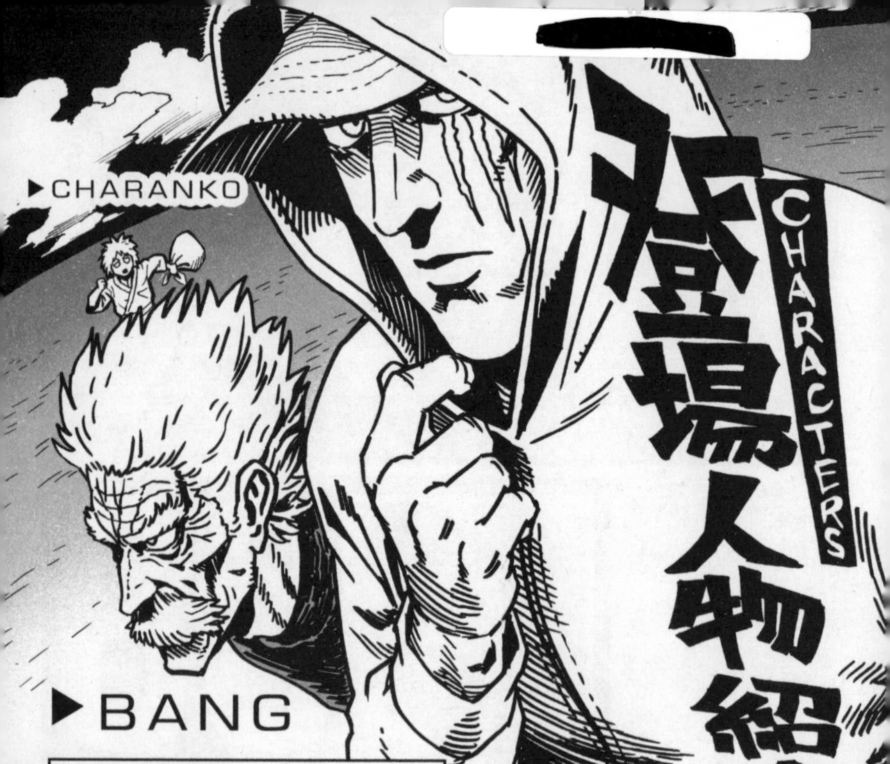

登場人物紹介
CHARACTERS
▶CHARANKO
▶BANG
▶KING

STORY

A single man arose to face the evil threatening humankind! His name was Saitama. He became a hero for fun!

With one punch, he has resolved every crisis so far, but no one believes he could be so extraordinarily strong.

Together with his pupil, Genos (Class S), Saitama has been active as a hero and risen from Class C to Class B.

One day, the seer Shibabawa predicts a great danger to Earth and dies. Soon after, a group of interstellar bandits led by an alien named Boros attacks Earth. Class-S heroes and Saitama defeat the alien invasion, but City A is destroyed. Later, the Hero Association erects a fortress where the city once stood...

RANKING
RANK NAME SCORE
1st KNG 9999999
2nd TBL 6871825
3rd OF 6623780
4th CON 5932200

CONTENTS

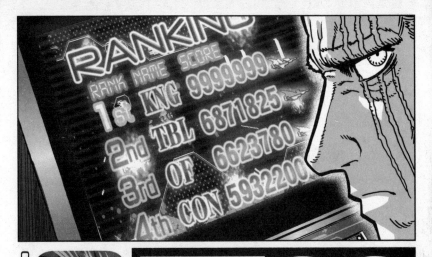

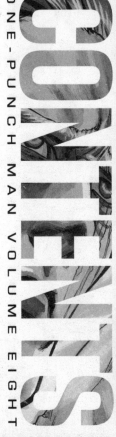

ONE-PUNCH MAN VOLUME EIGHT

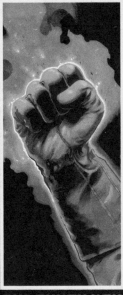

ONE-PUNCH MAN

ONE + YUSUKE MURATA

My name is Saitama. I am a hero. My hobby is heroic exploits. I got too strong. And that makes me sad. I can defeat any enemy with one blow. I lost my hair. And I lost all feeling. I want to feel the rush of battle. I would like to meet an incredibly strong enemy. And I would like to defeat it with one blow. That's because I am One-Punch Man.

08

THAT MAN

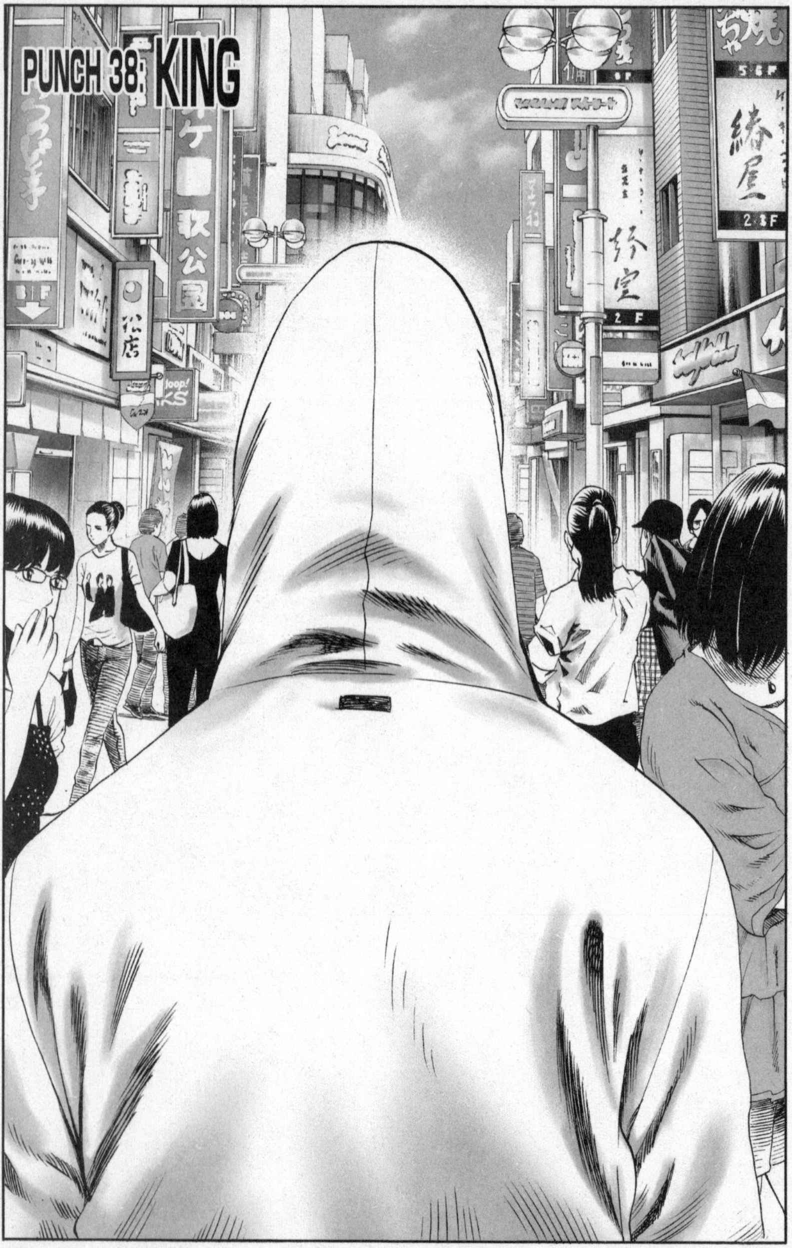
PUNCH 38: KING

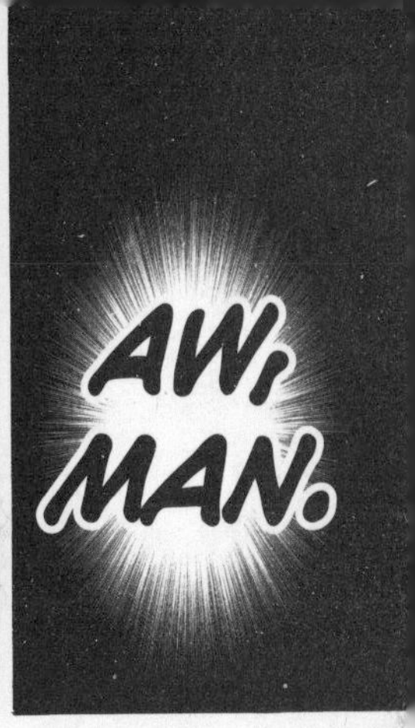
AW, MAN.
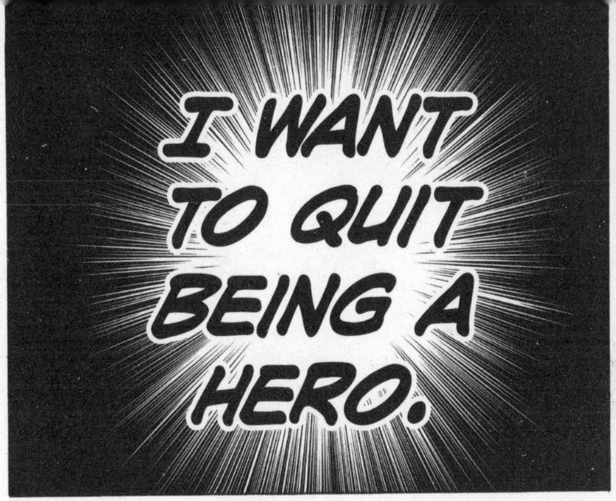
I WANT TO QUIT BEING A HERO.
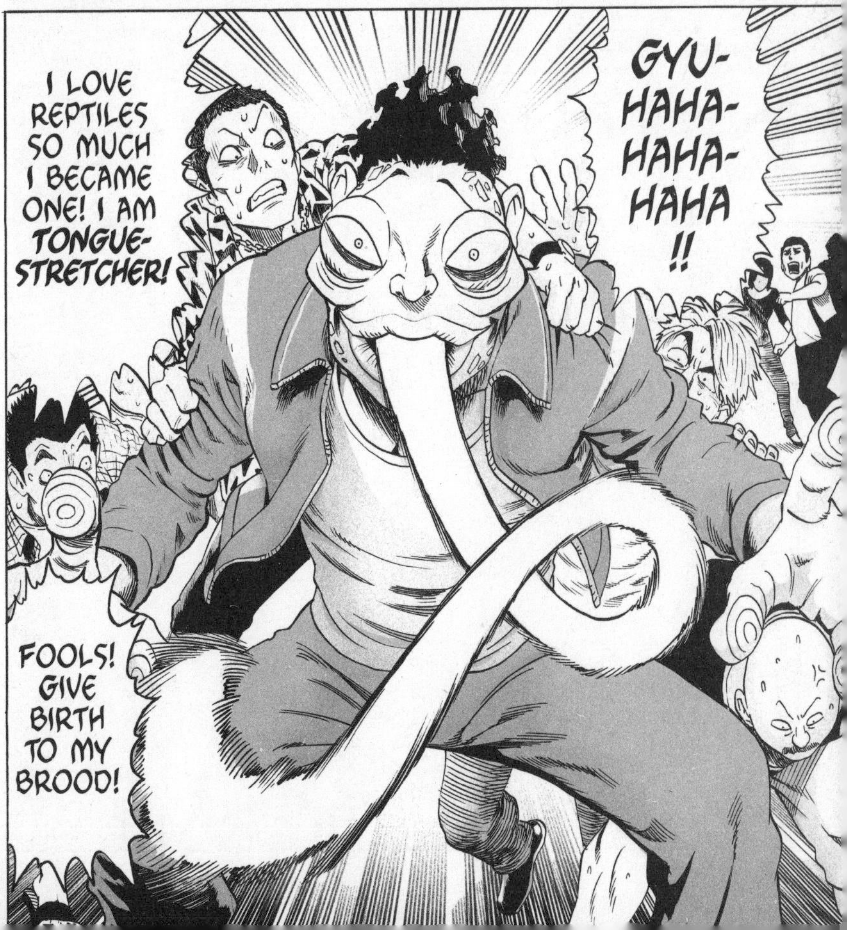
GYU-HAHA-HAHA-HAHA!!
I LOVE REPTILES SO MUCH I BECAME ONE! I AM TONGUE-STRETCHER!
FOOLS! GIVE BIRTH TO MY BROOD!

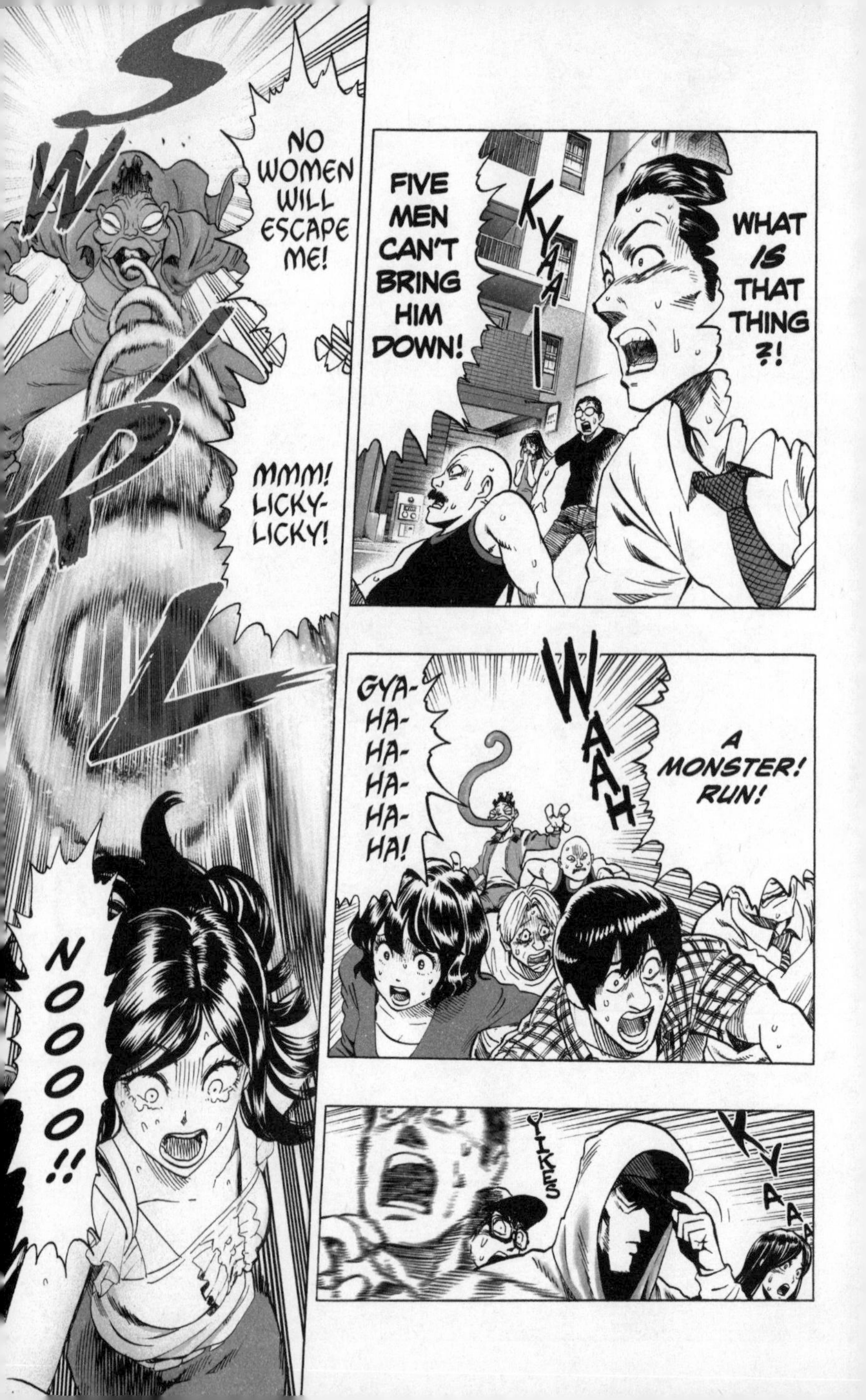
WHAT IS THAT THING?!
KYAAI
FIVE MEN CAN'T BRING HIM DOWN!
A MONSTER! RUN!
WAAH
GYA-HA-HA-HA-HA-HA-HA!
KYAAA
YIKES
NO WOMEN WILL ESCAPE ME!
MMM! LICKY-LICKY!
NOOOOO!!

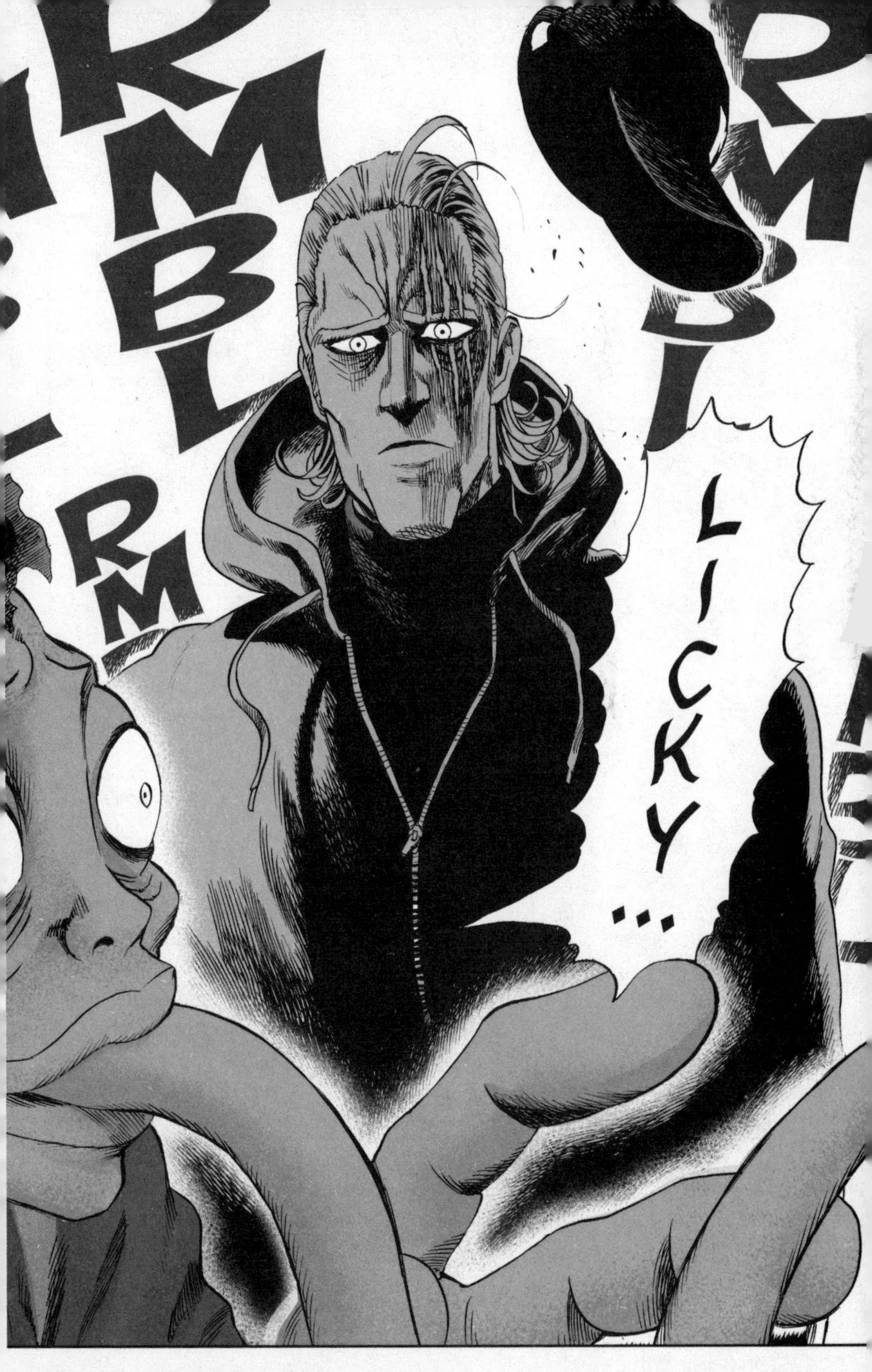
RMBL
LICKY...
RMBL
RM

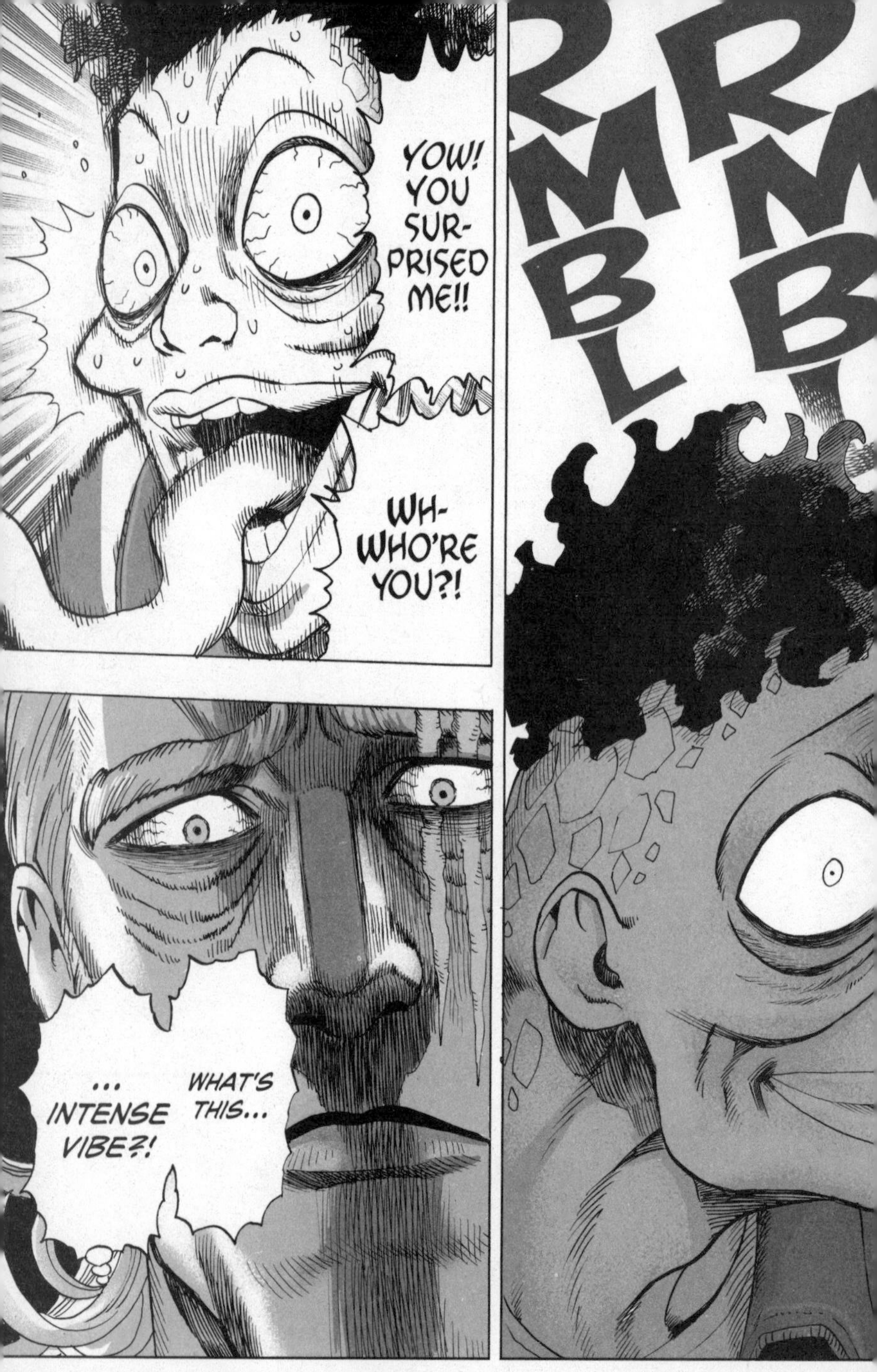
RMB
RMBL
YOW! YOU SURPRISED ME!!
WH-WHO'RE YOU?!
WHAT'S THIS... ...INTENSE VIBE?!

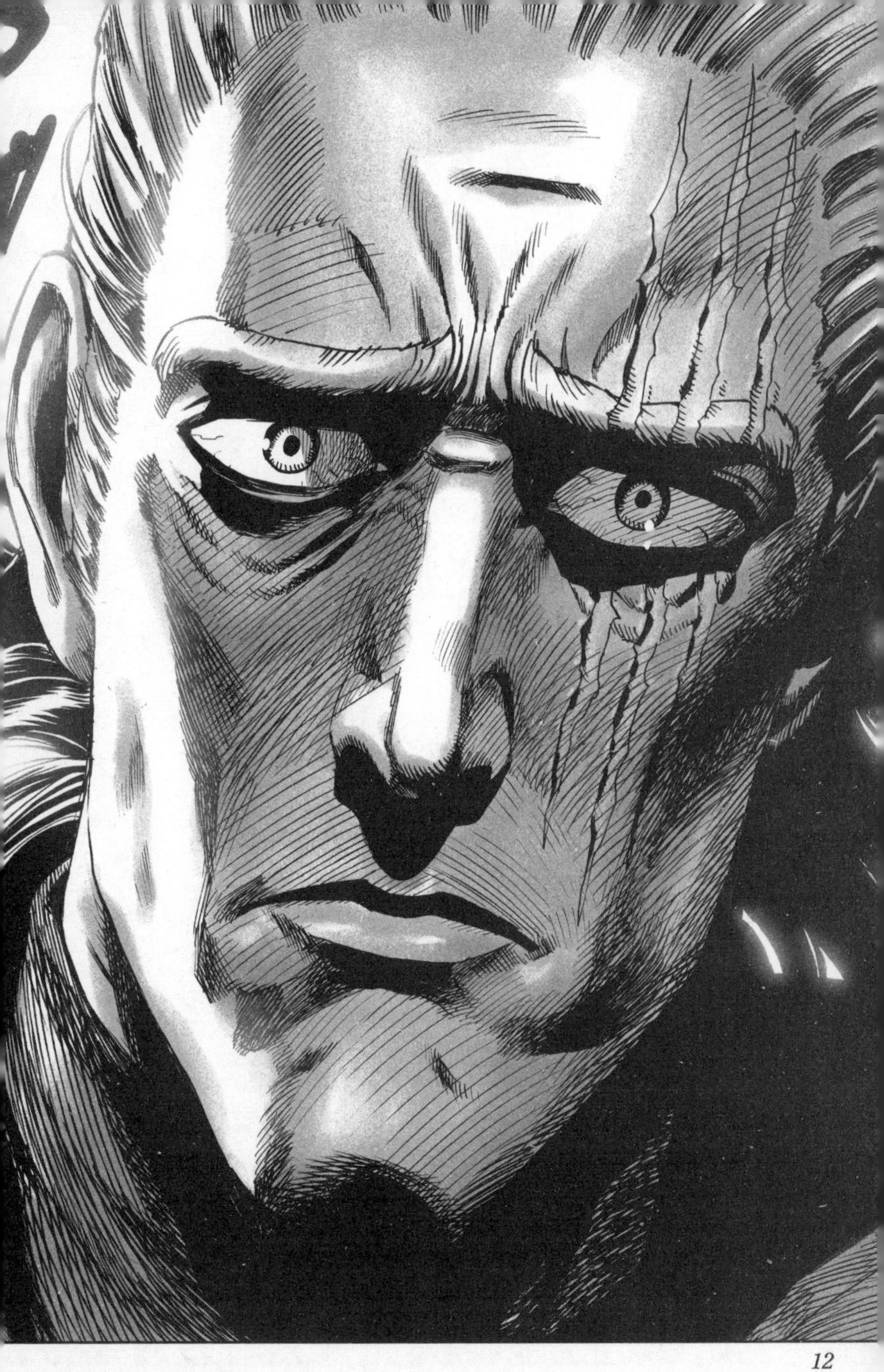

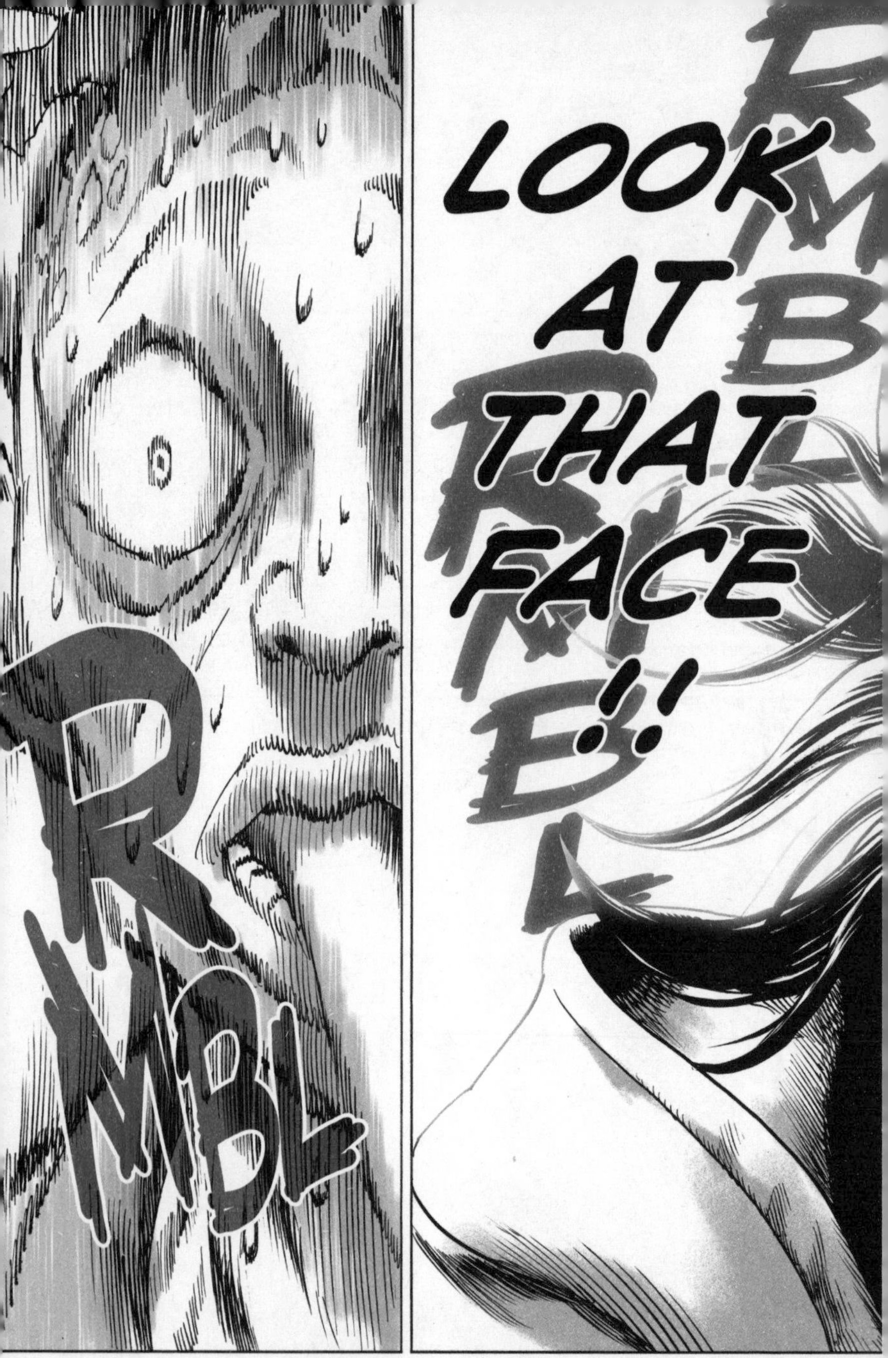
LOOK AT THAT FACE!!
RMBL
RMBL
RMBL

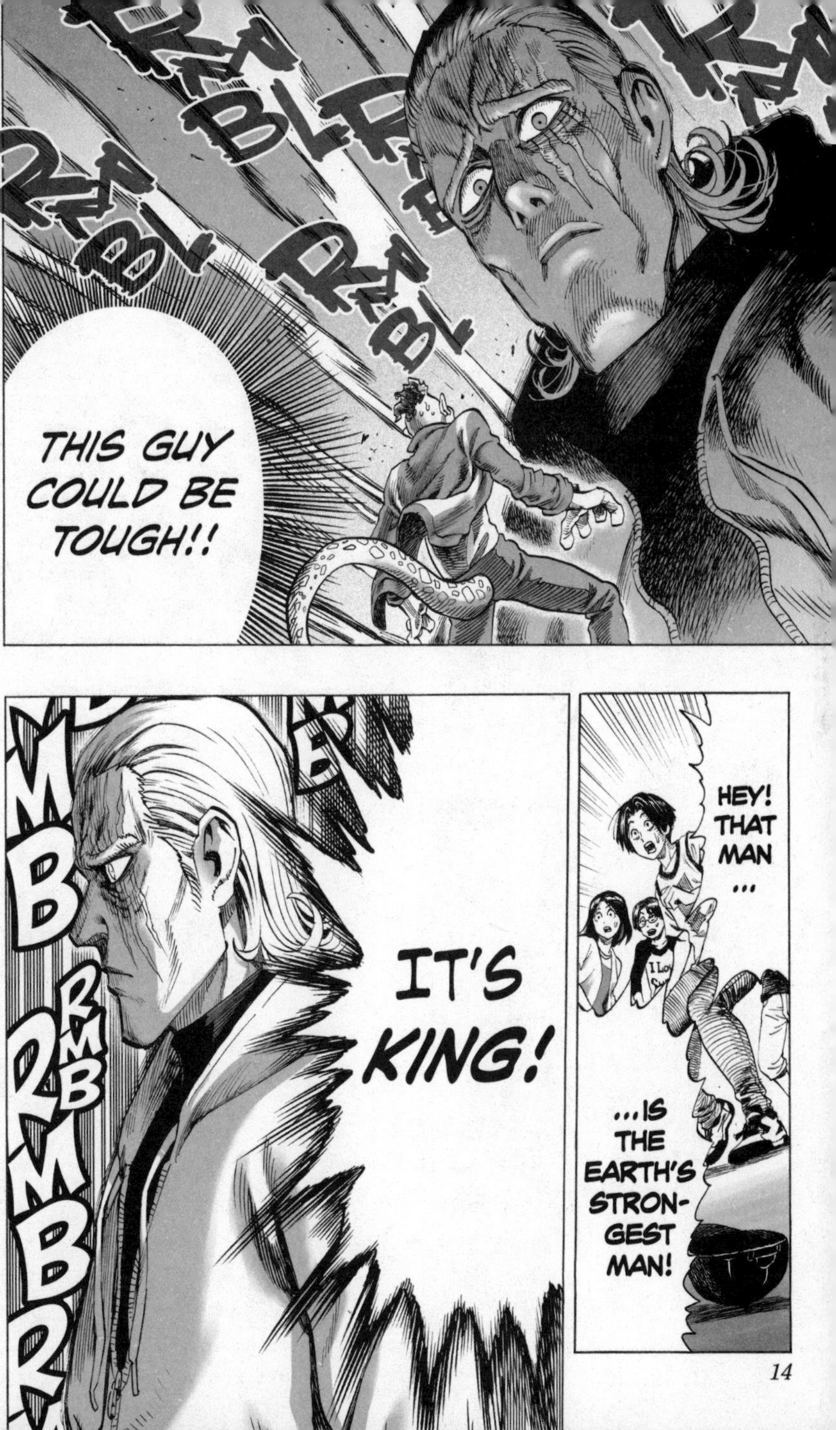
THIS GUY COULD BE TOUGH!!
HEY! THAT MAN ...
...IS THE EARTH'S STRON-GEST MAN!
IT'S KING!

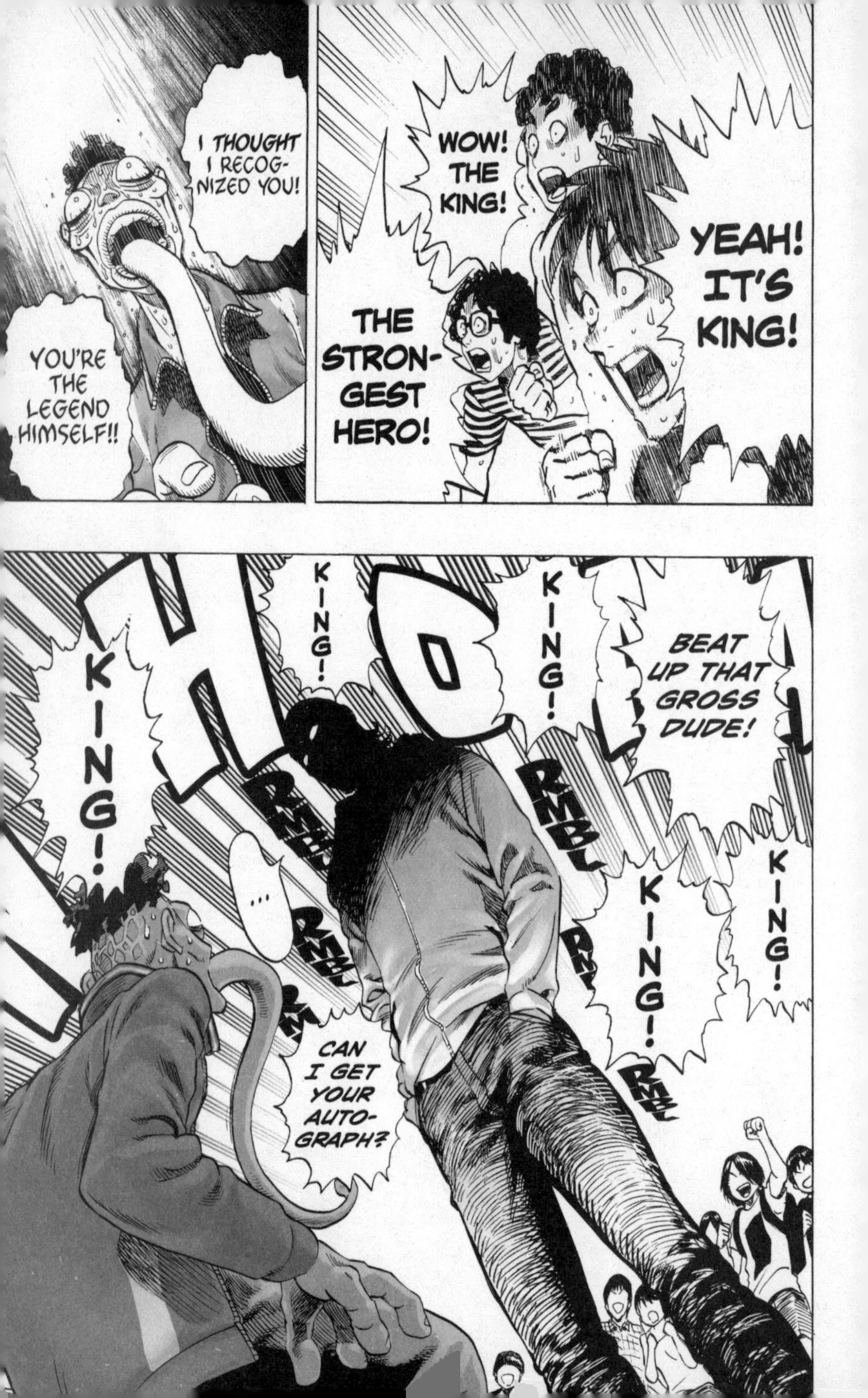

WOW! THE KING!
YEAH! IT'S KING!
THE STRONGEST HERO!
I THOUGHT I RECOGNIZED YOU!
YOU'RE THE LEGEND HIMSELF!!
BEAT UP THAT GROSS DUDE!
KING!
KING!
KING!
RMBL
RMBL
KING!
RMBL
RMBL
KING!
...
CAN I GET YOUR AUTOGRAPH?

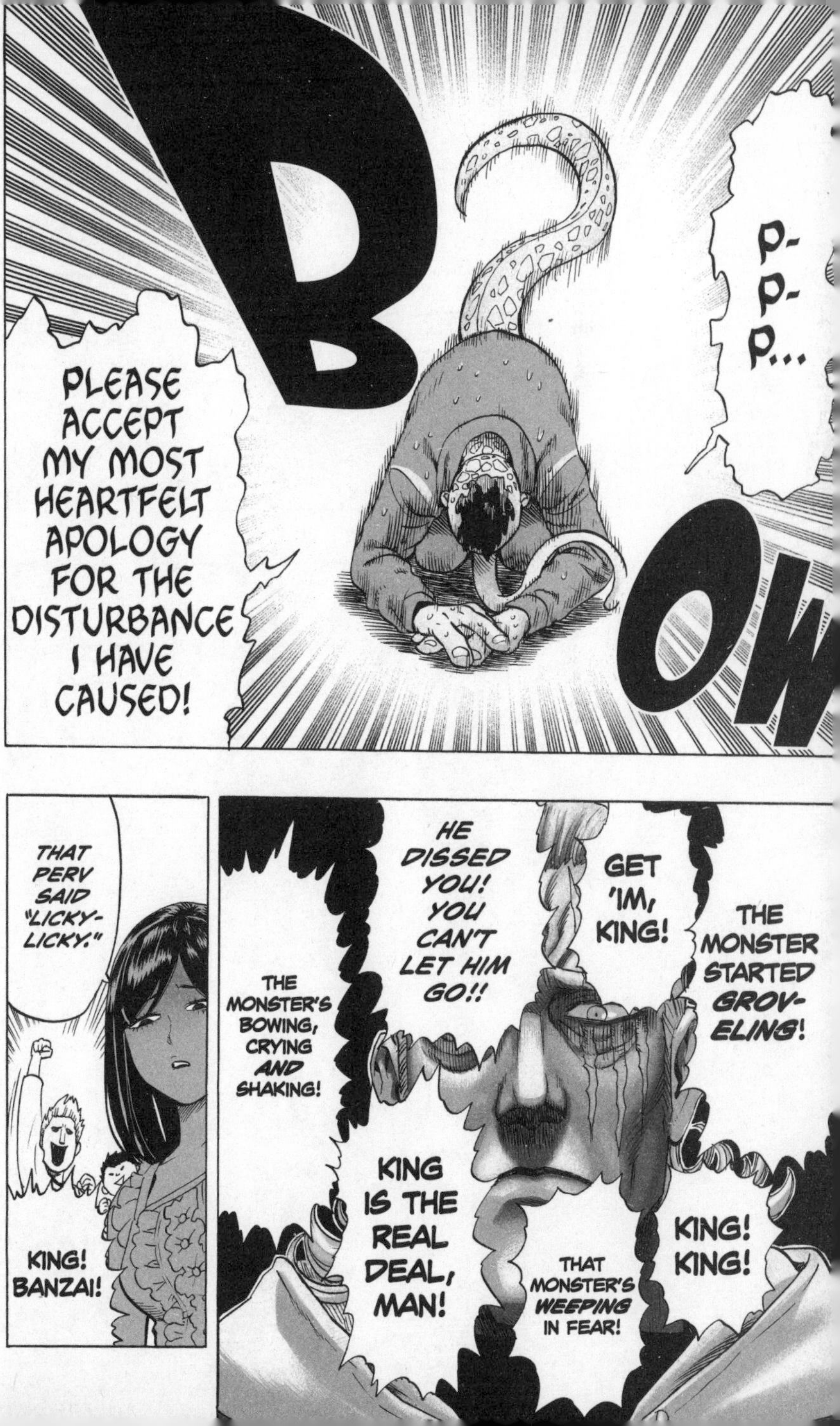
P-
P-
P...
BOW
PLEASE ACCEPT MY MOST HEARTFELT APOLOGY FOR THE DISTURBANCE I HAVE CAUSED!
THE MONSTER STARTED GROVELING!
GET 'IM, KING!
HE DISSED YOU! YOU CAN'T LET HIM GO!!
THE MONSTER'S BOWING, CRYING AND SHAKING!
KING! KING!
THAT MONSTER'S WEEPING IN FEAR!
KING IS THE REAL DEAL, MAN!
THAT PERV SAID "LICKY-LICKY."
KING! BANZAI!

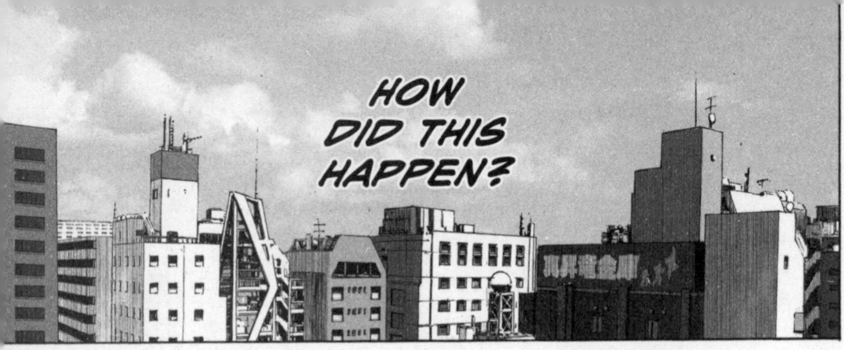
HOW DID THIS HAPPEN?

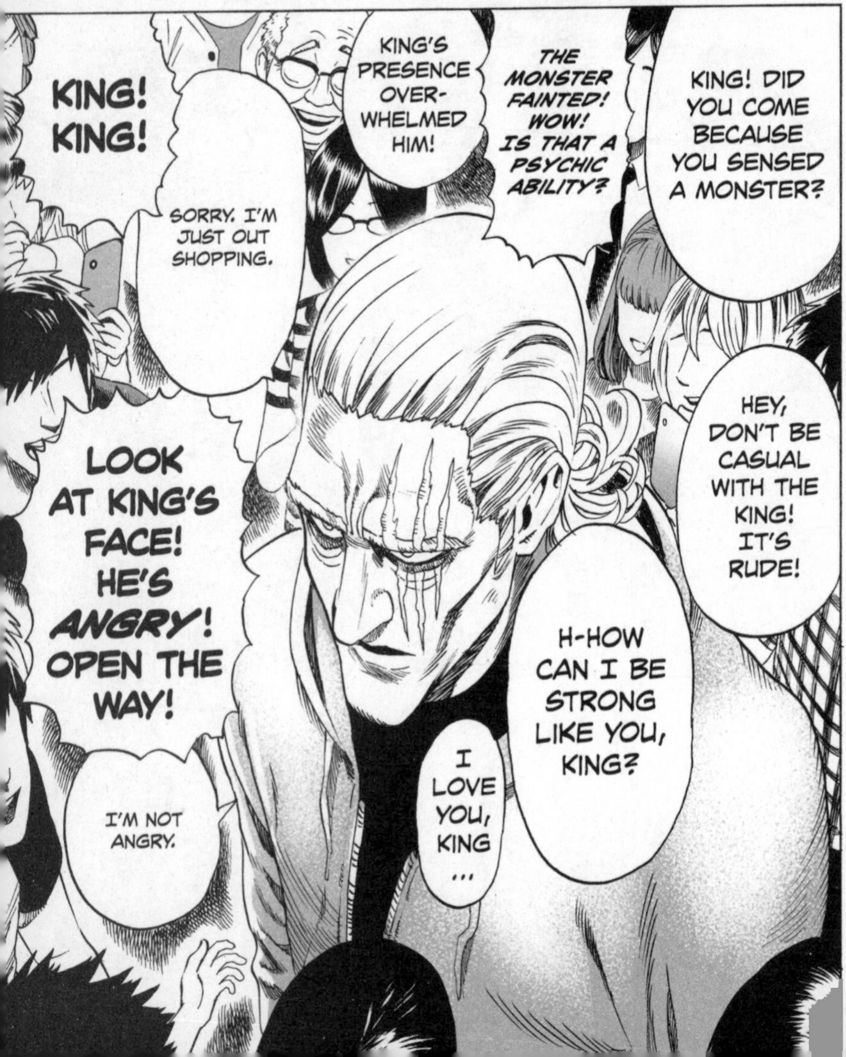
KING! DID YOU COME BECAUSE YOU SENSED A MONSTER?
THE MONSTER FAINTED! WOW! IS THAT A PSYCHIC ABILITY?
KING'S PRESENCE OVER-WHELMED HIM!
KING! KING!
SORRY. I'M JUST OUT SHOPPING.
HEY, DON'T BE CASUAL WITH THE KING! IT'S RUDE!
H-HOW CAN I BE STRONG LIKE YOU, KING?
I LOVE YOU, KING ...
LOOK AT KING'S FACE! HE'S ANGRY! OPEN THE WAY!
I'M NOT ANGRY.

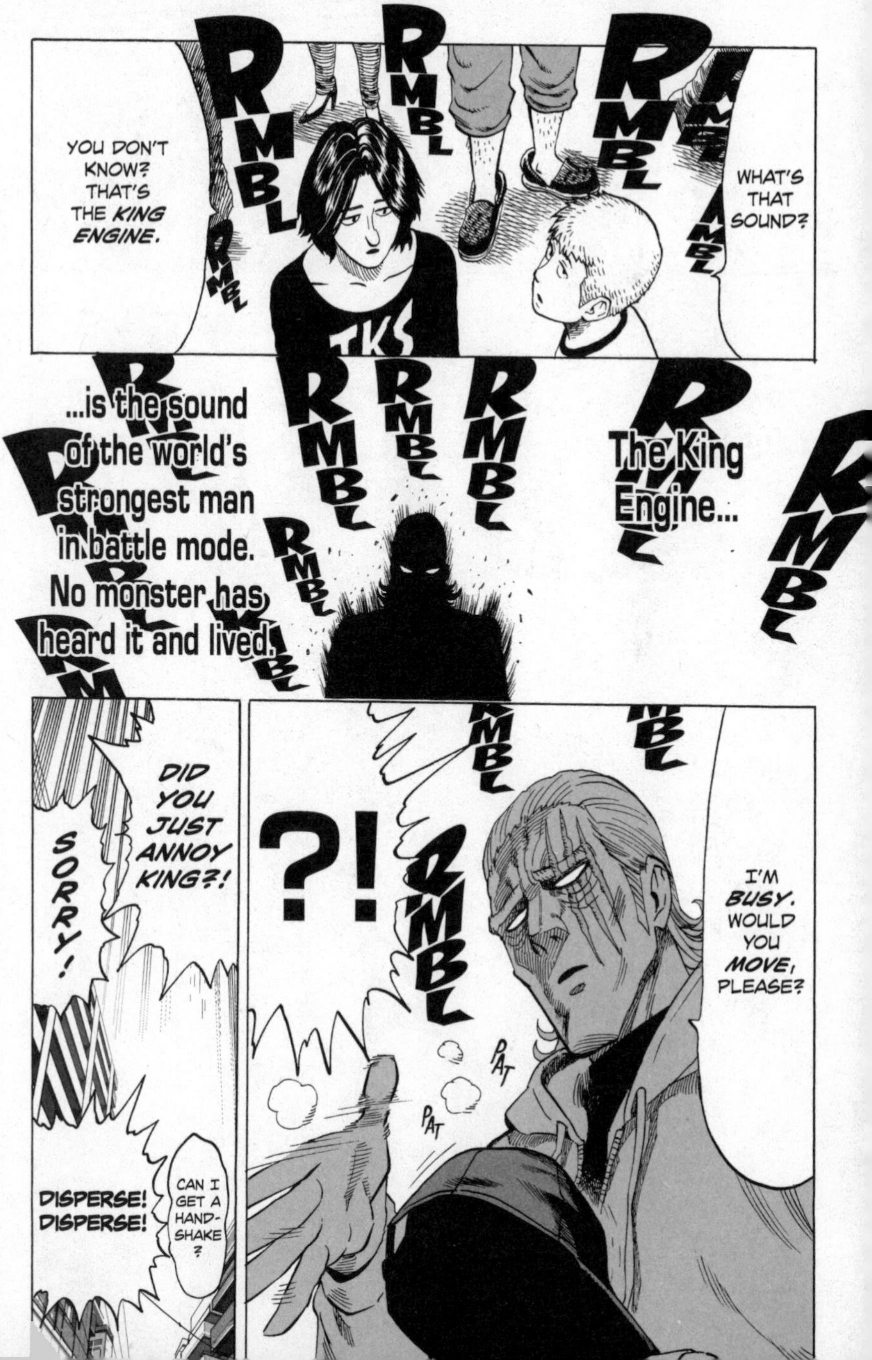
RMBL
WHAT'S THAT SOUND?
YOU DON'T KNOW? THAT'S THE KING ENGINE.
The King Engine...
...is the sound of the world's strongest man in battle mode. No monster has heard it and lived.
RMBL
I'M BUSY. WOULD YOU MOVE, PLEASE?
PAT
PAT
?!
DID YOU JUST ANNOY KING?!
SORRY!
CAN I GET A HANDSHAKE?
DISPERSE! DISPERSE!

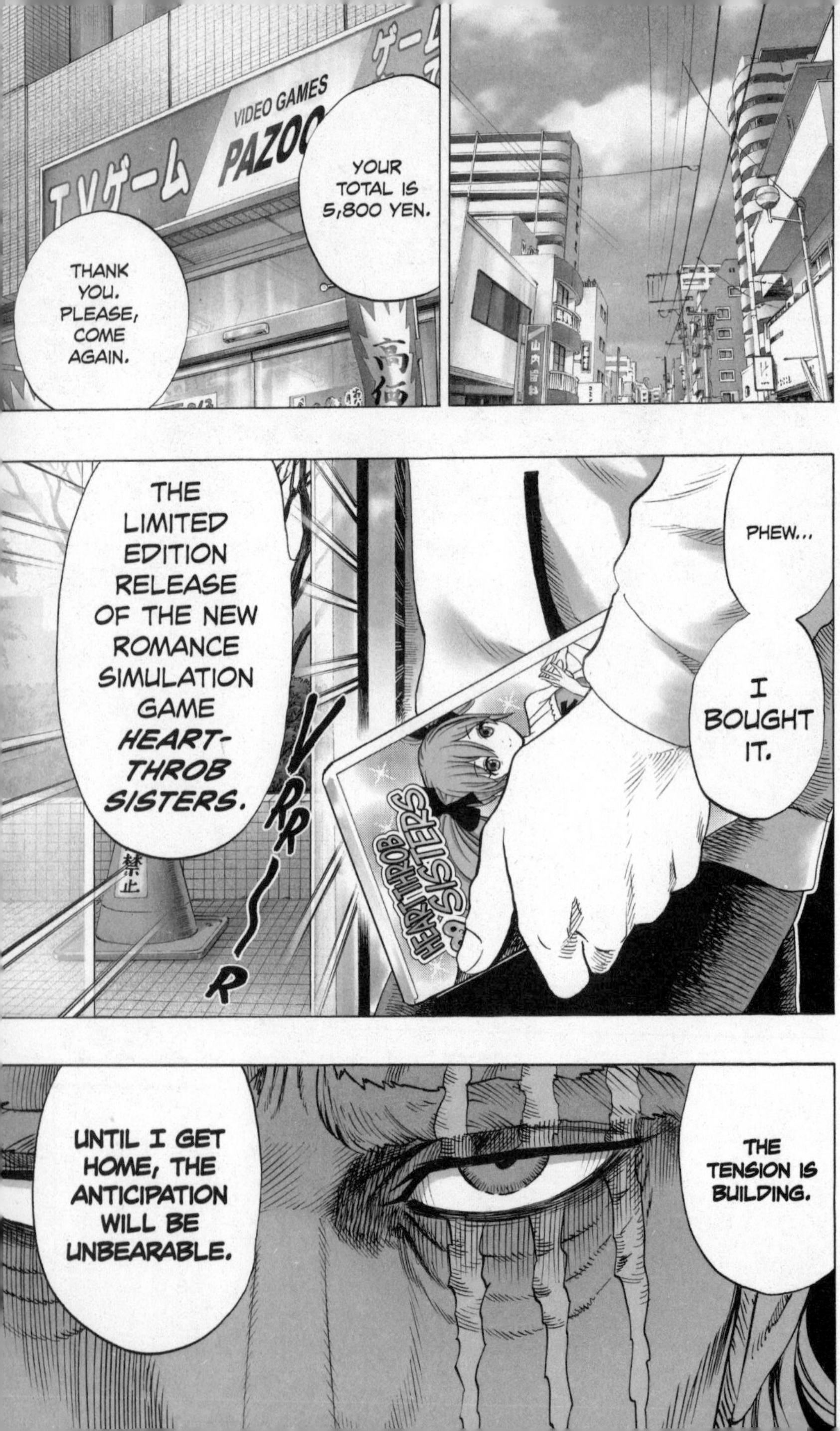
VIDEO GAMES
TVゲーム
YOUR TOTAL IS 5,800 YEN.
THANK YOU. PLEASE, COME AGAIN.
PHEW...
I BOUGHT IT.
THE LIMITED EDITION RELEASE OF THE NEW ROMANCE SIMULATION GAME *HEART-THROB SISTERS*.
VRRR——R
HEARTTHROB SISTERS
THE TENSION IS BUILDING.
UNTIL I GET HOME, THE ANTICIPATION WILL BE UNBEARABLE.

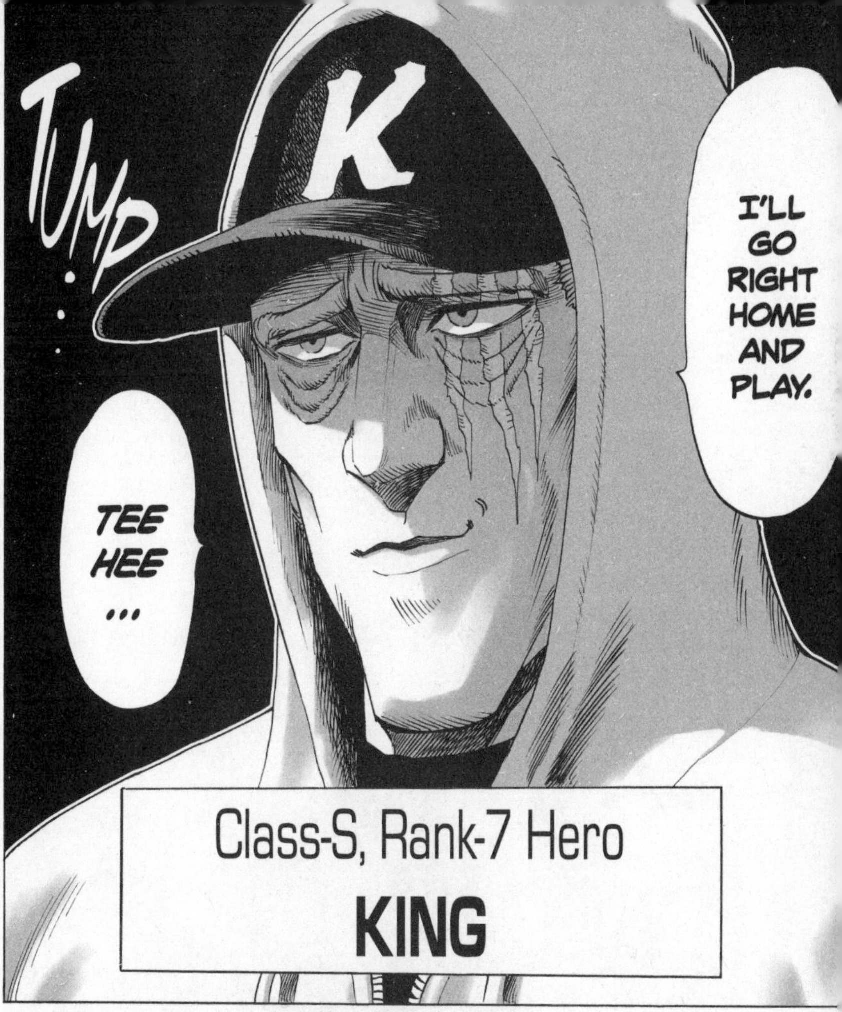
I'LL GO RIGHT HOME AND PLAY.
TUMP
TEE HEE ...
Class-S, Rank-7 Hero
KING

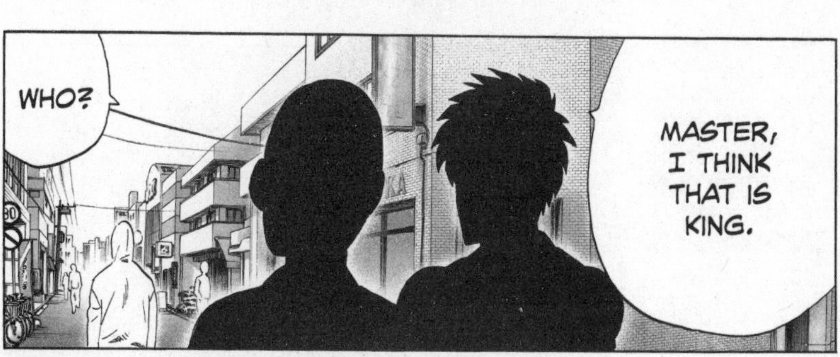
MASTER, I THINK THAT IS KING.
WHO?

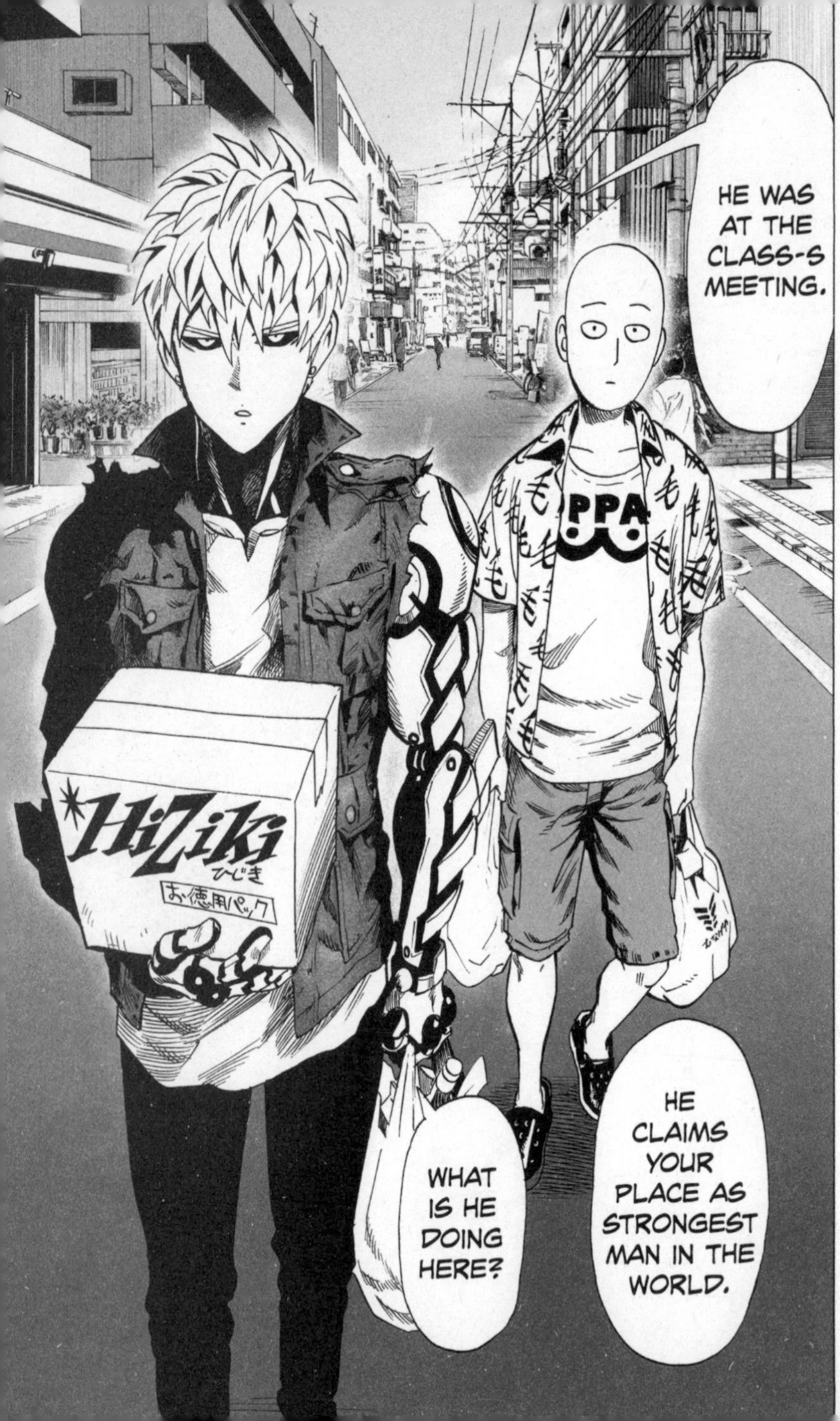
HE WAS AT THE CLASS-S MEETING.
PPA
HiZiKi
ひじき
お徳用パック
HE CLAIMS YOUR PLACE AS STRONGEST MAN IN THE WORLD.
WHAT IS HE DOING HERE?

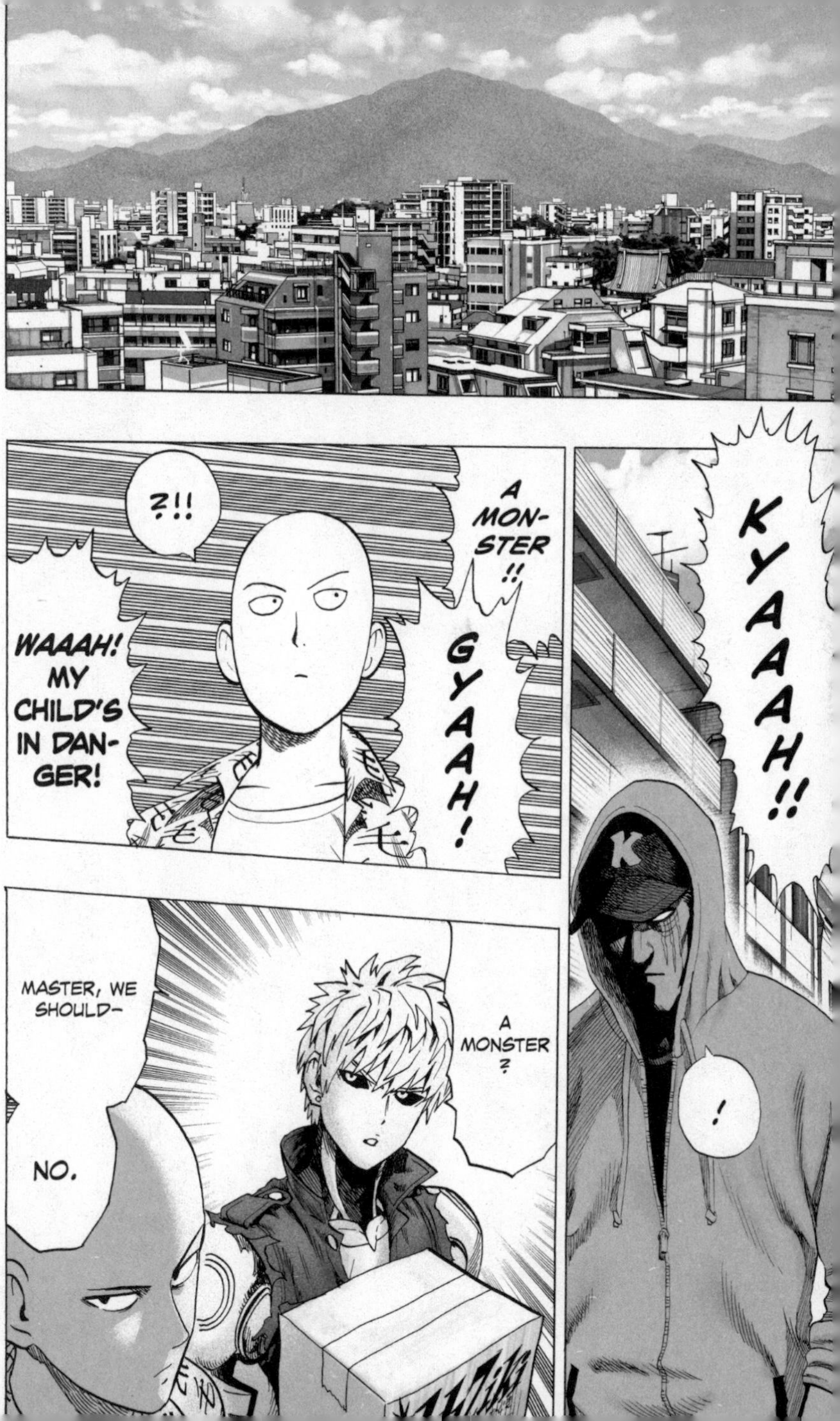
KYAAAAH!!
!
A MON-STER!!
GYAAAH!
?!!
WAAAH! MY CHILD'S IN DAN-GER!
A MONSTER?
MASTER, WE SHOULD-
NO.

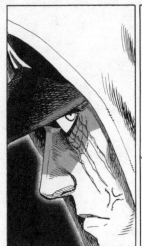

LET US WATCH!

THIS IS A GOOD OPPORTUNITY TO SEE KING'S ABILITY.

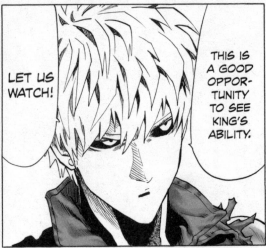

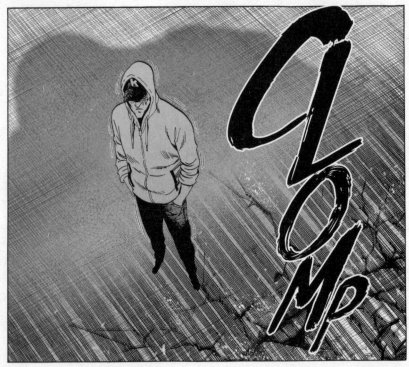

GLOMP

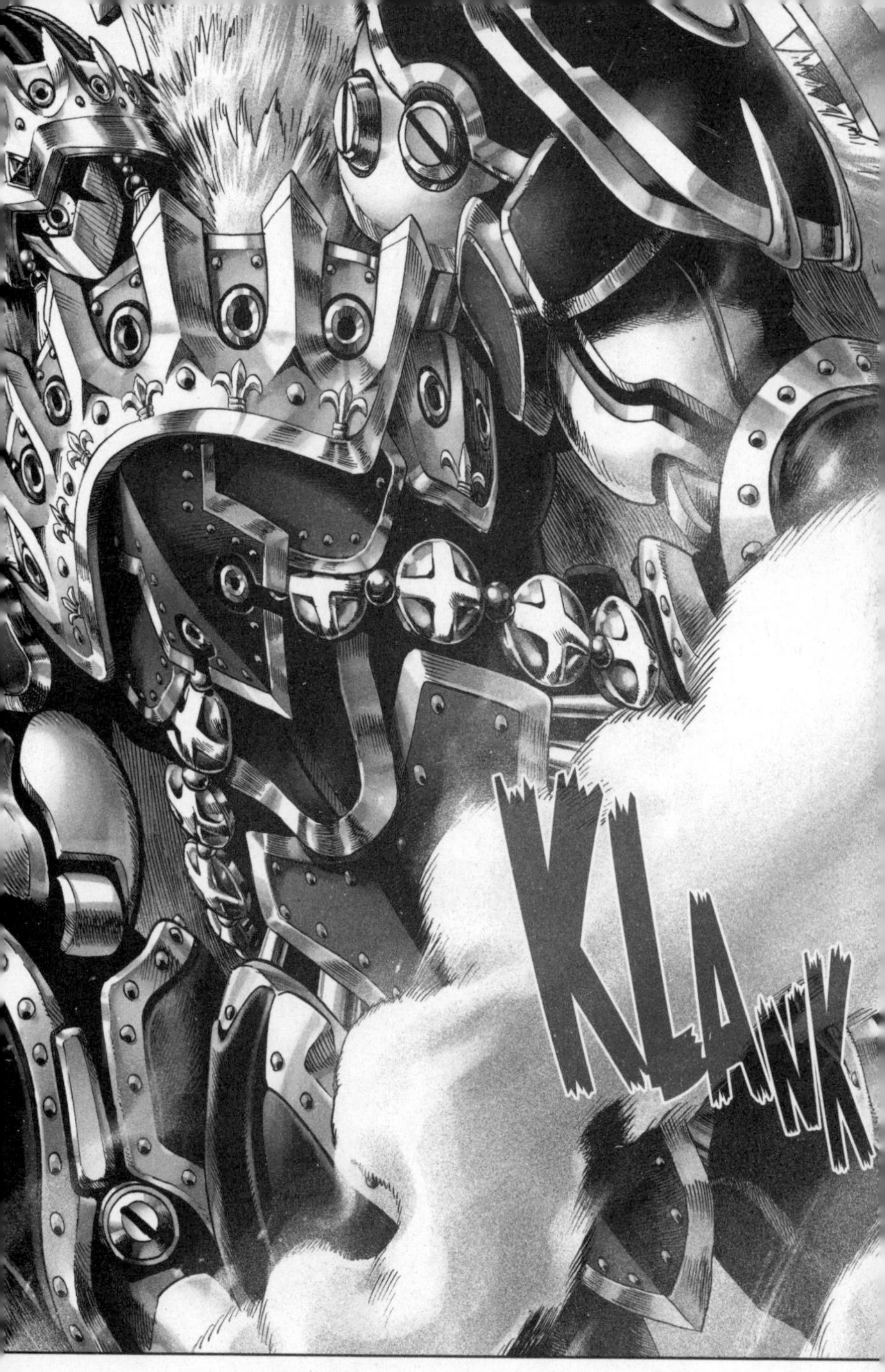
KLANK

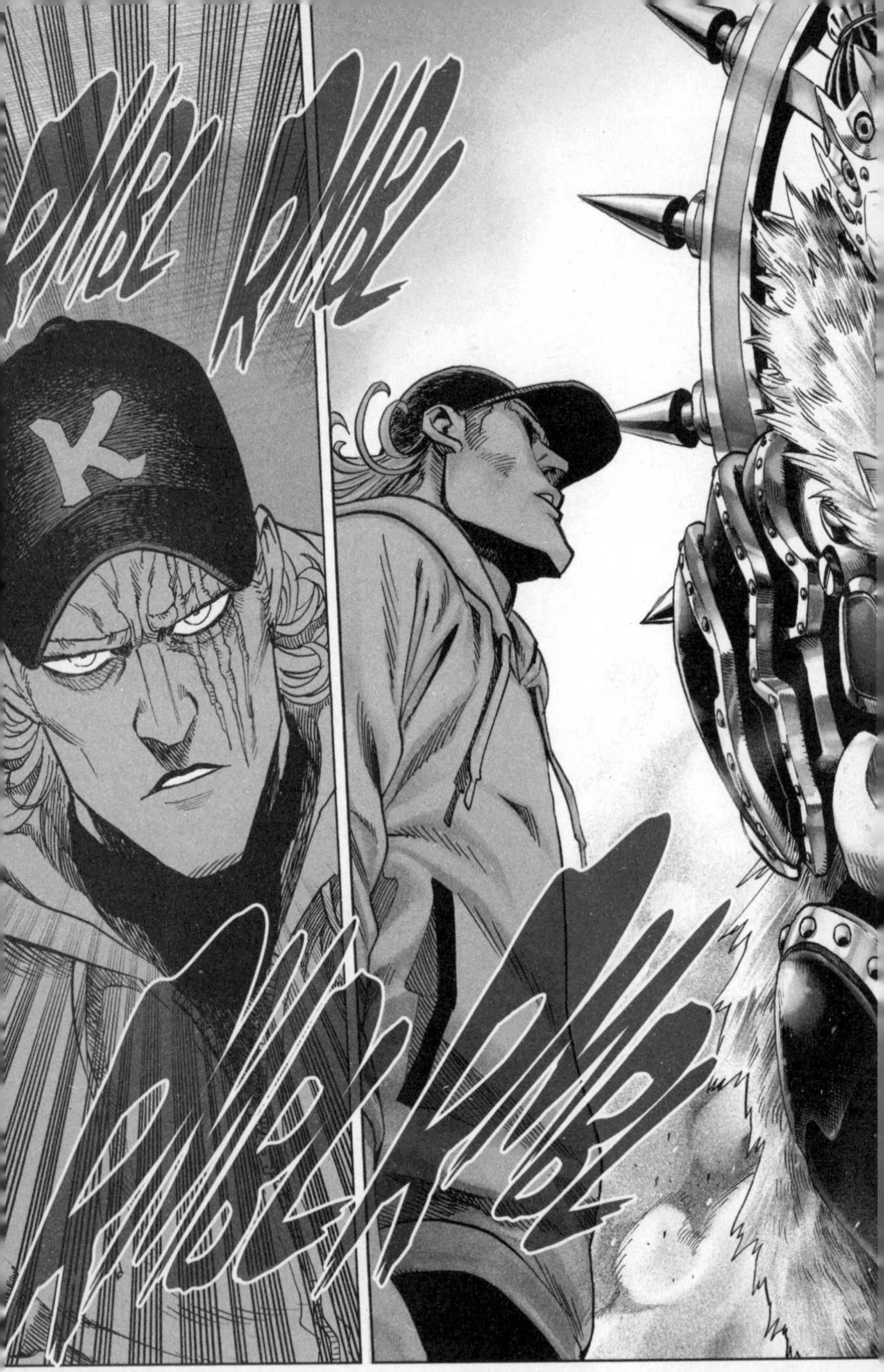

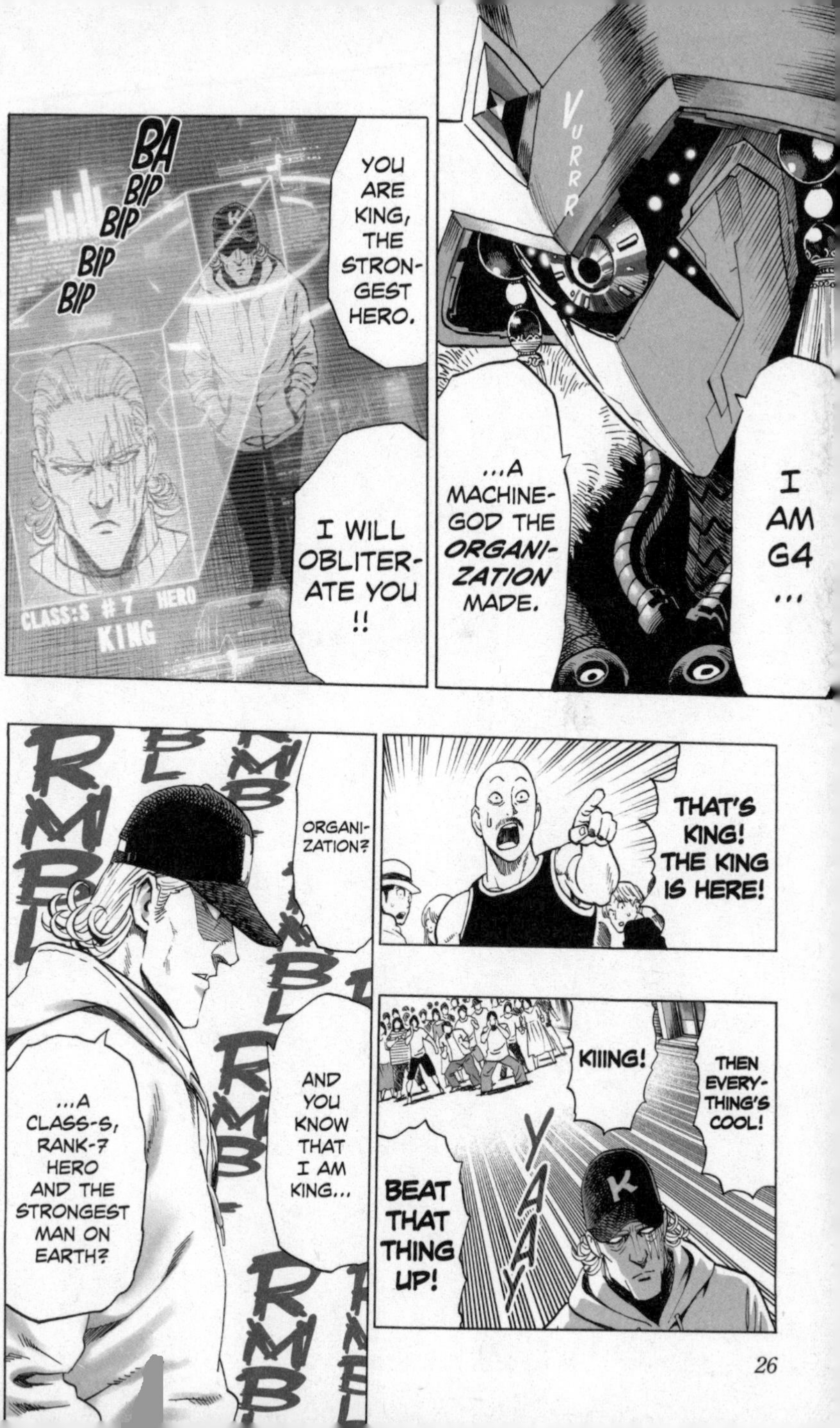
VURRR
I AM G4...
...A MACHINE-GOD THE ORGANIZATION MADE.
YOU ARE KING, THE STRONGEST HERO.
I WILL OBLITERATE YOU!!
BA BIP BIP BIP BIP
CLASS:S # 7 HERO
KING
THAT'S KING! THE KING IS HERE!
THEN EVERYTHING'S COOL!
KIIING!
YAAAY
BEAT THAT THING UP!
RMBL RMBL RMBL
ORGANIZATION?
AND YOU KNOW THAT I AM KING...
...A CLASS-S, RANK-7 HERO AND THE STRONGEST MAN ON EARTH?

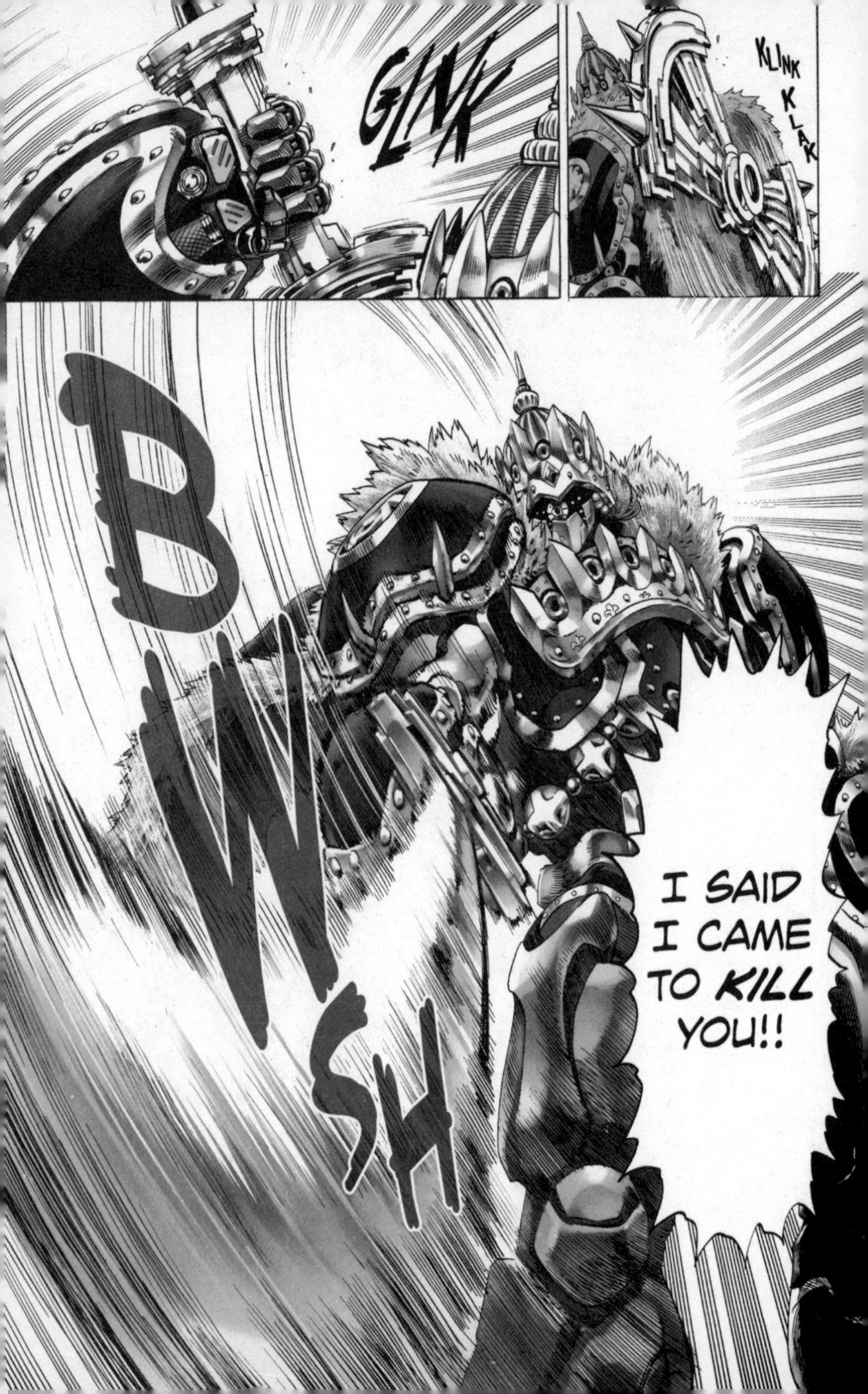
KLINK KLAK
GLINK
I SAID I CAME TO *KILL* YOU!!
BWSH

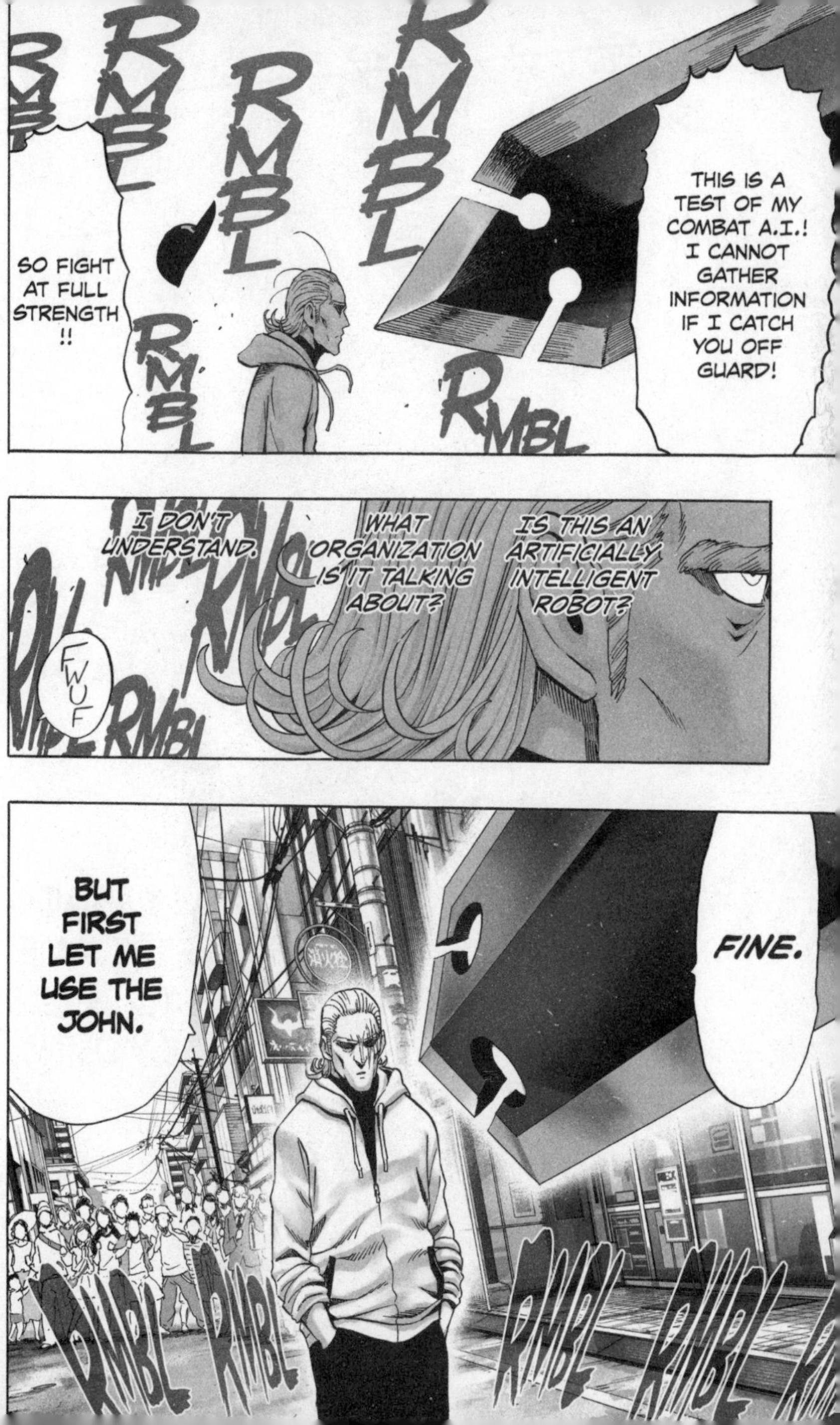
THIS IS A TEST OF MY COMBAT A.I.! I CANNOT GATHER INFORMATION IF I CATCH YOU OFF GUARD!
KMBL
RMBL
RMBL
SO FIGHT AT FULL STRENGTH!!
RMBL
IS THIS AN ARTIFICIALLY INTELLIGENT ROBOT?
WHAT ORGANIZATION IS IT TALKING ABOUT?
I DON'T UNDERSTAND.
FWUF
RMBL
FINE.
BUT FIRST LET ME USE THE JOHN.
RMBL RMBL

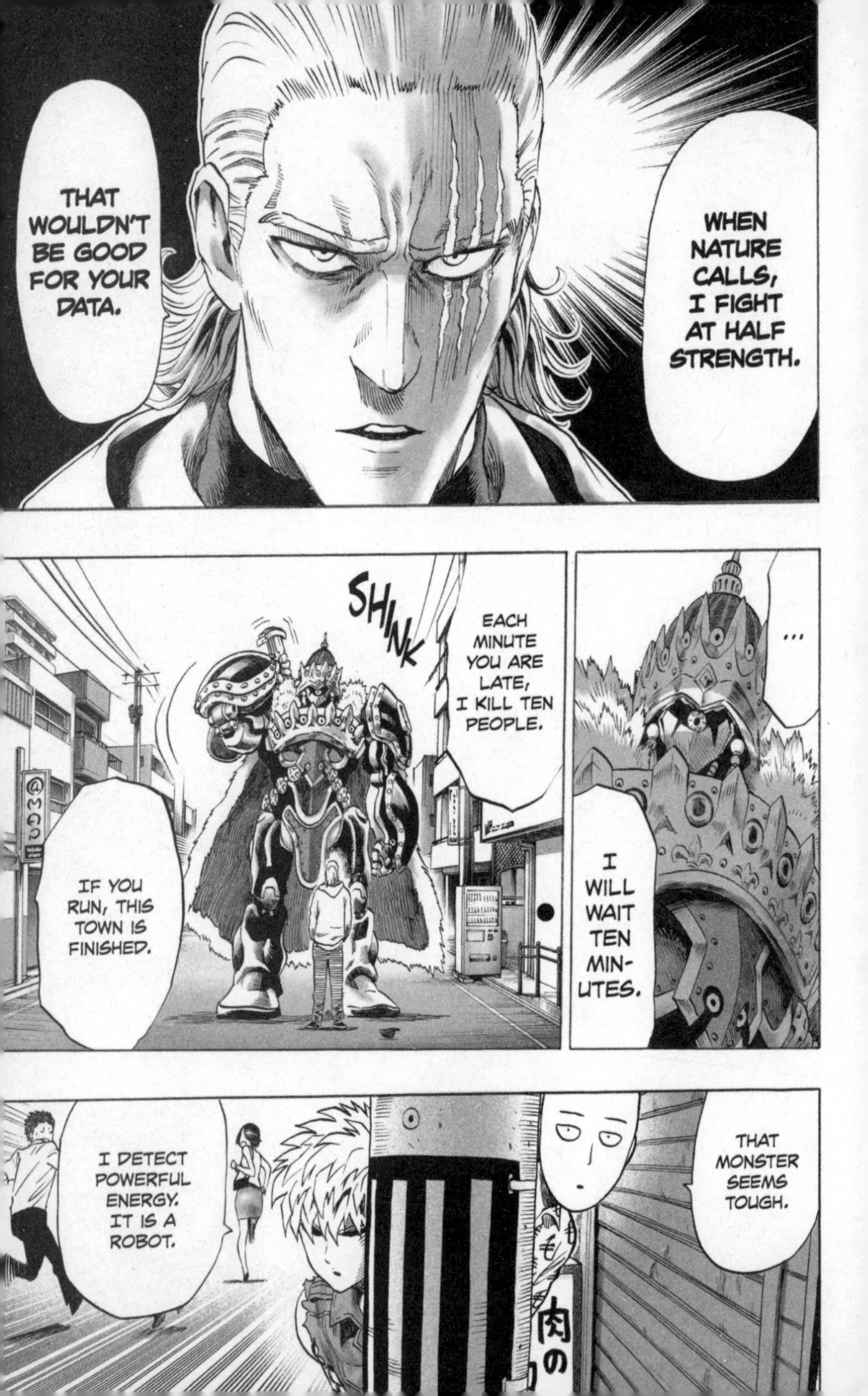
WHEN NATURE CALLS, I FIGHT AT HALF STRENGTH.
THAT WOULDN'T BE GOOD FOR YOUR DATA.
...
I WILL WAIT TEN MIN- UTES.
SHINK
EACH MINUTE YOU ARE LATE, I KILL TEN PEOPLE.
IF YOU RUN, THIS TOWN IS FINISHED.
THAT MONSTER SEEMS TOUGH.
肉の
I DETECT POWERFUL ENERGY. IT IS A ROBOT.

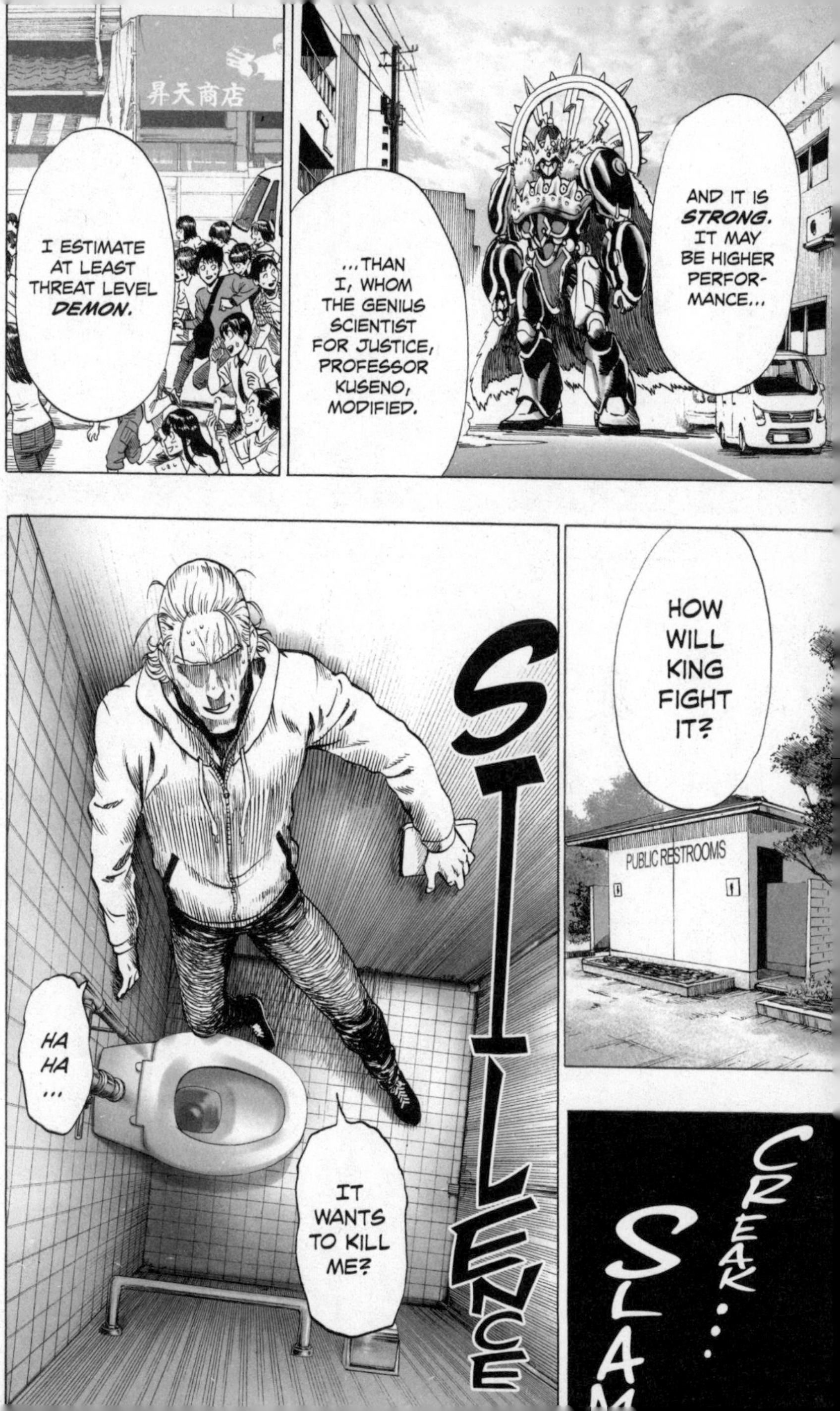
AND IT IS STRONG. IT MAY BE HIGHER PERFORMANCE...
...THAN I, WHOM THE GENIUS SCIENTIST FOR JUSTICE, PROFESSOR KUSENO, MODIFIED.
昇天商店
I ESTIMATE AT LEAST THREAT LEVEL DEMON.
HOW WILL KING FIGHT IT?
PUBLIC RESTROOMS
CREAK...
SLAM
SILENCE
HA HA ...
IT WANTS TO KILL ME?

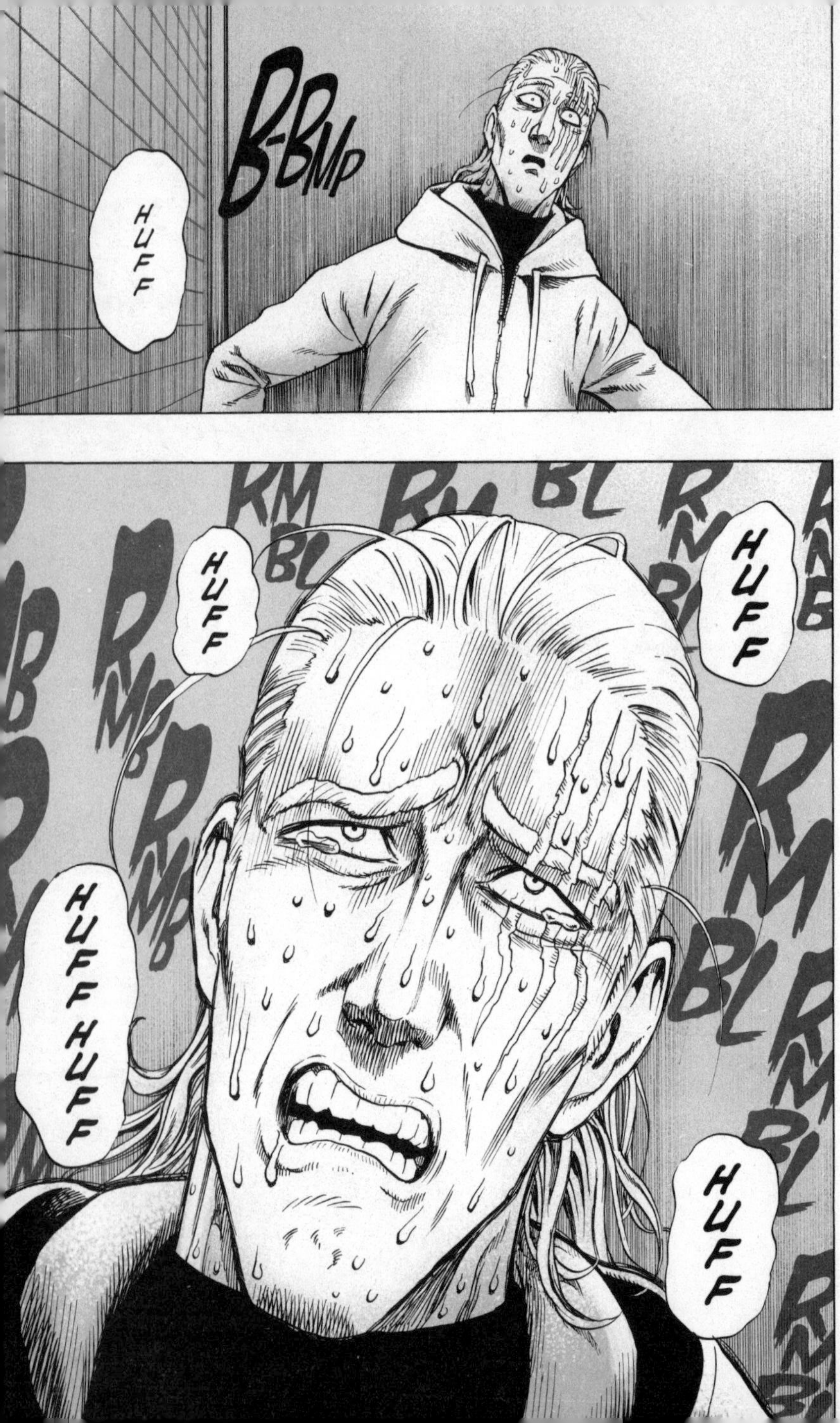
B-BMP
HUFF HUFF
RMBL RMBL
HUFF HUFF
HUFF HUFF
HUFF HUFF HUFF HUFF
HUFF HUFF

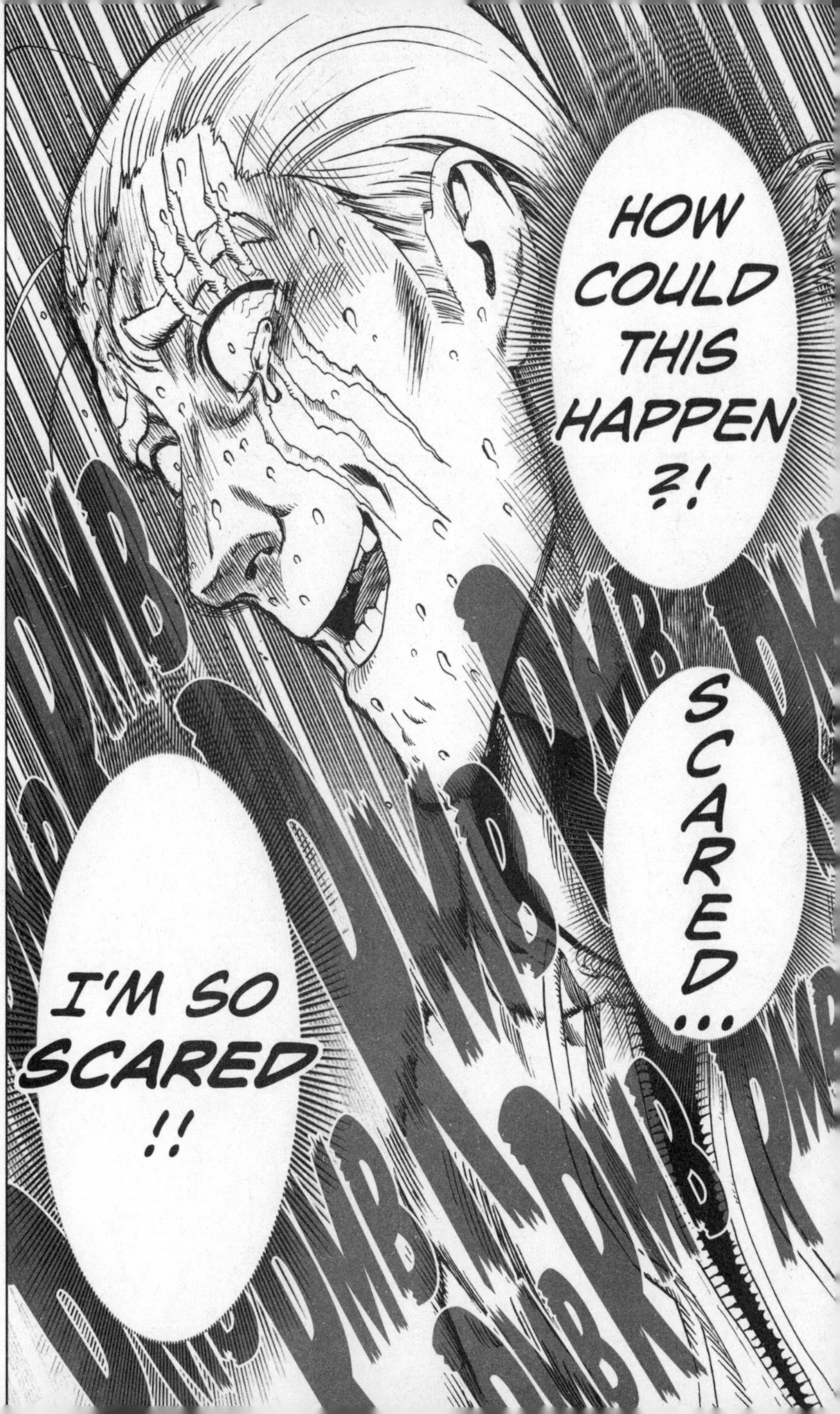
HOW COULD THIS HAPPEN?!
SCARED...
I'M SO SCARED!!

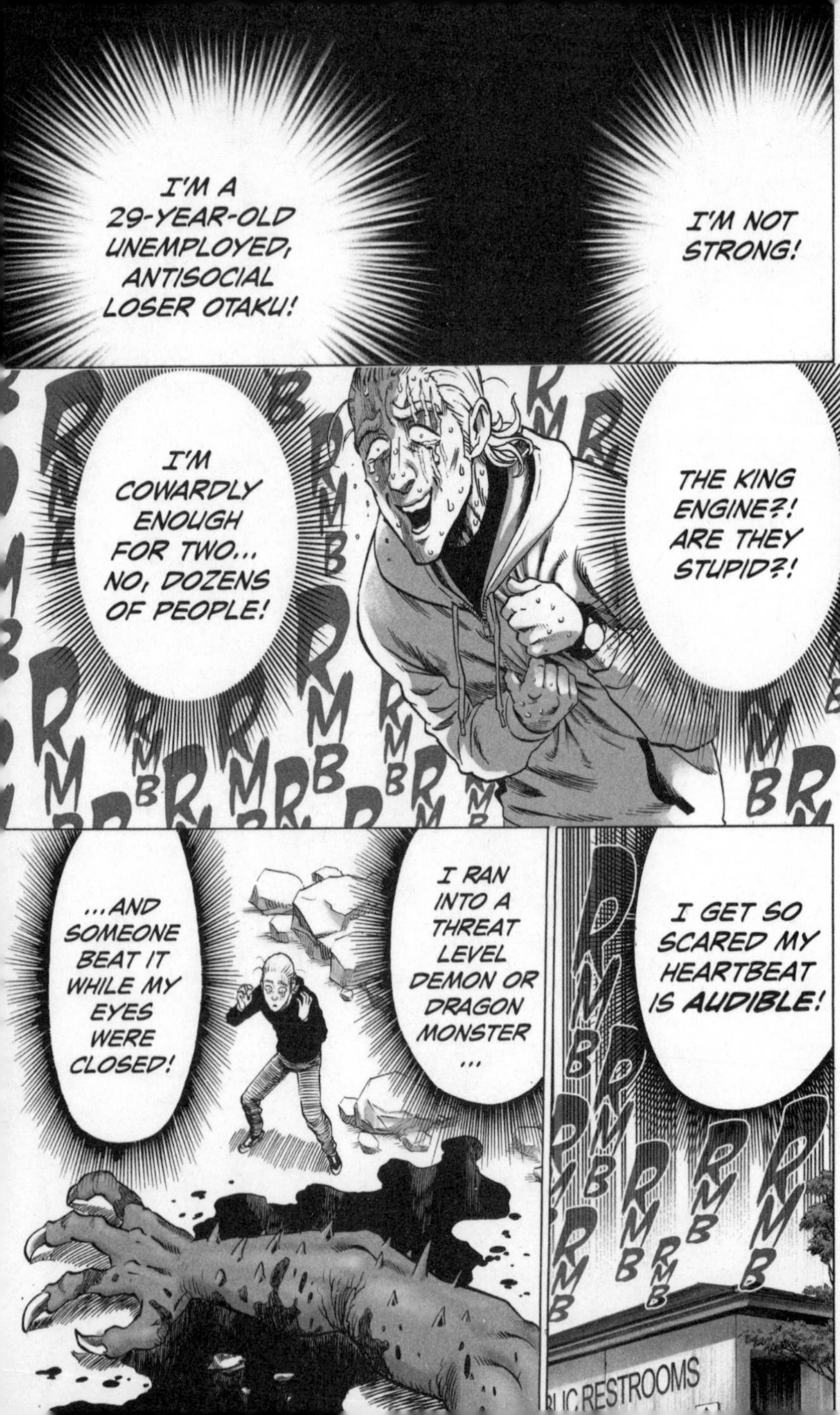
I'M NOT STRONG!
I'M A 29-YEAR-OLD UNEMPLOYED, ANTISOCIAL LOSER OTAKU!
BRMB BRMB BRMB
THE KING ENGINE?! ARE THEY STUPID?!
I'M COWARDLY ENOUGH FOR TWO... NO, DOZENS OF PEOPLE!
BRMB BRMB BRMB
I GET SO SCARED MY HEARTBEAT IS AUDIBLE!
RESTROOMS
I RAN INTO A THREAT LEVEL DEMON OR DRAGON MONSTER...
...AND SOMEONE BEAT IT WHILE MY EYES WERE CLOSED!

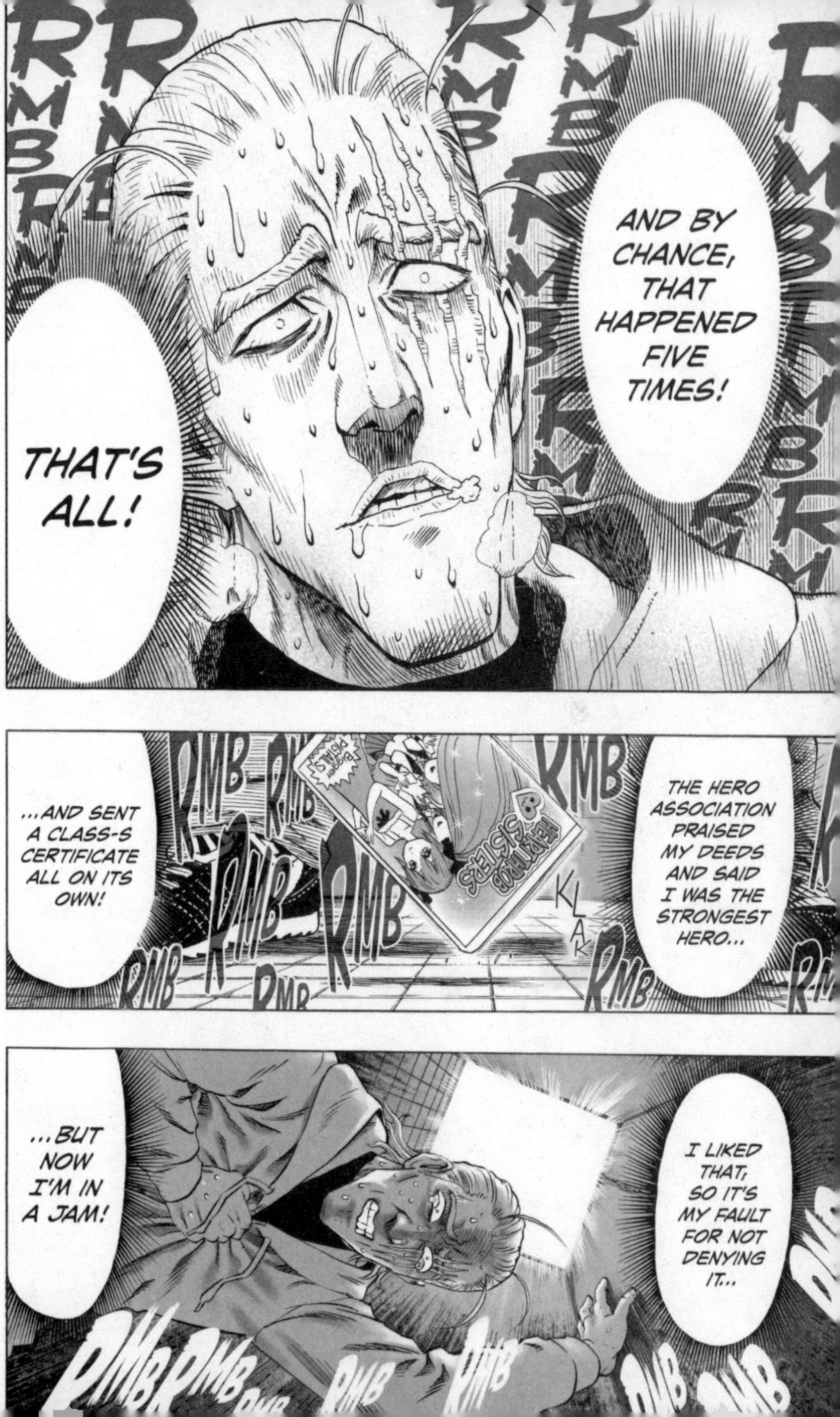
AND BY CHANCE, THAT HAPPENED FIVE TIMES!
THAT'S ALL!
THE HERO ASSOCIATION PRAISED MY DEEDS AND SAID I WAS THE STRONGEST HERO...
KLAK
RMB
...AND SENT A CLASS-S CERTIFICATE ALL ON ITS OWN!
I LIKED THAT, SO IT'S MY FAULT FOR NOT DENYING IT...
...BUT NOW I'M IN A JAM!

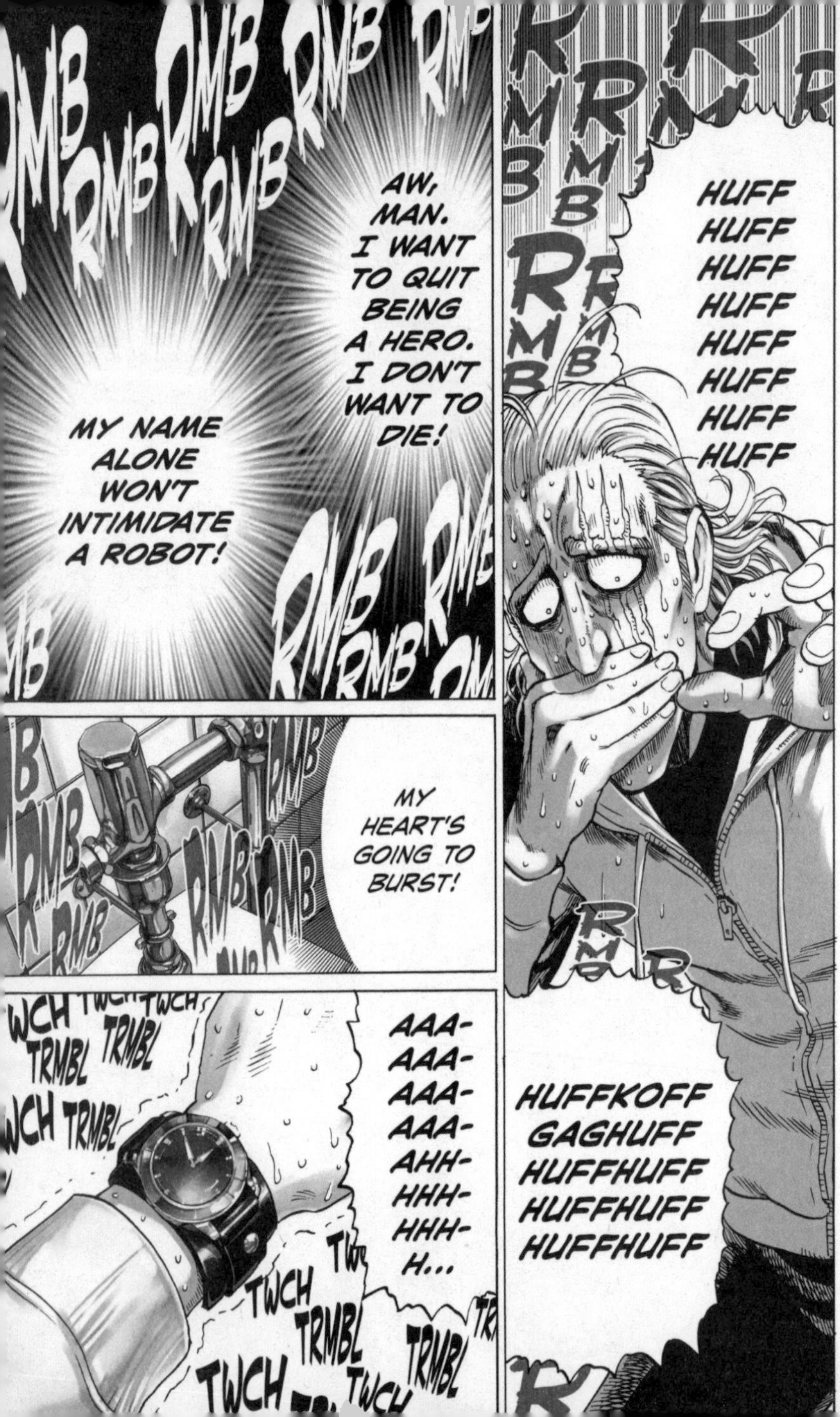
RMB RMB
HUFF HUFF HUFF HUFF HUFF HUFF HUFF HUFF
RMB
HUFFKOFF GAGHUFF HUFFHUFF HUFFHUFF HUFFHUFF
RMB RMB RMB RMB RMB RMB RMB
AW, MAN. I WANT TO QUIT BEING A HERO. I DON'T WANT TO DIE!
MY NAME ALONE WON'T INTIMIDATE A ROBOT!
RMB RMB RMB
RMB RMB RMB RMB
MY HEART'S GOING TO BURST!
AAA-AAA-AAA-AAA-AHH-HHH-HHH-H...
TWCH TWCH TRMBL TWCH TRMBL TWCH TRMBL
TWCH TRMBL TWCH TRMBL TWCH TWCH

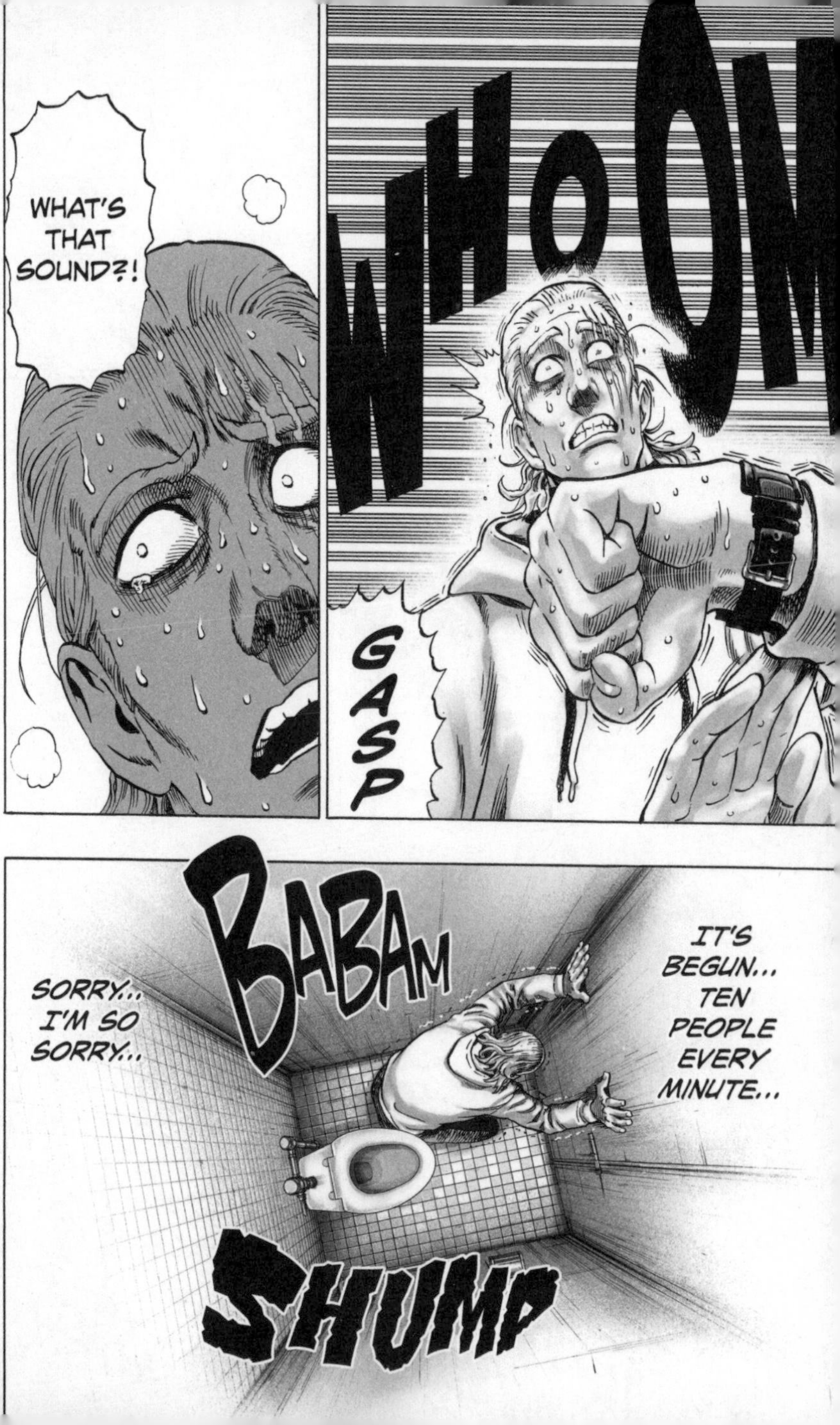
WHOOM
GASP
WHAT'S THAT SOUND?!
IT'S BEGUN... TEN PEOPLE EVERY MINUTE...
BABAM
SORRY... I'M SO SORRY...
SHUMP

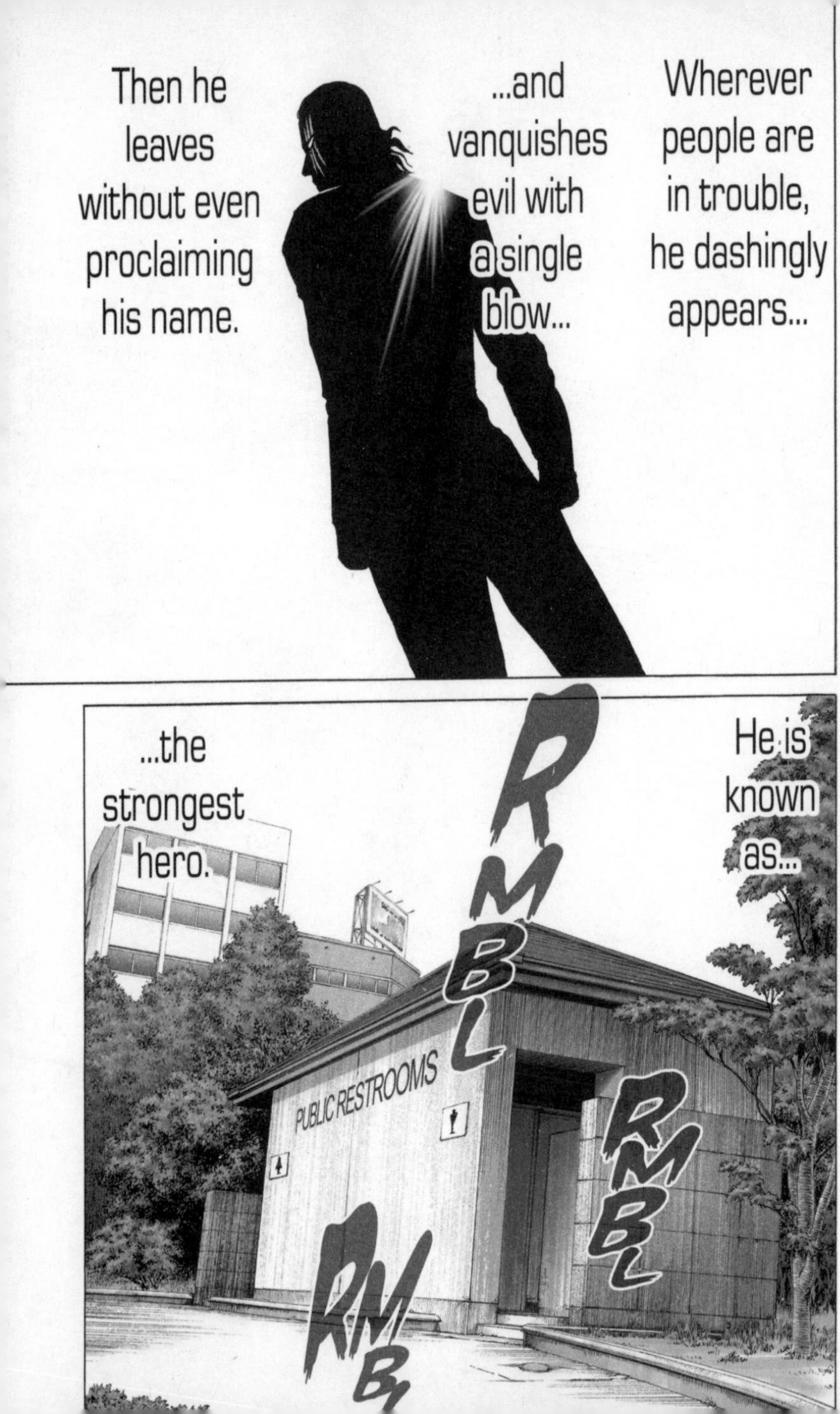
Wherever people are in trouble, he dashingly appears...
...and vanquishes evil with a single blow...
Then he leaves without even proclaiming his name.
He is known as...
RMBL
...the strongest hero.
PUBLIC RESTROOMS
RMBL
RMB

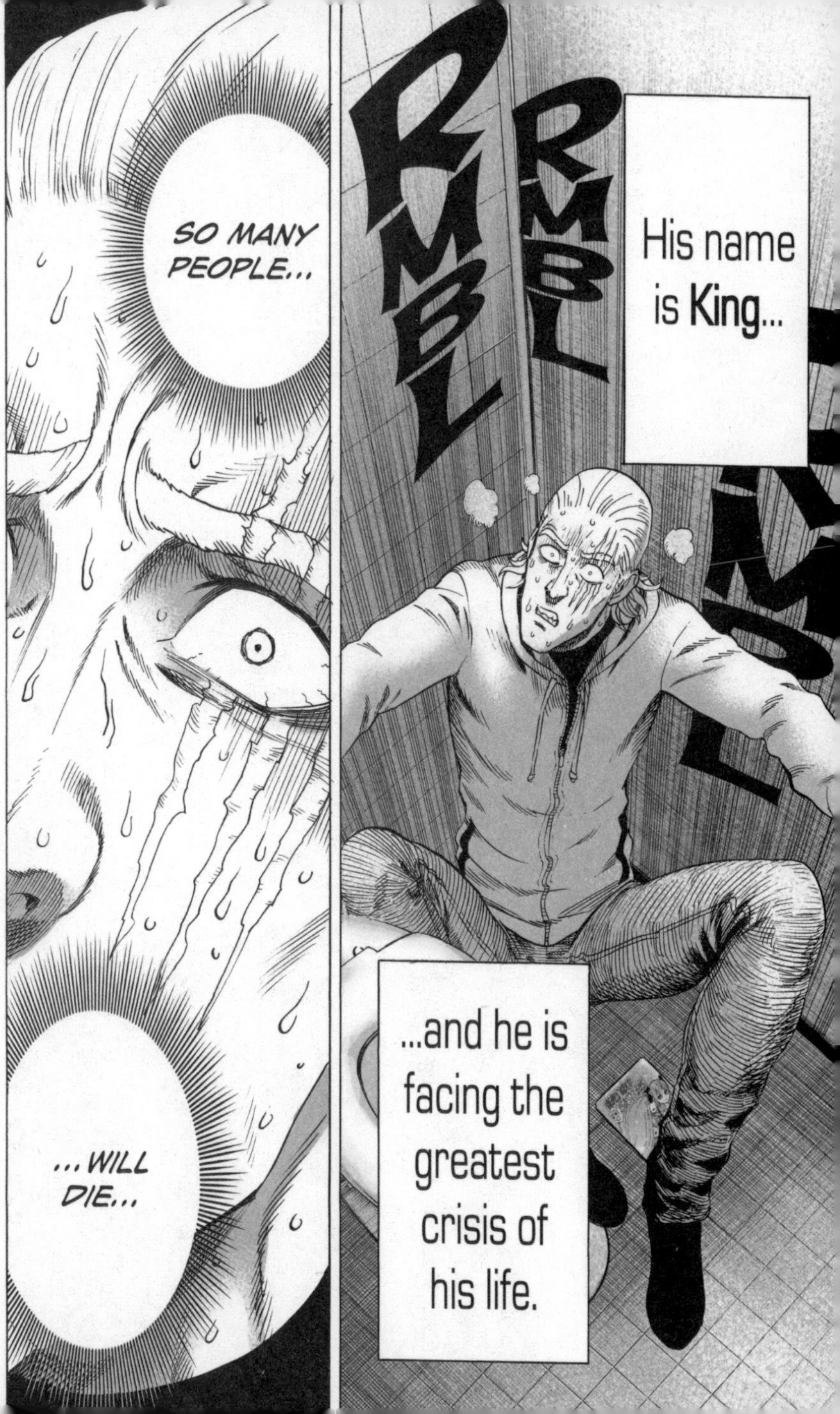
His name is King...
...and he is facing the greatest crisis of his life.
SO MANY PEOPLE...
...WILL DIE...

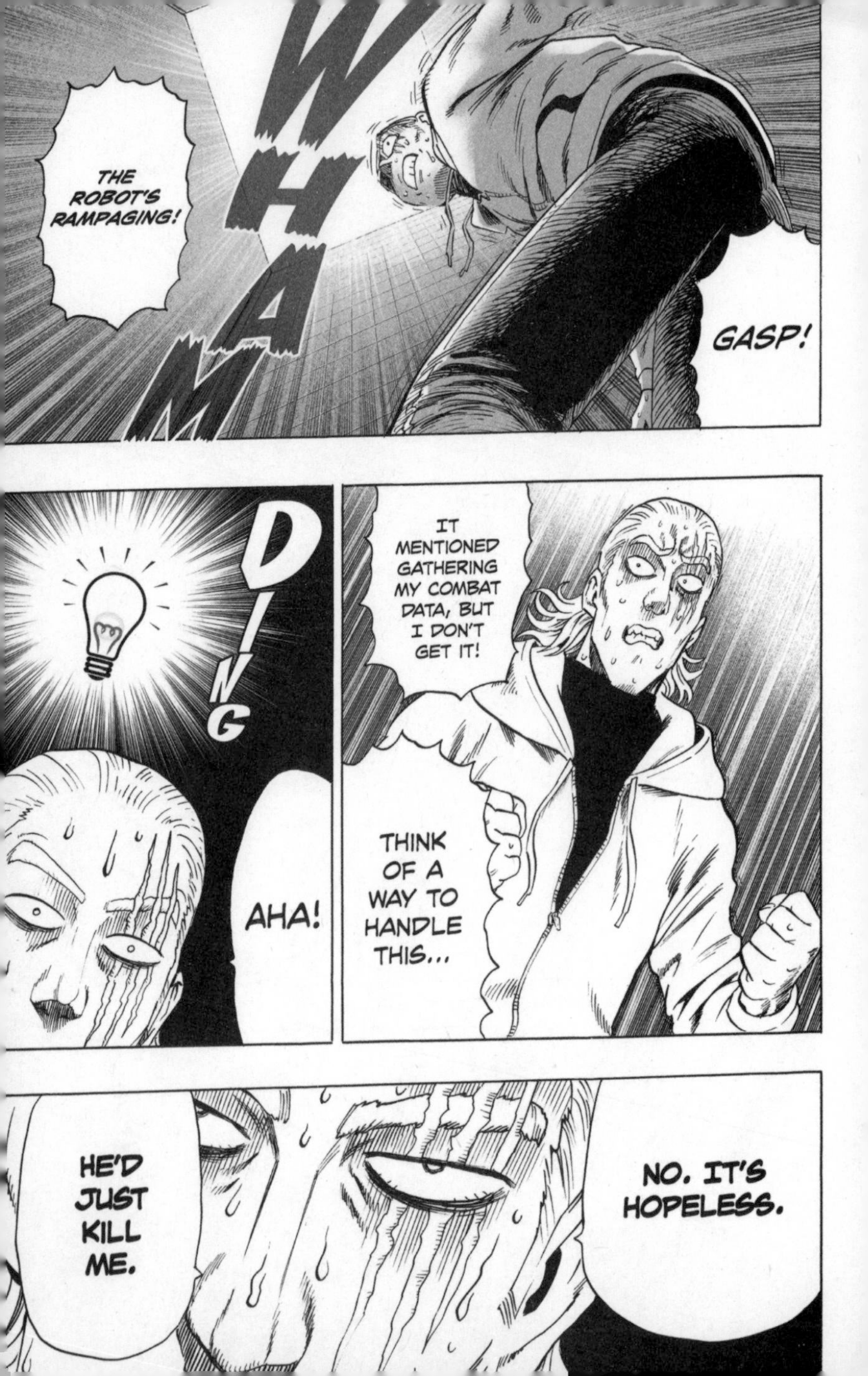
GASP!
WHAM
THE ROBOT'S RAMPAGING!
IT MENTIONED GATHERING MY COMBAT DATA, BUT I DON'T GET IT!
THINK OF A WAY TO HANDLE THIS...
DING
AHA!
NO. IT'S HOPELESS.
HE'D JUST KILL ME.

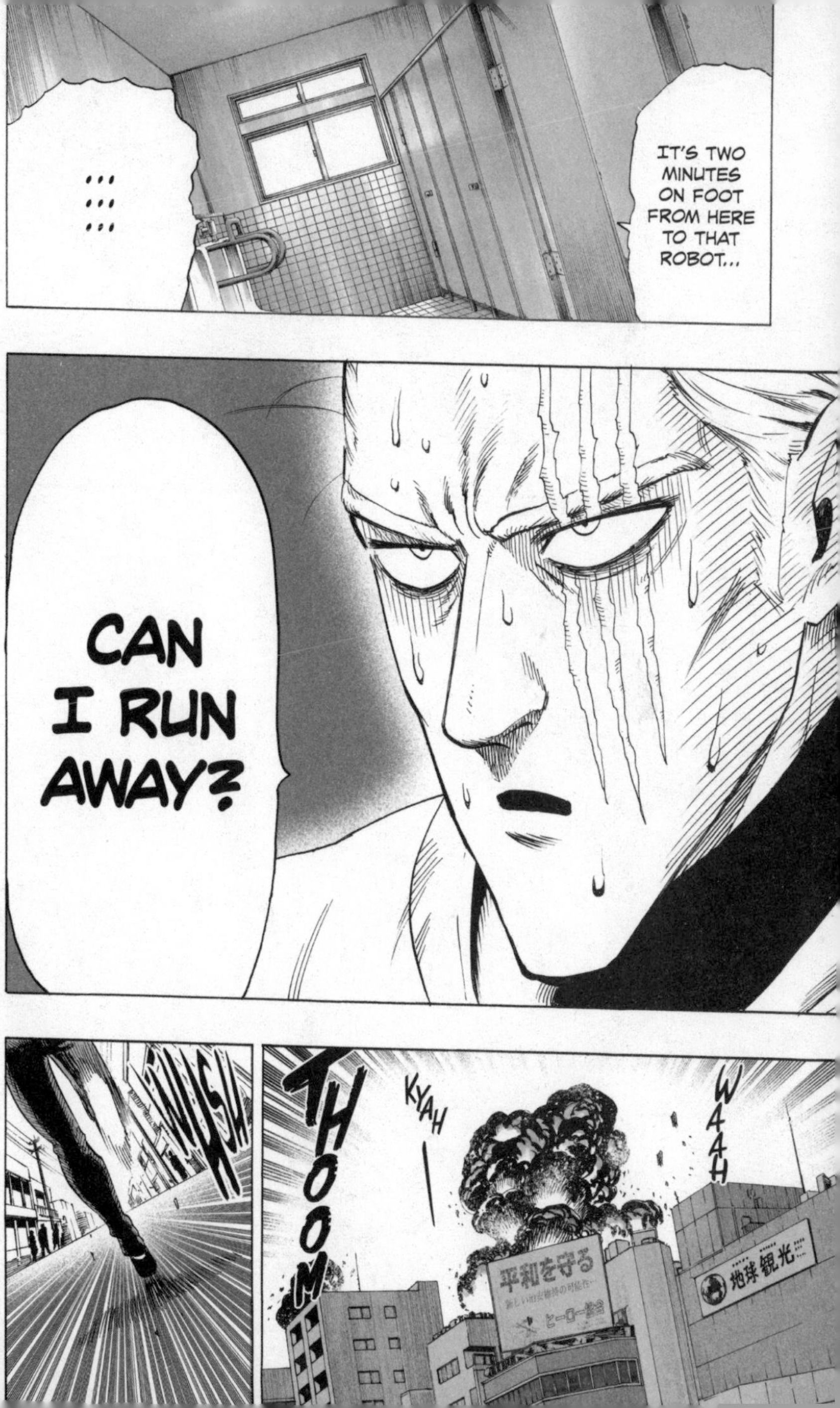
IT'S TWO MINUTES ON FOOT FROM HERE TO THAT ROBOT...
...
...
...
CAN I RUN AWAY?
WAAH
KYAH
THOOOM
地球観光
平和を守る
SWISH

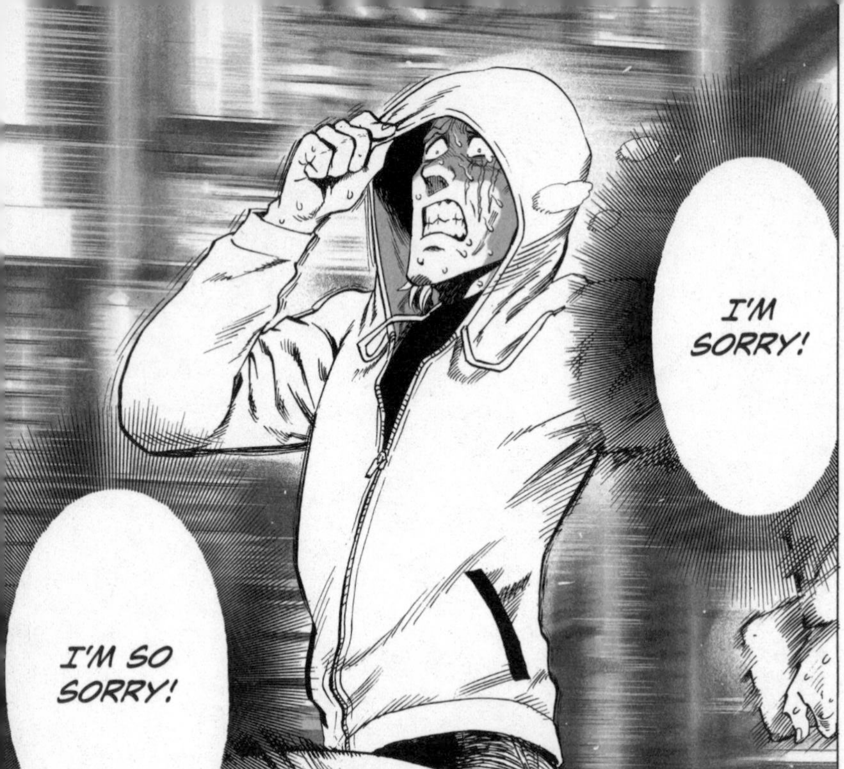
I'M SORRY!
I'M SO SORRY!

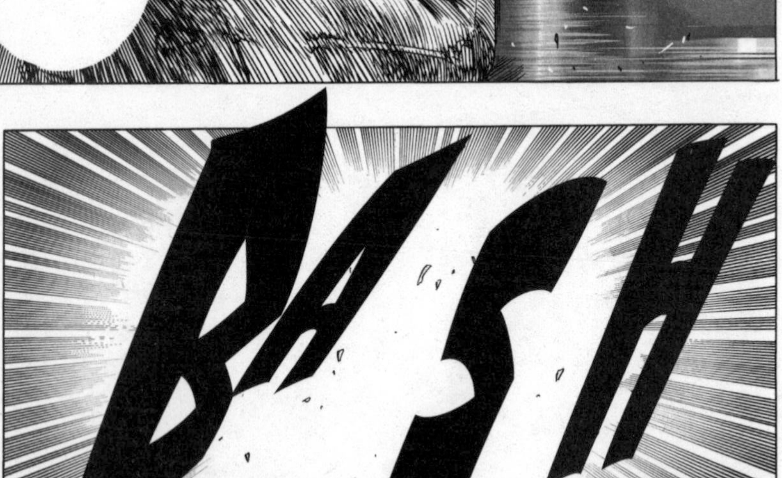
BASH

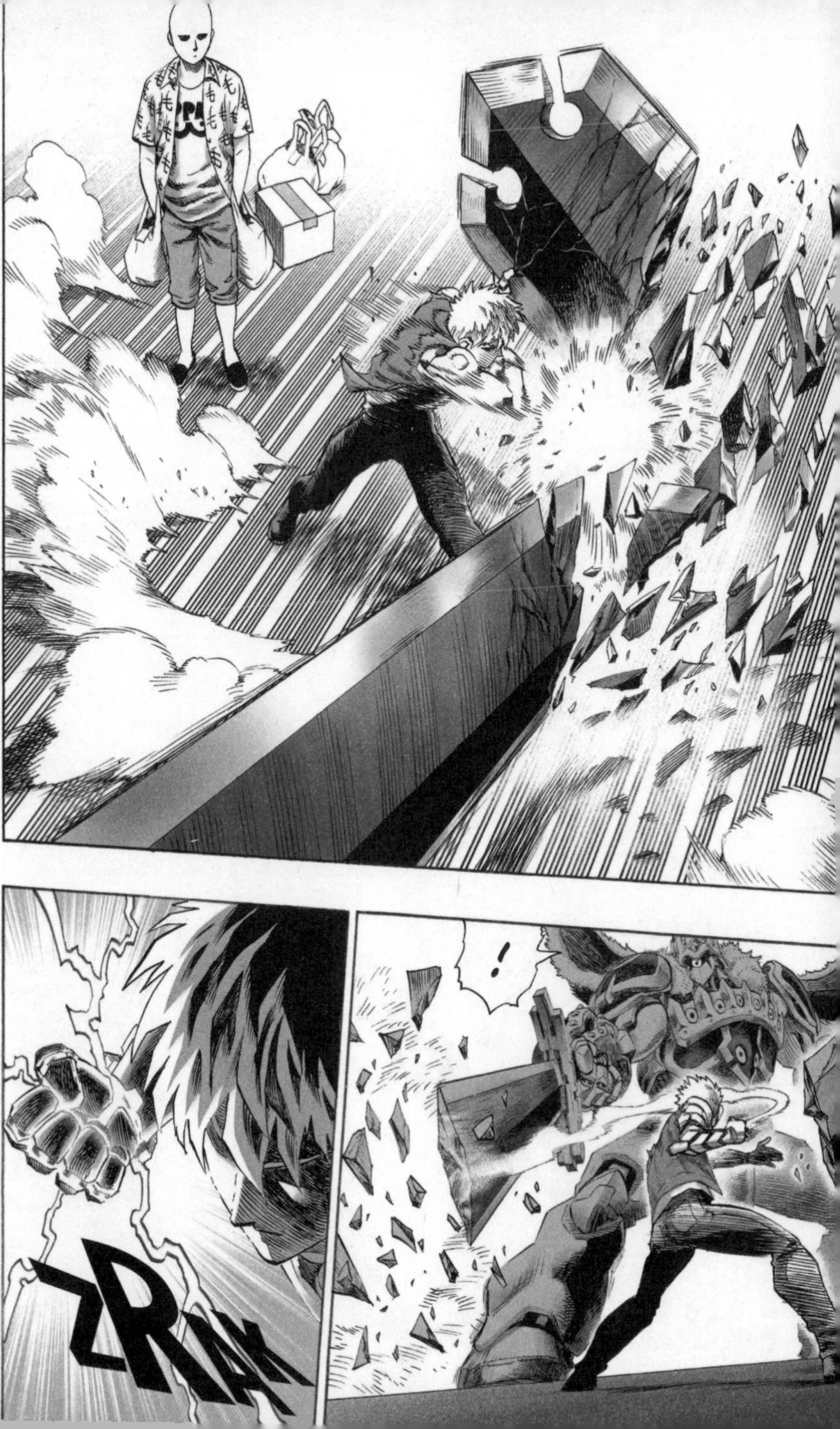
!
ZRAK

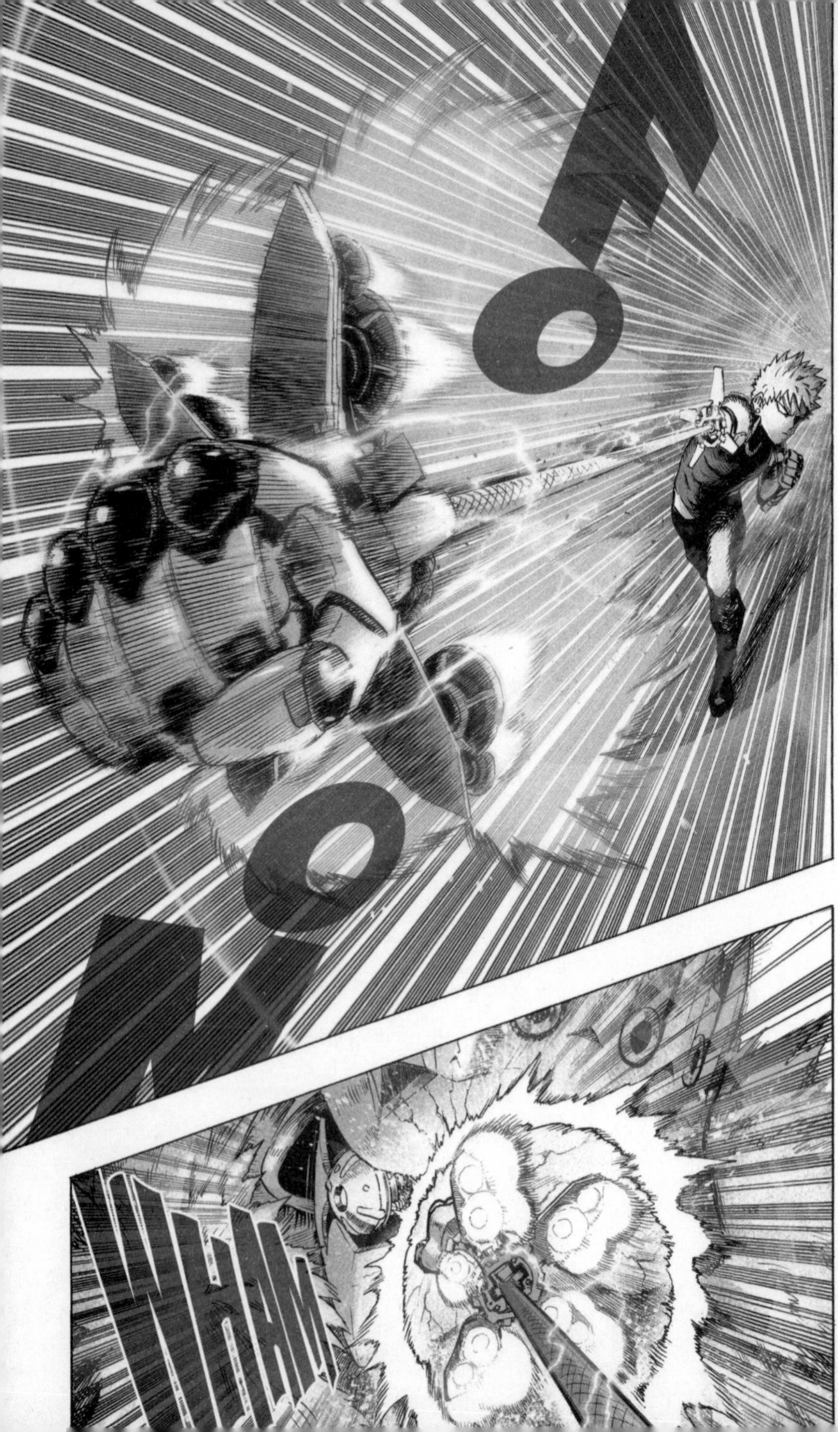
WHAM

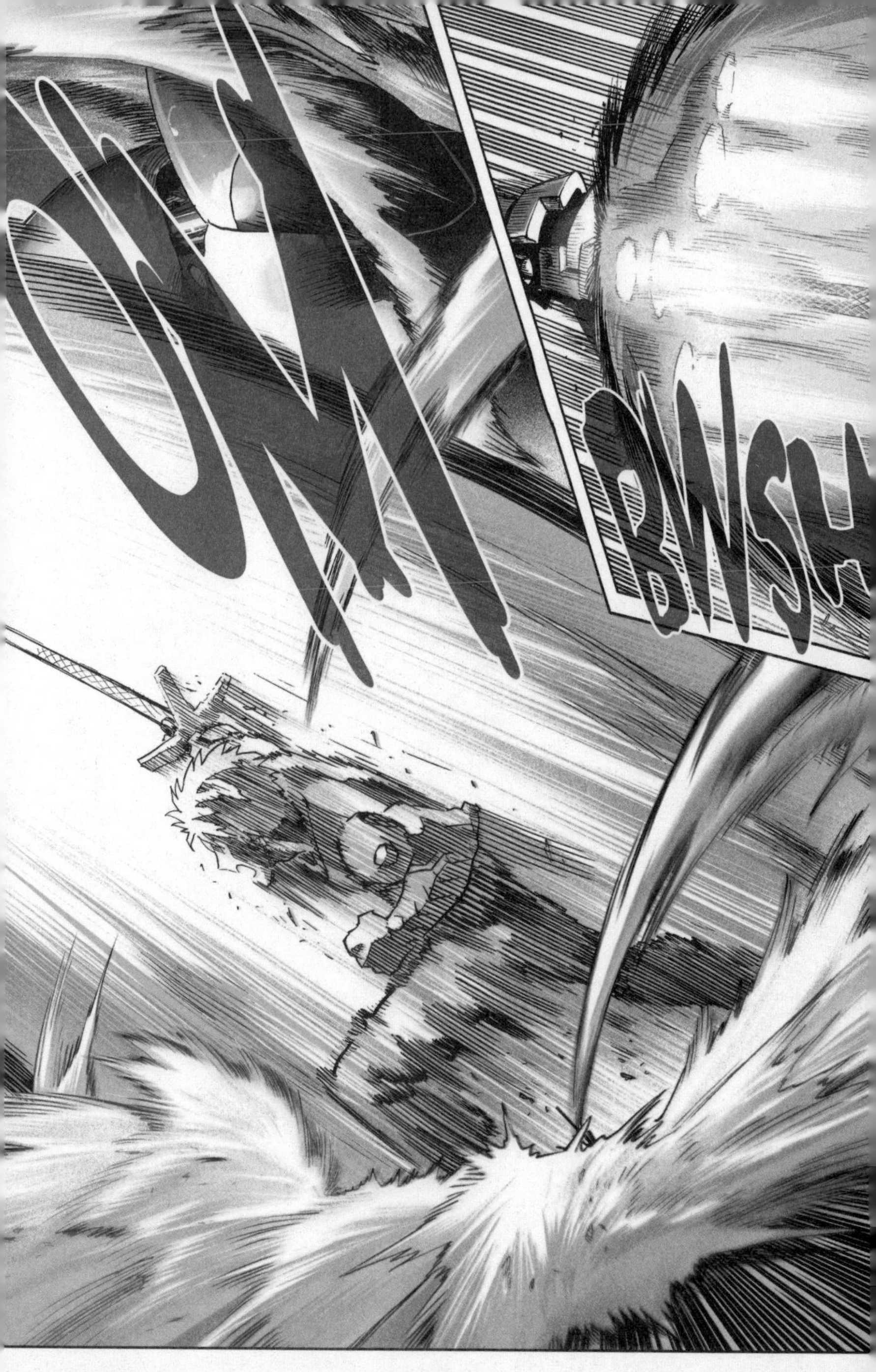

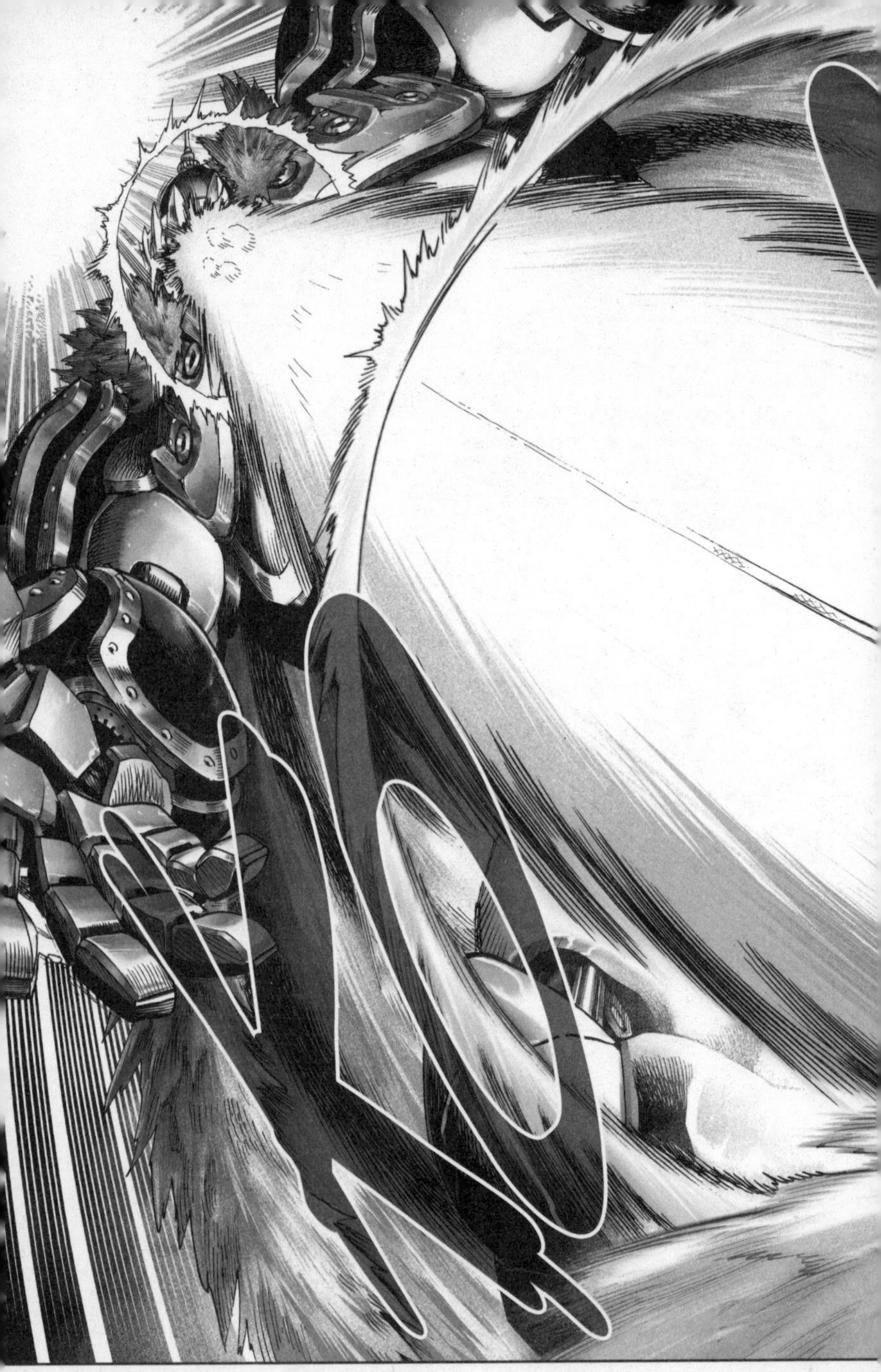

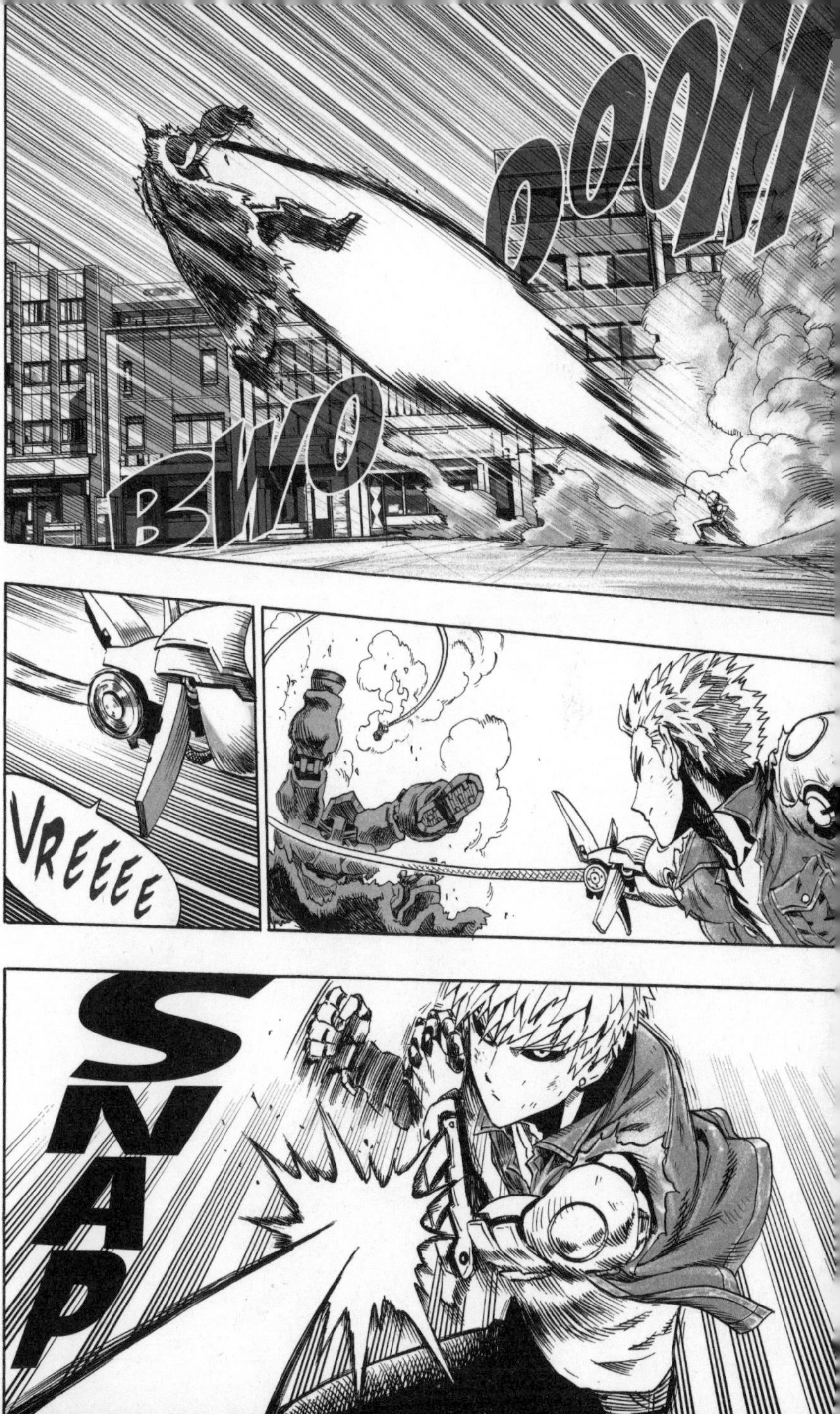
BWO
OOOM
VREEEE
SNAP

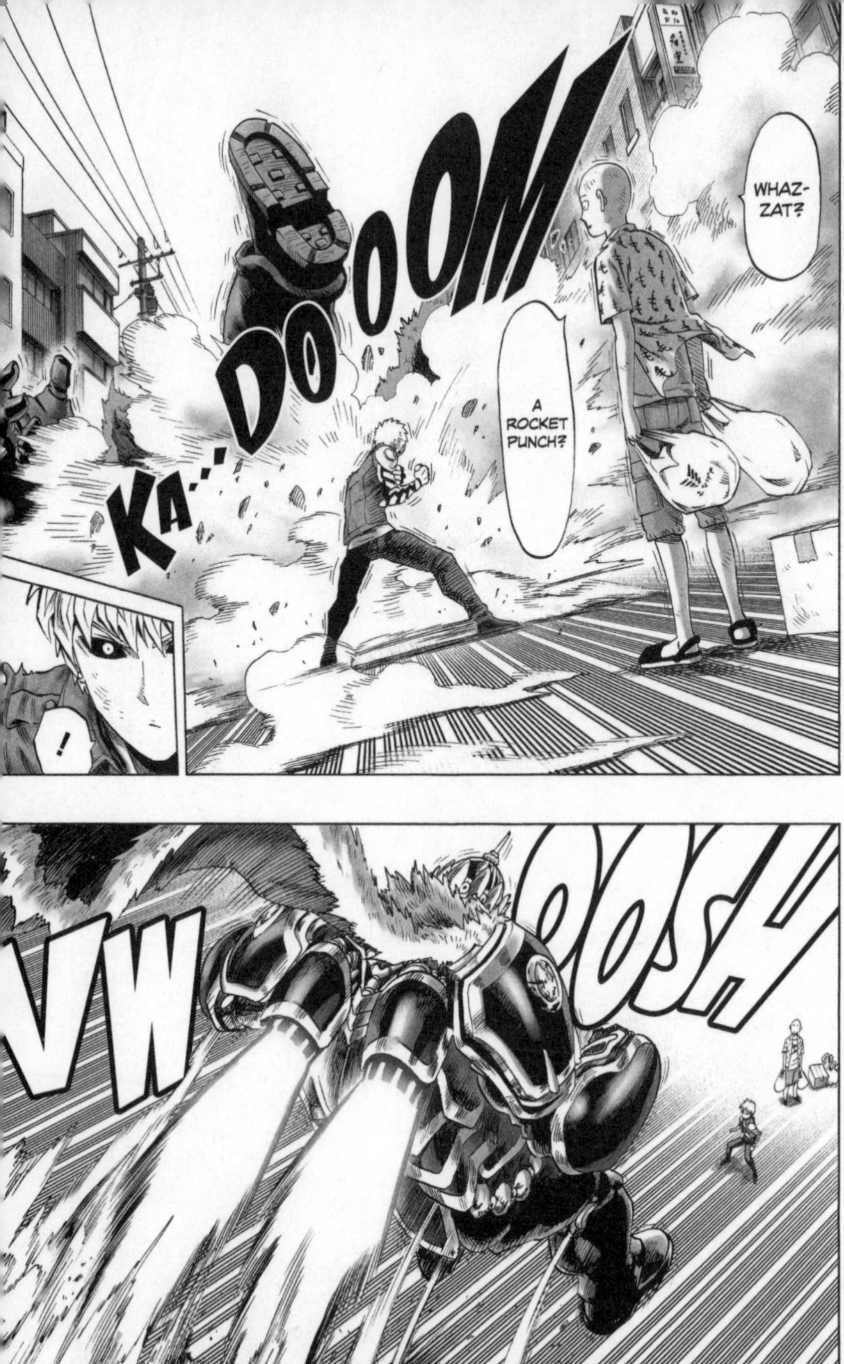
WHAZ-ZAT?
A ROCKET PUNCH?
DOOOOM
KA...
!
VWOOSH

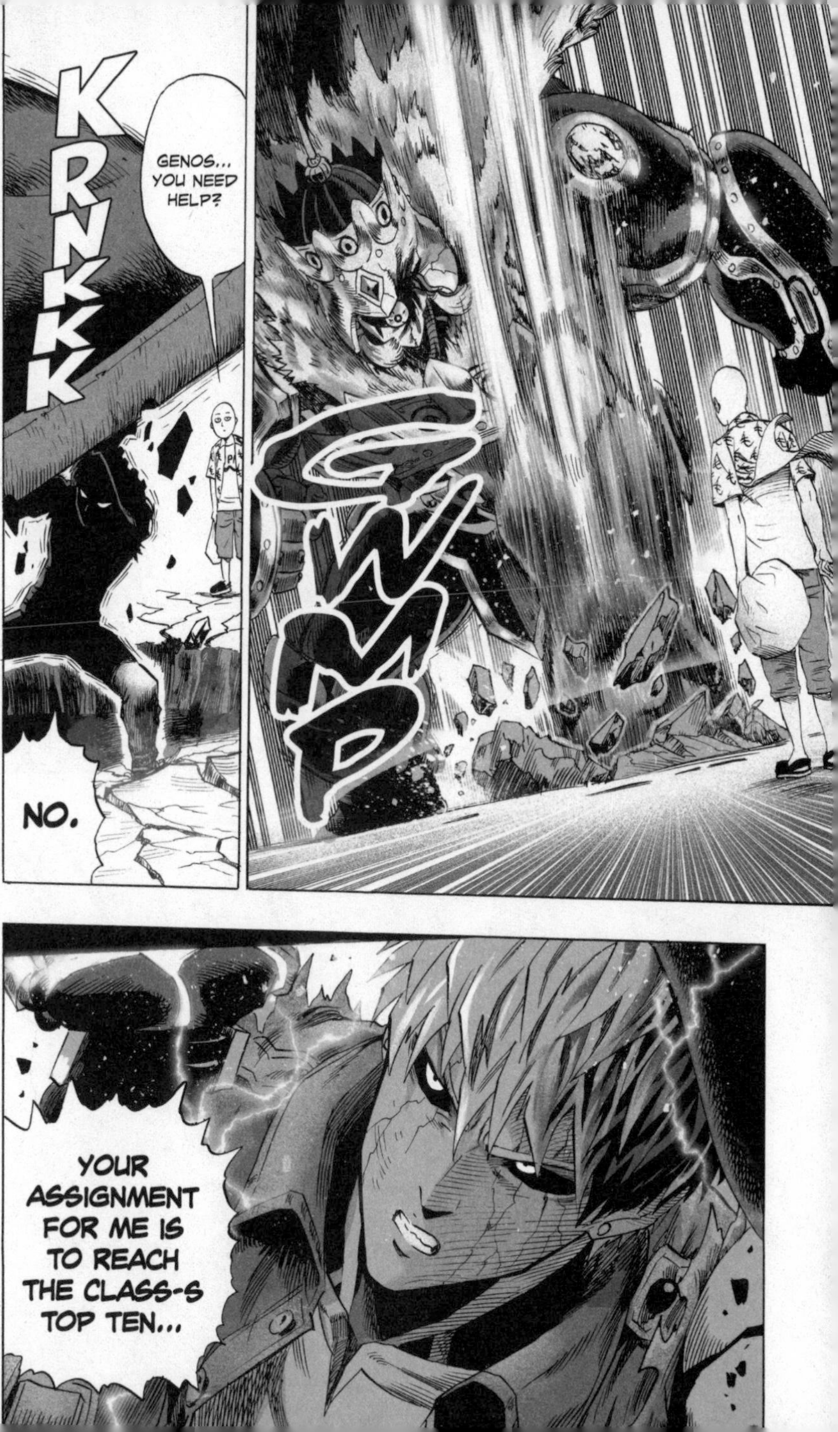
GWMP
KRNKKK
GENOS... YOU NEED HELP?
NO.
YOUR ASSIGNMENT FOR ME IS TO REACH THE CLASS-S TOP TEN...

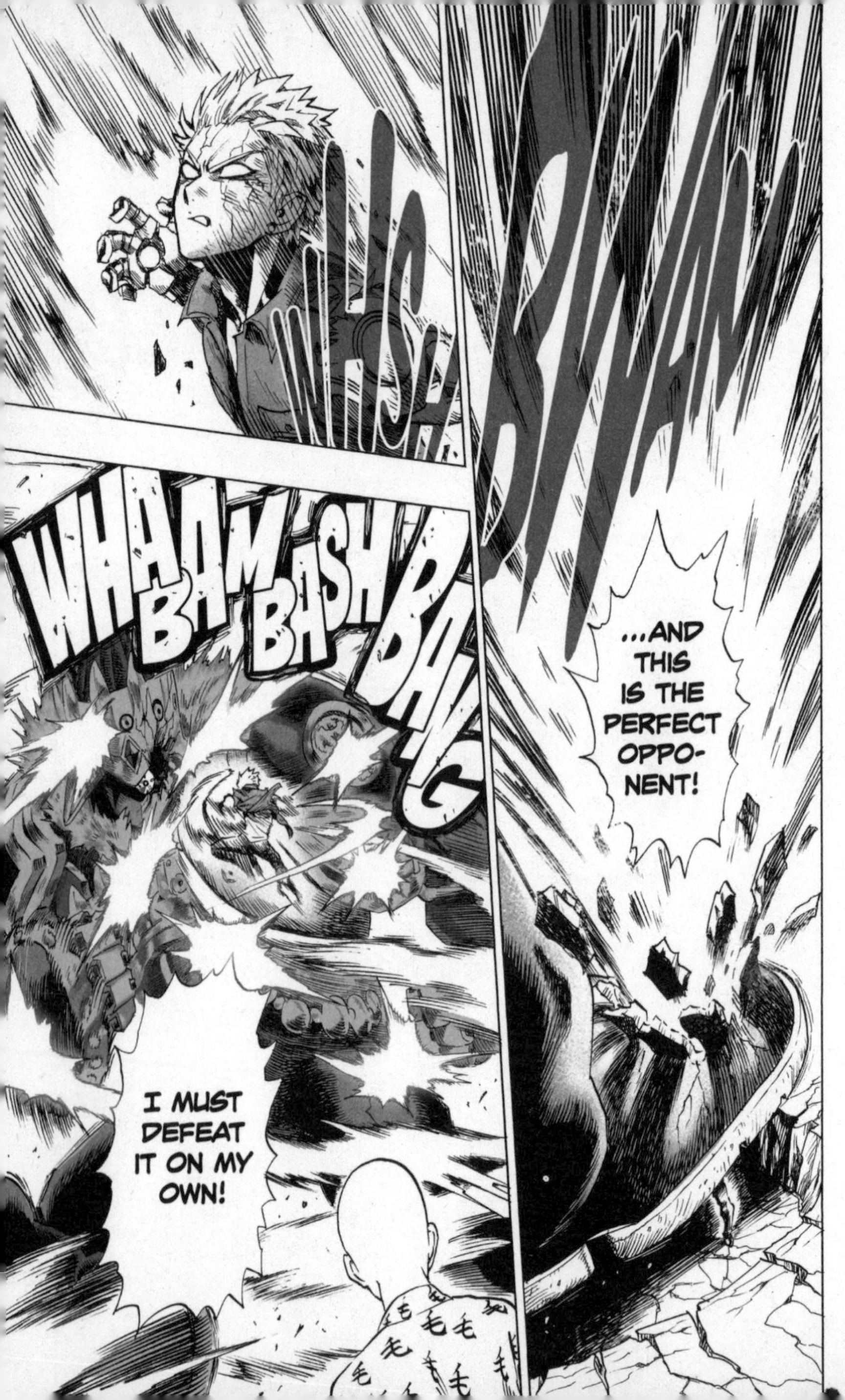
...AND THIS IS THE PERFECT OPPONENT!
WHAM BAM BASH
I MUST DEFEAT IT ON MY OWN!

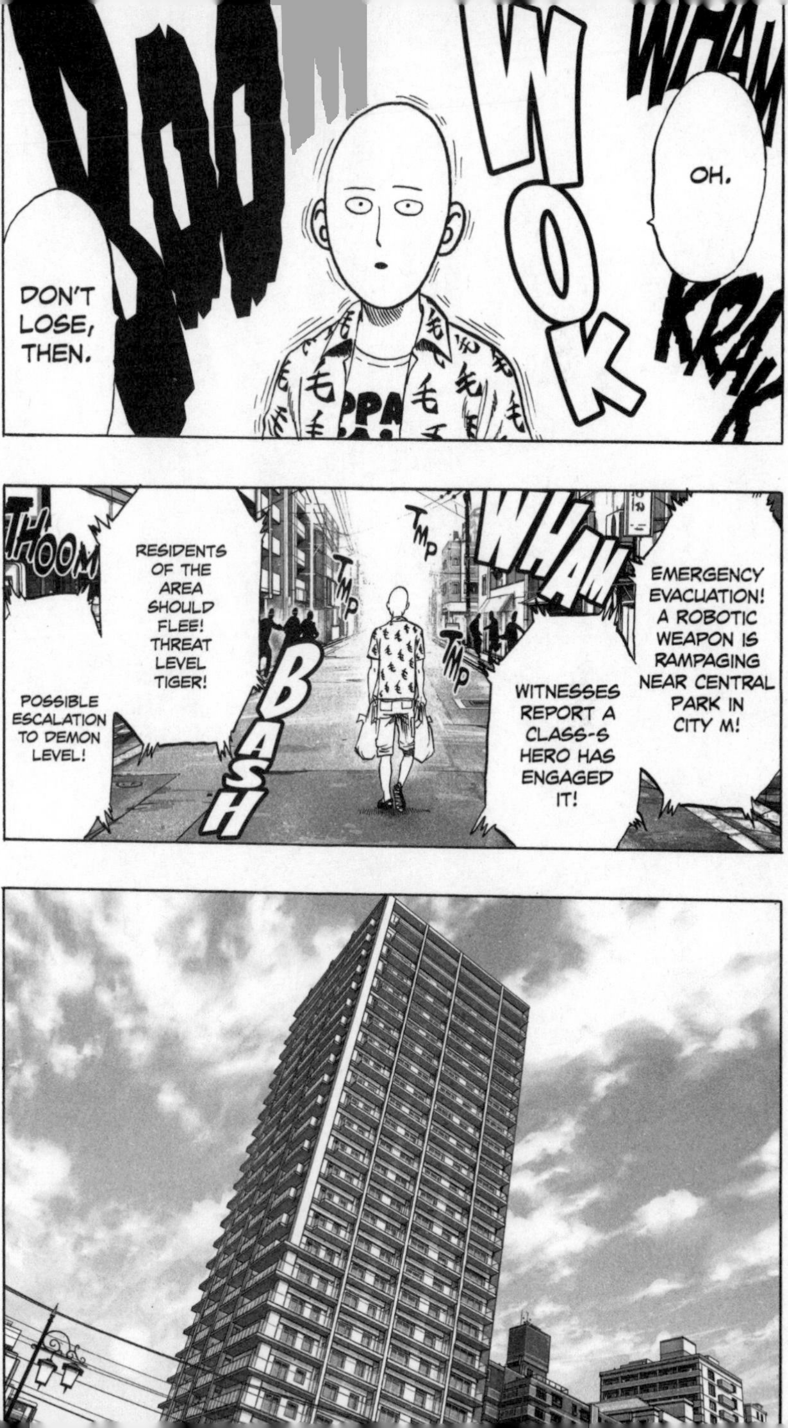
WHAM
OH.
KRAK
DON'T LOSE, THEN.
EMERGENCY EVACUATION! A ROBOTIC WEAPON IS RAMPAGING NEAR CENTRAL PARK IN CITY M!
WITNESSES REPORT A CLASS-S HERO HAS ENGAGED IT!
WHAM
TMP
TMP
TMP
BASH
RESIDENTS OF THE AREA SHOULD FLEE! THREAT LEVEL TIGER!
THOOM
POSSIBLE ESCALATION TO DEMON LEVEL!

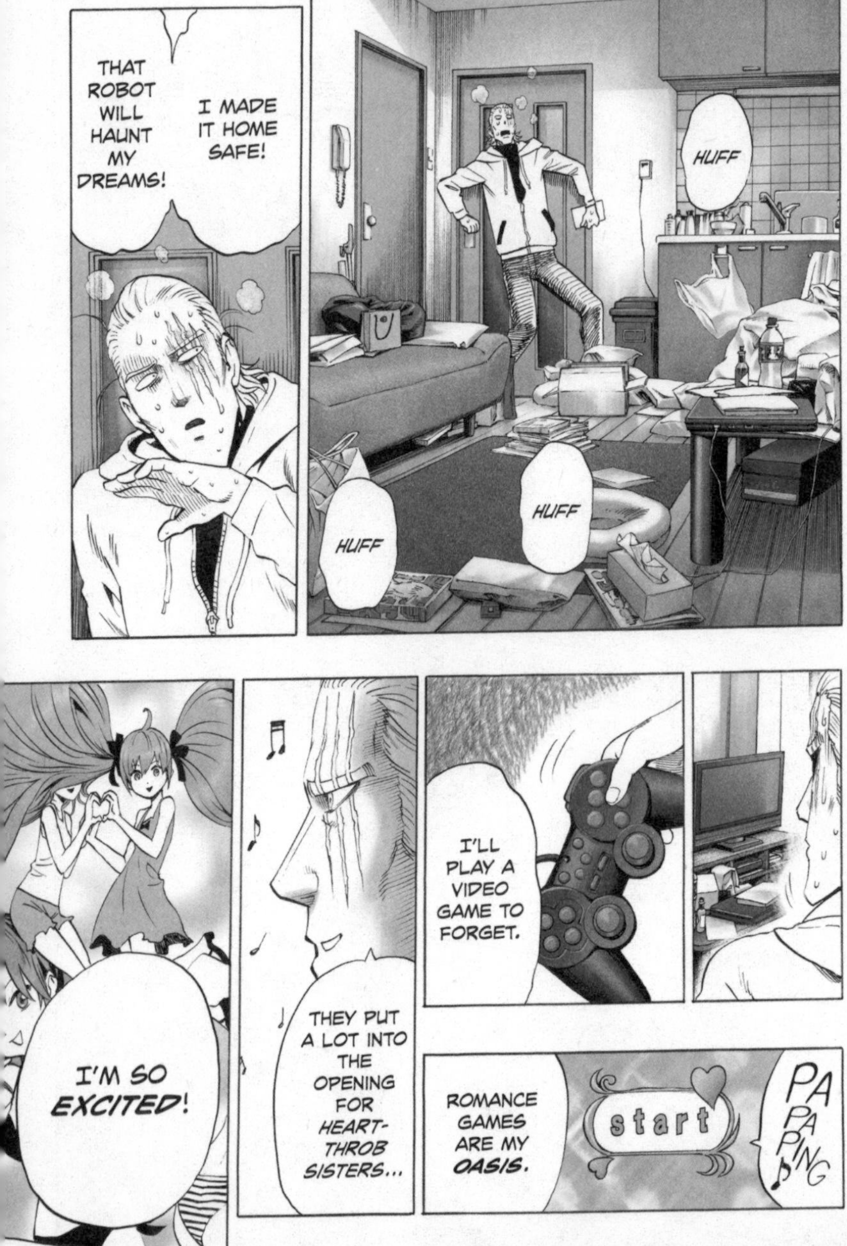
HUFF
HUFF
HUFF
I MADE IT HOME SAFE!
THAT ROBOT WILL HAUNT MY DREAMS!
I'LL PLAY A VIDEO GAME TO FORGET.
PAPAPING
start
ROMANCE GAMES ARE MY OASIS.
THEY PUT A LOT INTO THE OPENING FOR HEART-THROB SISTERS...
I'M SO EXCITED!

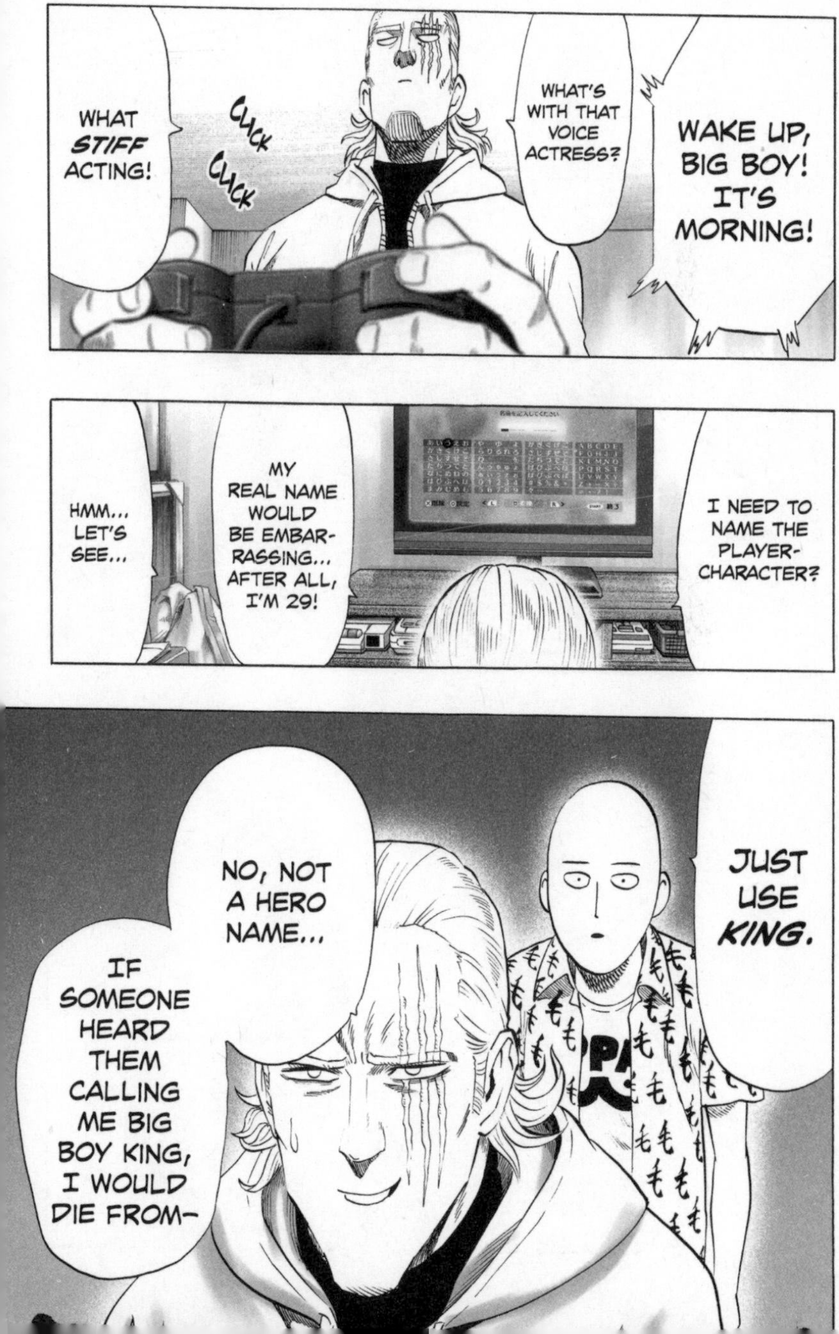
WAKE UP, BIG BOY! IT'S MORNING!
WHAT'S WITH THAT VOICE ACTRESS?
CLACK
CLACK
WHAT *STIFF* ACTING!
I NEED TO NAME THE PLAYER-CHARACTER?
MY REAL NAME WOULD BE EMBARRASSING... AFTER ALL, I'M 29!
HMM... LET'S SEE...
JUST USE *KING*.
NO, NOT A HERO NAME...
IF SOMEONE HEARD THEM CALLING ME BIG BOY KING, I WOULD DIE FROM-

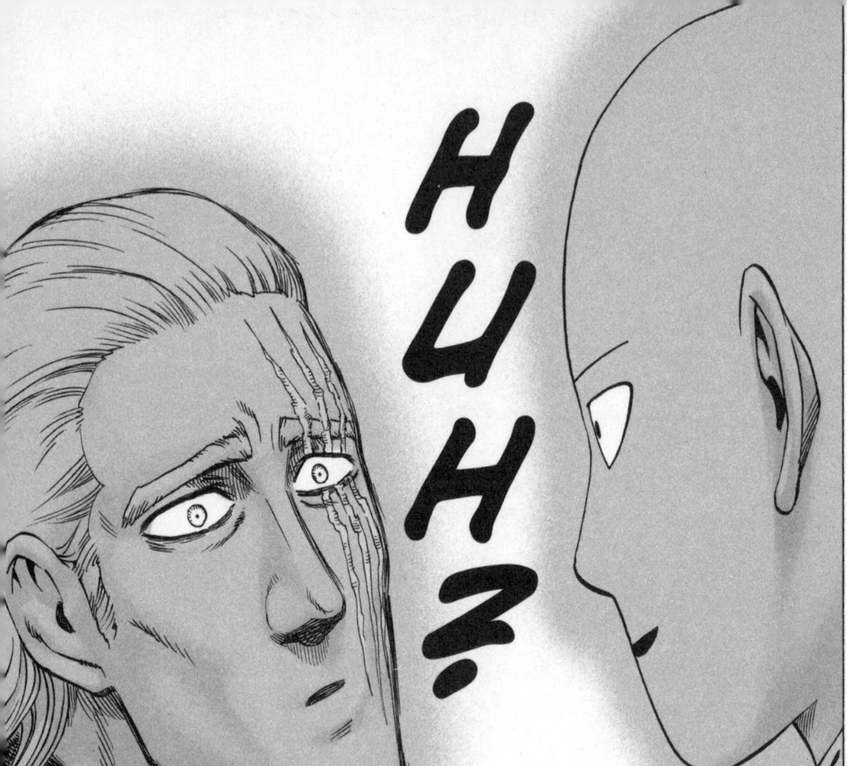
HUH?!

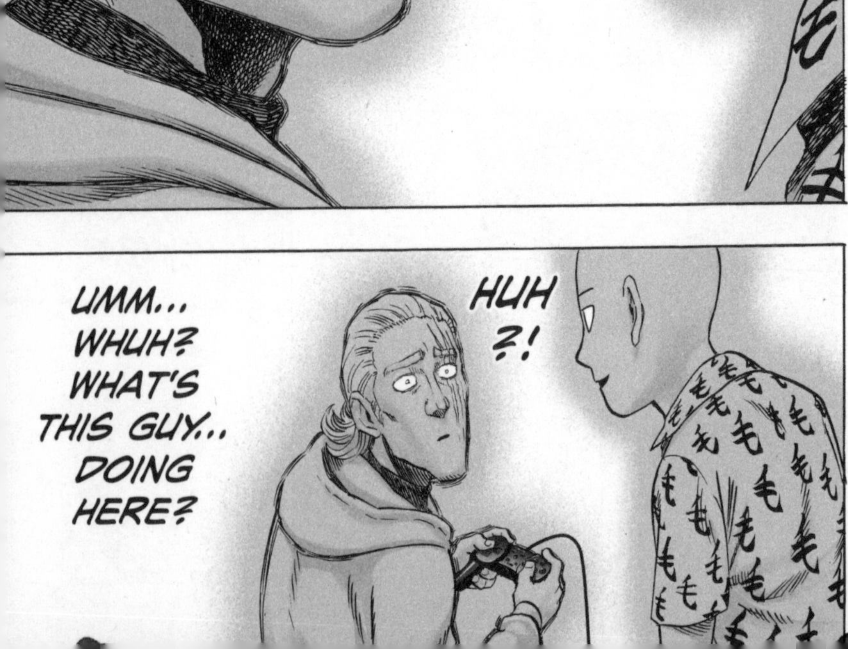
HUH ?!
UMM... WHUH? WHAT'S THIS GUY... DOING HERE?

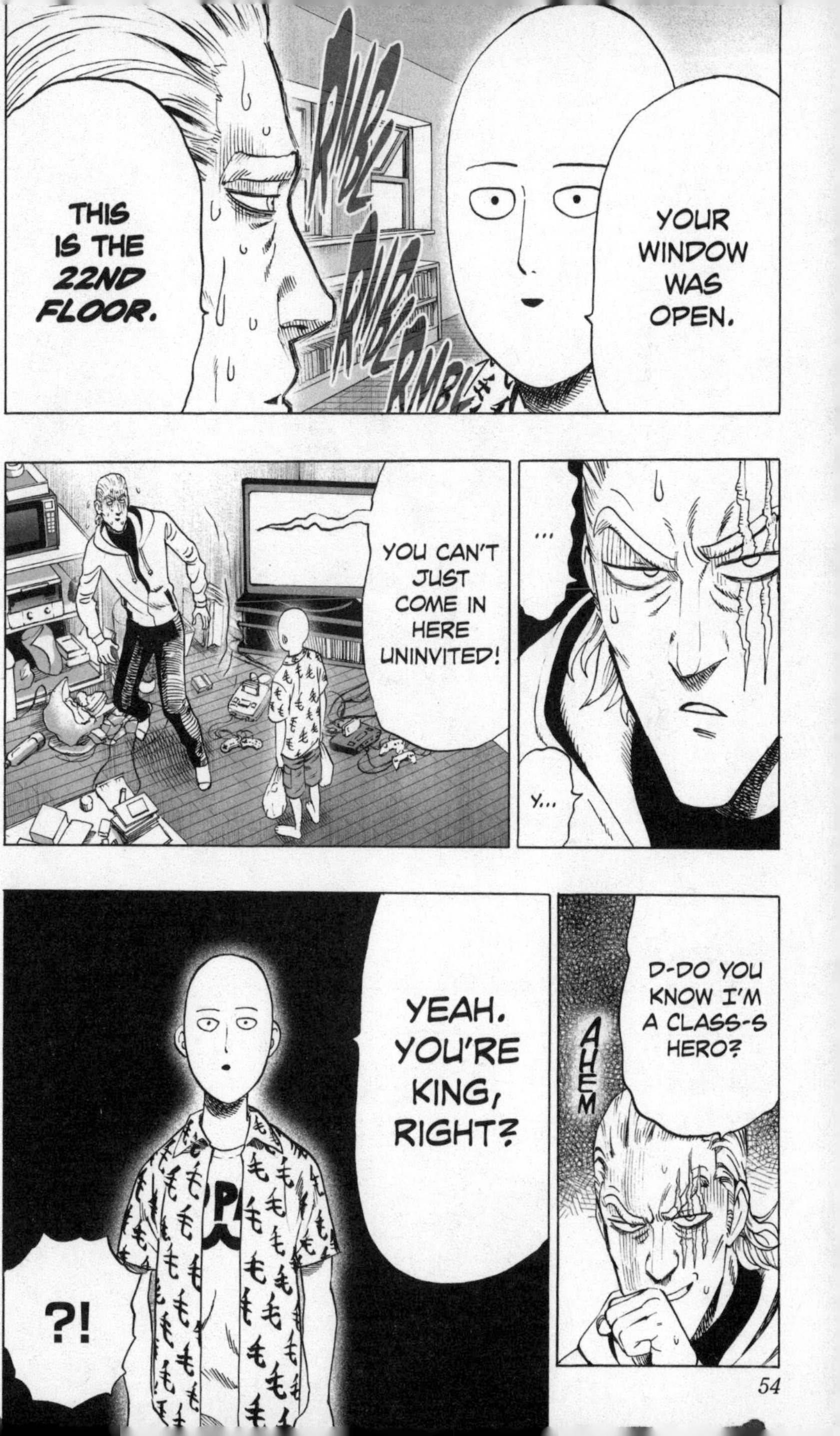
YOUR WINDOW WAS OPEN.
THIS IS THE 22ND FLOOR.
RMBL RMBL RMBL RMBL
...
Y...
YOU CAN'T JUST COME IN HERE UNINVITED!
AHEM
D-DO YOU KNOW I'M A CLASS-S HERO?
YEAH. YOU'RE KING, RIGHT?
?!

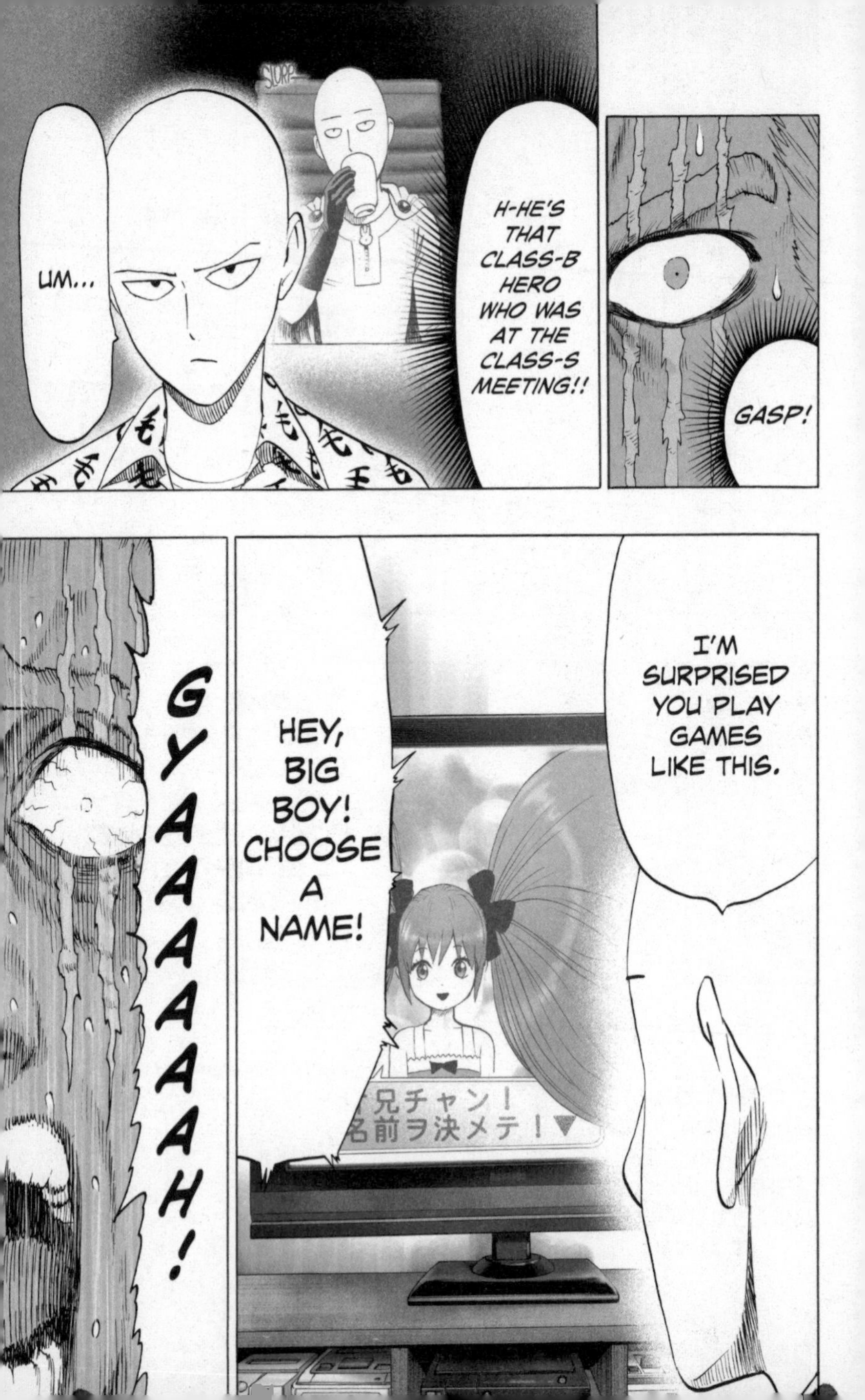
GASP!
H-HE'S THAT CLASS-B HERO WHO WAS AT THE CLASS-S MEETING!!
SLURP
UM...
I'M SURPRISED YOU PLAY GAMES LIKE THIS.
HEY, BIG BOY! CHOOSE A NAME!
兄チャン！
名前ヲ決メテ！
GYAAAAAAAH!

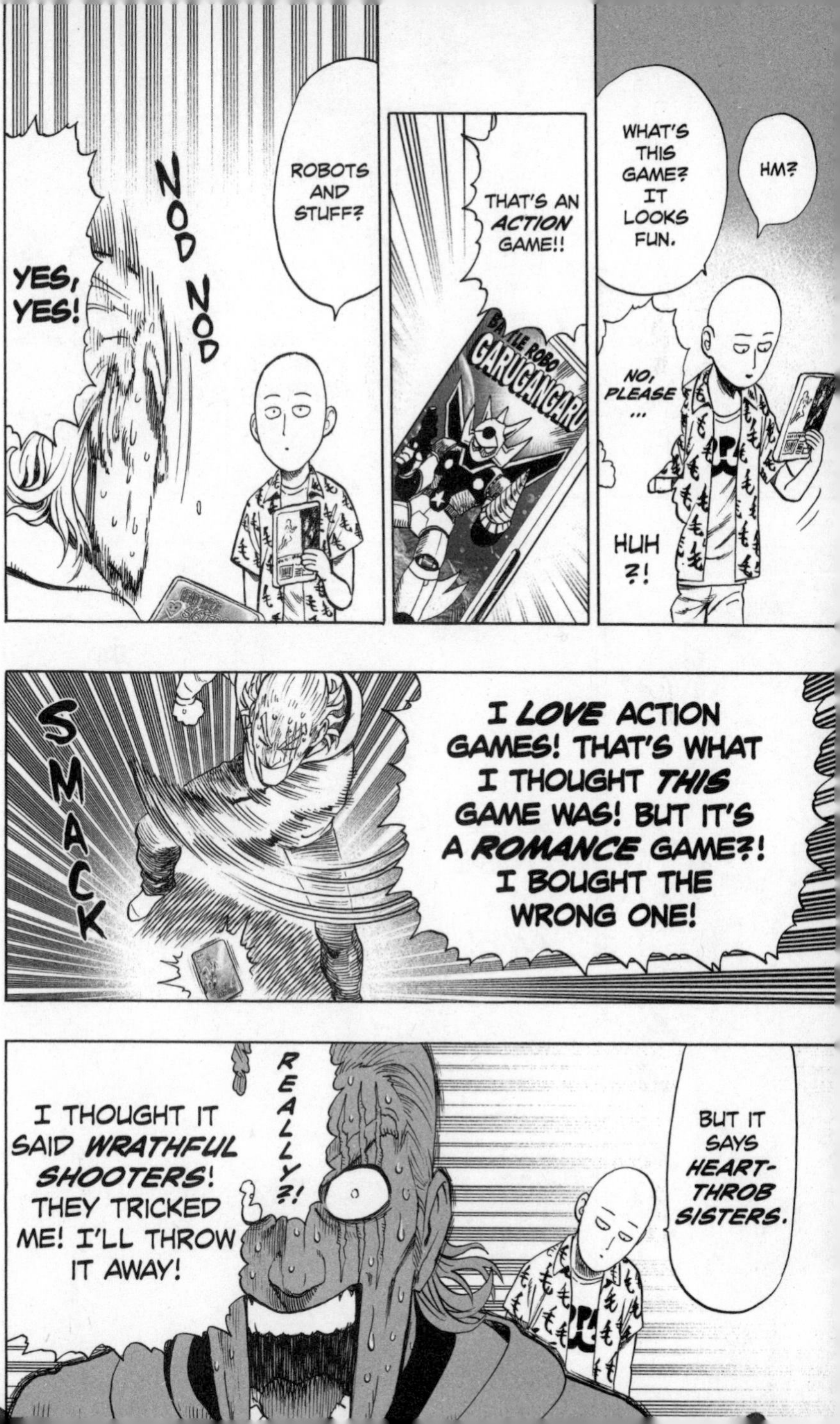
HM?
WHAT'S THIS GAME? IT LOOKS FUN.
NO, PLEASE ...
HUH ?!
BATTLE ROBO GARUGANGARU
THAT'S AN ACTION GAME!!
ROBOTS AND STUFF?
NOD NOD
YES, YES!
I LOVE ACTION GAMES! THAT'S WHAT I THOUGHT THIS GAME WAS! BUT IT'S A ROMANCE GAME?! I BOUGHT THE WRONG ONE!
SMACK
BUT IT SAYS HEART-THROB SISTERS.
REALLY?!
I THOUGHT IT SAID WRATHFUL SHOOTERS! THEY TRICKED ME! I'LL THROW IT AWAY!

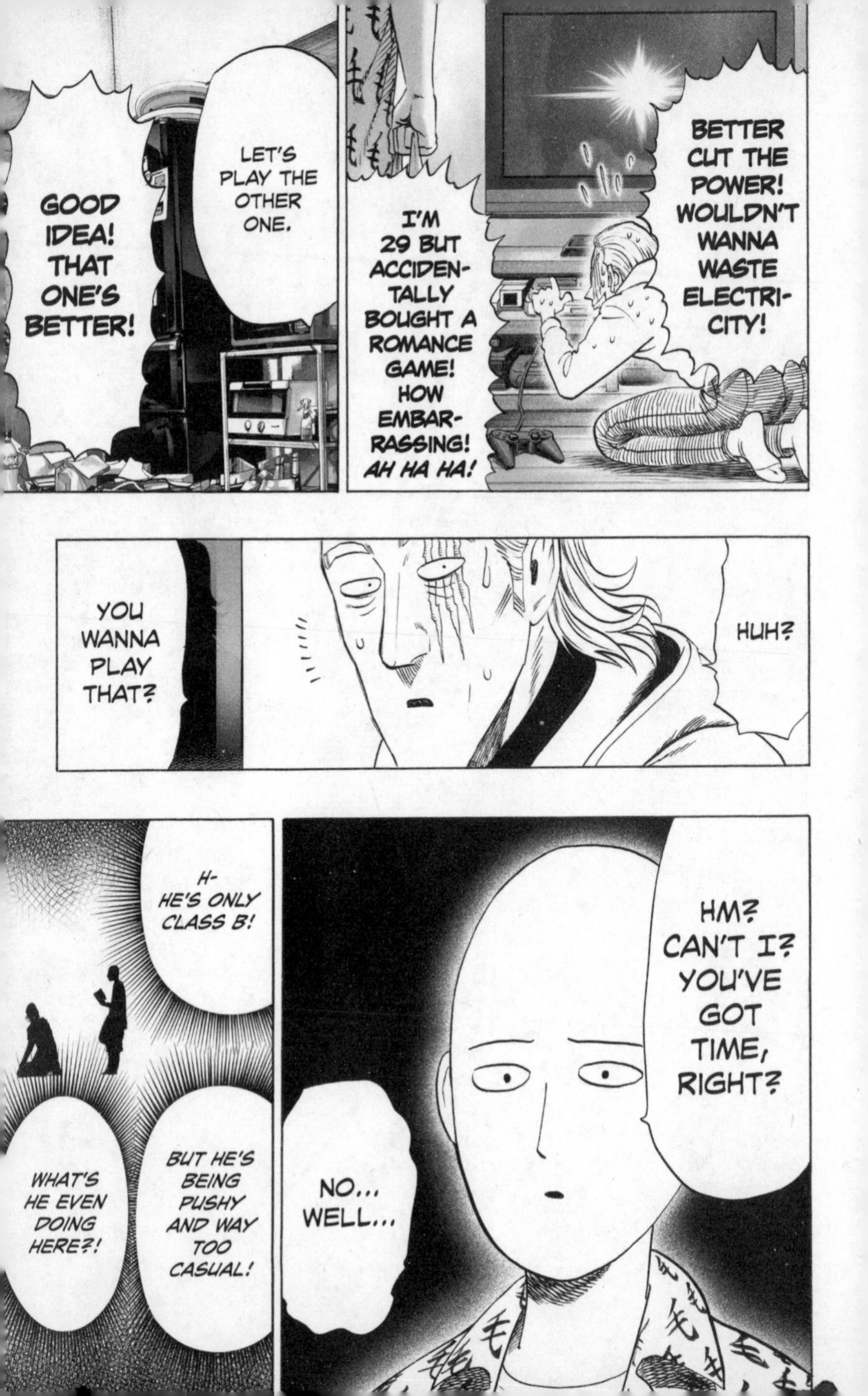
BETTER CUT THE POWER! WOULDN'T WANNA WASTE ELECTRICITY!
I'M 29 BUT ACCIDENTALLY BOUGHT A ROMANCE GAME! HOW EMBARRASSING! AH HA HA!
LET'S PLAY THE OTHER ONE.
GOOD IDEA! THAT ONE'S BETTER!
HUH?
YOU WANNA PLAY THAT?
HM? CAN'T I? YOU'VE GOT TIME, RIGHT?
NO... WELL...
H-HE'S ONLY CLASS B!
BUT HE'S BEING PUSHY AND WAY TOO CASUAL!
WHAT'S HE EVEN DOING HERE?!

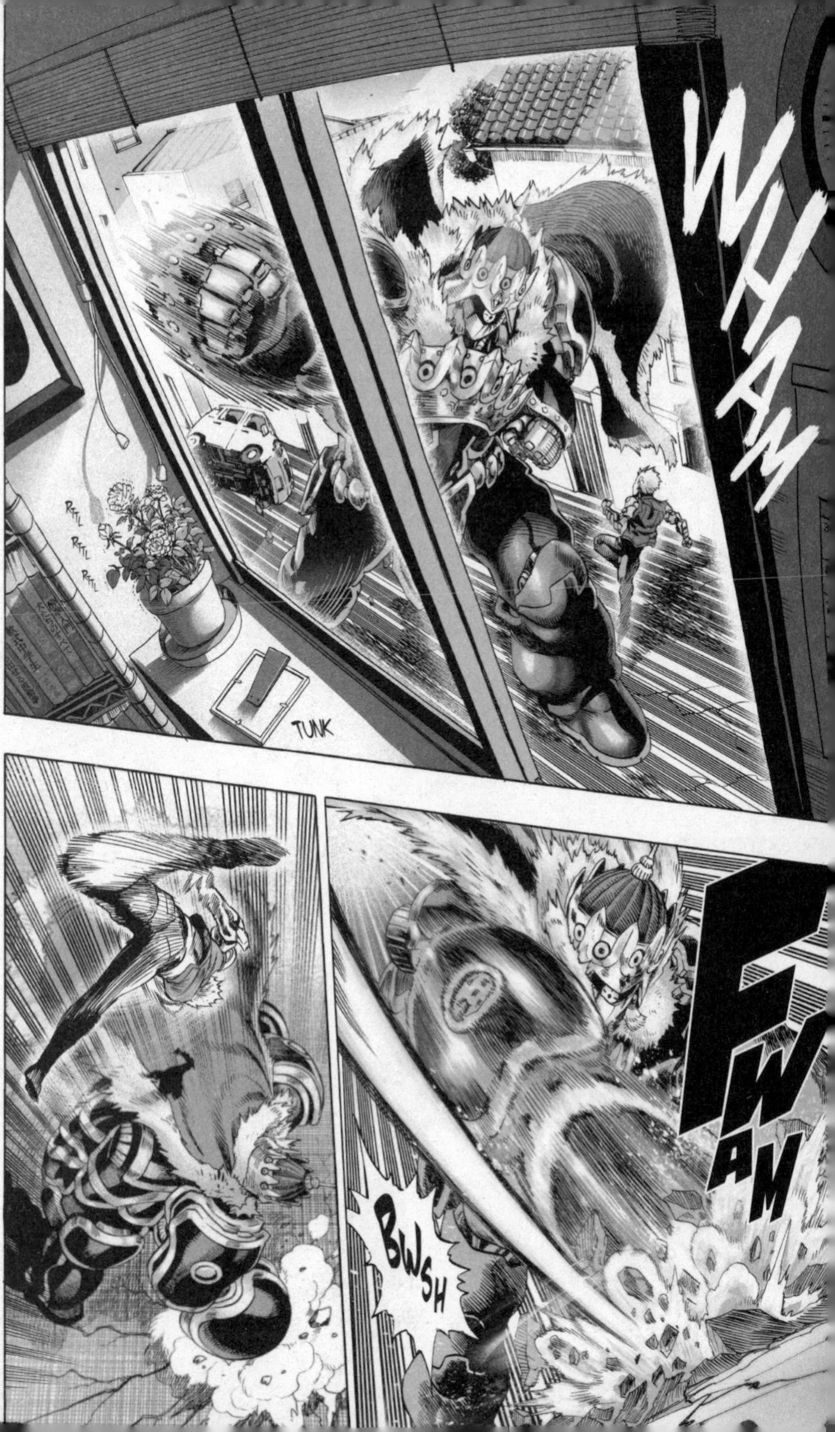
WHAM
RTTL
RTTL
RTTL
TUNK
FWAM
BWSH

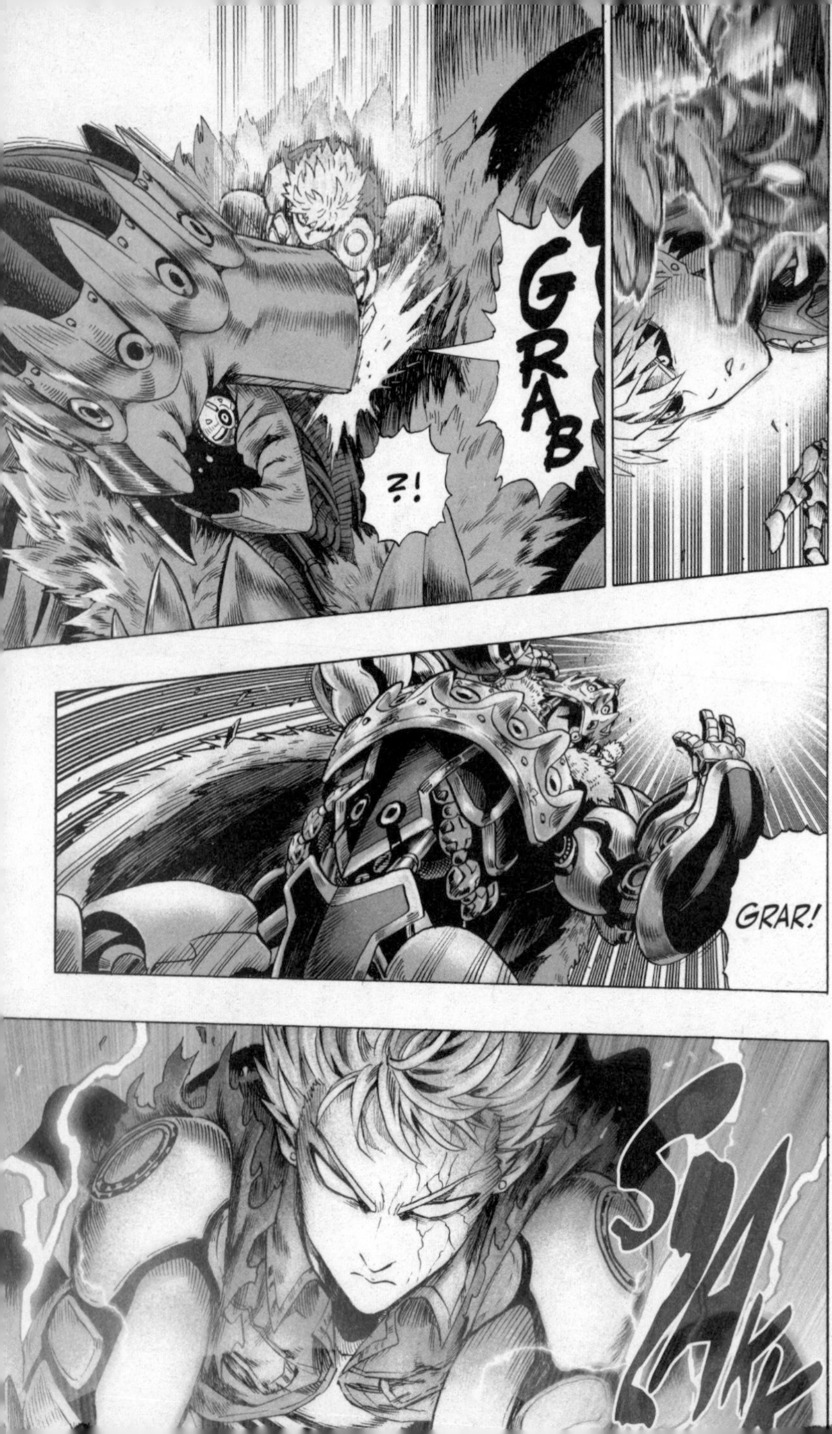
GRAB
?!
GRAR!

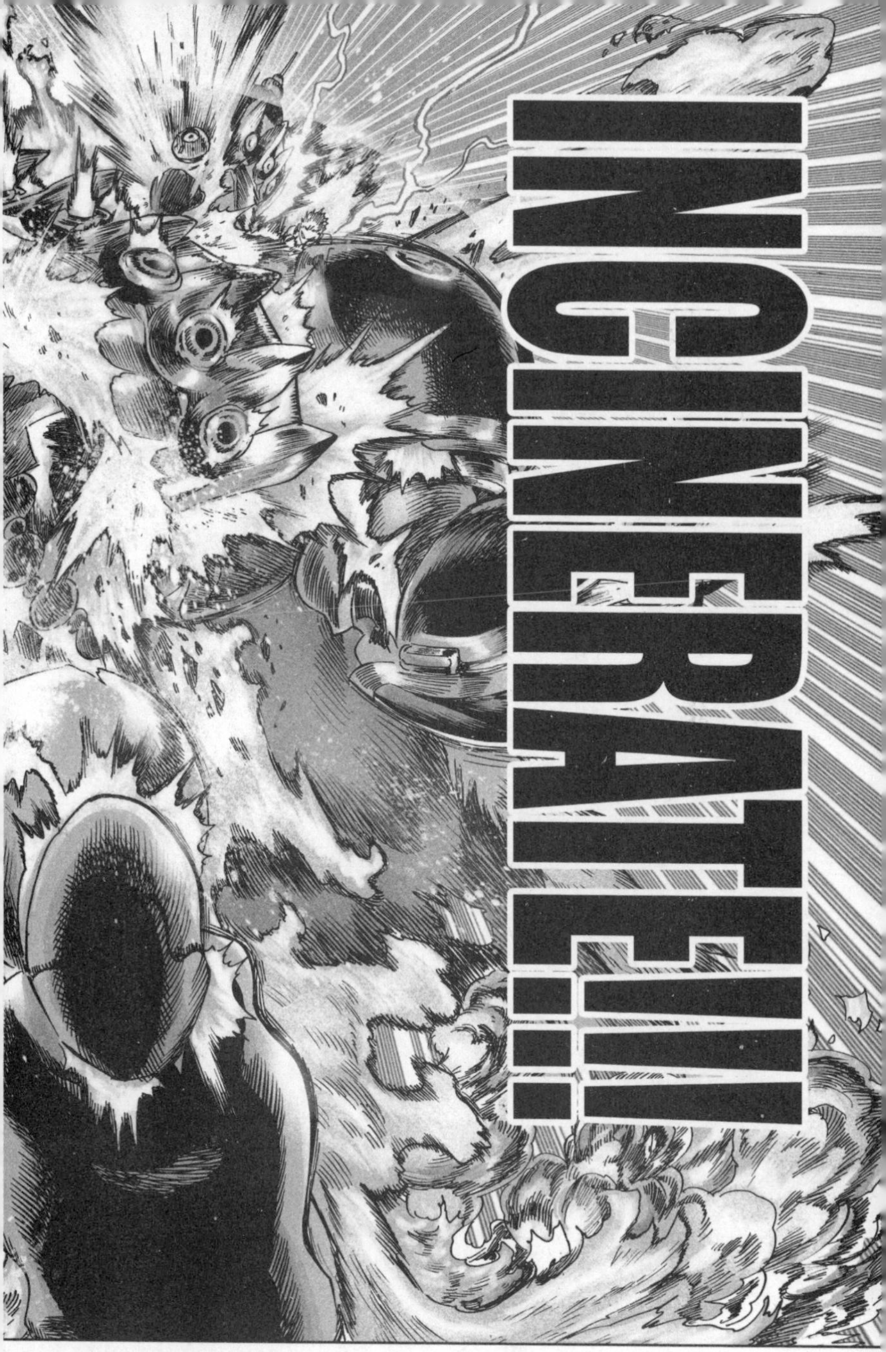
INCINERATE!!

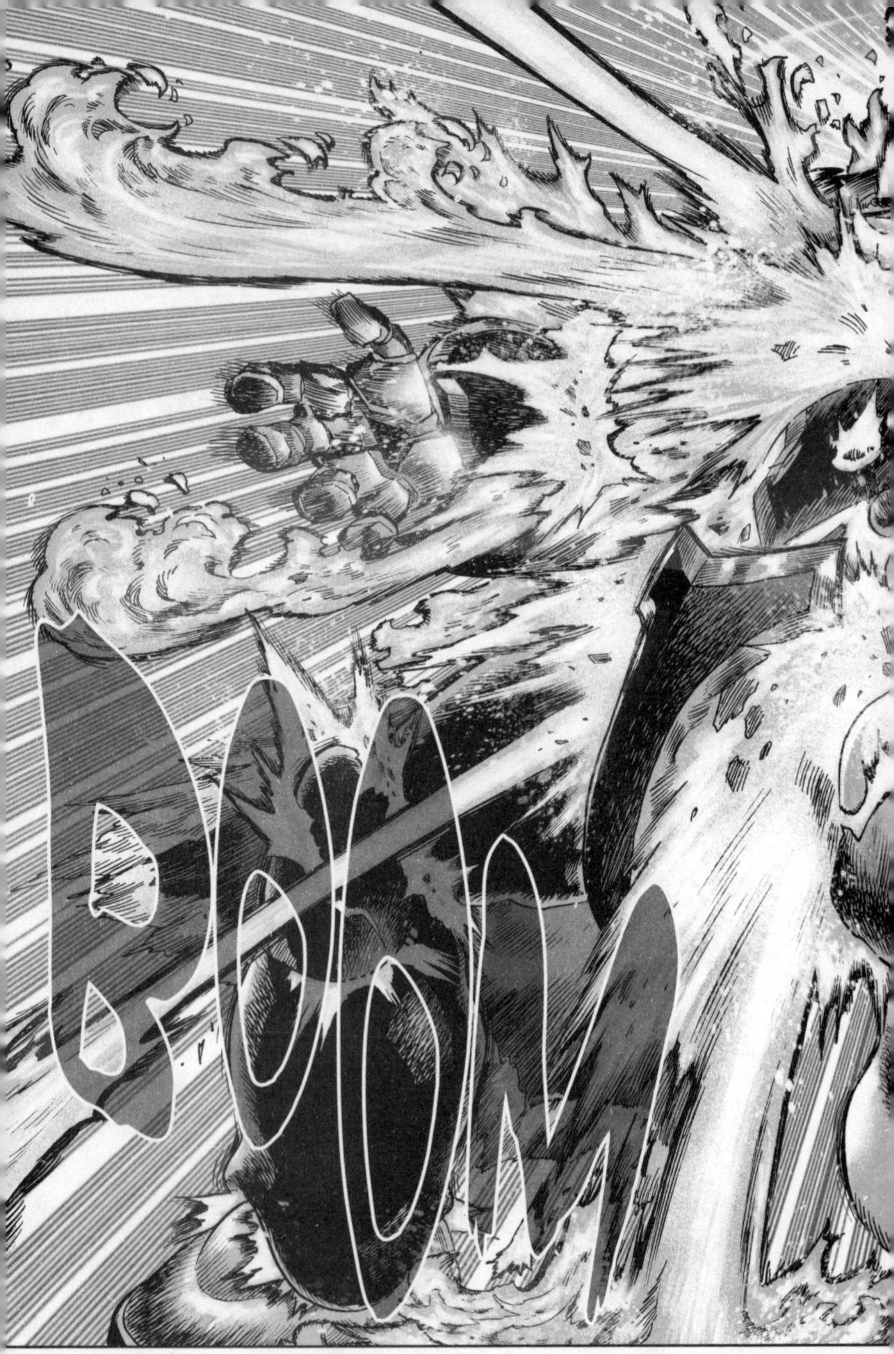
DOOOM

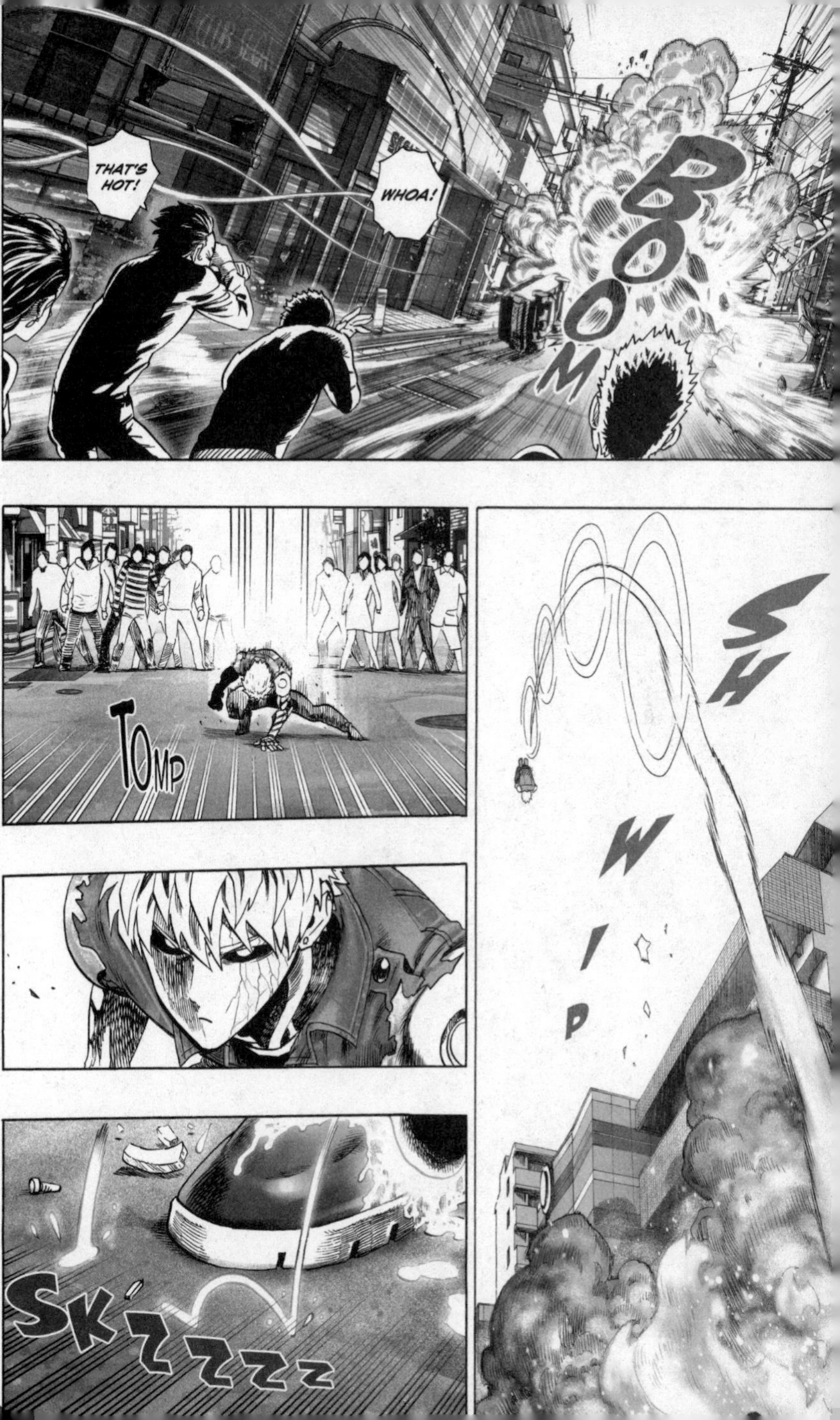
BOOM
WHOA!
THAT'S HOT!
SHWIP
TOMP
SKZZZZZ

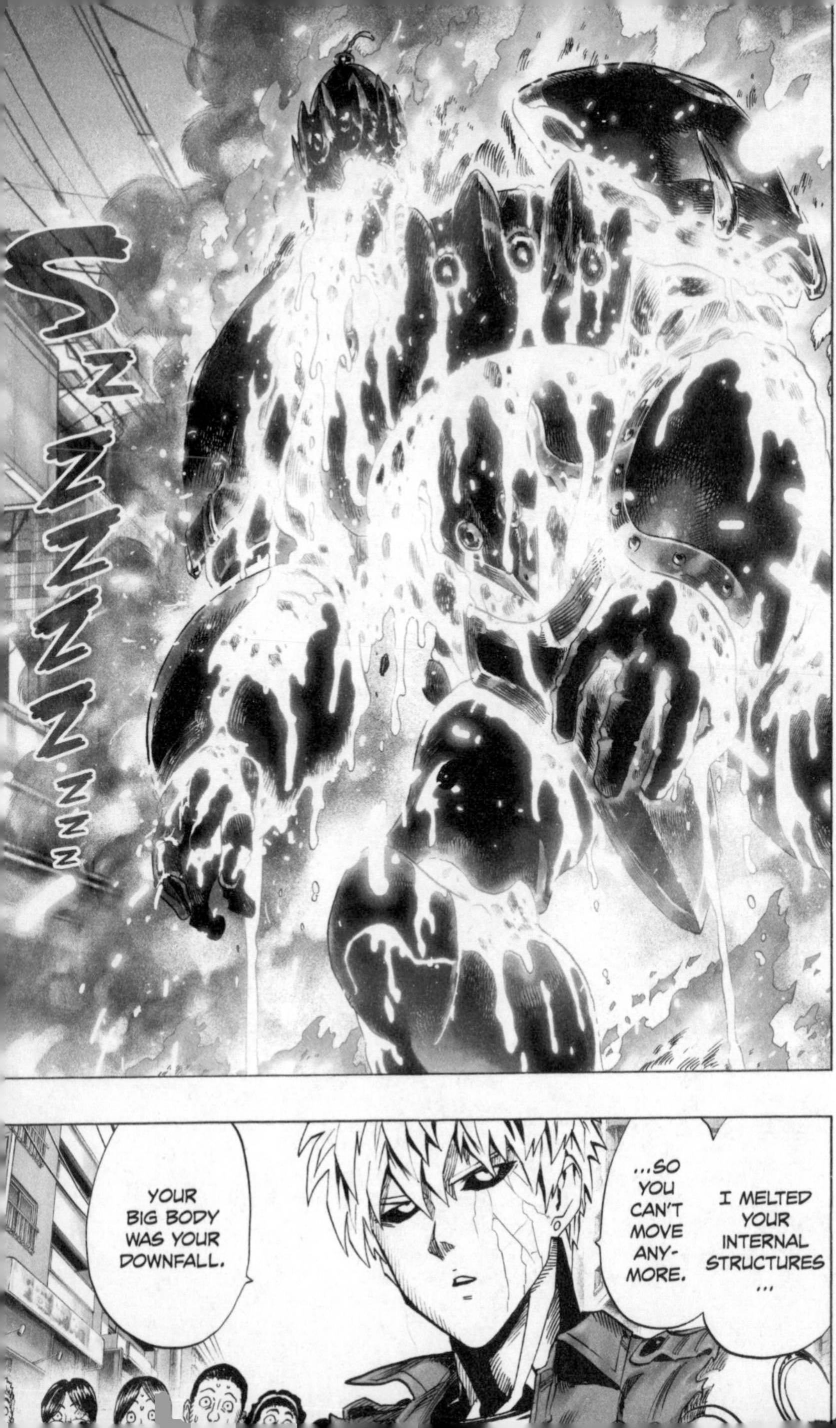
SZZZZZZZZzzzz
I MELTED YOUR INTERNAL STRUCTURES ...
...SO YOU CAN'T MOVE ANY-MORE.
YOUR BIG BODY WAS YOUR DOWNFALL.

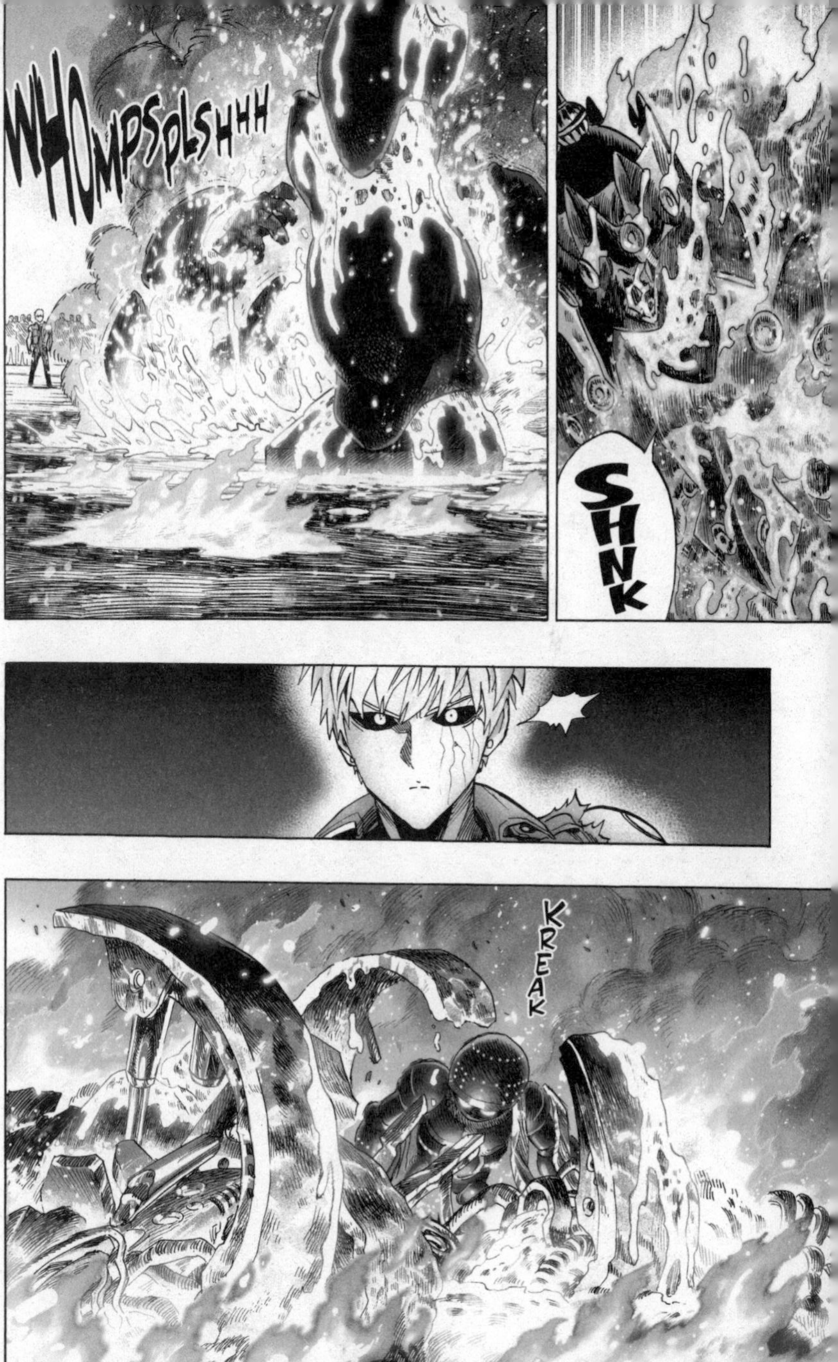
SHNK
WHOMPSPLSHHH
KREAK

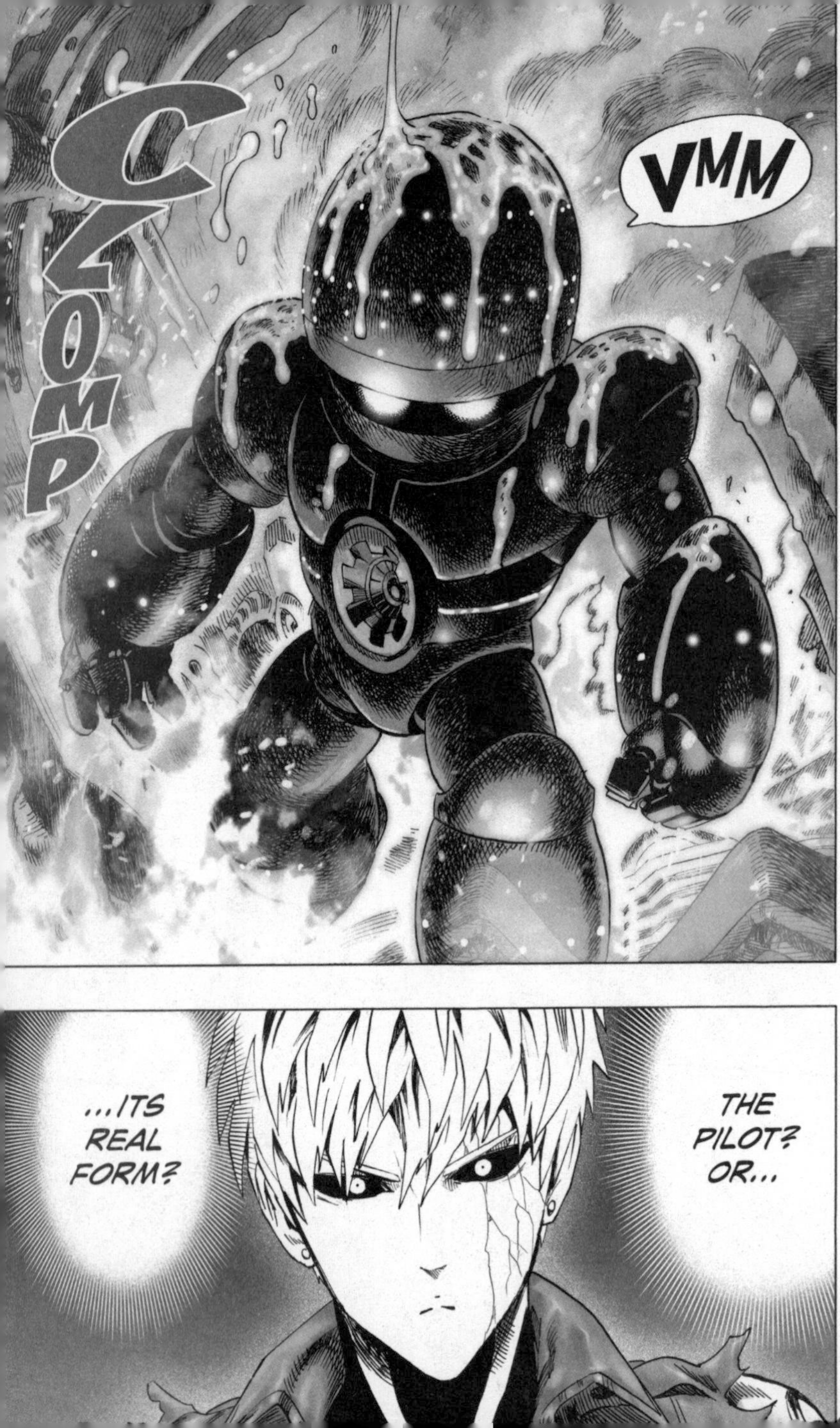
VMM
CLOMP
THE PILOT? OR...
...ITS REAL FORM?

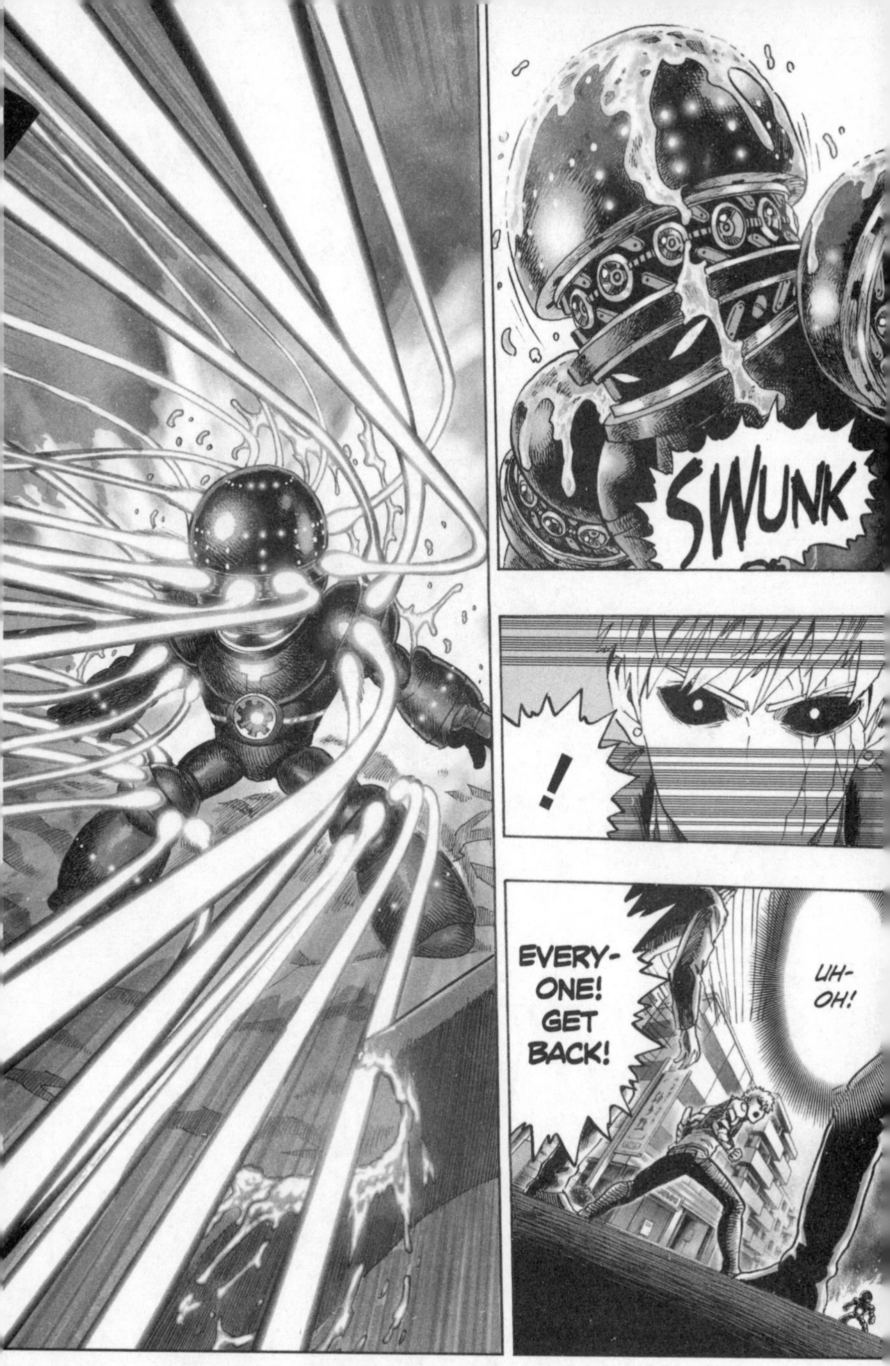
SWUNK
!
EVERY-ONE! GET BACK!
UH-OH!

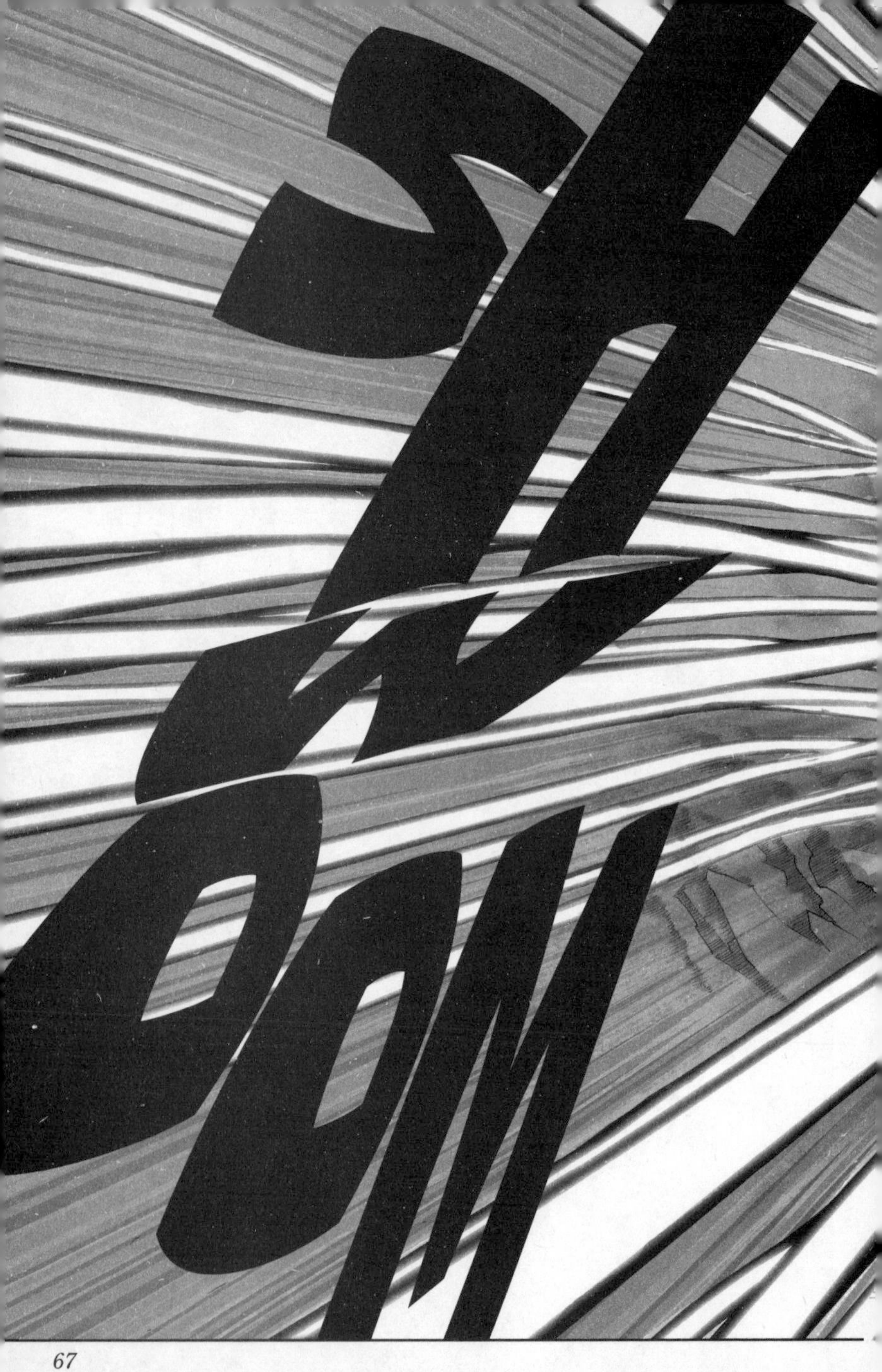
SHUBOM

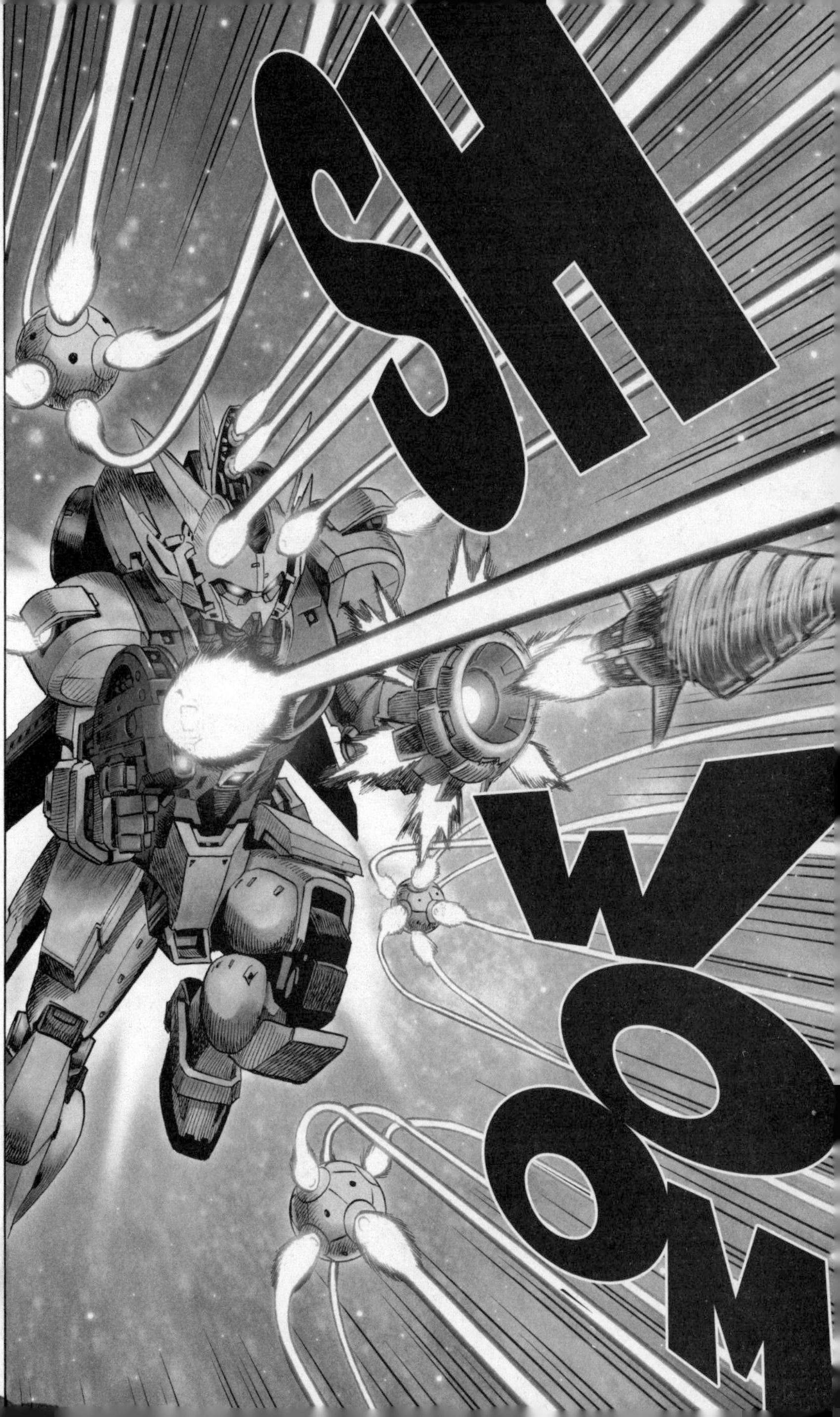
SHWOOM

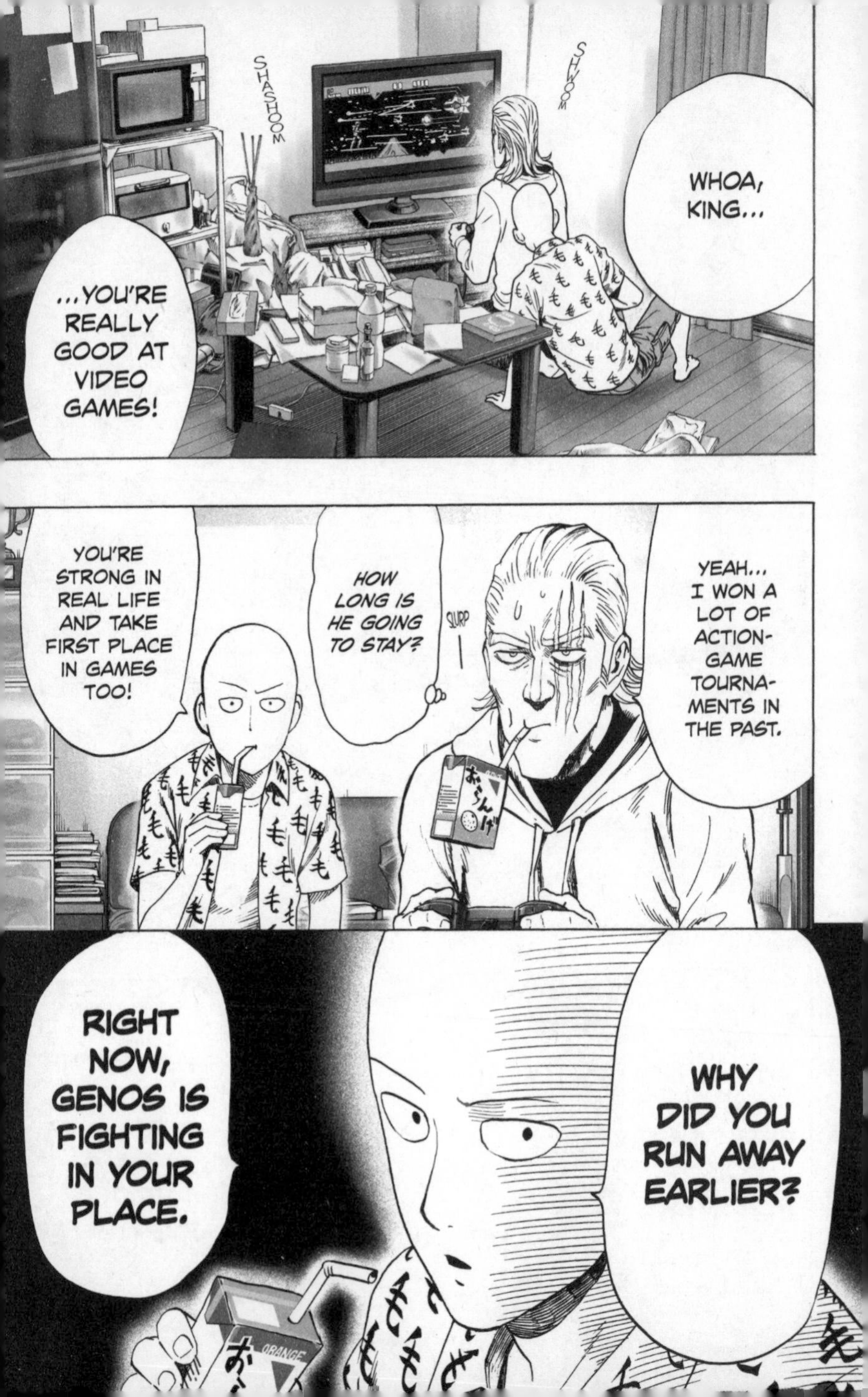
WHOA, KING...
SHWOOM
SHASHOOM
...YOU'RE REALLY GOOD AT VIDEO GAMES!
YEAH... I WON A LOT OF ACTION-GAME TOURNAMENTS IN THE PAST.
SLURP
HOW LONG IS HE GOING TO STAY?
YOU'RE STRONG IN REAL LIFE AND TAKE FIRST PLACE IN GAMES TOO!
WHY DID YOU RUN AWAY EARLIER?
RIGHT NOW, GENOS IS FIGHTING IN YOUR PLACE.
ORANGE

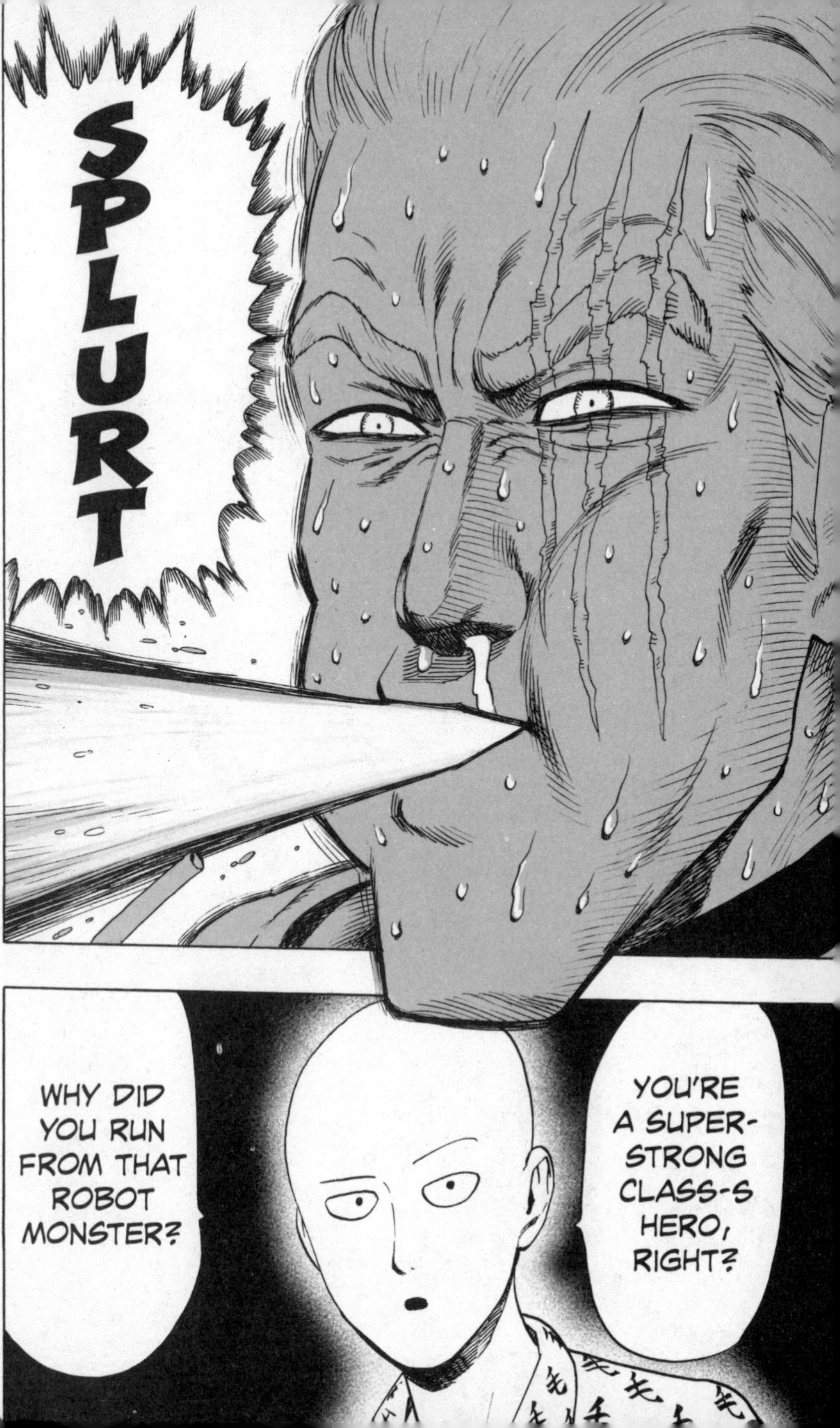
SPLURT
YOU'RE A SUPER-STRONG CLASS-S HERO, RIGHT?
WHY DID YOU RUN FROM THAT ROBOT MONSTER?

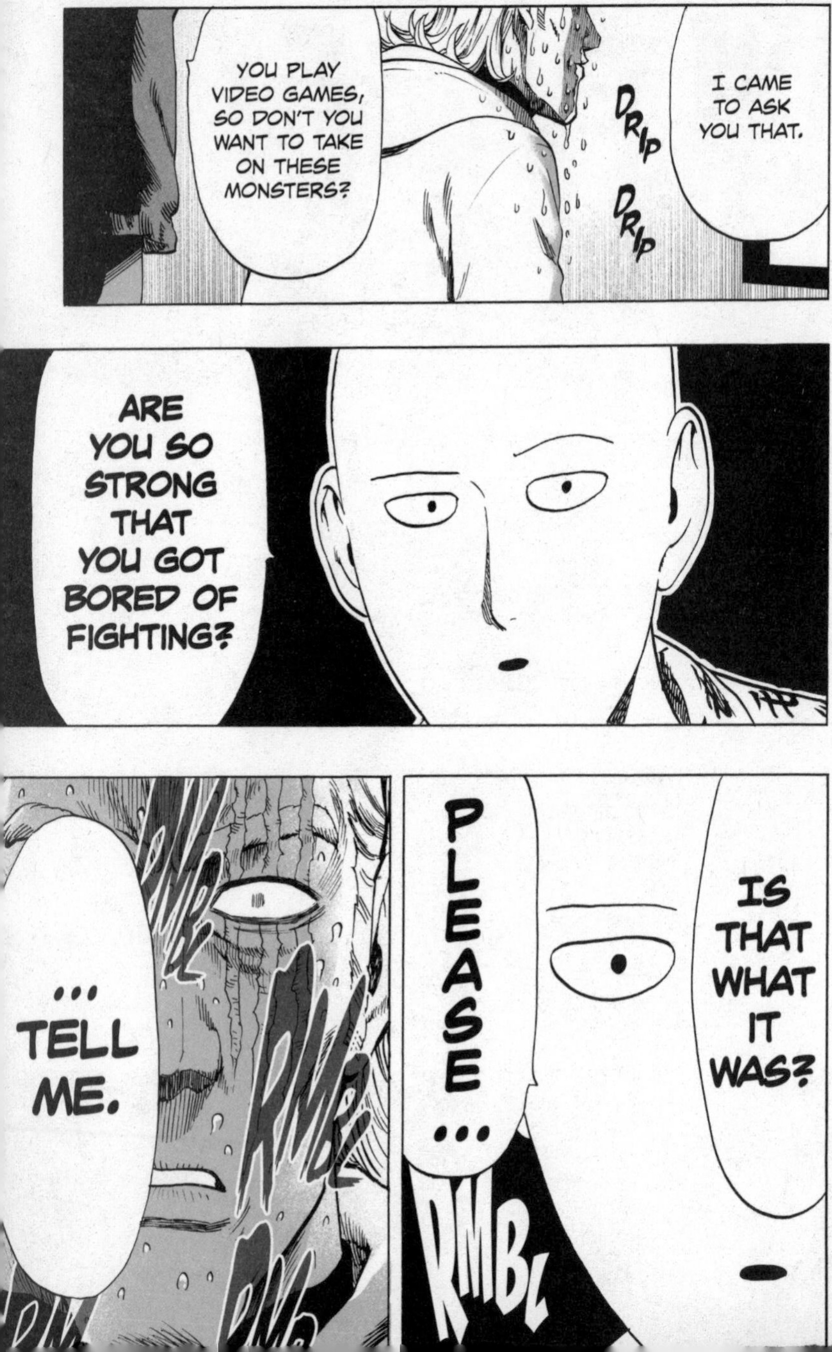
I CAME TO ASK YOU THAT.
DRIP
DRIP
YOU PLAY VIDEO GAMES, SO DON'T YOU WANT TO TAKE ON THESE MONSTERS?
ARE YOU SO STRONG THAT YOU GOT BORED OF FIGHTING?
IS THAT WHAT IT WAS?
PLEASE...
RMBL
...TELL ME.

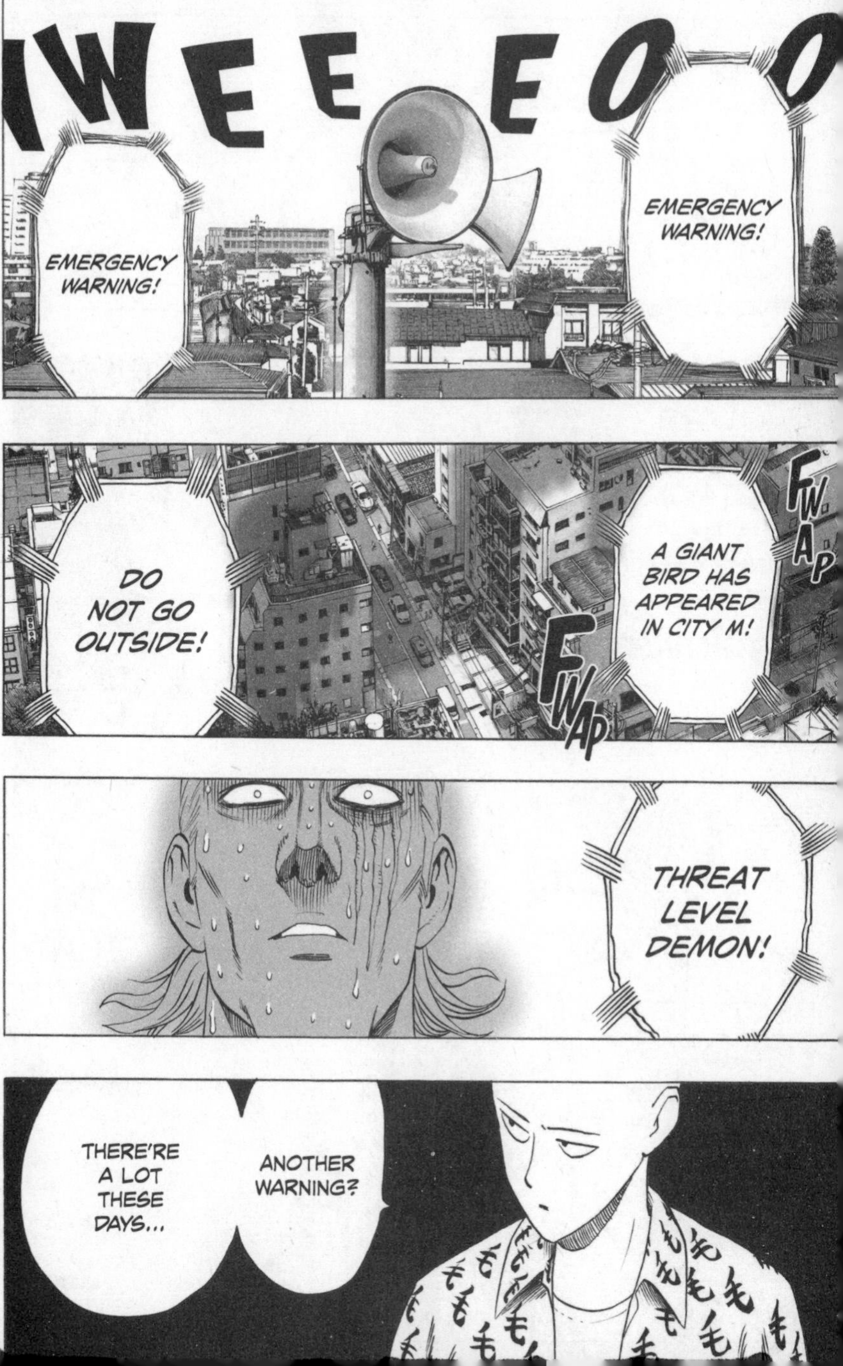
IWEEEOO
EMERGENCY WARNING!
EMERGENCY WARNING!
A GIANT BIRD HAS APPEARED IN CITY M!
FWAP
DO NOT GO OUTSIDE!
FWAP
THREAT LEVEL DEMON!
ANOTHER WARNING?
THERE'RE A LOT THESE DAYS...

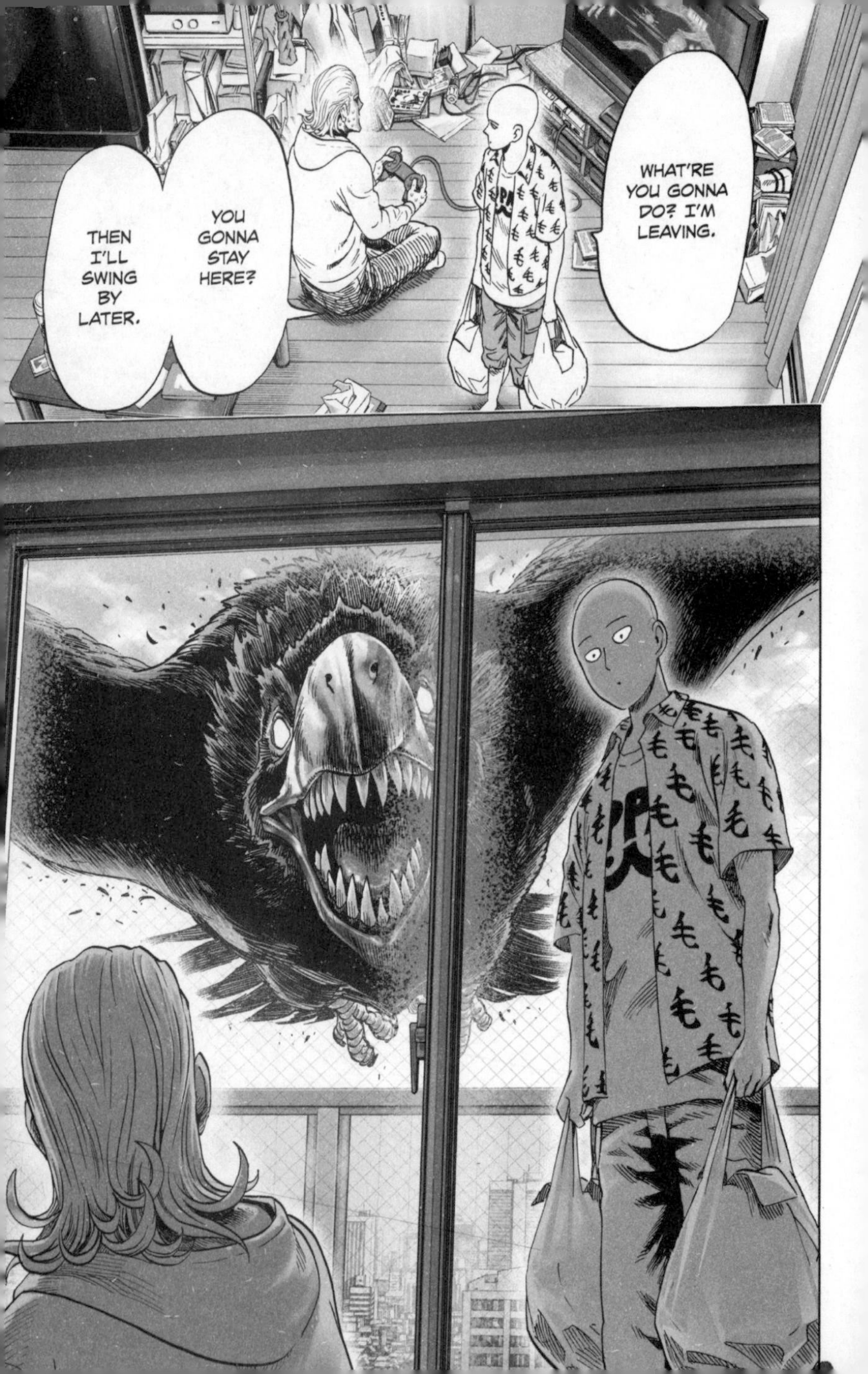
WHAT'RE YOU GONNA DO? I'M LEAVING.
YOU GONNA STAY HERE?
THEN I'LL SWING BY LATER.

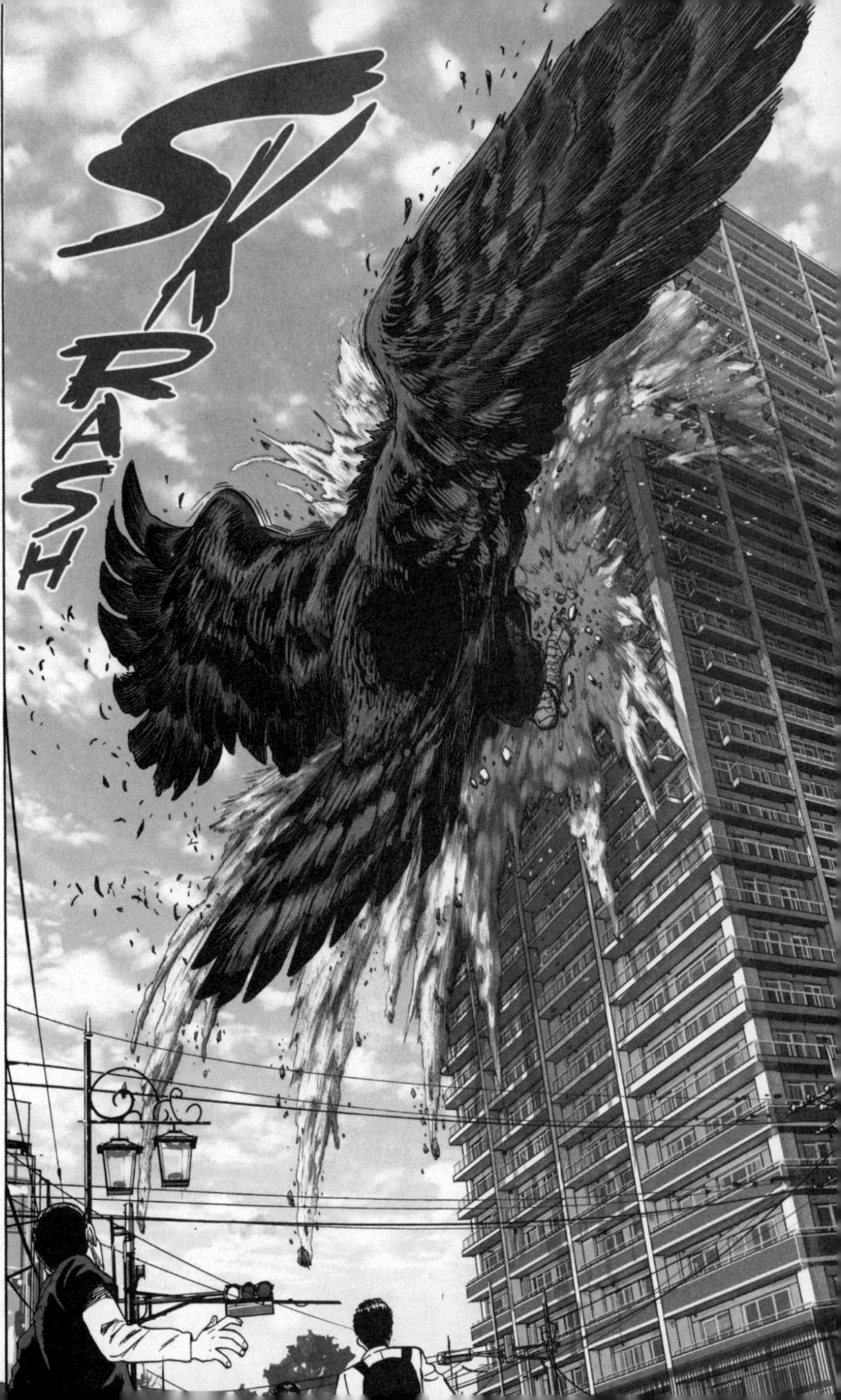
SKRASH

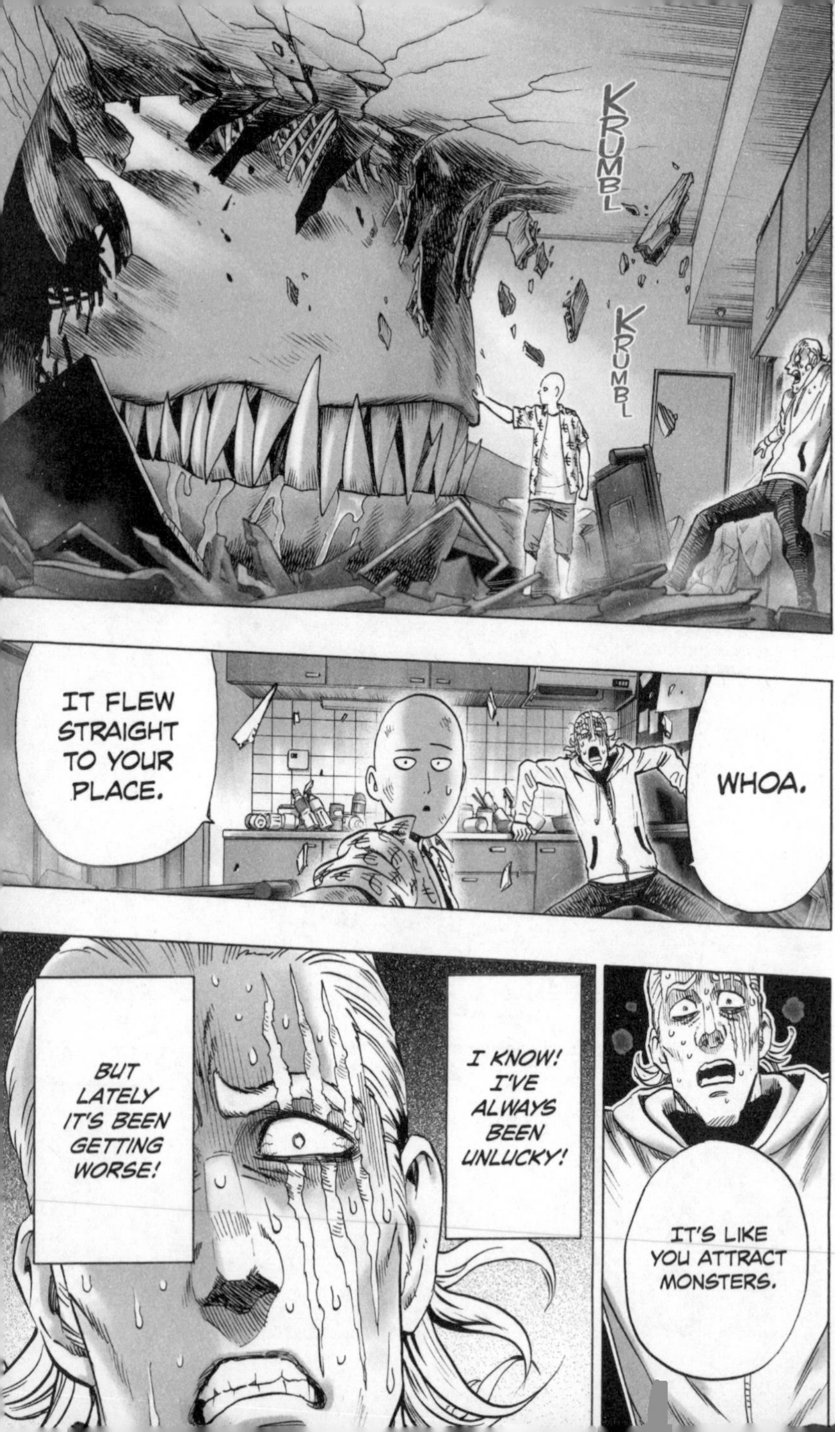
KRUMBL
KRUMBL
WHOA.
IT FLEW STRAIGHT TO YOUR PLACE.
IT'S LIKE YOU ATTRACT MONSTERS.
I KNOW! I'VE ALWAYS BEEN UNLUCKY!
BUT LATELY IT'S BEEN GETTING WORSE!

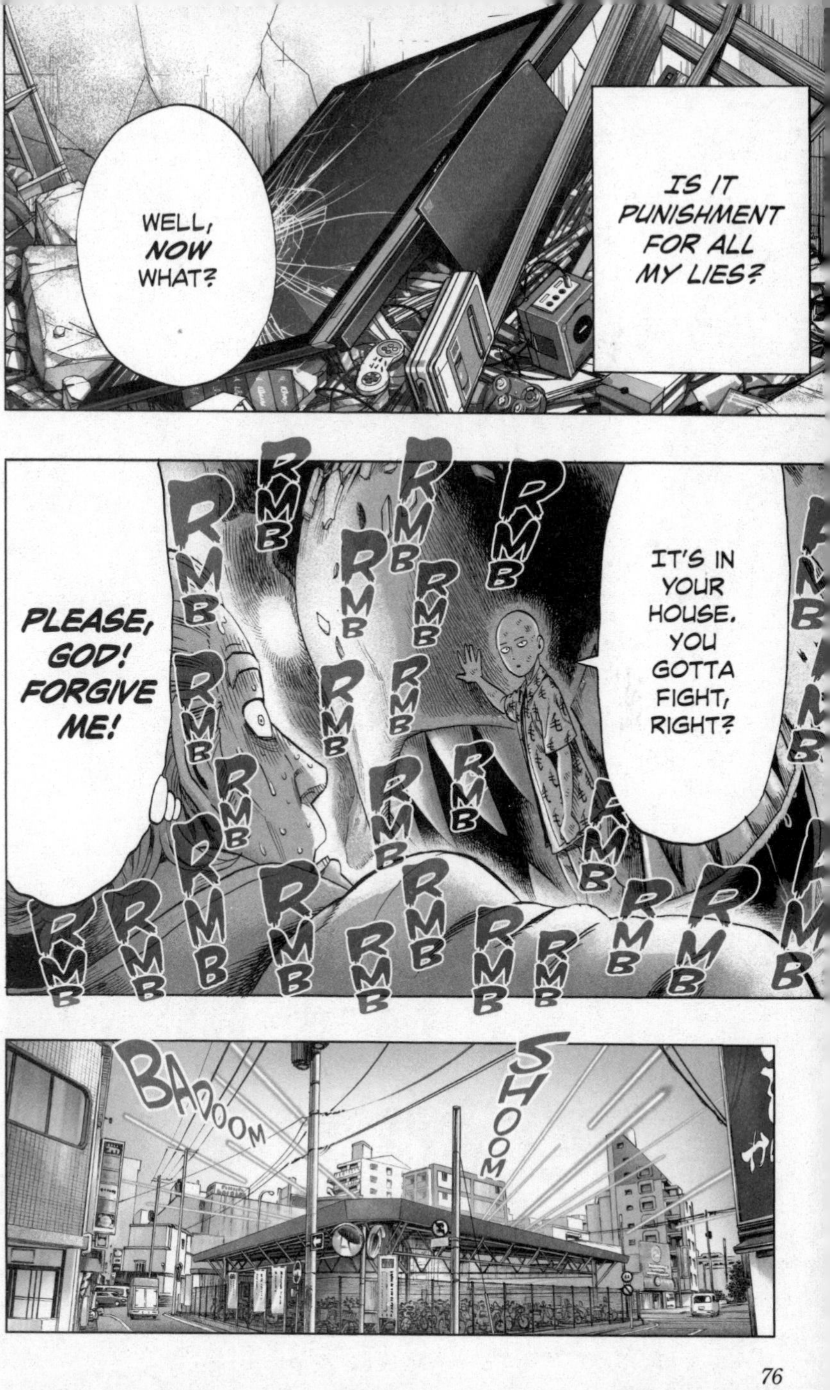
IS IT PUNISHMENT FOR ALL MY LIES?
WELL, NOW WHAT?
IT'S IN YOUR HOUSE. YOU GOTTA FIGHT, RIGHT?
PLEASE, GOD! FORGIVE ME!
RMB
SHOOM
BADOOM

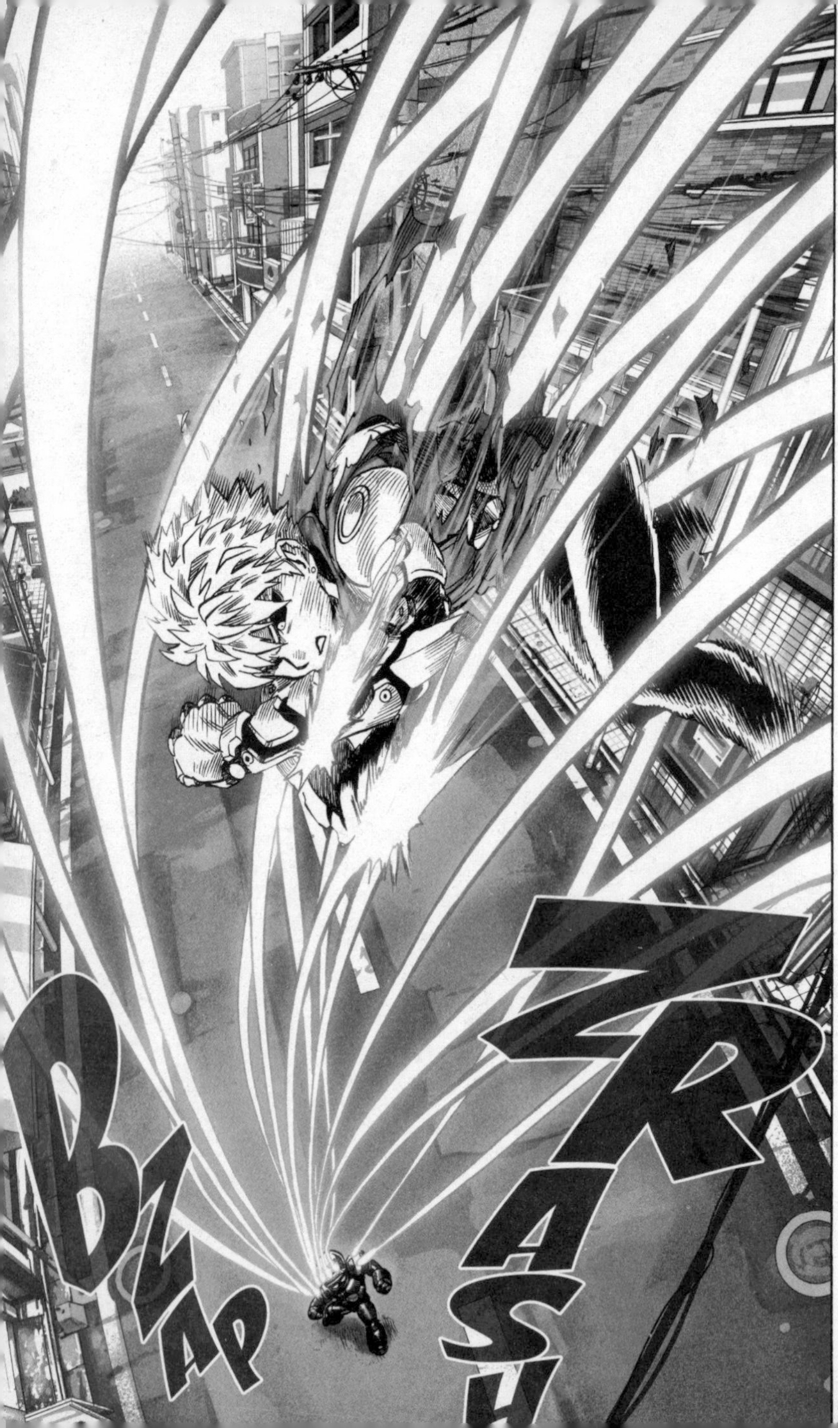
ZRASH
BZZAP

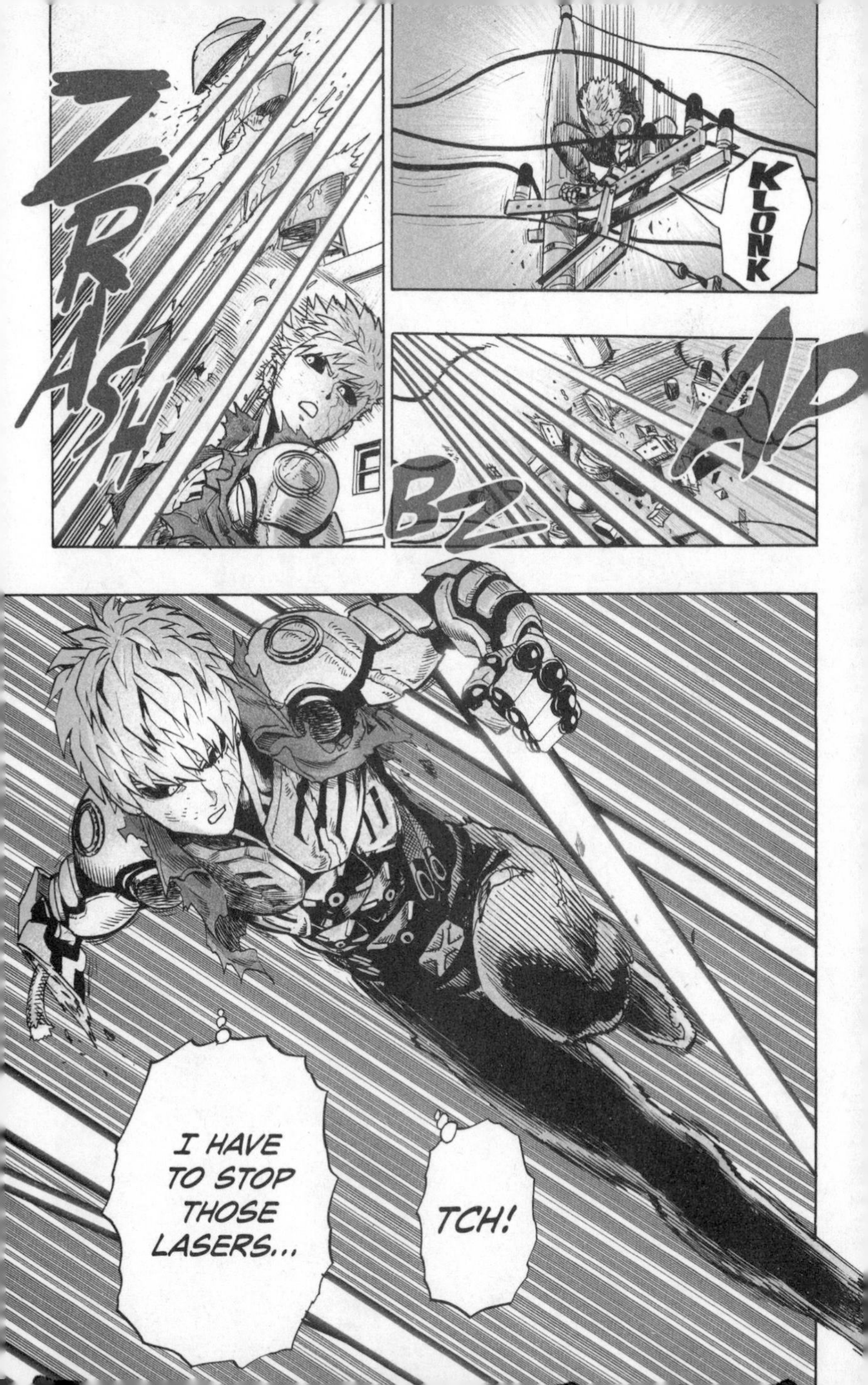
KLONK
BZ
AP
ZRASH
TCH!
I HAVE TO STOP THOSE LASERS...

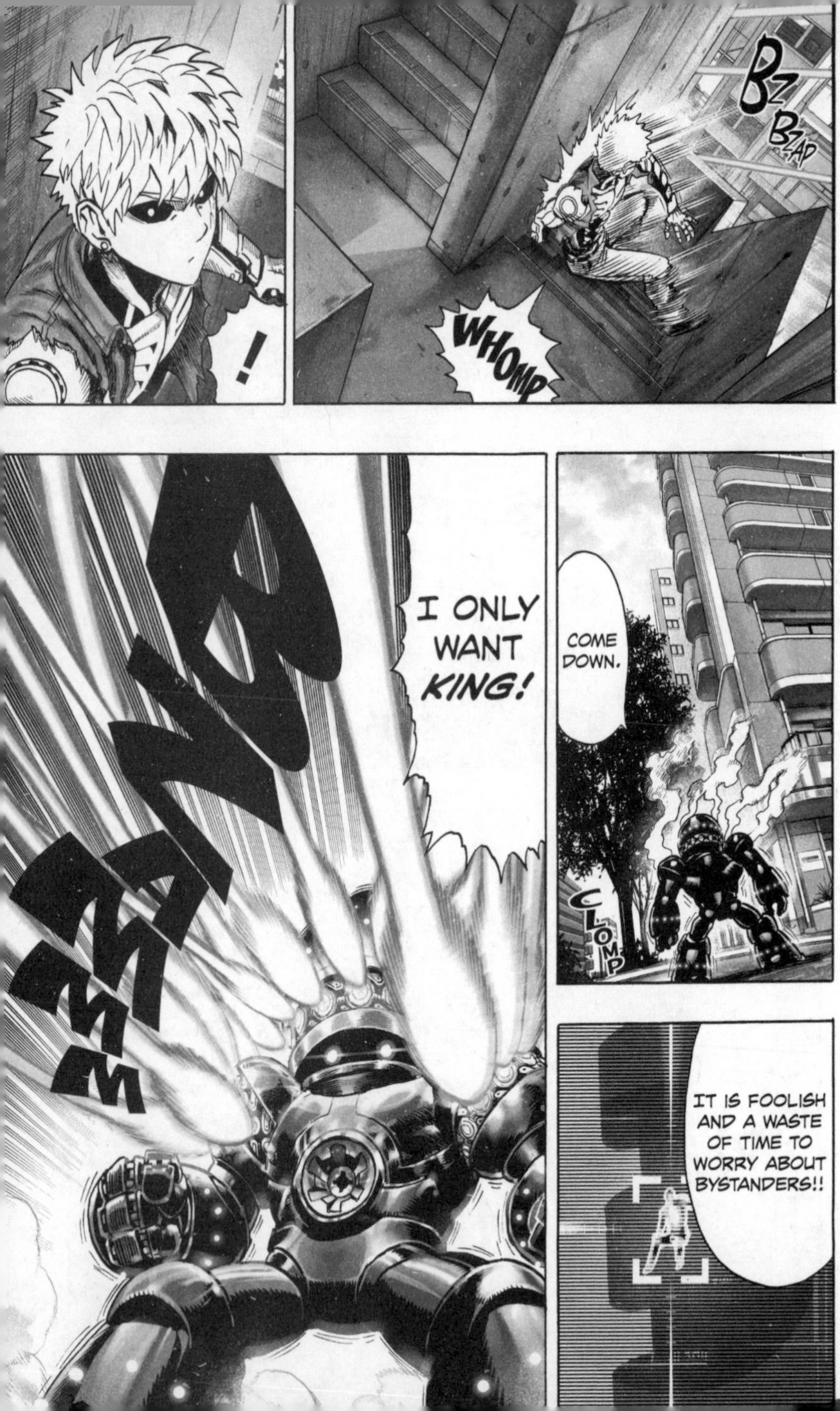
BZ
BZAP
WHOMP
!
COME DOWN.
CLOMP
IT IS FOOLISH AND A WASTE OF TIME TO WORRY ABOUT BYSTANDERS!!
I ONLY WANT KING!

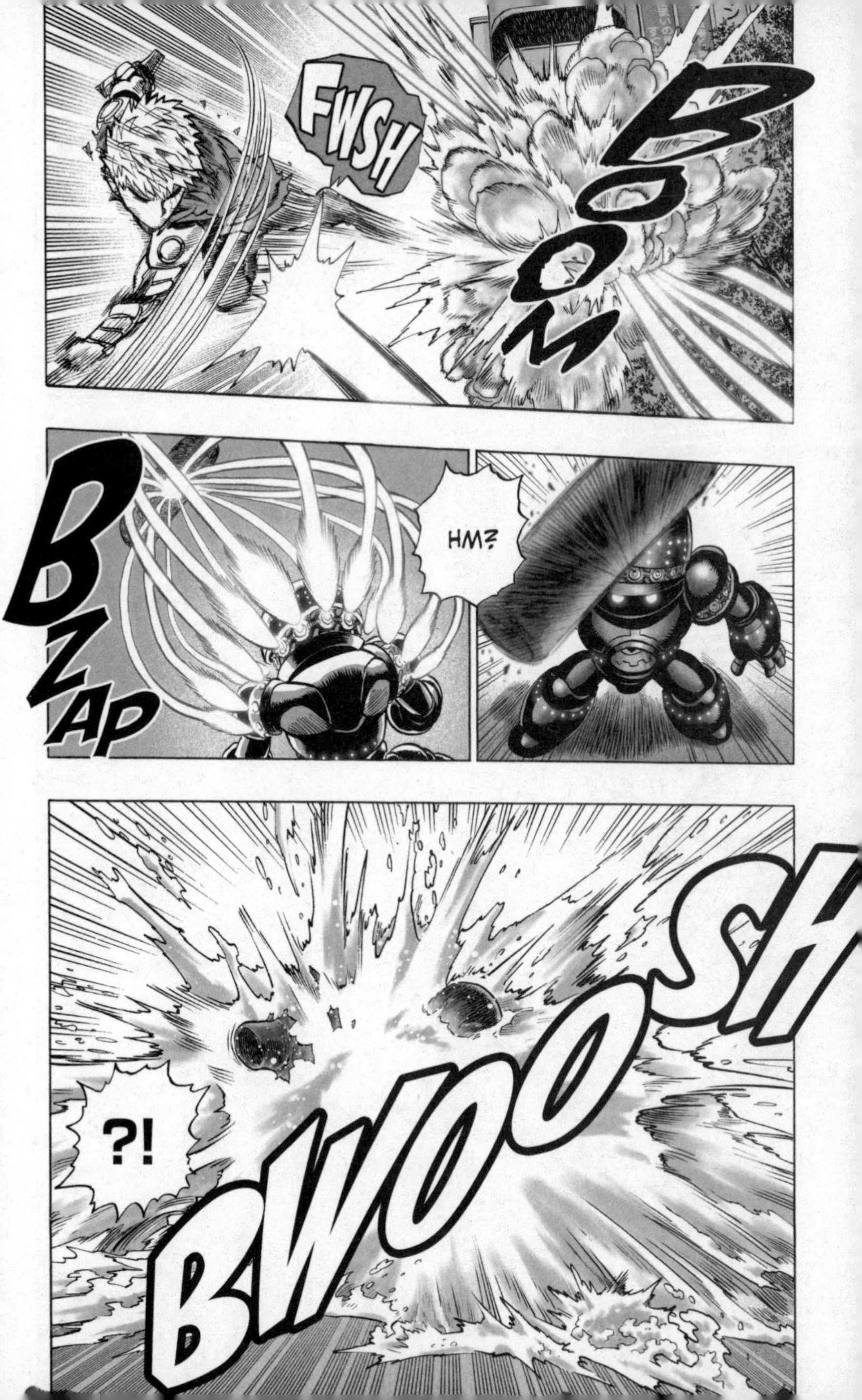
BOOM
FWSH
HM?
BZZAP
BWOOOSH
?!

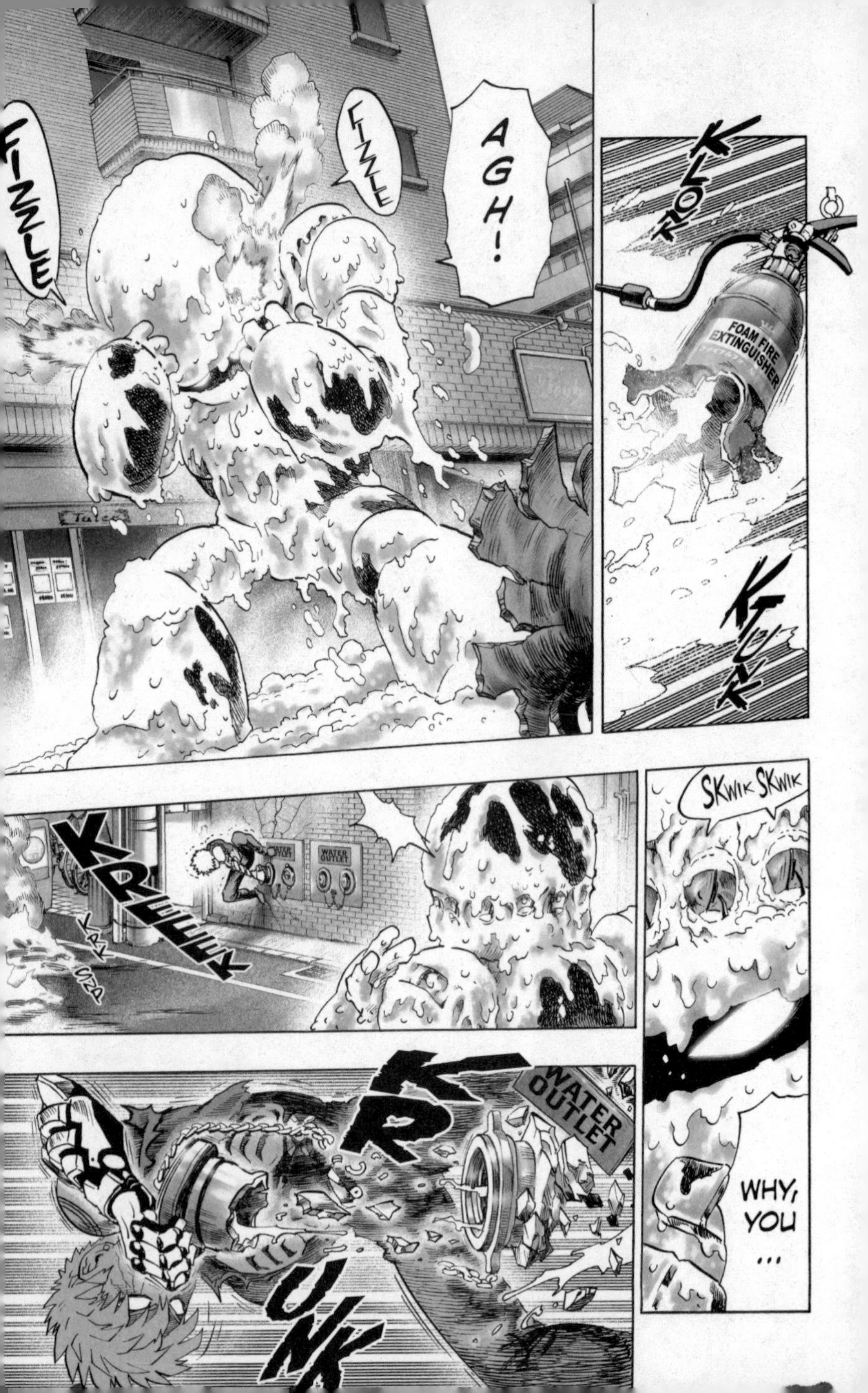
KLONK
FOAM FIRE EXTINGUISHER
KTUNK
AGH!
FIZZLE
FIZZLE
SKWIK SKWIK
WHY, YOU ...
KREEEEK
WATER OUTLET
WATER OUTLET
KRUNK
WATER OUTLET

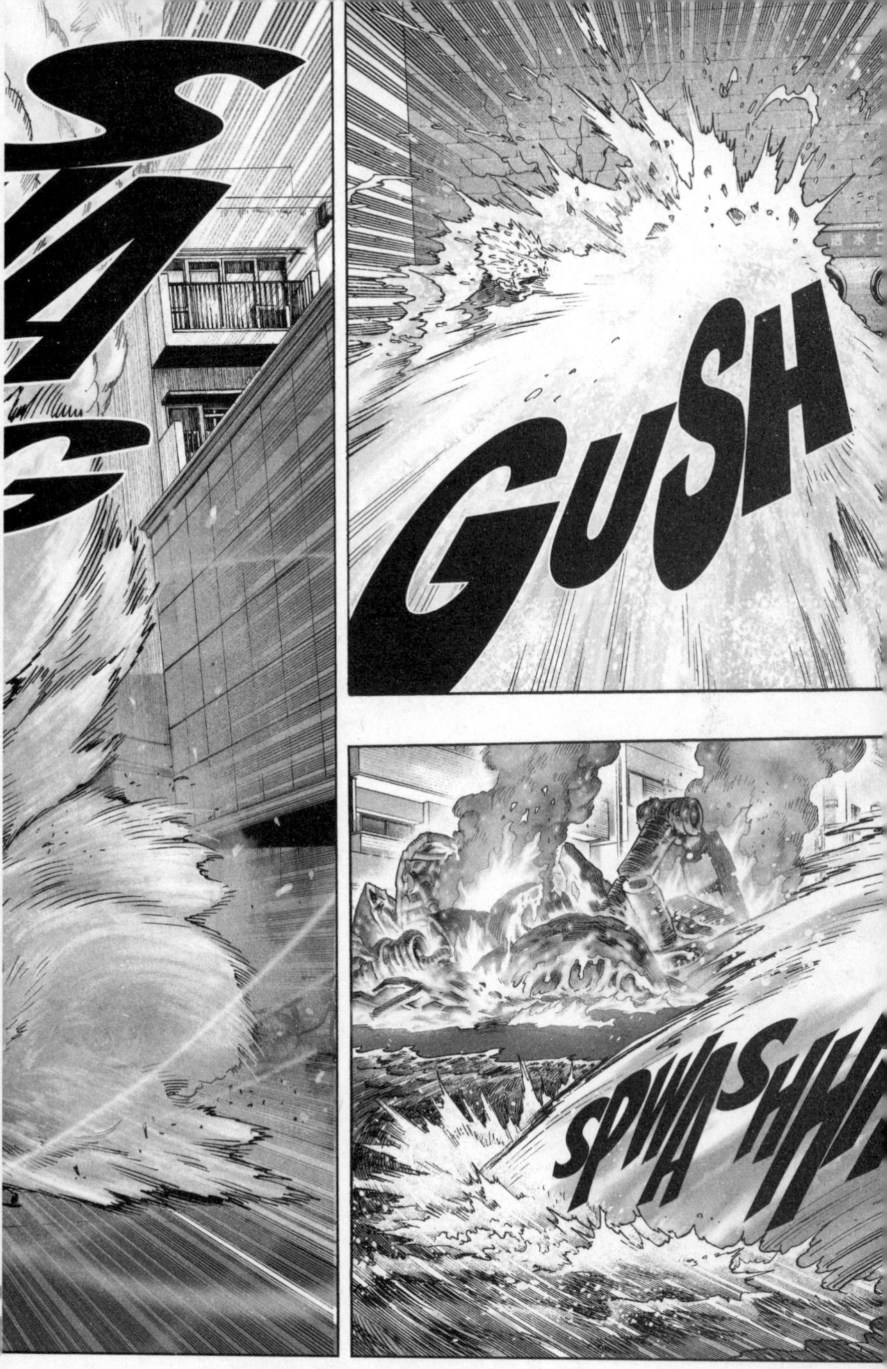
GUSH
SPWASHH

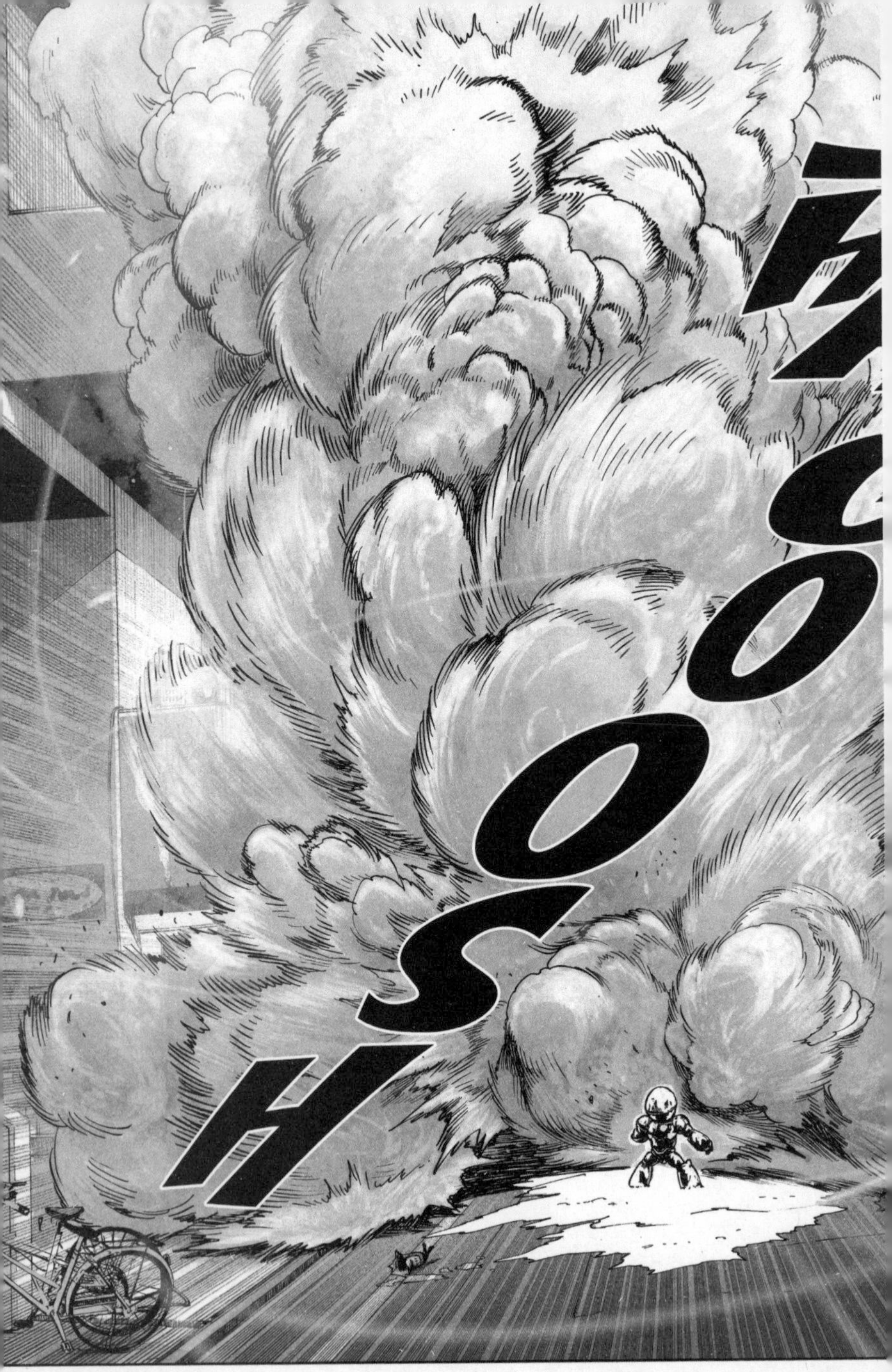
WOOOSH

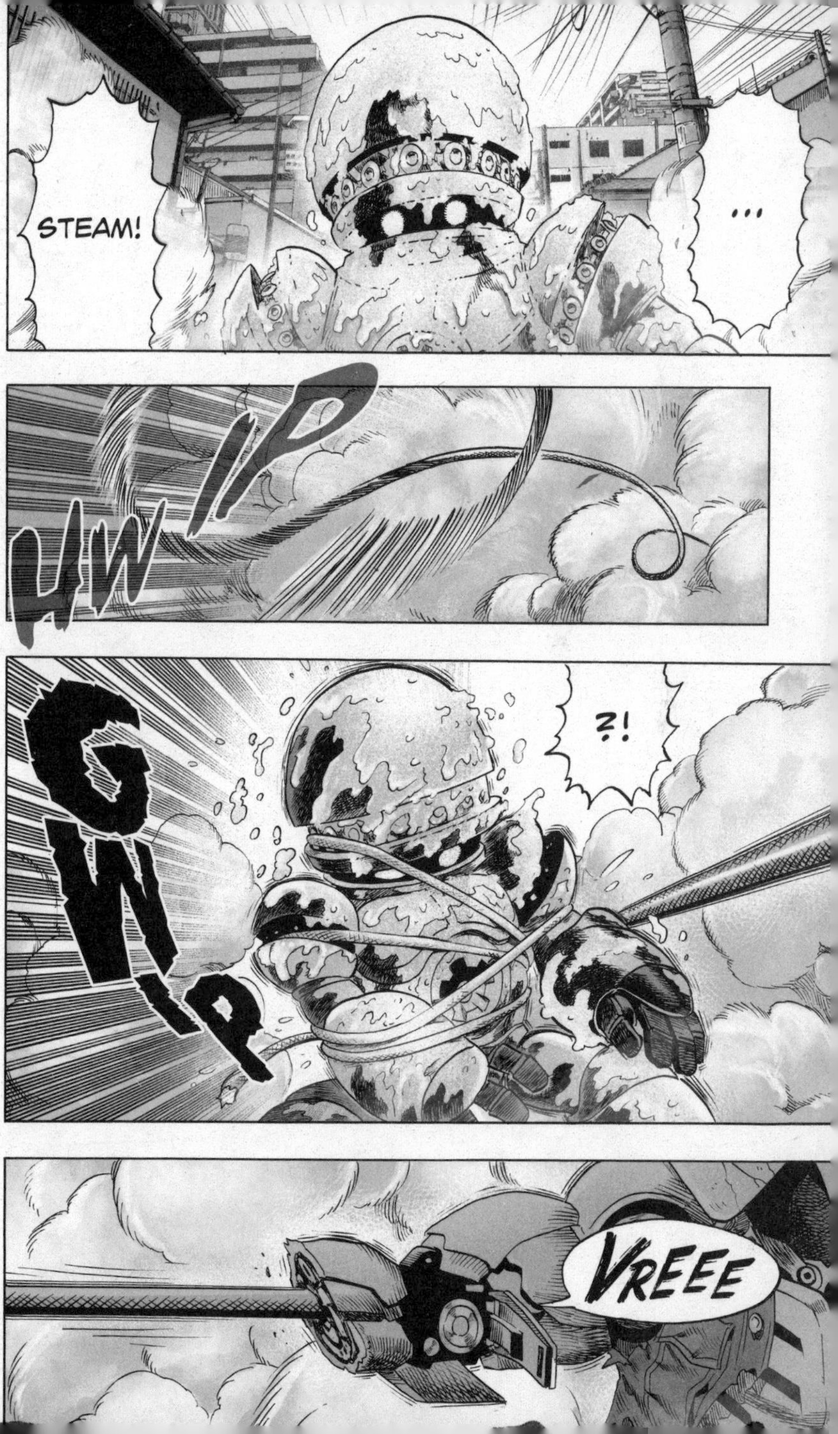
...
STEAM!
HWIP
?!
GWIP
VREEE

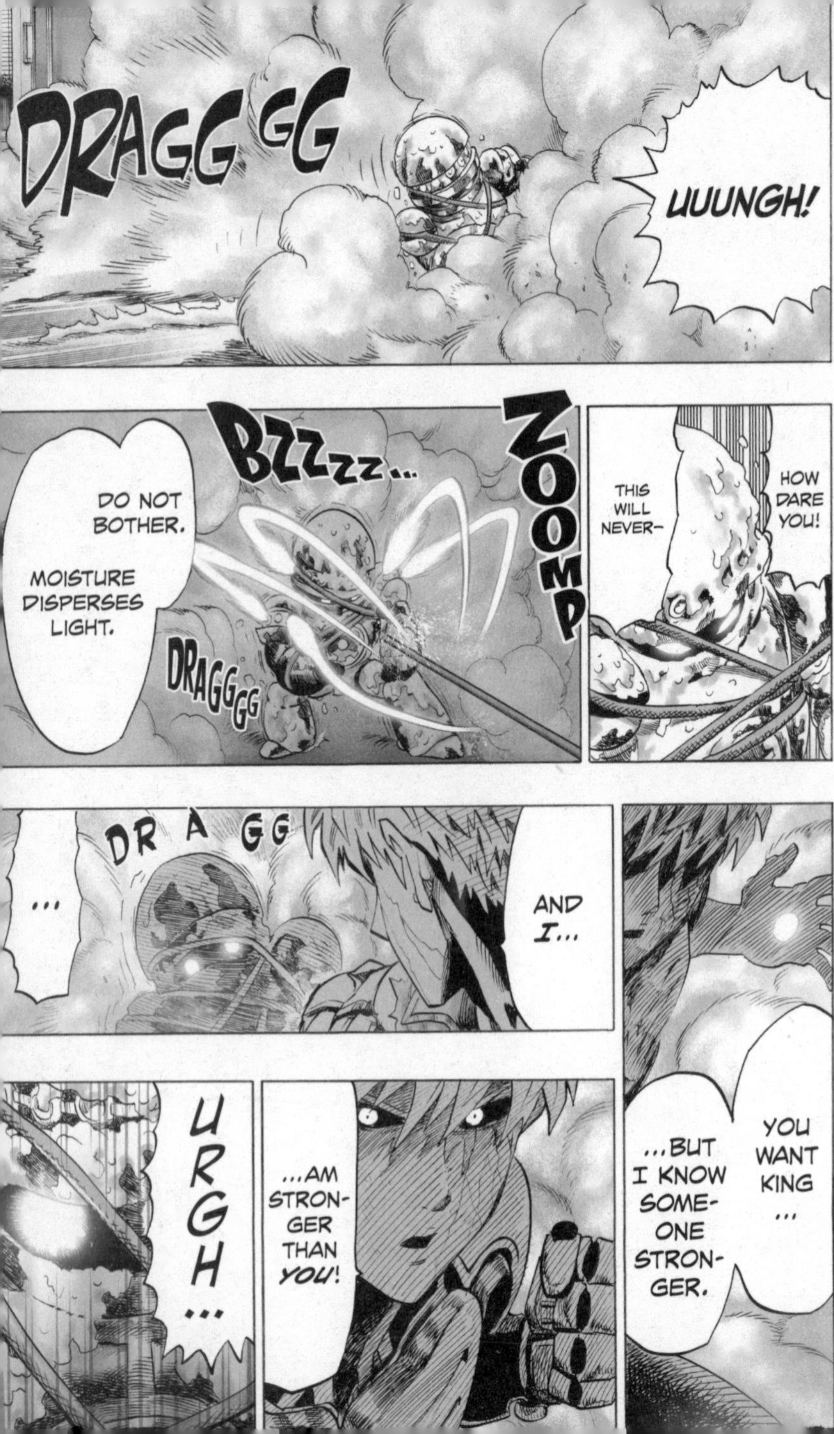
UUUNGH!
DRAGG GG
HOW DARE YOU!
THIS WILL NEVER—
ZOOMP
BZZzz...
DO NOT BOTHER.
MOISTURE DISPERSES LIGHT.
DRAGGGG
YOU WANT KING...
...BUT I KNOW SOME-ONE STRON-GER.
AND I...
DR A GG
...
...AM STRON-GER THAN YOU!
URGH...

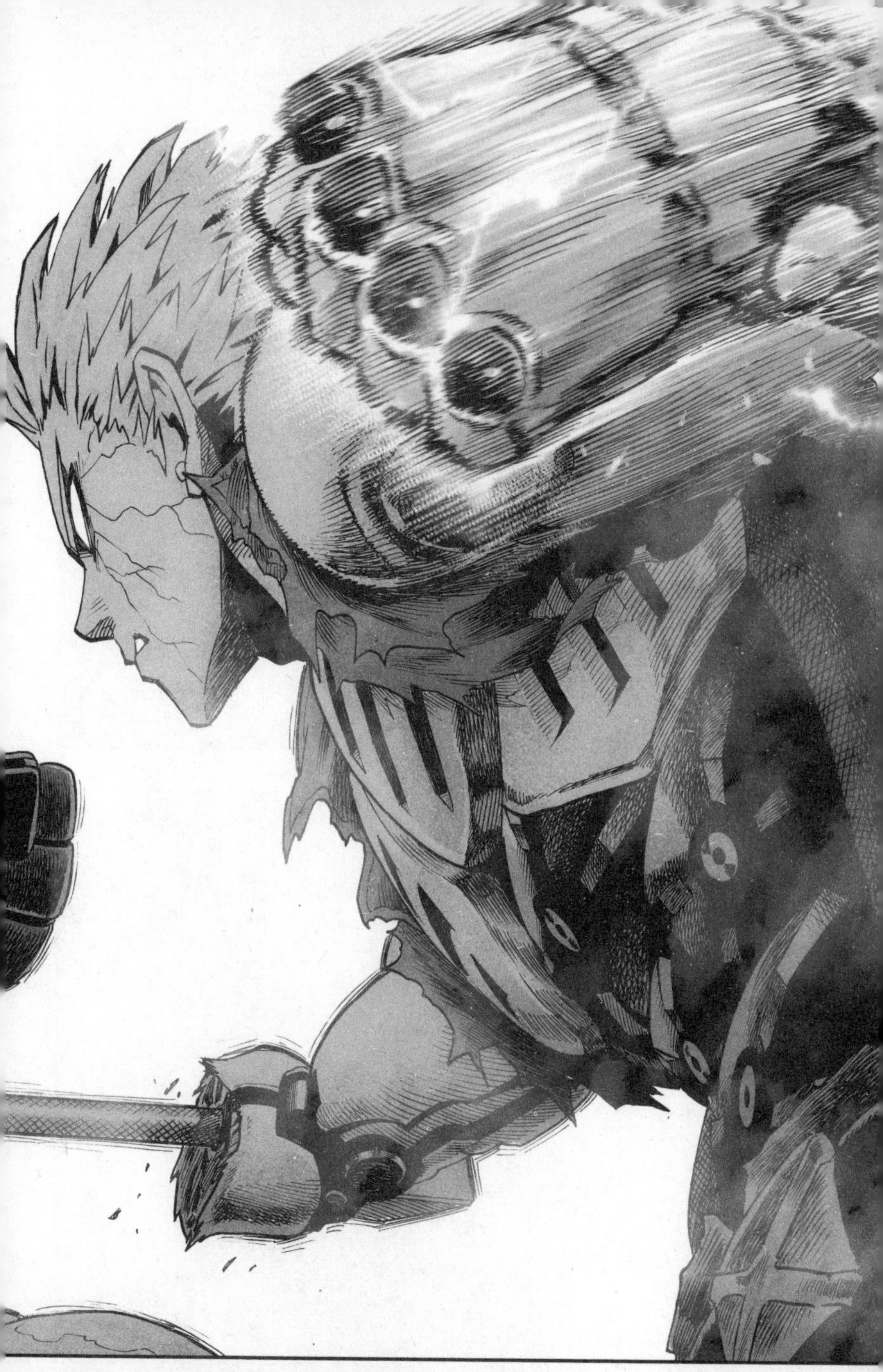

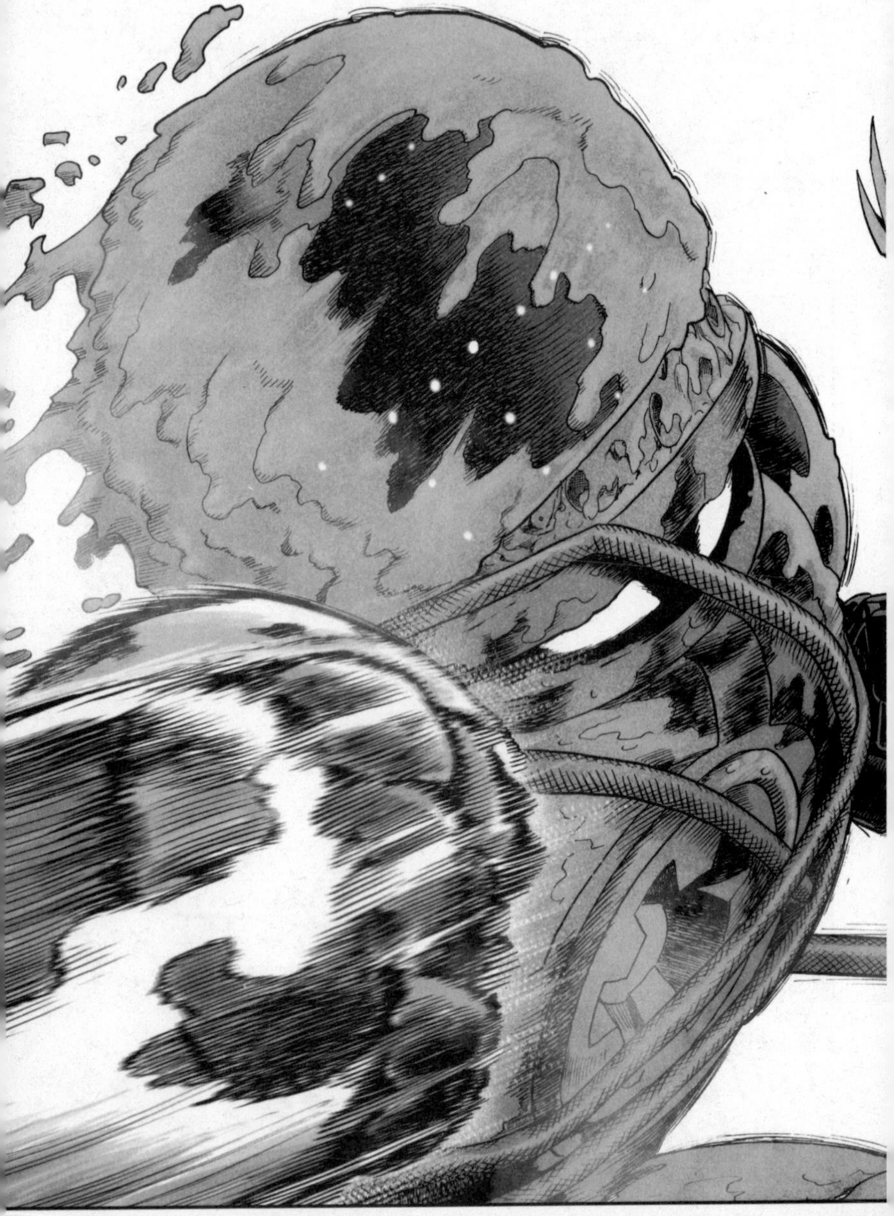

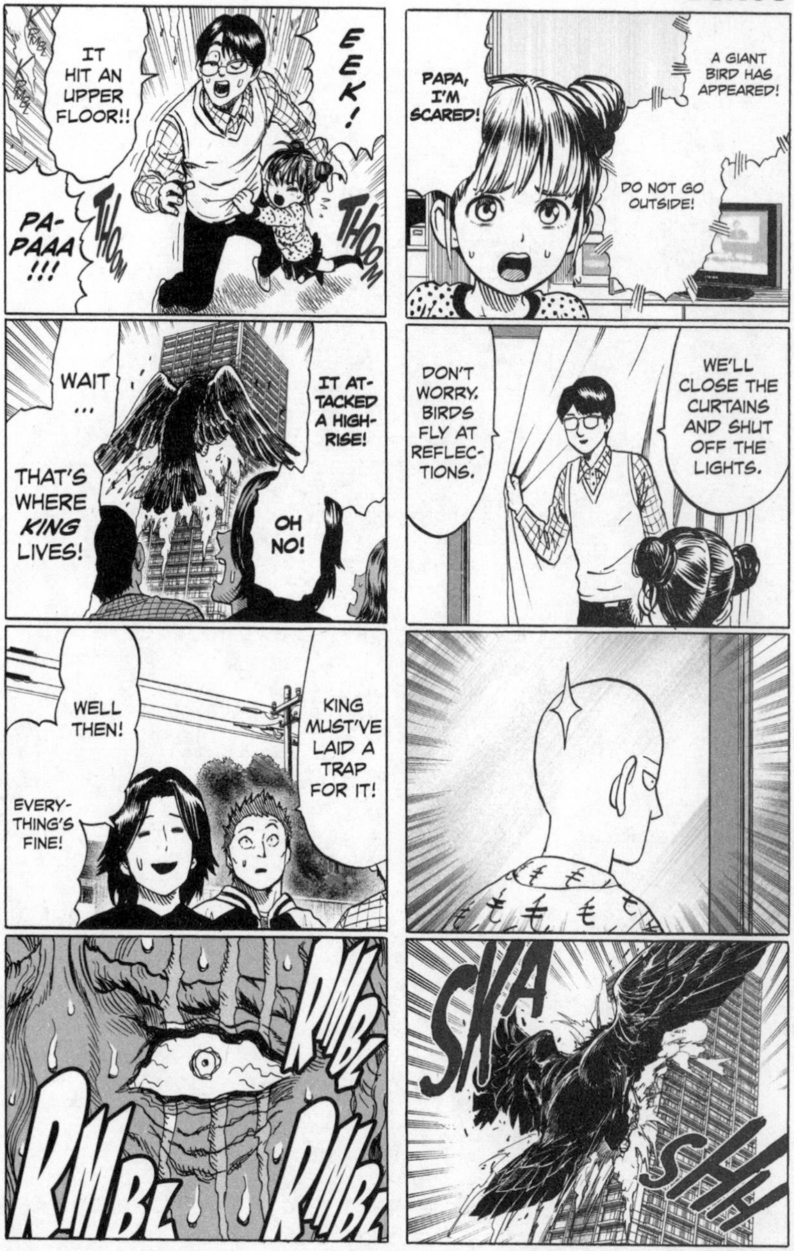
A GIANT BIRD HAS APPEARED!
PAPA, I'M SCARED!
DO NOT GO OUTSIDE!
EEK!
IT HIT AN UPPER FLOOR!!
THOOM
PA-PAAA!!!
THOOM
WE'LL CLOSE THE CURTAINS AND SHUT OFF THE LIGHTS.
DON'T WORRY. BIRDS FLY AT REFLECTIONS.
IT AT-TACKED A HIGH-RISE!
WAIT ...
OH NO!
THAT'S WHERE KING LIVES!
KING MUST'VE LAID A TRAP FOR IT!
WELL THEN!
EVERY-THING'S FINE!
SKA
SHH
RMBL
RMBL
RMBL

PUNCH 39: THAT MAN

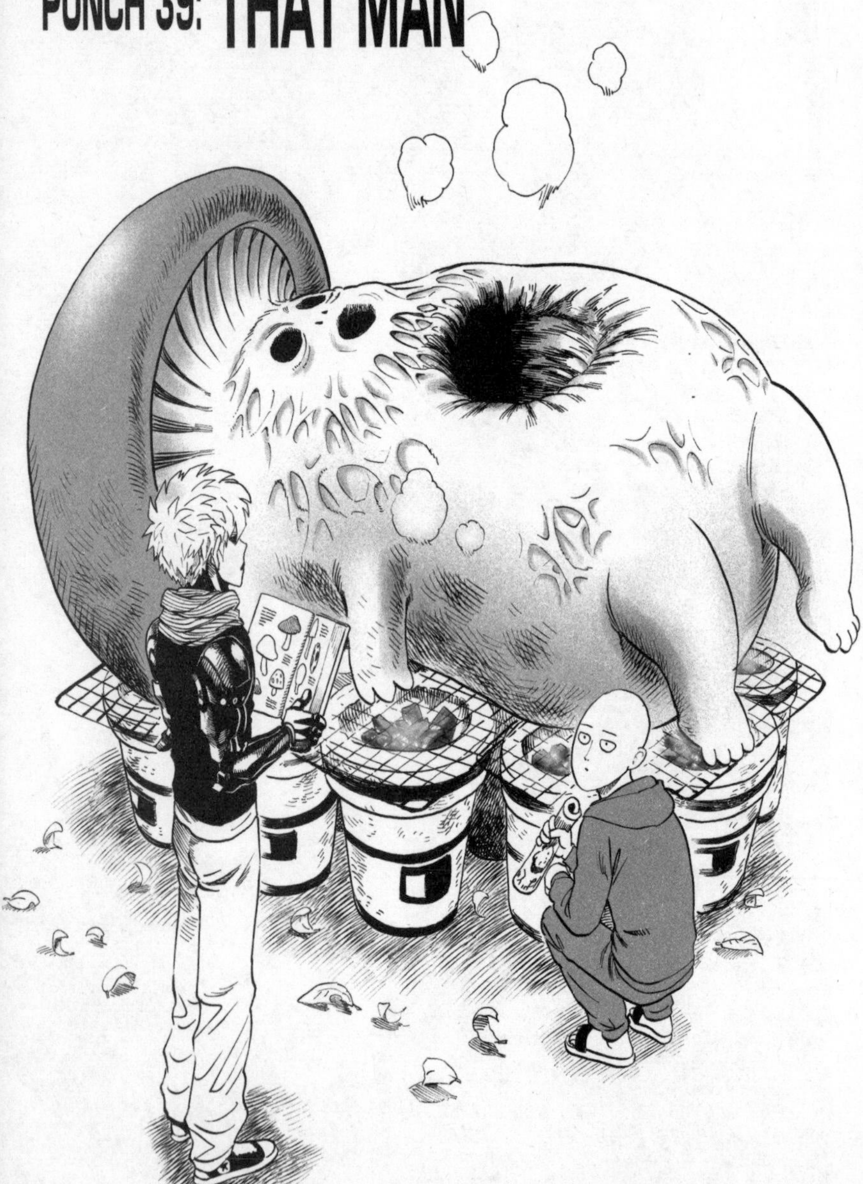

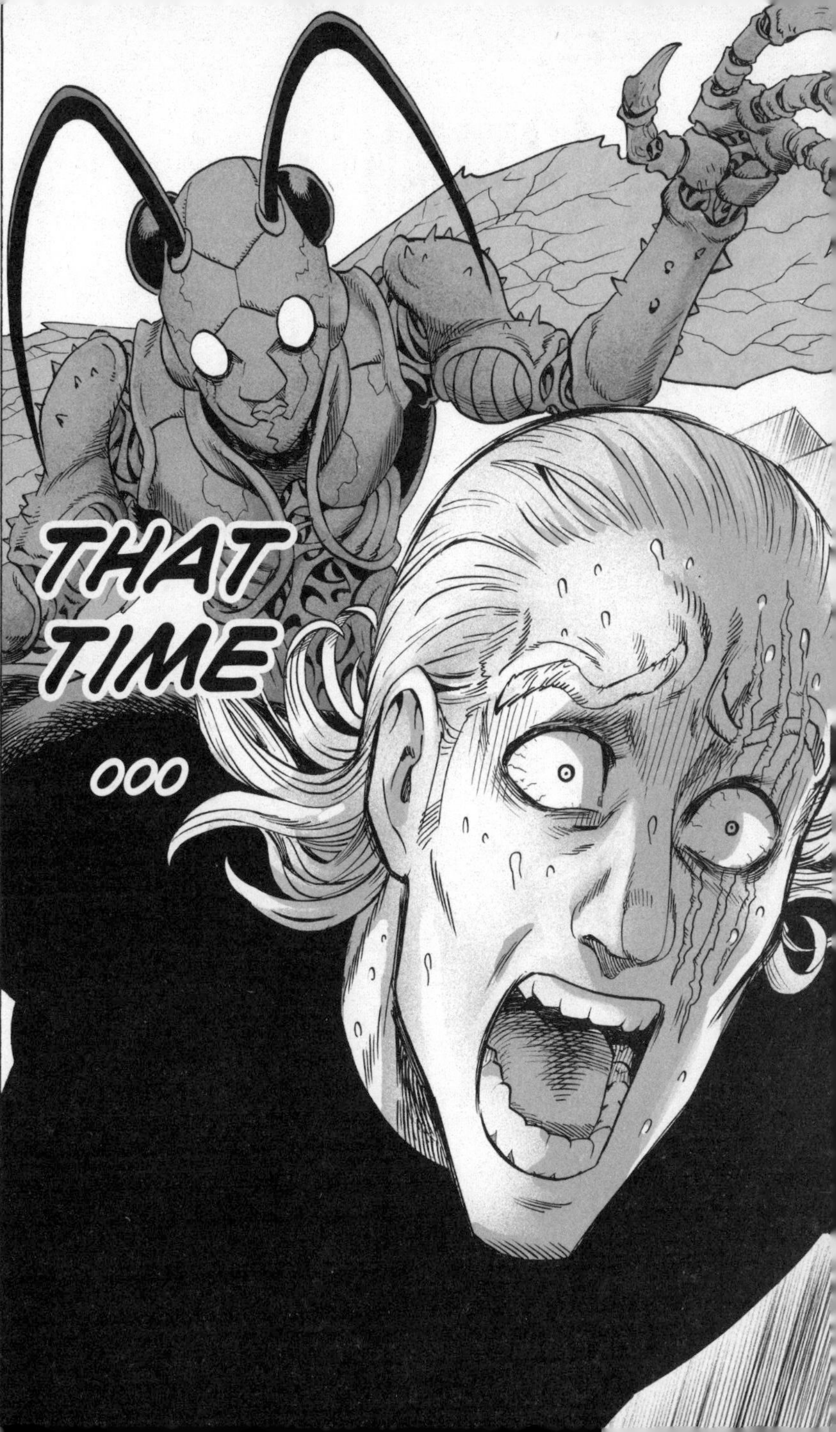
THAT TIME
...

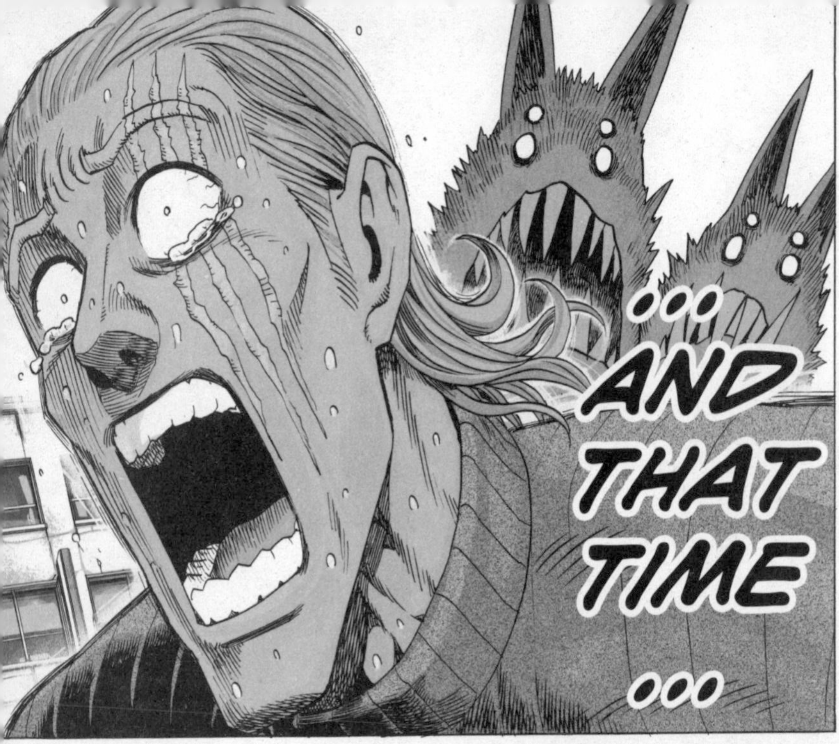
...AND THAT TIME ...

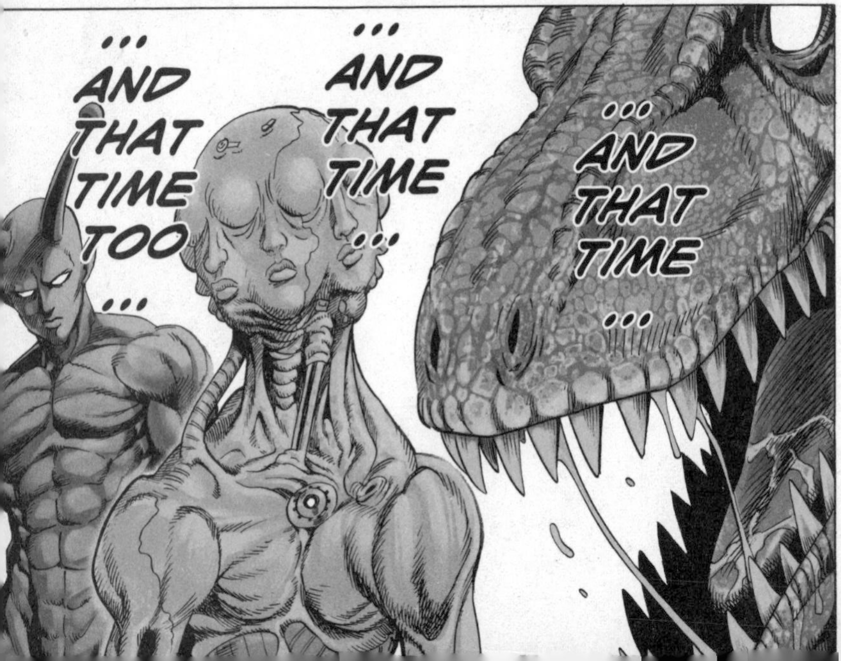
...AND THAT TIME ...
...AND THAT TIME ...
...AND THAT TIME TOO ...

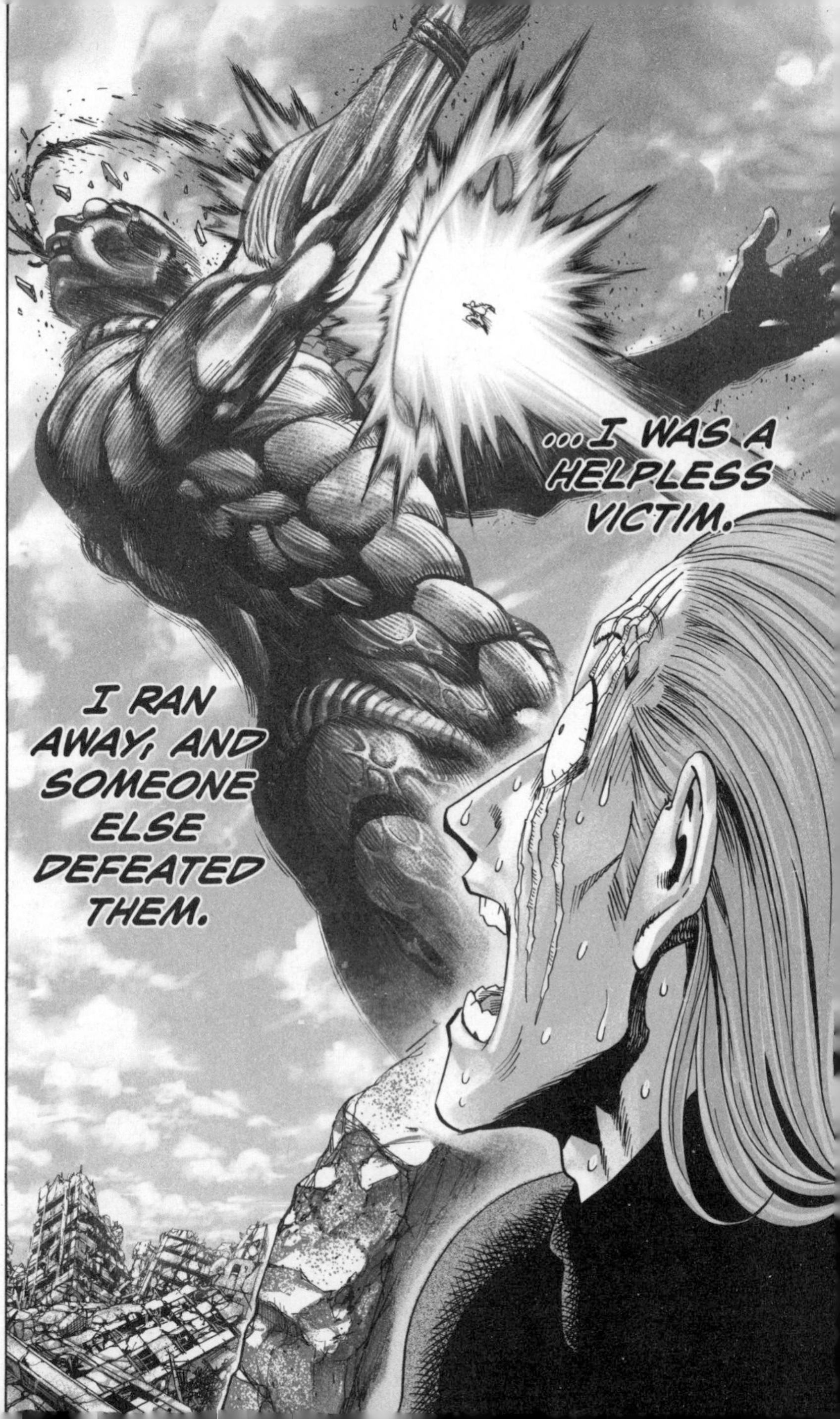
...I WAS A HELPLESS VICTIM.
I RAN AWAY, AND SOMEONE ELSE DEFEATED THEM.

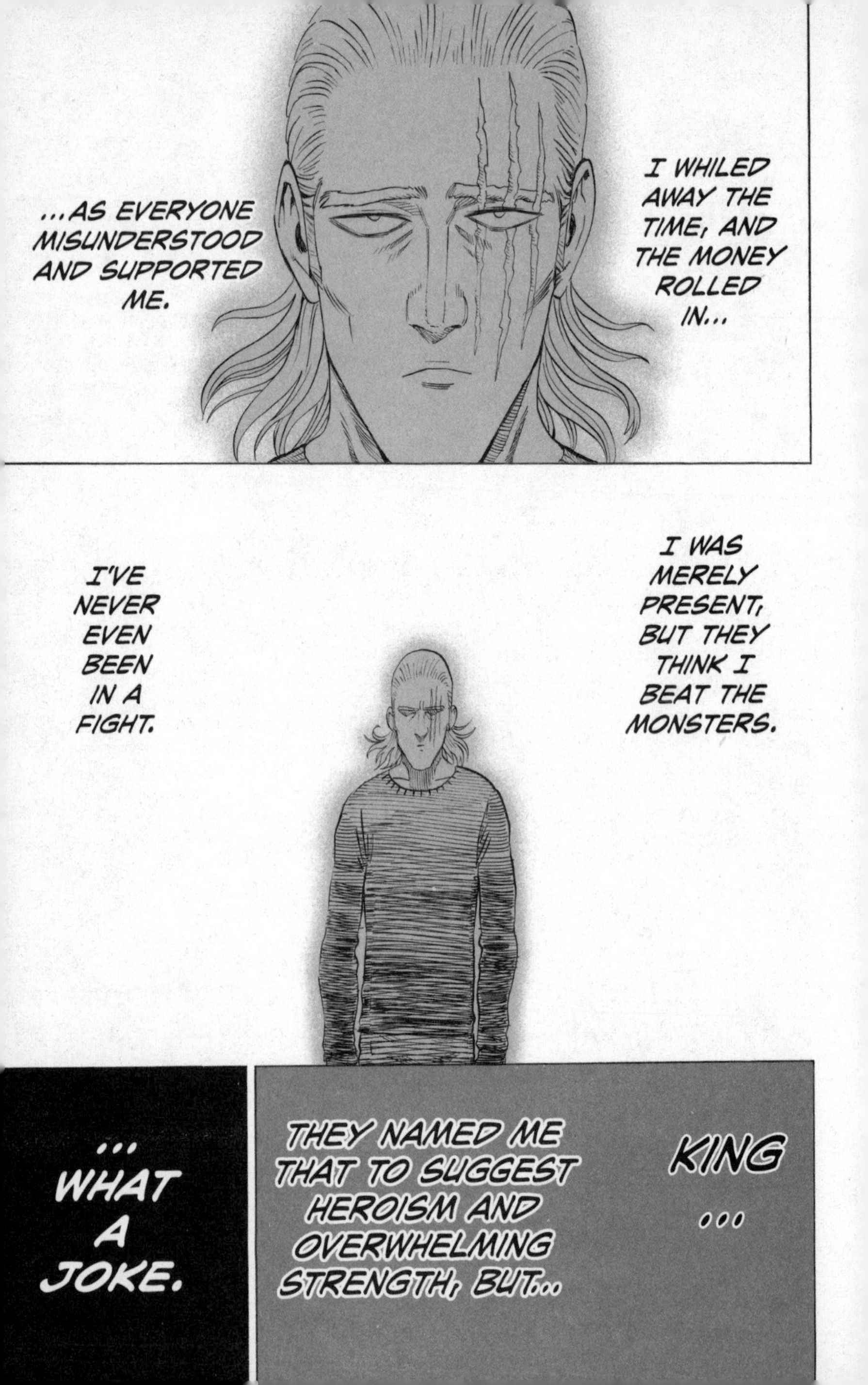
I WHILED AWAY THE TIME, AND THE MONEY ROLLED IN...
...AS EVERYONE MISUNDERSTOOD AND SUPPORTED ME.
I WAS MERELY PRESENT, BUT THEY THINK I BEAT THE MONSTERS.
I'VE NEVER EVEN BEEN IN A FIGHT.
KING...
THEY NAMED ME THAT TO SUGGEST HEROISM AND OVERWHELMING STRENGTH, BUT...
... WHAT A JOKE.

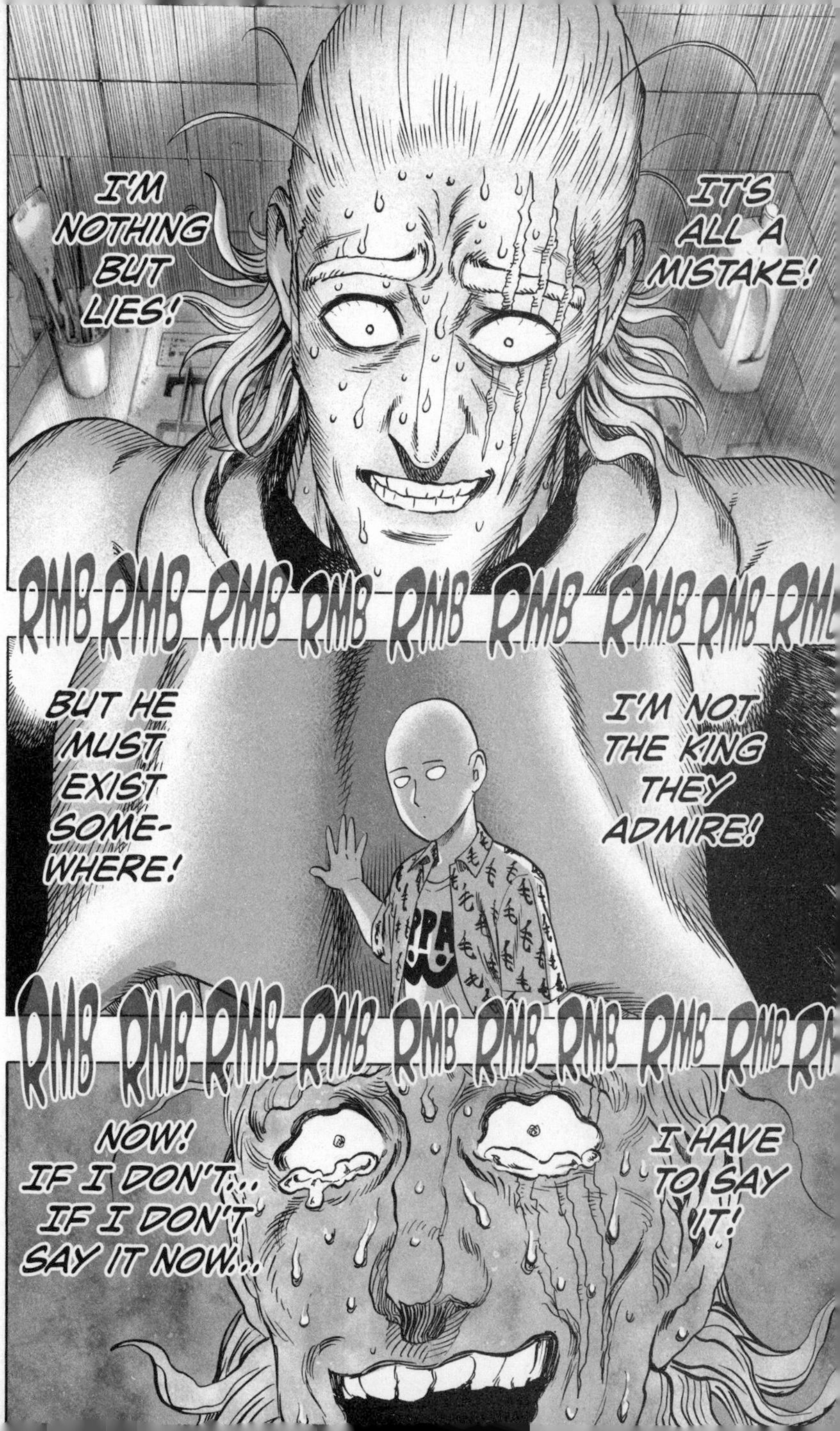
IT'S ALL A MISTAKE!
I'M NOTHING BUT LIES!
RMB RMB RMB RMB RMB RMB RMB RMB
I'M NOT THE KING THEY ADMIRE!
BUT HE MUST EXIST SOME-WHERE!
RMB RMB RMB RMB RMB RMB RMB RMB RMB
I HAVE TO SAY IT!
NOW! IF I DON'T... IF I DON'T SAY IT NOW...

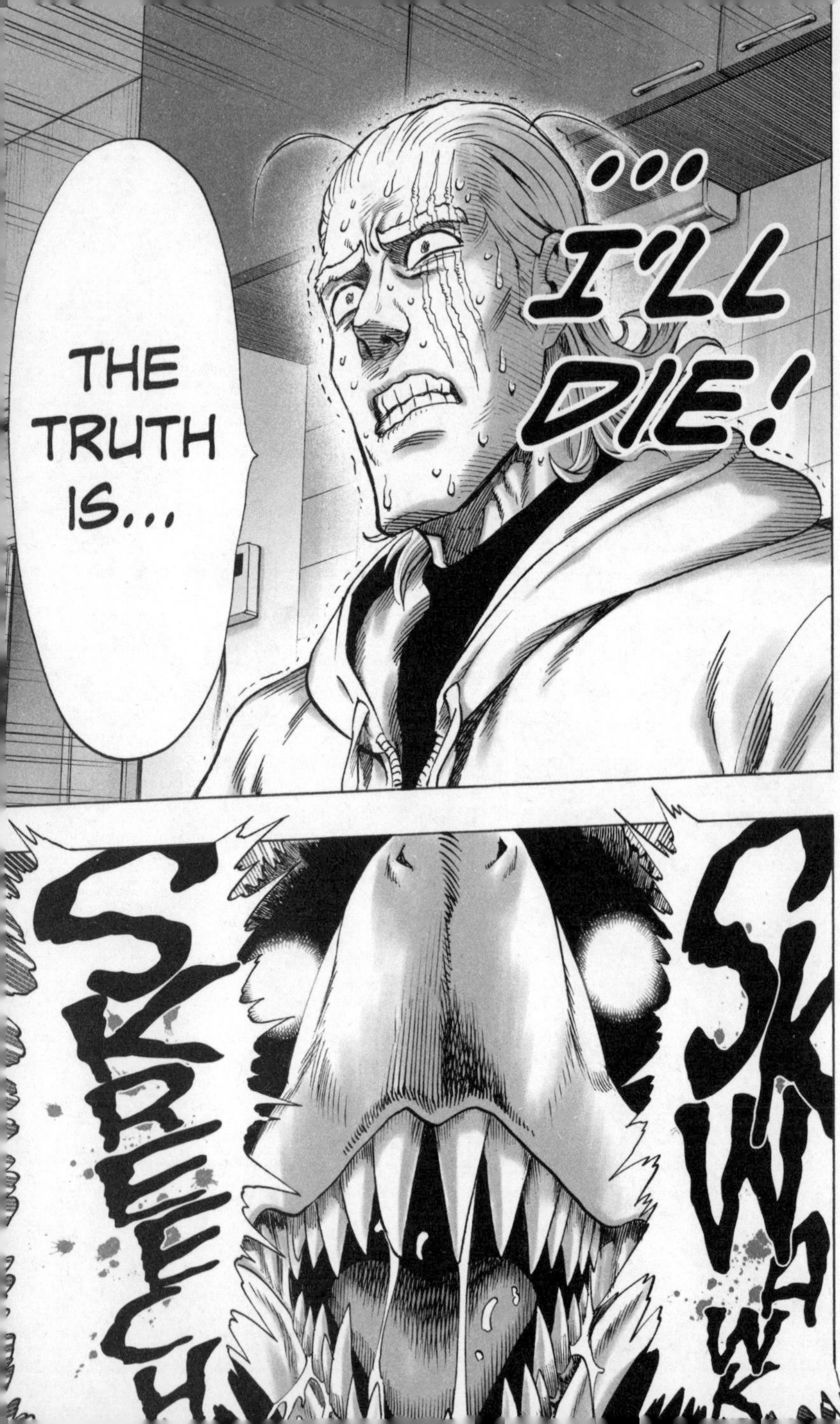
...I'LL DIE!
THE TRUTH IS...
SKWAWK
SKREEECH

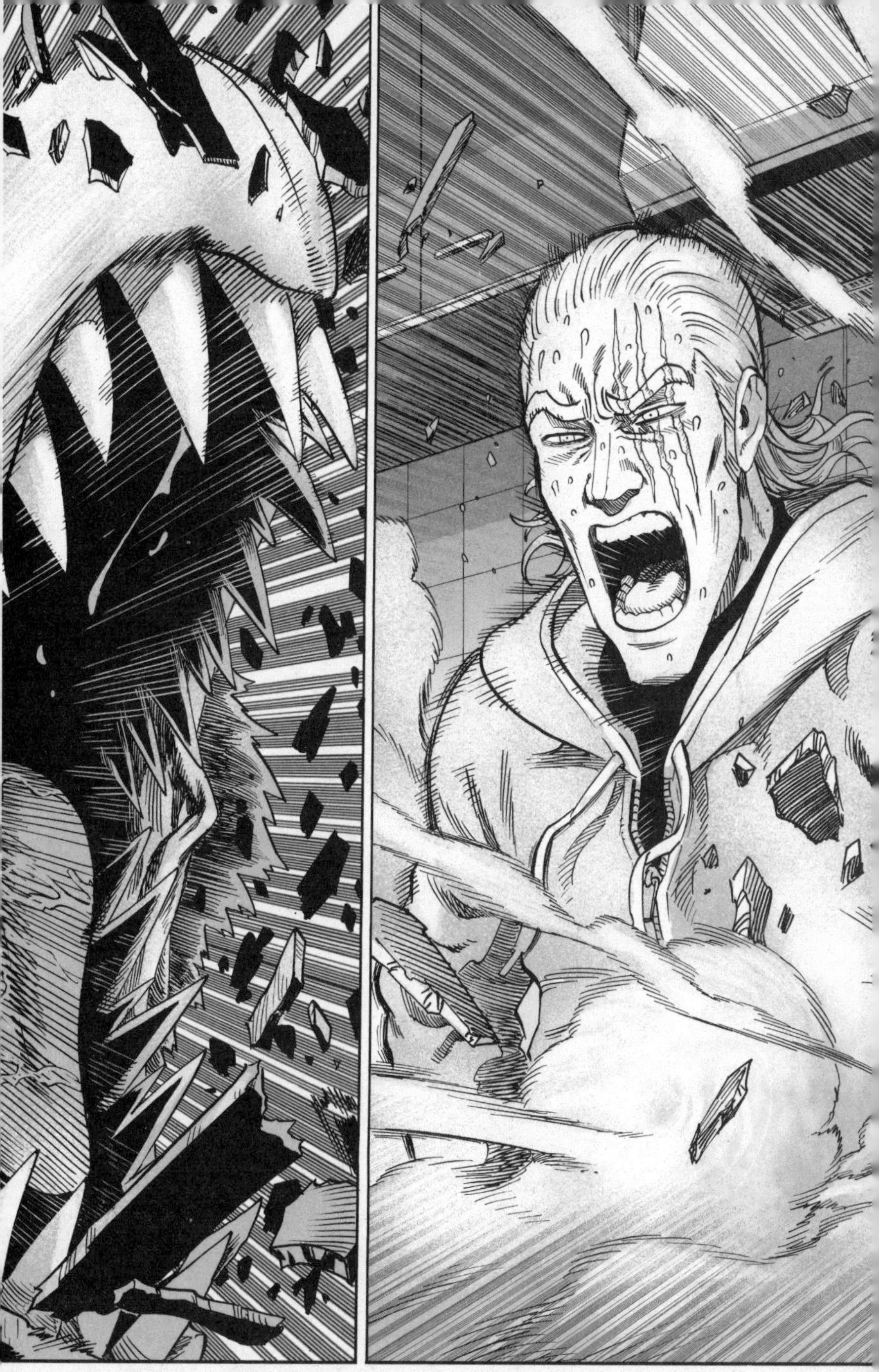

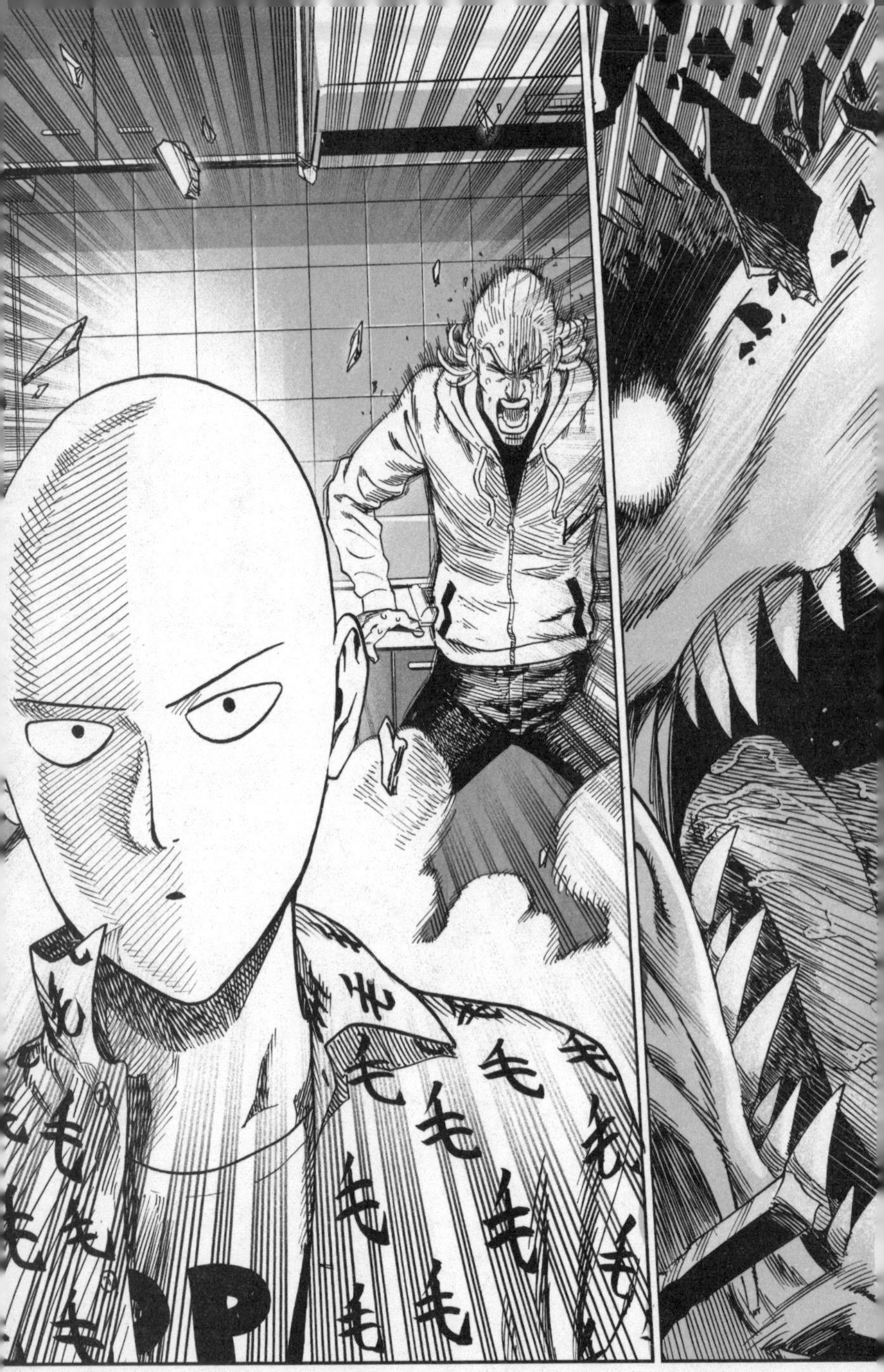

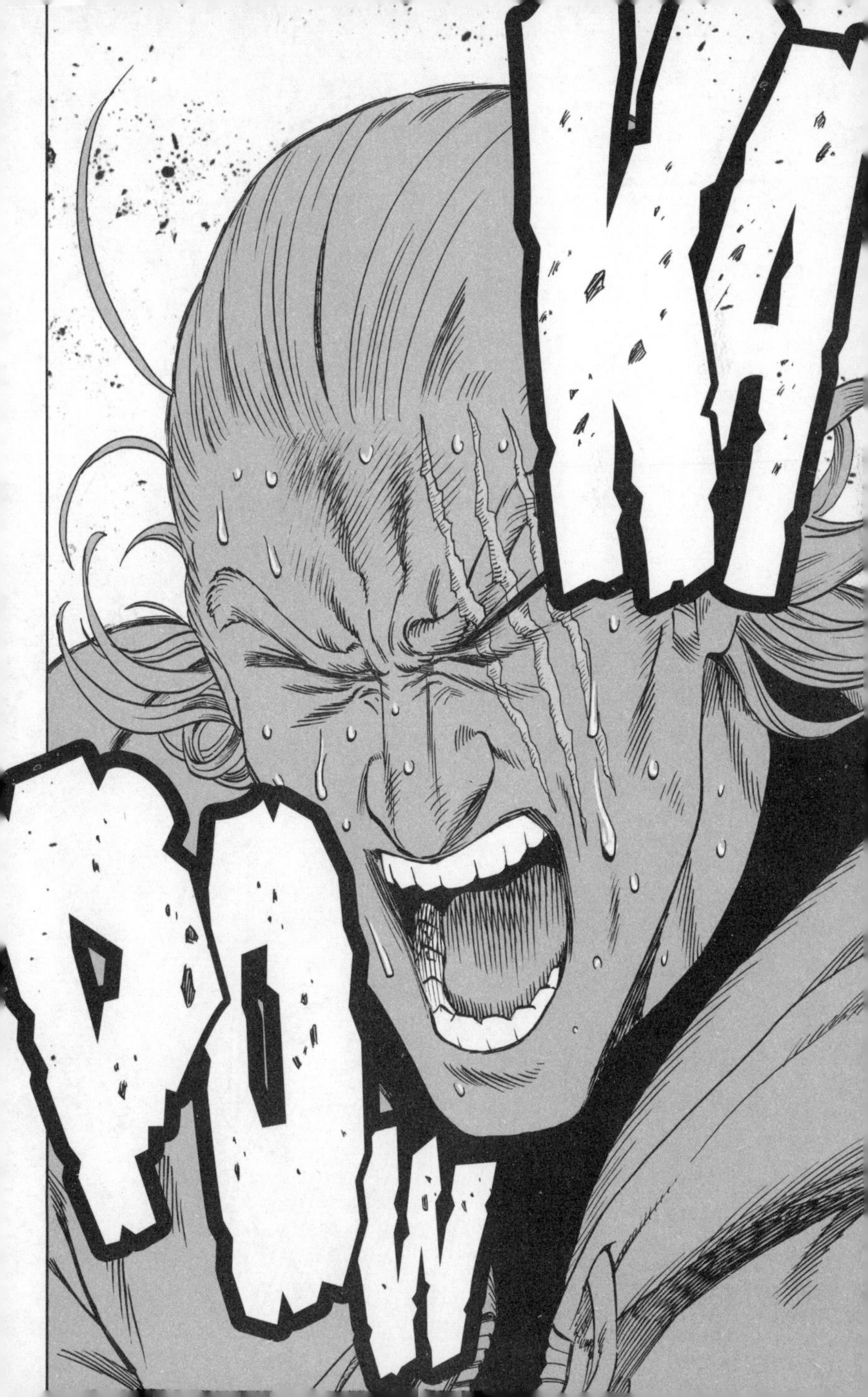
WA
POW

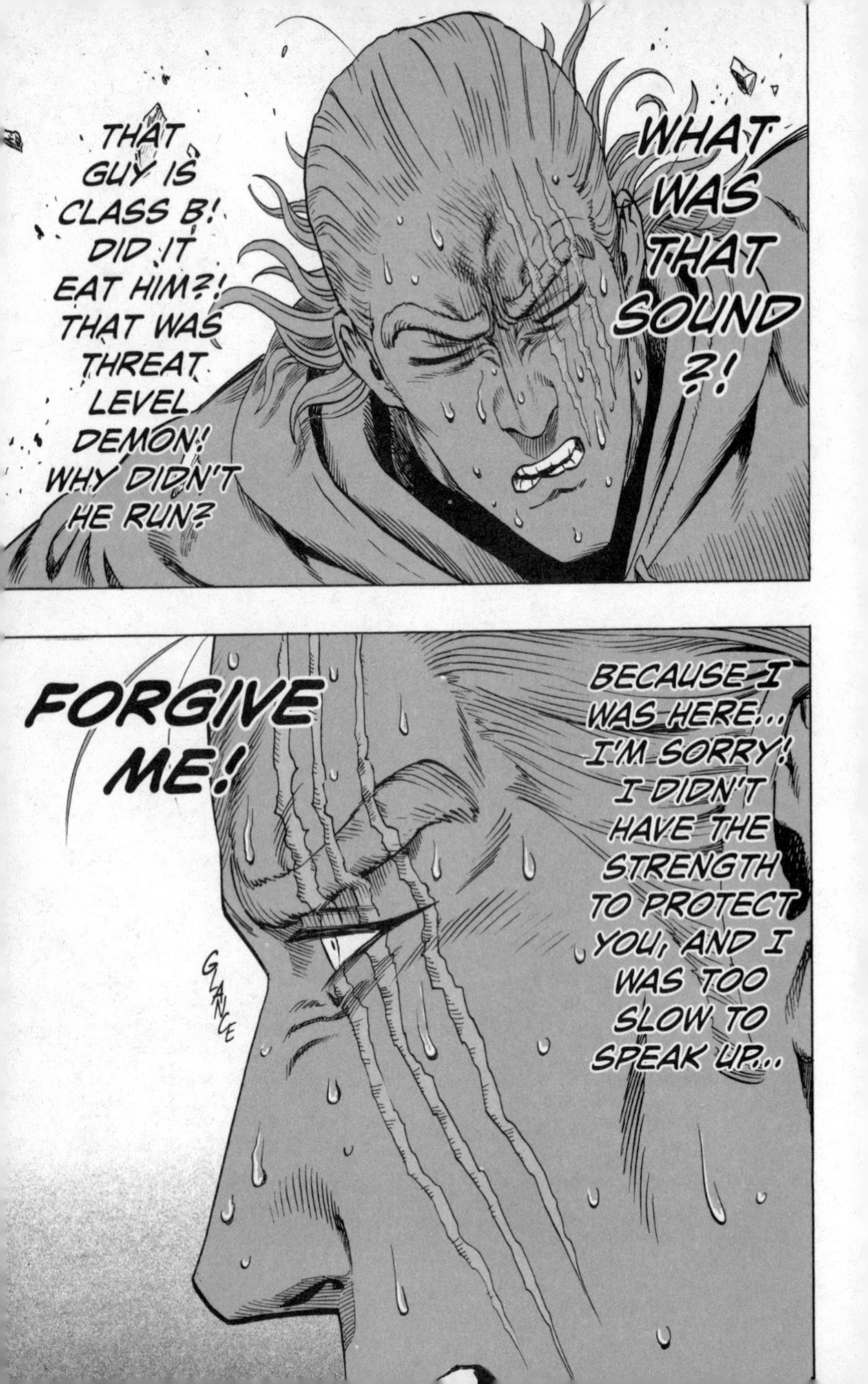
WHAT WAS THAT SOUND?!
THAT GUY IS CLASS B! DID IT EAT HIM?! THAT WAS THREAT LEVEL DEMON! WHY DIDN'T HE RUN?
BECAUSE I WAS HERE... I'M SORRY! I DIDN'T HAVE THE STRENGTH TO PROTECT YOU, AND I WAS TOO SLOW TO SPEAK UP...
FORGIVE ME!
GLANCE

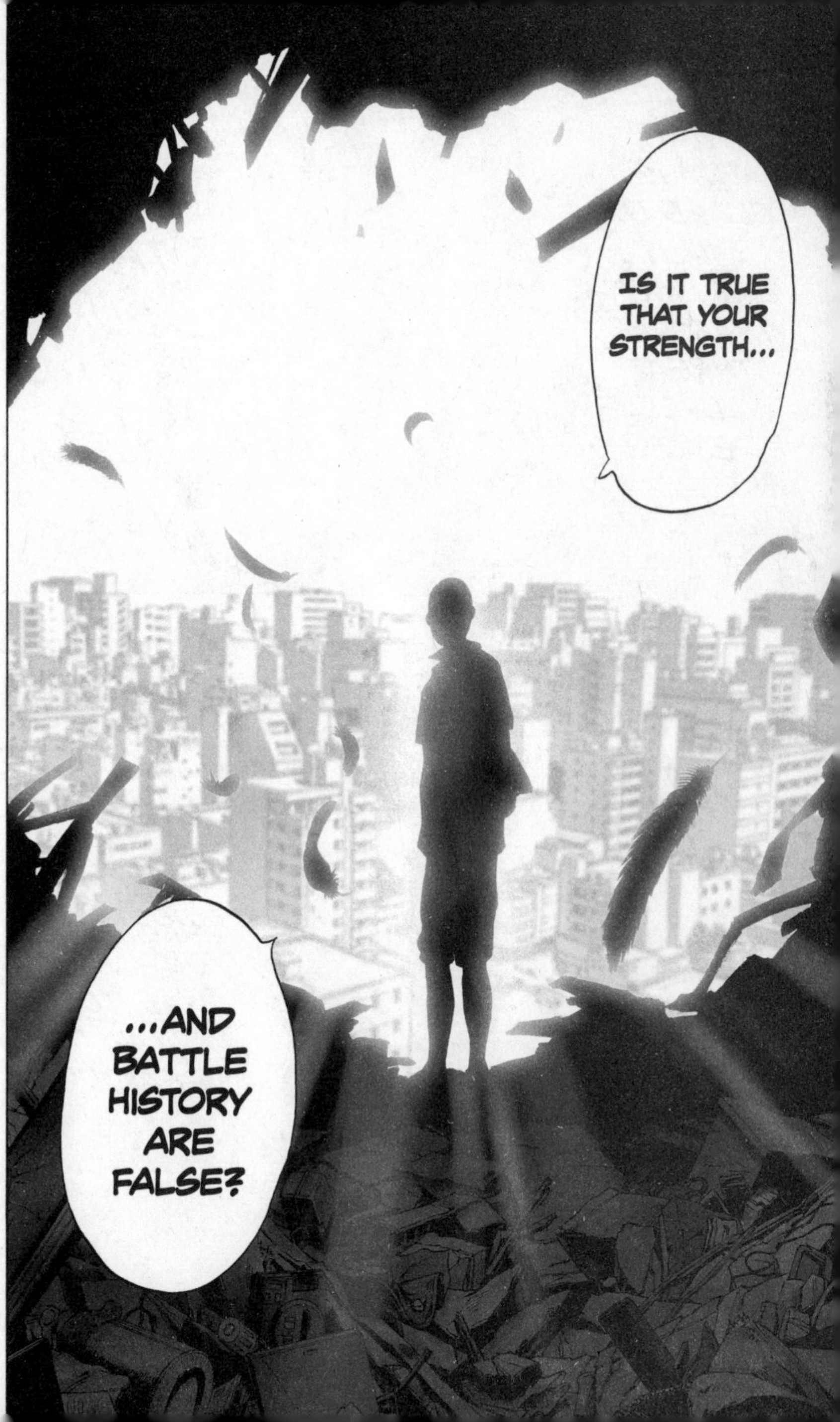
IS IT TRUE THAT YOUR STRENGTH...
...AND BATTLE HISTORY ARE FALSE?

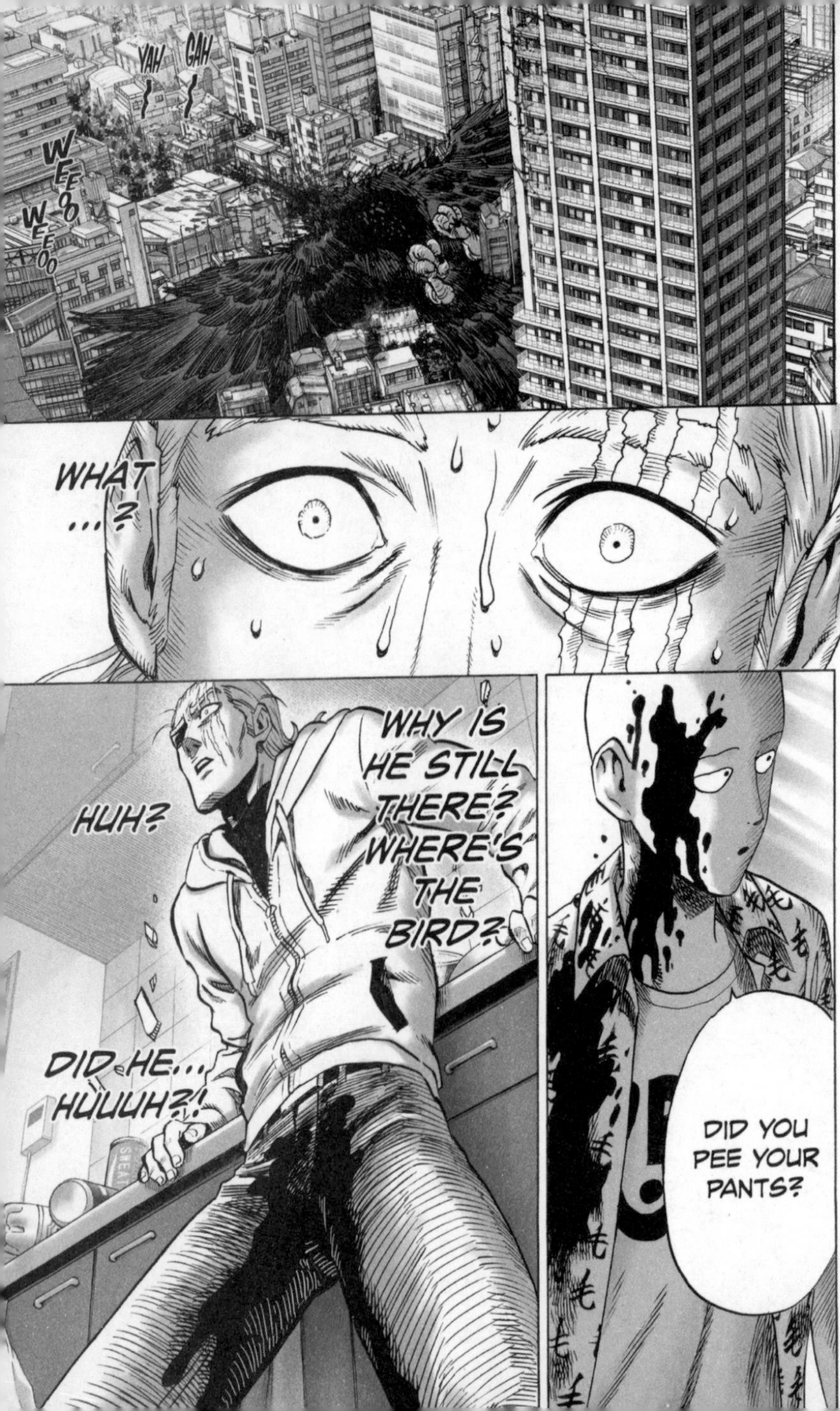
GAH
YAH
WEEOO
WEEOO
WHAT ...?
DID YOU PEE YOUR PANTS?
WHY IS HE STILL THERE? WHERE'S THE BIRD?
HUH?
DID HE... HUUUH?!

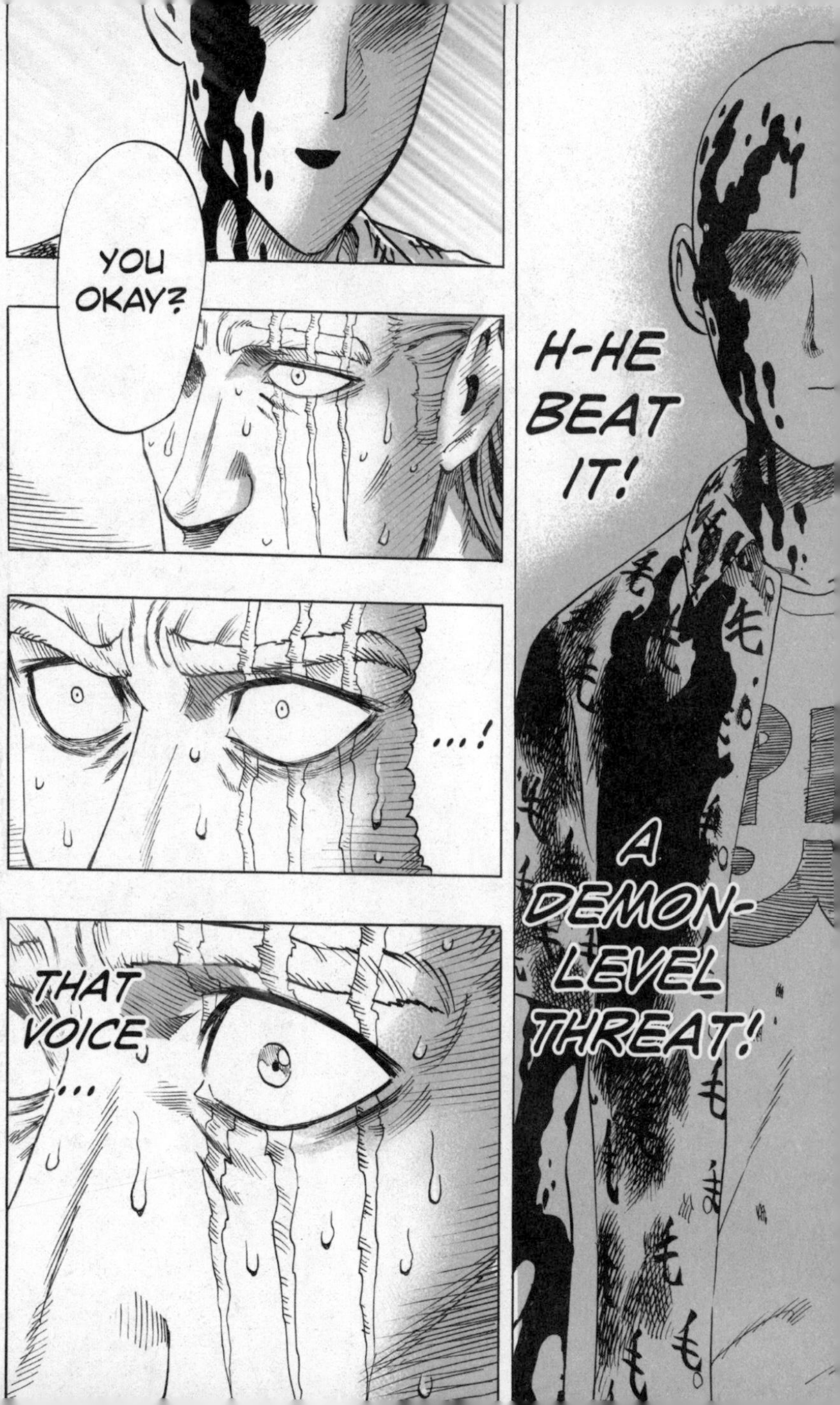

H-HE BEAT IT!
A DEMON-LEVEL THREAT!
YOU OKAY?
...!
THAT VOICE...

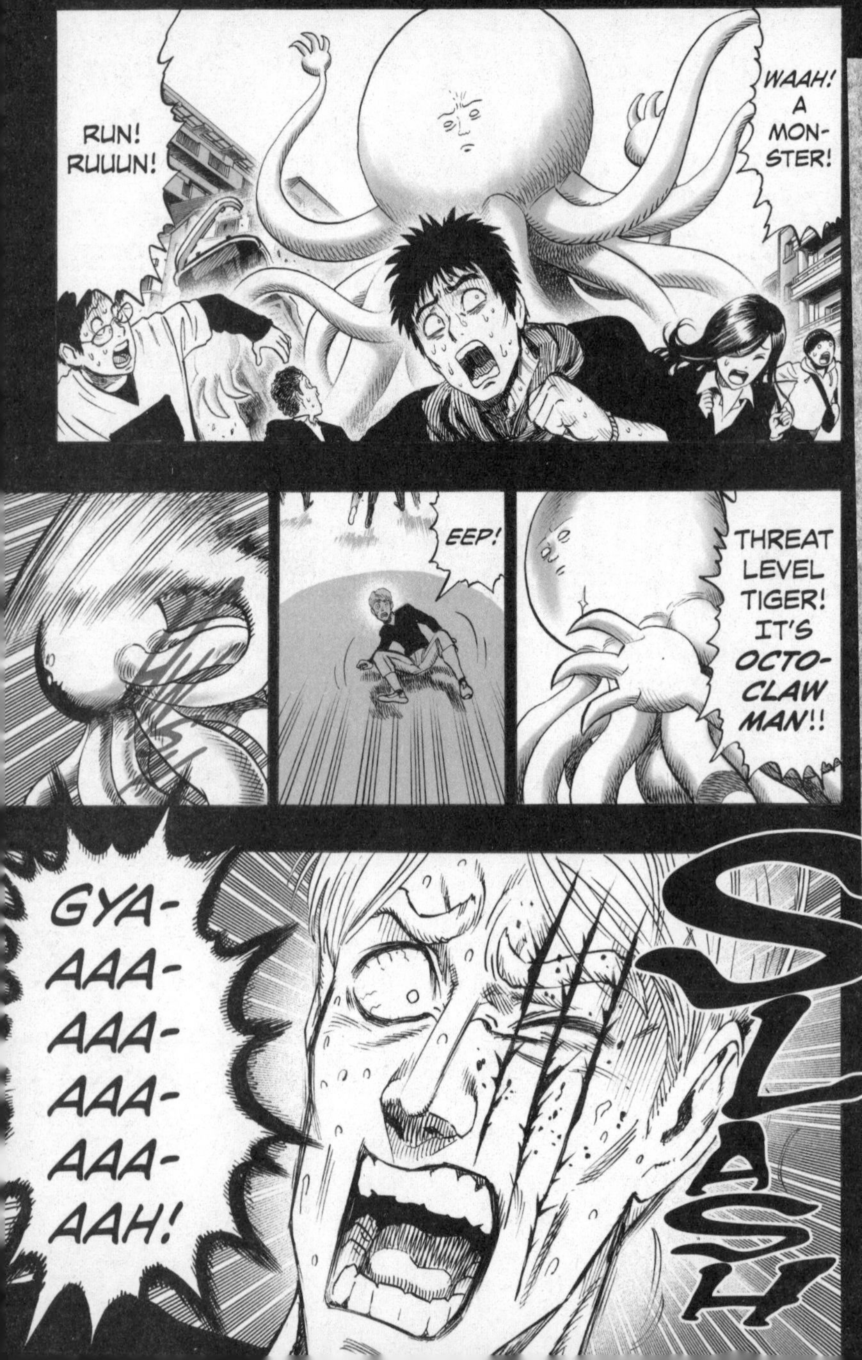
WAAH! A MON-STER!
RUN! RUUUN!
THREAT LEVEL TIGER! IT'S OCTO-CLAW MAN!!
EEP!
SLASH
GYA-AAA-AAA-AAA-AAA-AAH!

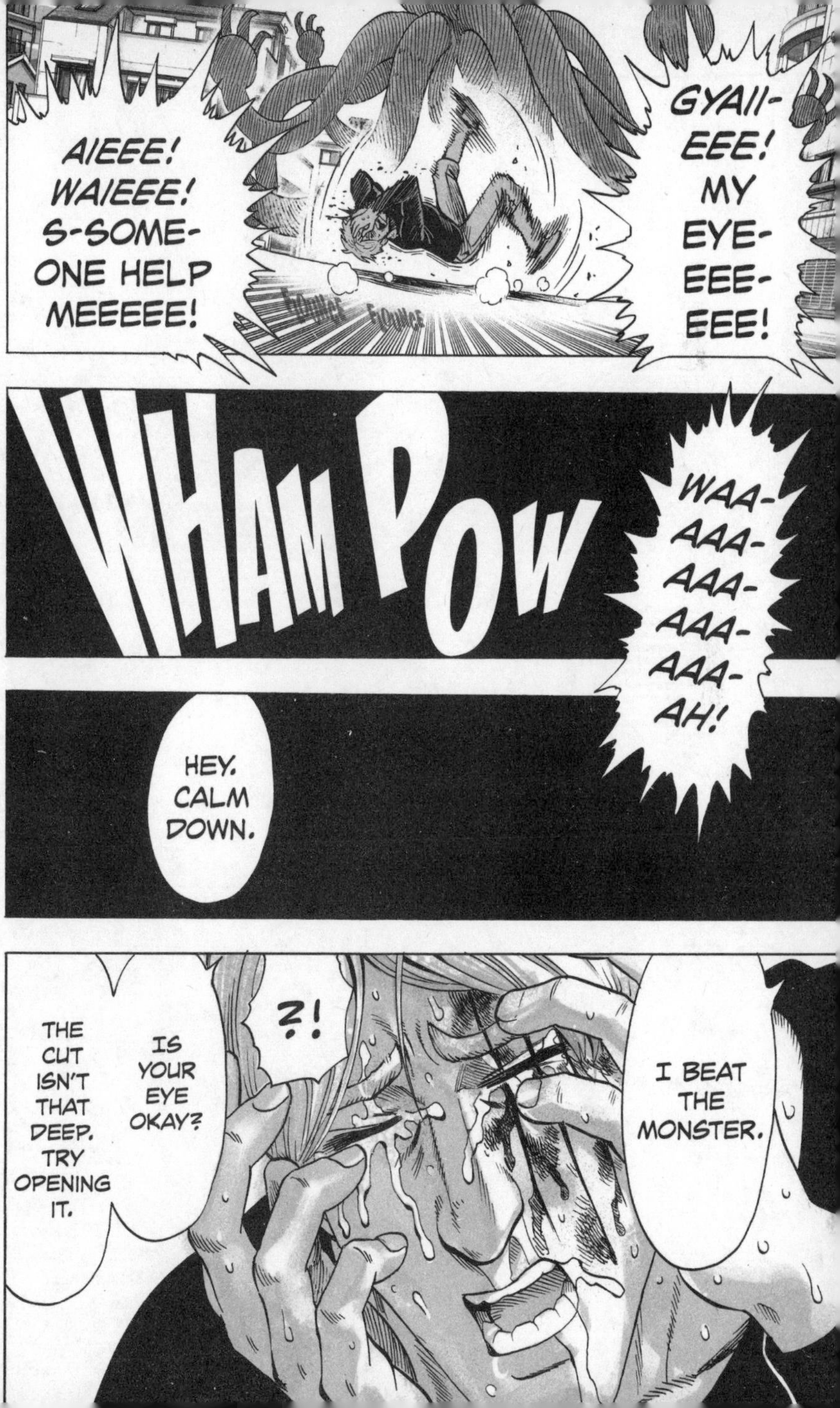
GYAII-EEE! MY EYE-EEE-EEE!
AIEEE! WAIEEE! S-SOME-ONE HELP MEEEEE!
WAA-AAA-AAA-AAA-AAA-AH!
WHAM POW
HEY. CALM DOWN.
I BEAT THE MONSTER.
?!
IS YOUR EYE OKAY?
THE CUT ISN'T THAT DEEP. TRY OPENING IT.

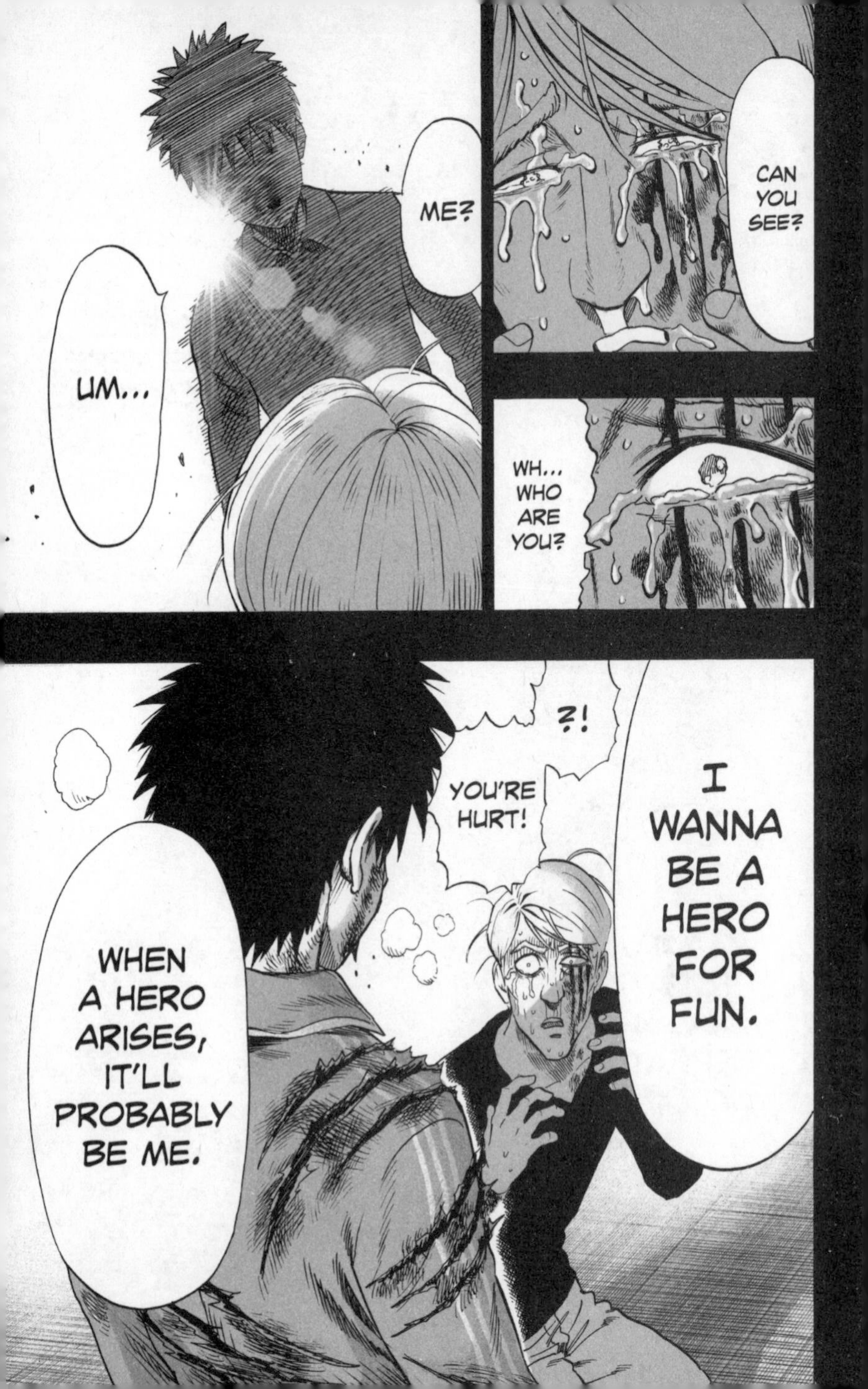
CAN YOU SEE?
WH... WHO ARE YOU?
ME?
UM...
I WANNA BE A HERO FOR FUN.
?!
YOU'RE HURT!
WHEN A HERO ARISES, IT'LL PROBABLY BE ME.

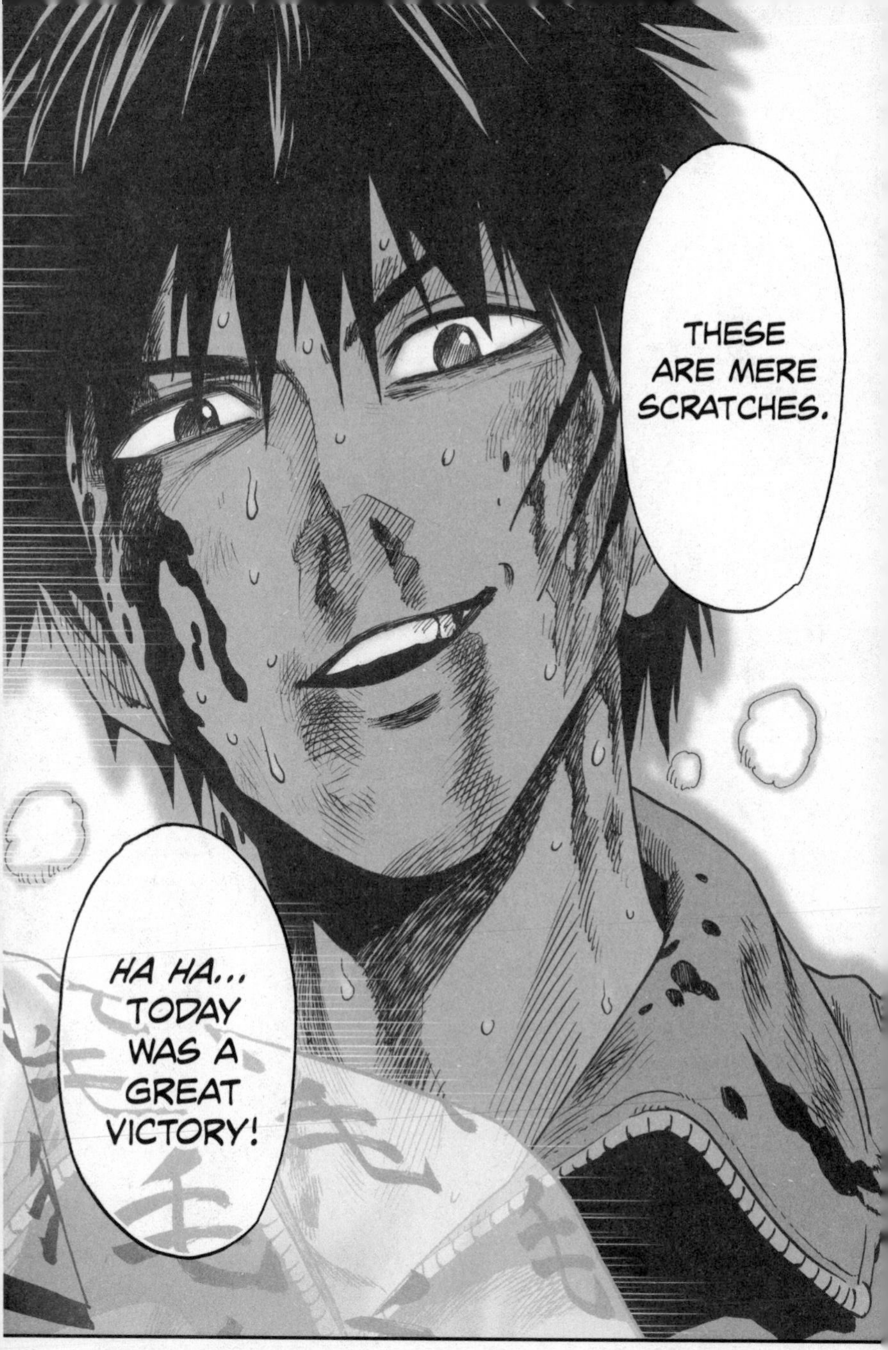
THESE ARE MERE SCRATCHES.
HA HA... TODAY WAS A GREAT VICTORY!

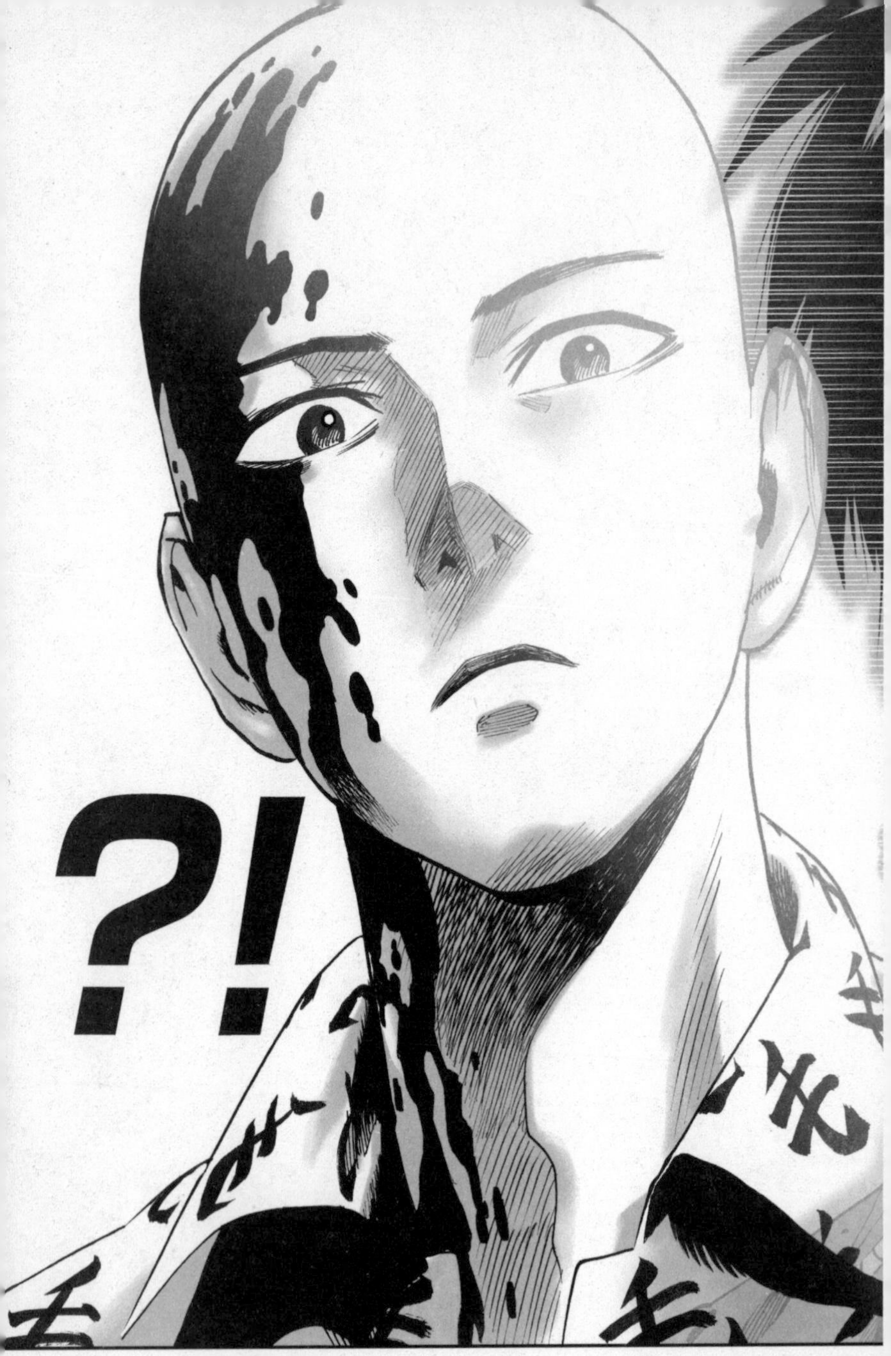
?!

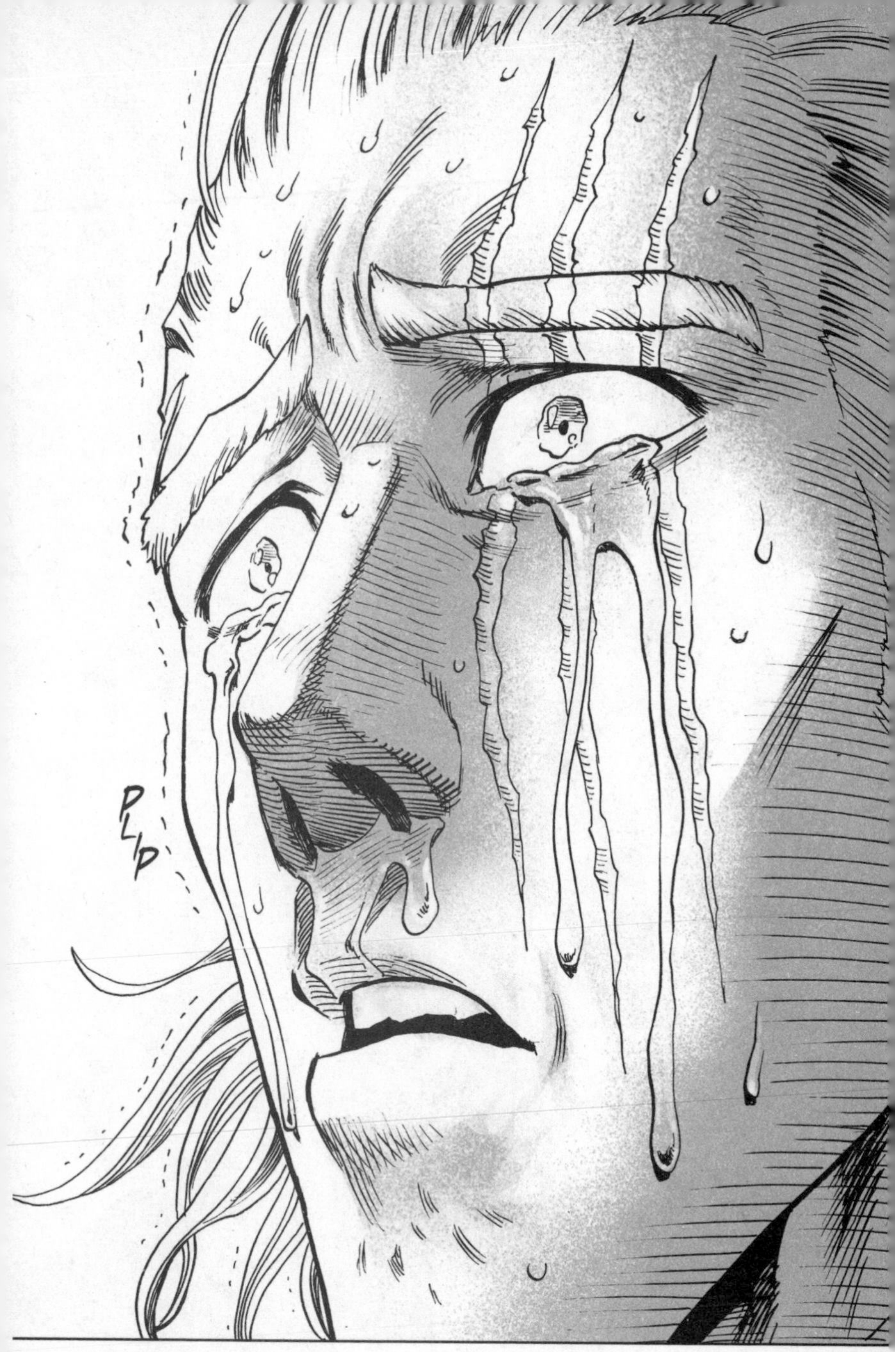
PLIP

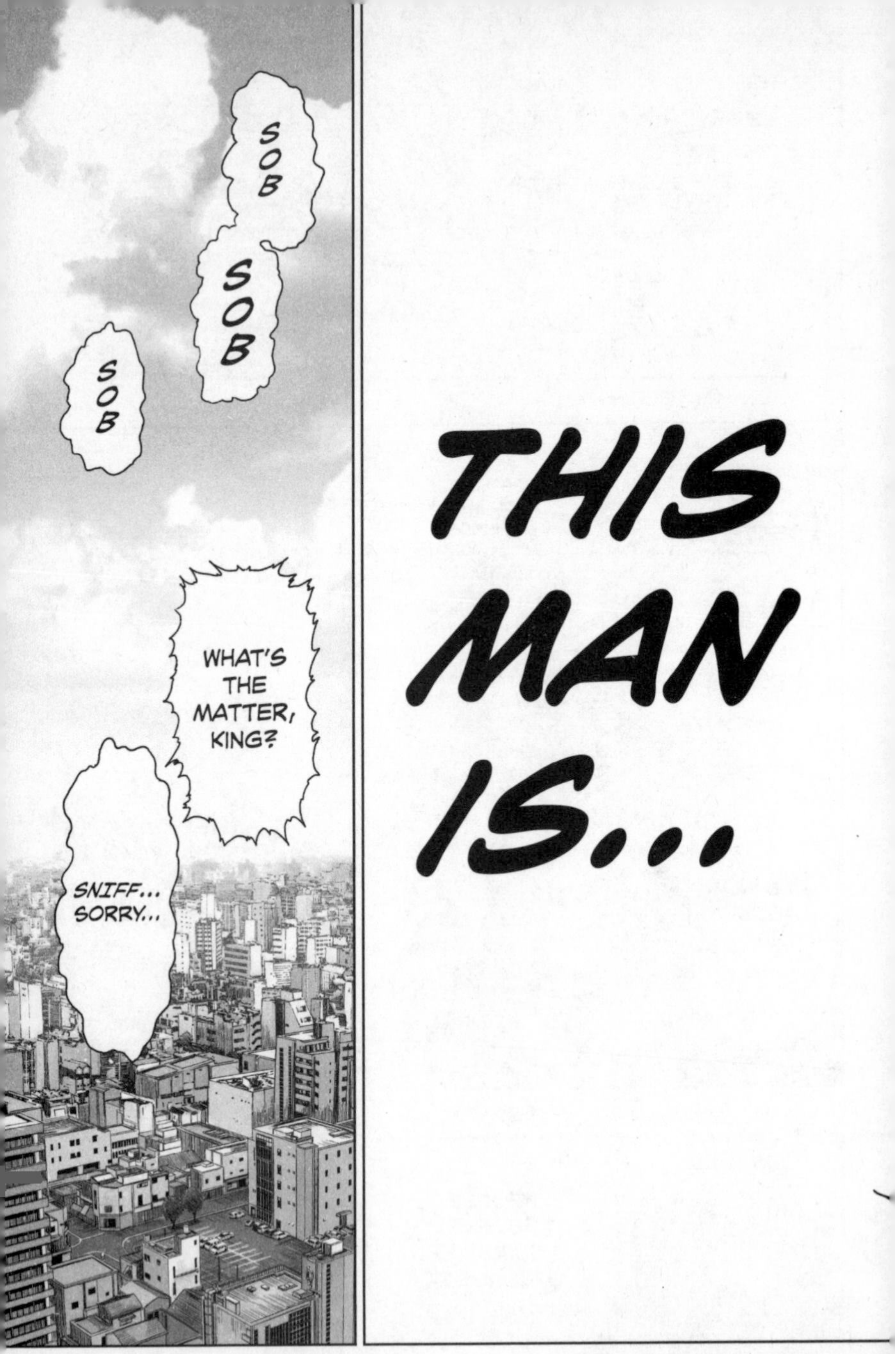
THIS MAN IS...
SOB
SOB
SOB
WHAT'S THE MATTER, KING?
SNIFF... SORRY...

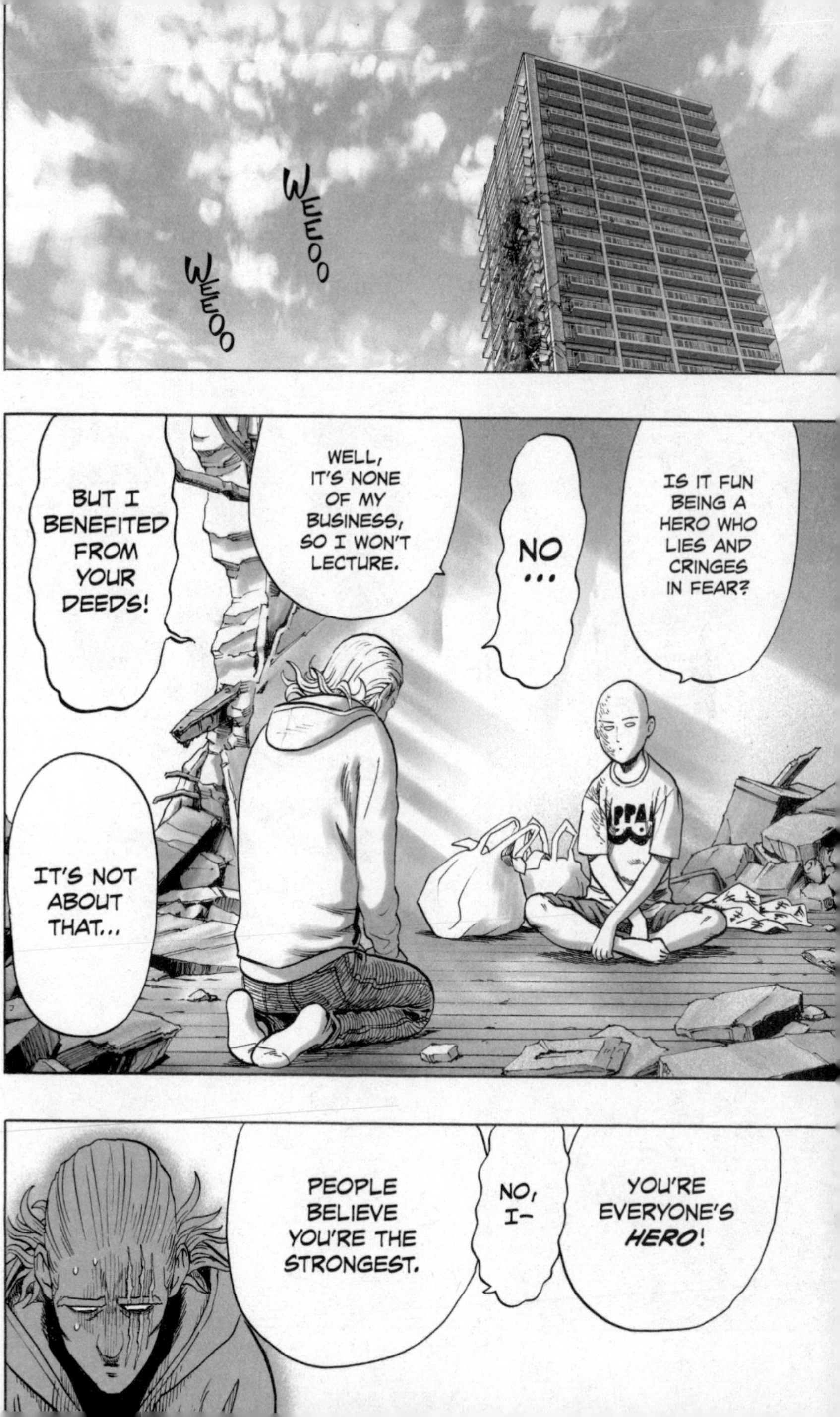
WEEOO
WEEOO
IS IT FUN BEING A HERO WHO LIES AND CRINGES IN FEAR?
NO...
WELL, IT'S NONE OF MY BUSINESS, SO I WON'T LECTURE.
BUT I BENEFITED FROM YOUR DEEDS!
IT'S NOT ABOUT THAT...
YOU'RE EVERYONE'S ***HERO***!
NO, I—
PEOPLE BELIEVE YOU'RE THE STRONGEST.

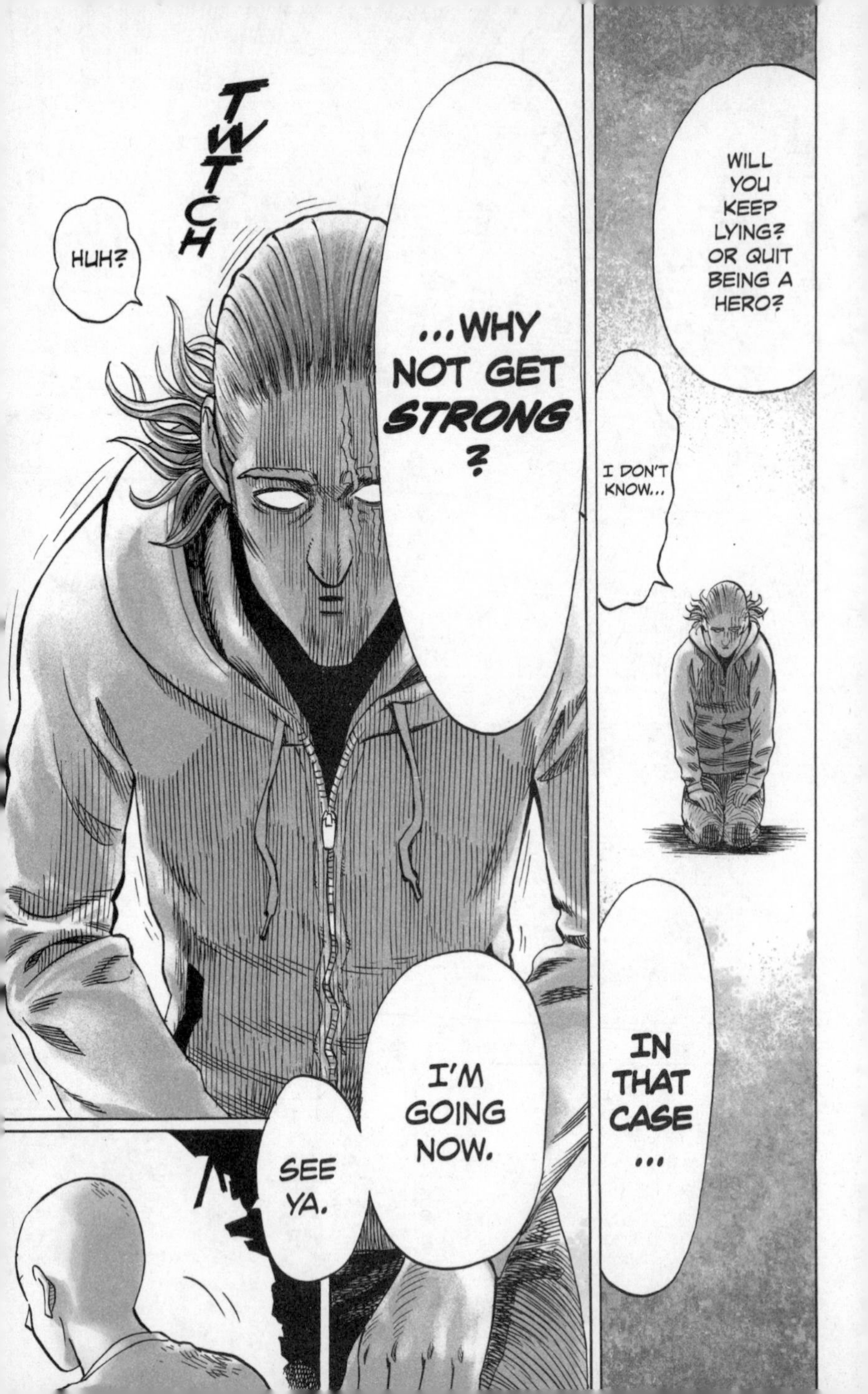
WILL YOU KEEP LYING? OR QUIT BEING A HERO?
I DON'T KNOW...
IN THAT CASE...
...WHY NOT GET STRONG?
TWTCH
HUH?
I'M GOING NOW.
SEE YA.

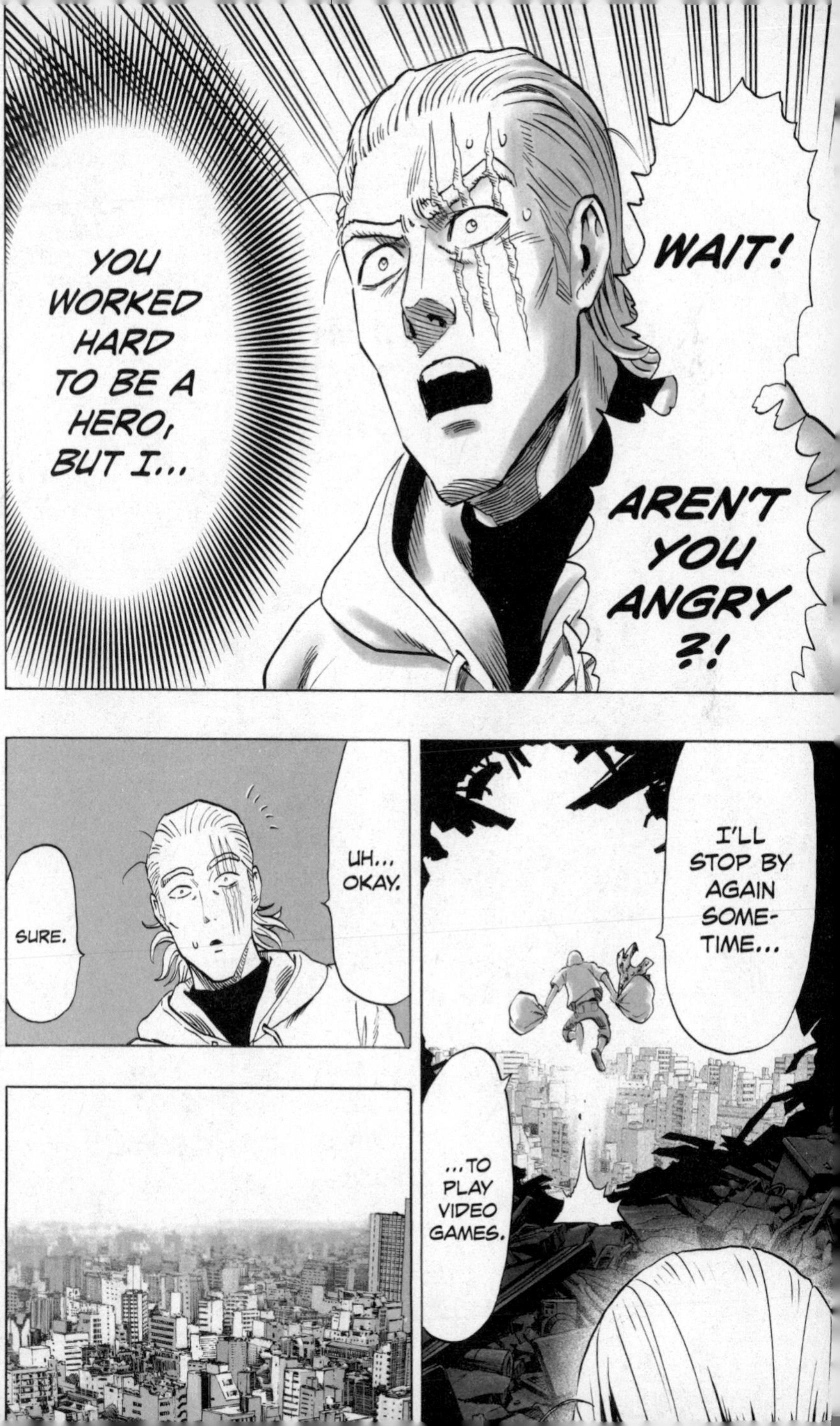
WAIT!
AREN'T YOU ANGRY ?!
YOU WORKED HARD TO BE A HERO, BUT I...
I'LL STOP BY AGAIN SOME-TIME...
...TO PLAY VIDEO GAMES.
UH... OKAY.
SURE.

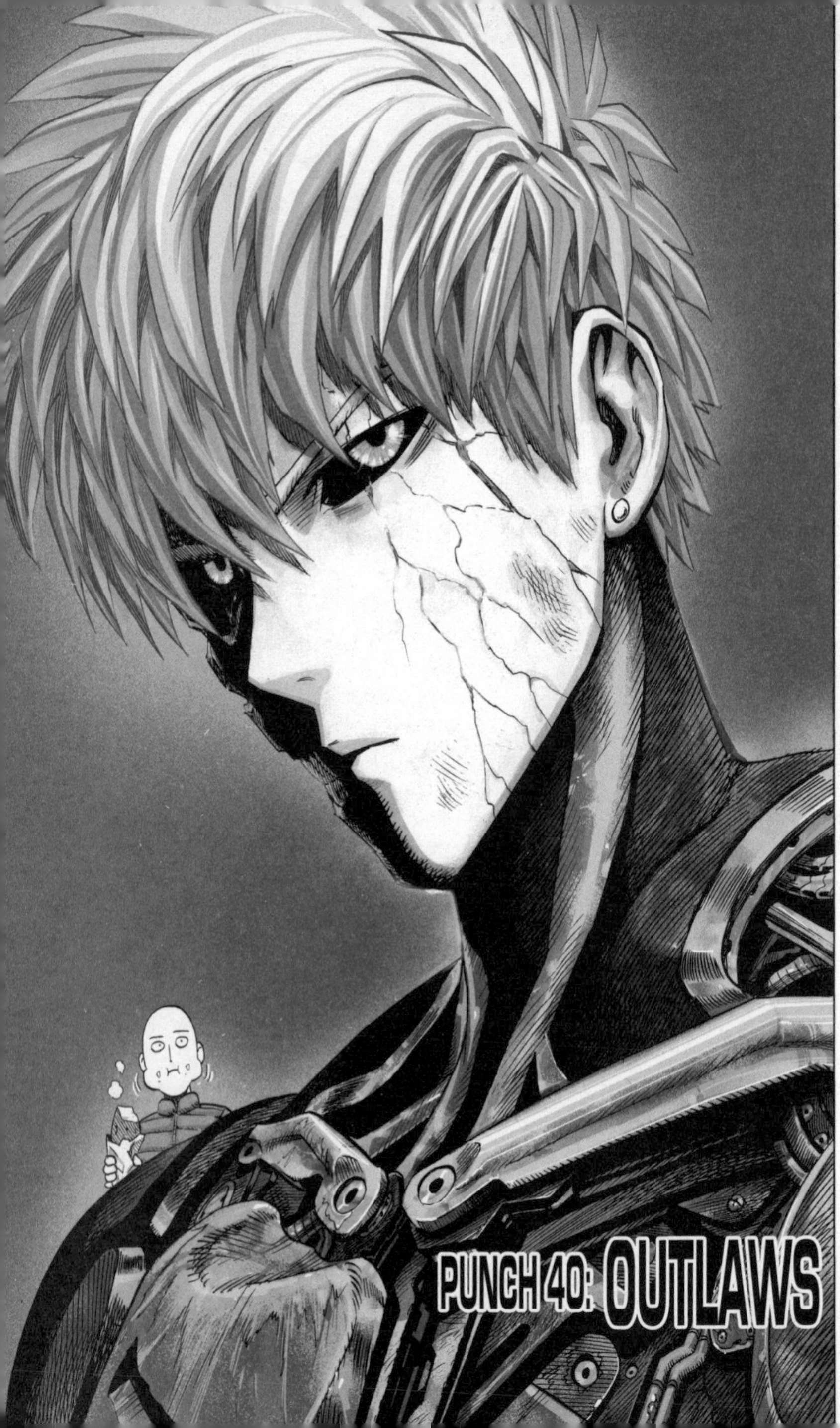
PUNCH 40: OUTLAWS

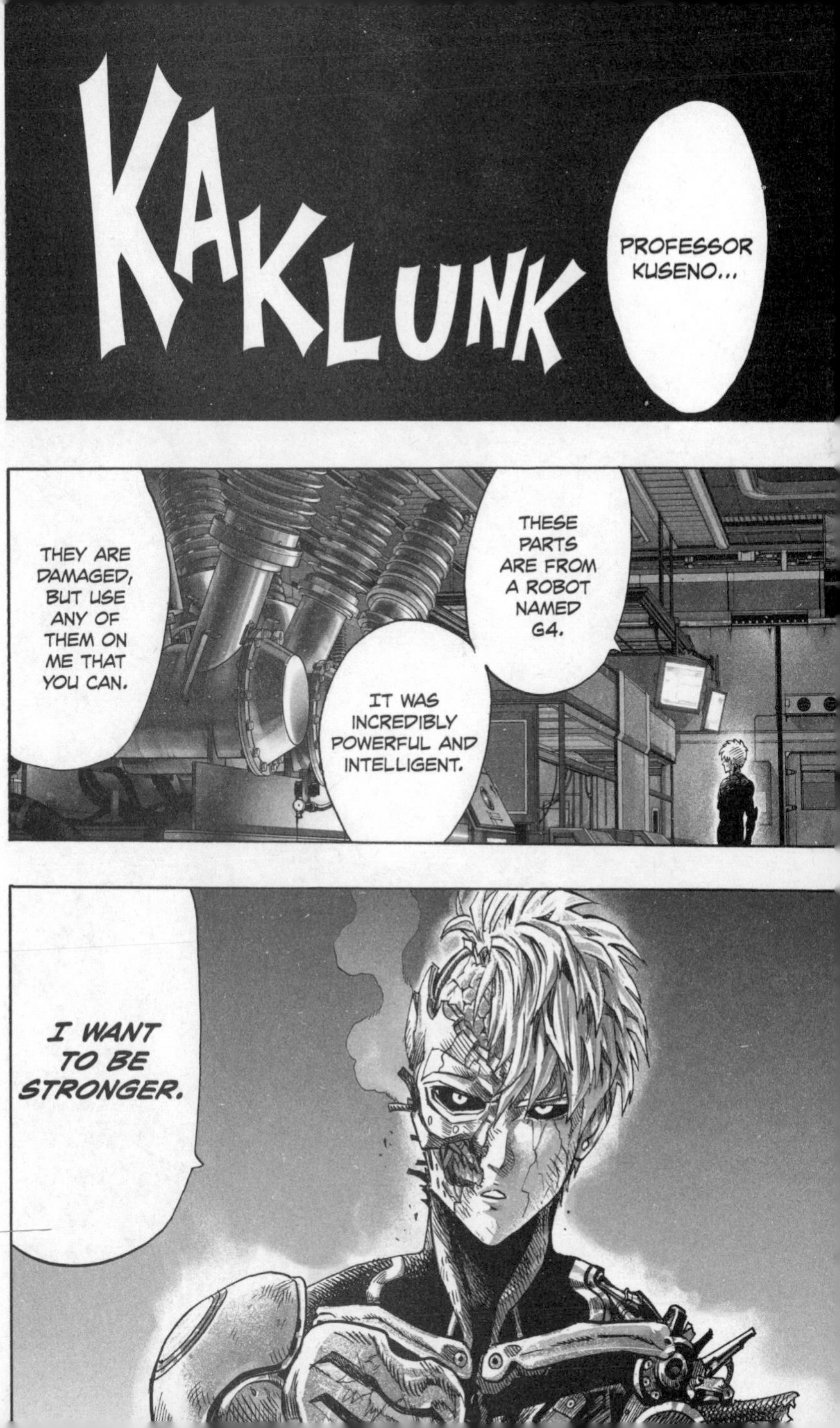
PROFESSOR KUSENO...
KAKLUNK
THESE PARTS ARE FROM A ROBOT NAMED G4.
IT WAS INCREDIBLY POWERFUL AND INTELLIGENT.
THEY ARE DAMAGED, BUT USE ANY OF THEM ON ME THAT YOU CAN.
I WANT TO BE STRONGER.

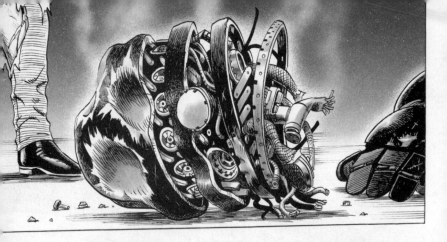

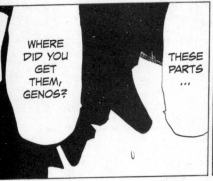

TH...
THESE PARTS ...
WHERE DID YOU GET THEM, GENOS?
VERY WELL! I'LL DO IT!
YOU HAVE ROOM TO GROW STRONGER!

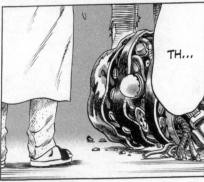

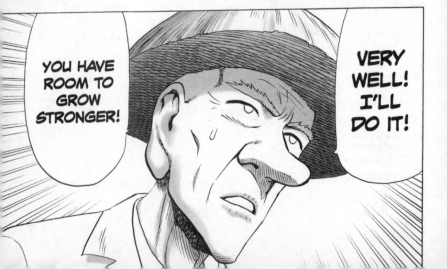

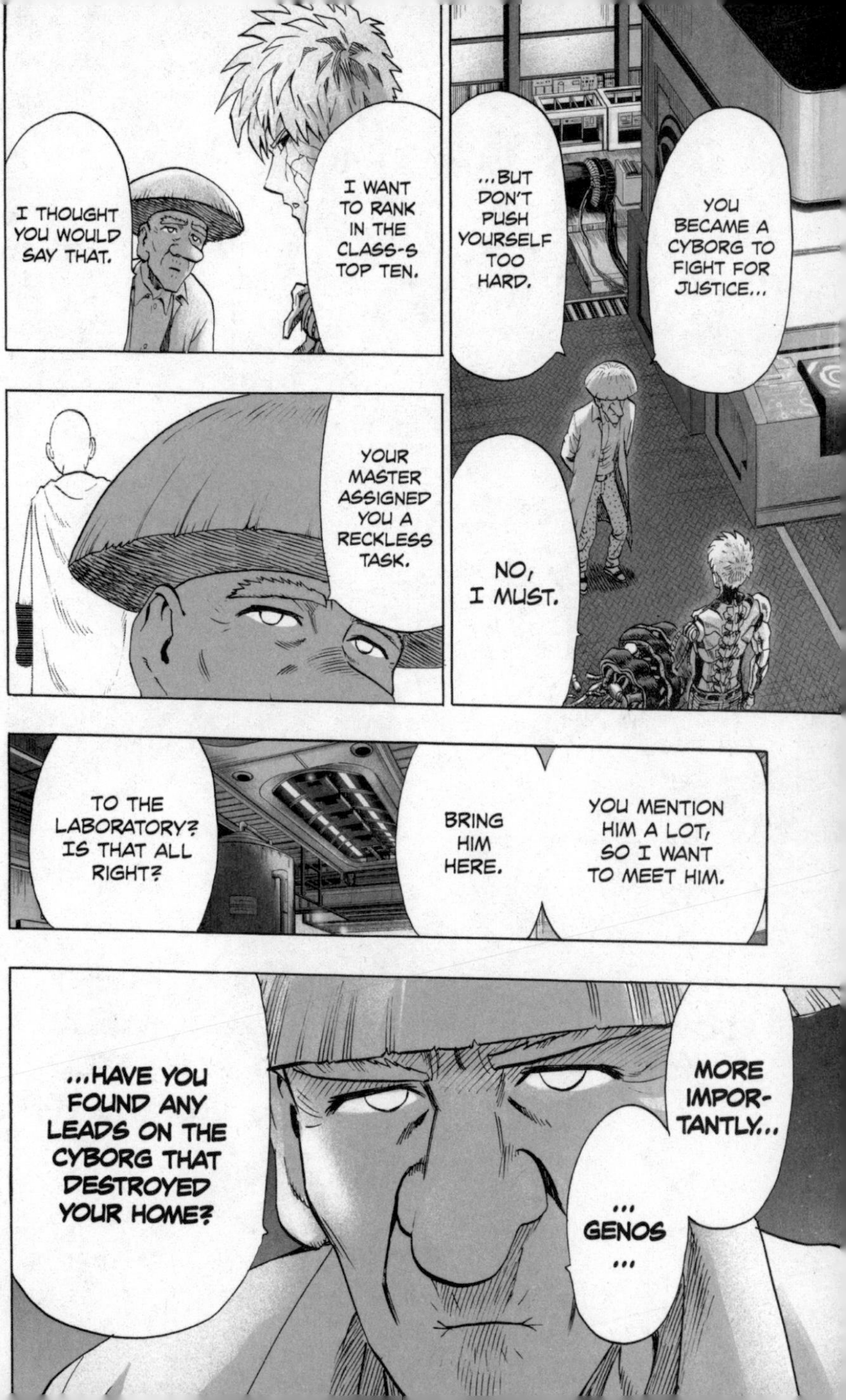
YOU BECAME A CYBORG TO FIGHT FOR JUSTICE...
...BUT DON'T PUSH YOURSELF TOO HARD.
NO, I MUST.
I WANT TO RANK IN THE CLASS-S TOP TEN.
I THOUGHT YOU WOULD SAY THAT.
YOUR MASTER ASSIGNED YOU A RECKLESS TASK.
YOU MENTION HIM A LOT, SO I WANT TO MEET HIM.
BRING HIM HERE.
TO THE LABORATORY? IS THAT ALL RIGHT?
MORE IMPORTANTLY...
...GENOS...
...HAVE YOU FOUND ANY LEADS ON THE CYBORG THAT DESTROYED YOUR HOME?

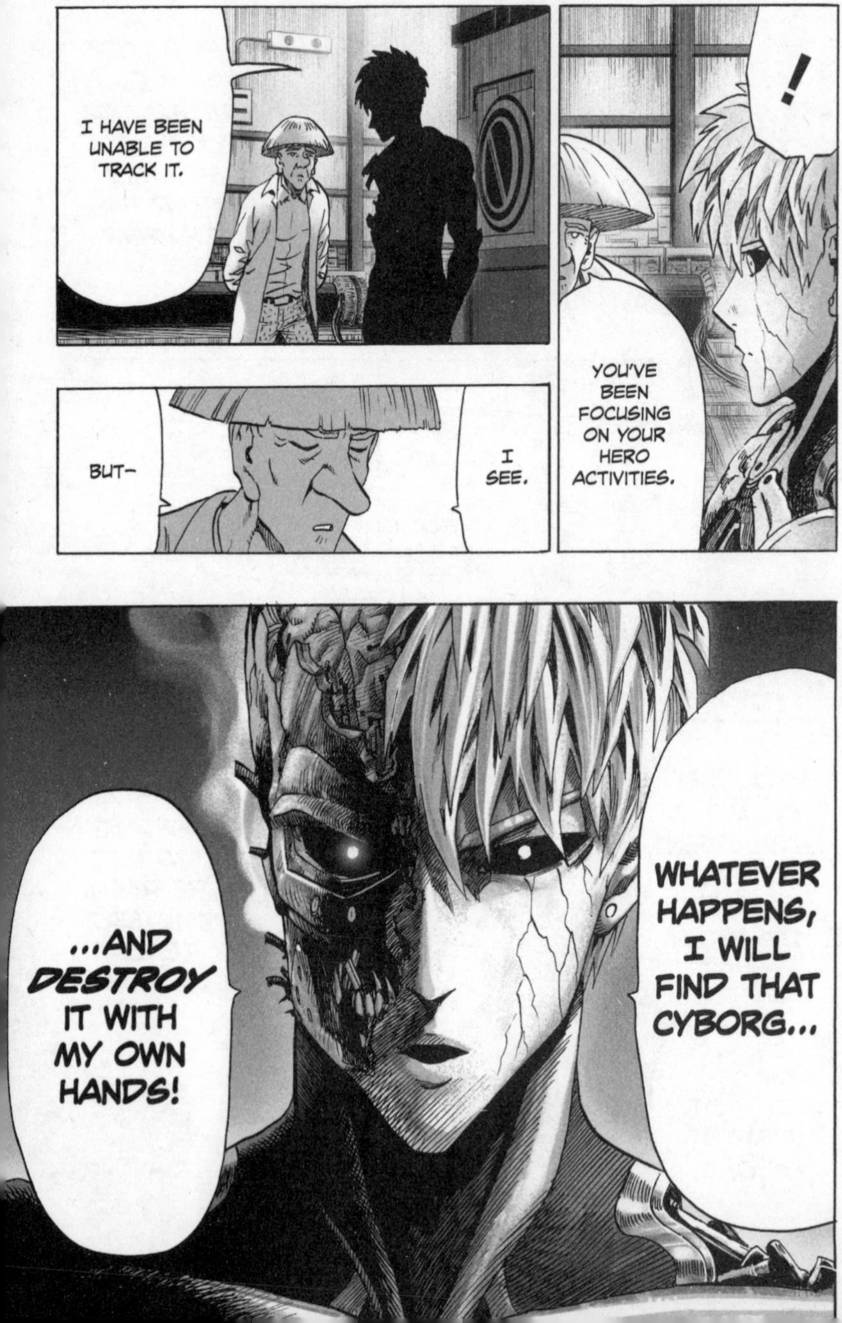
!
YOU'VE BEEN FOCUSING ON YOUR HERO ACTIVITIES.
I HAVE BEEN UNABLE TO TRACK IT.
I SEE.
BUT-
WHATEVER HAPPENS, I WILL FIND THAT CYBORG...
...AND DESTROY IT WITH MY OWN HANDS!

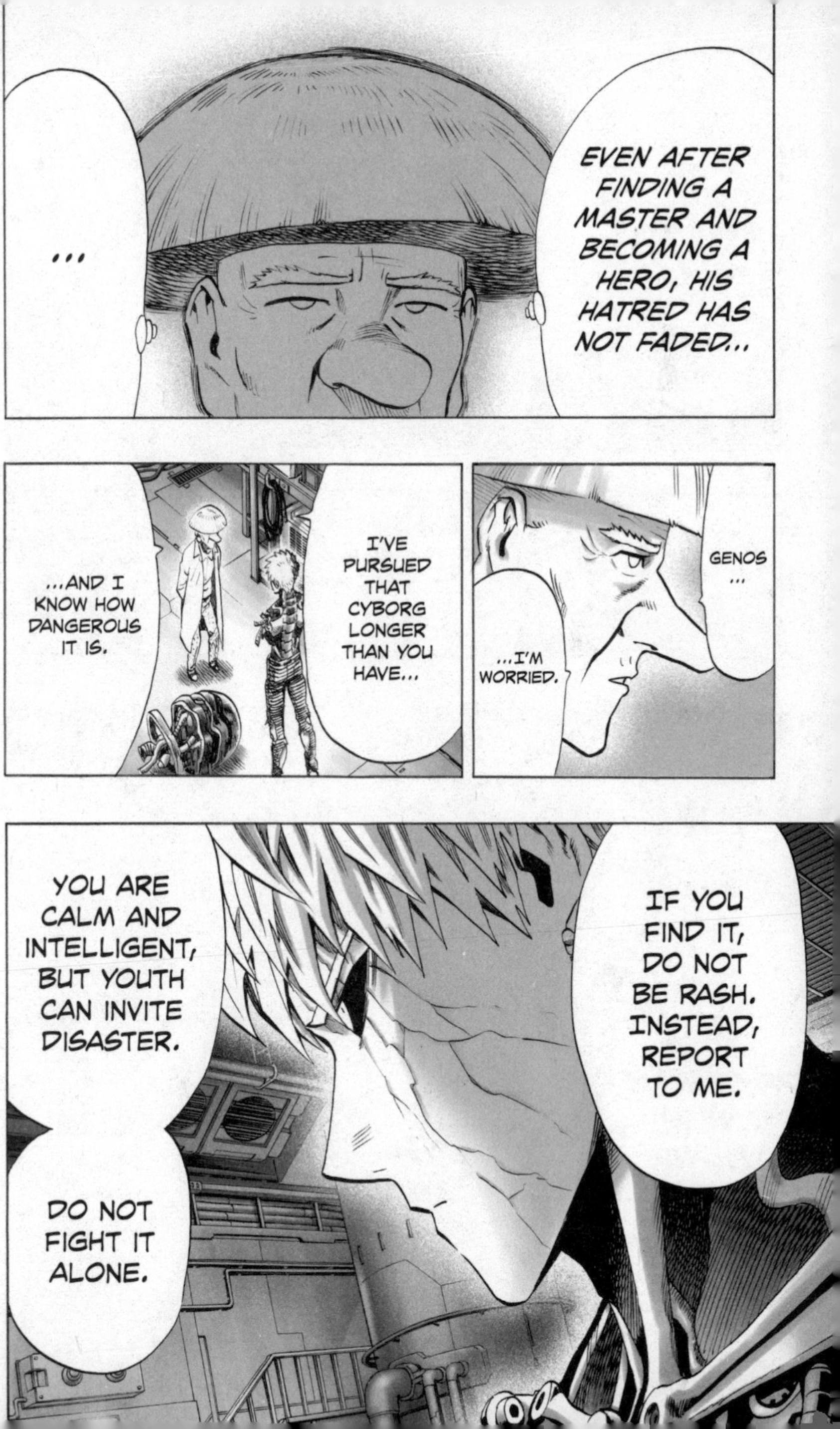
EVEN AFTER FINDING A MASTER AND BECOMING A HERO, HIS HATRED HAS NOT FADED...
...
GENOS ...
...I'M WORRIED.
I'VE PURSUED THAT CYBORG LONGER THAN YOU HAVE...
...AND I KNOW HOW DANGEROUS IT IS.
IF YOU FIND IT, DO NOT BE RASH. INSTEAD, REPORT TO ME.
YOU ARE CALM AND INTELLIGENT, BUT YOUTH CAN INVITE DISASTER.
DO NOT FIGHT IT ALONE.

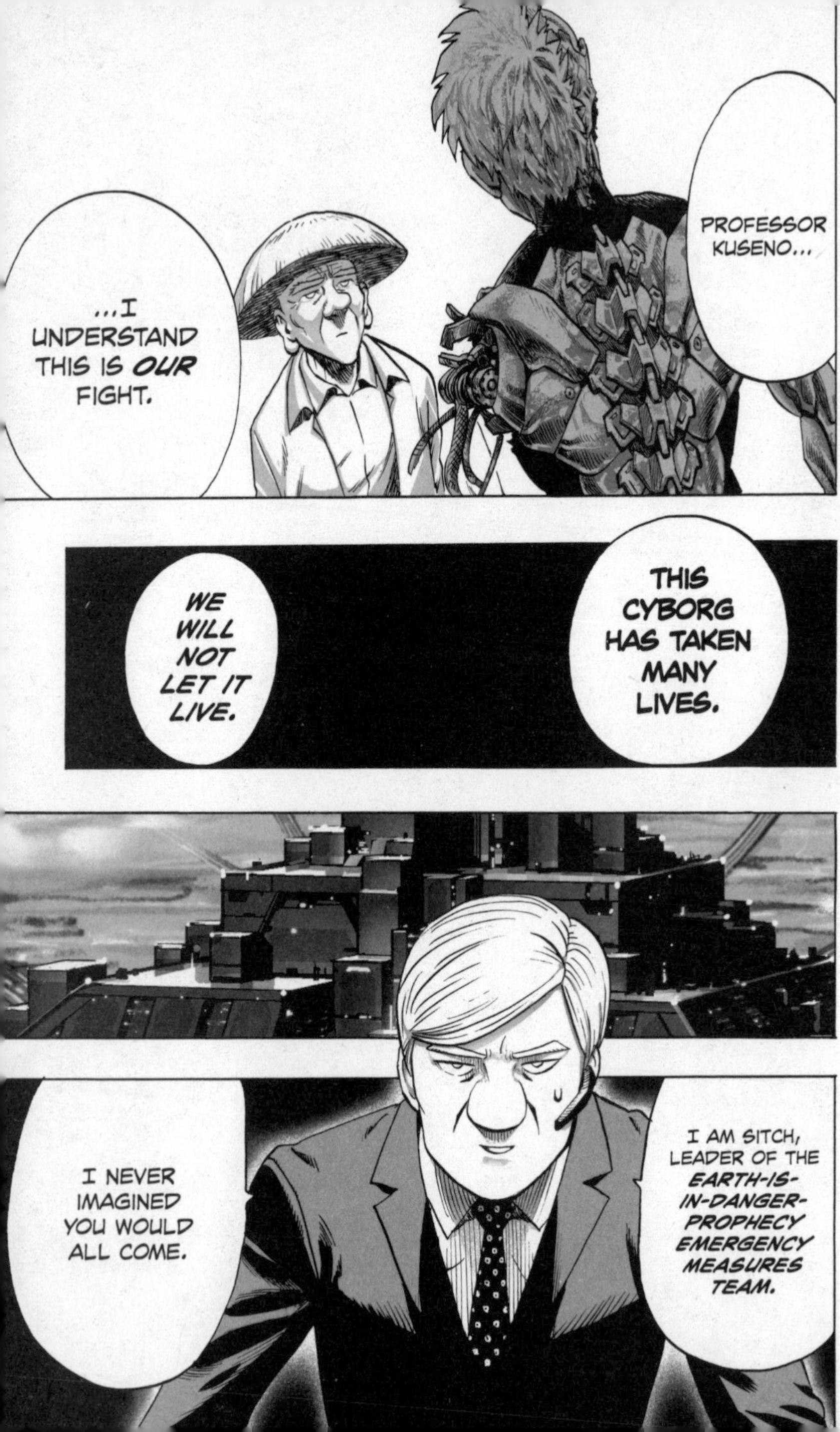
PROFESSOR KUSENO...
...I UNDERSTAND THIS IS *OUR* FIGHT.
THIS CYBORG HAS TAKEN MANY LIVES.
WE WILL NOT LET IT LIVE.
I AM SITCH, LEADER OF THE *EARTH-IS-IN-DANGER-PROPHECY EMERGENCY MEASURES TEAM.*
I NEVER IMAGINED YOU WOULD ALL COME.

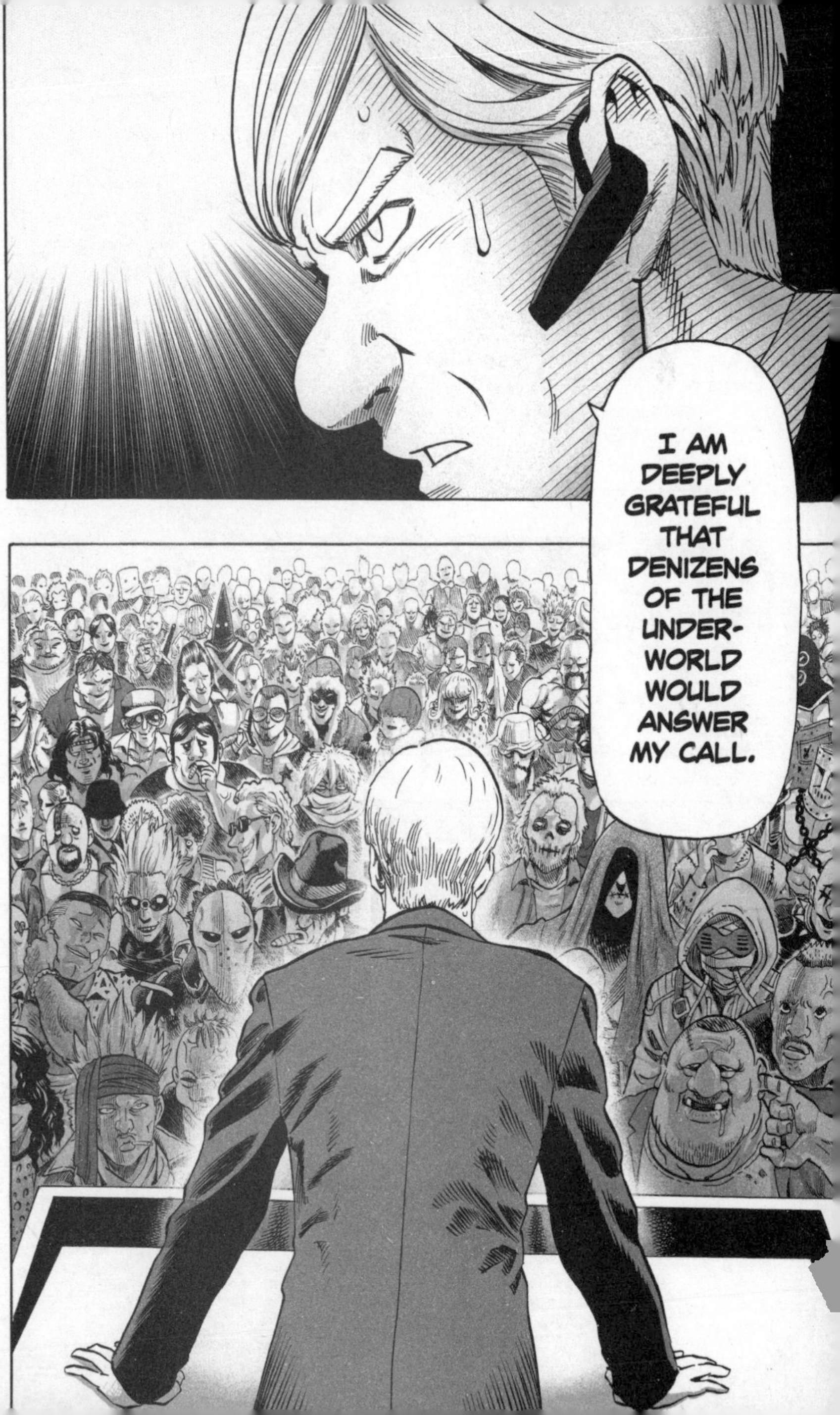
I AM DEEPLY GRATEFUL THAT DENIZENS OF THE UNDER-WORLD WOULD ANSWER MY CALL.

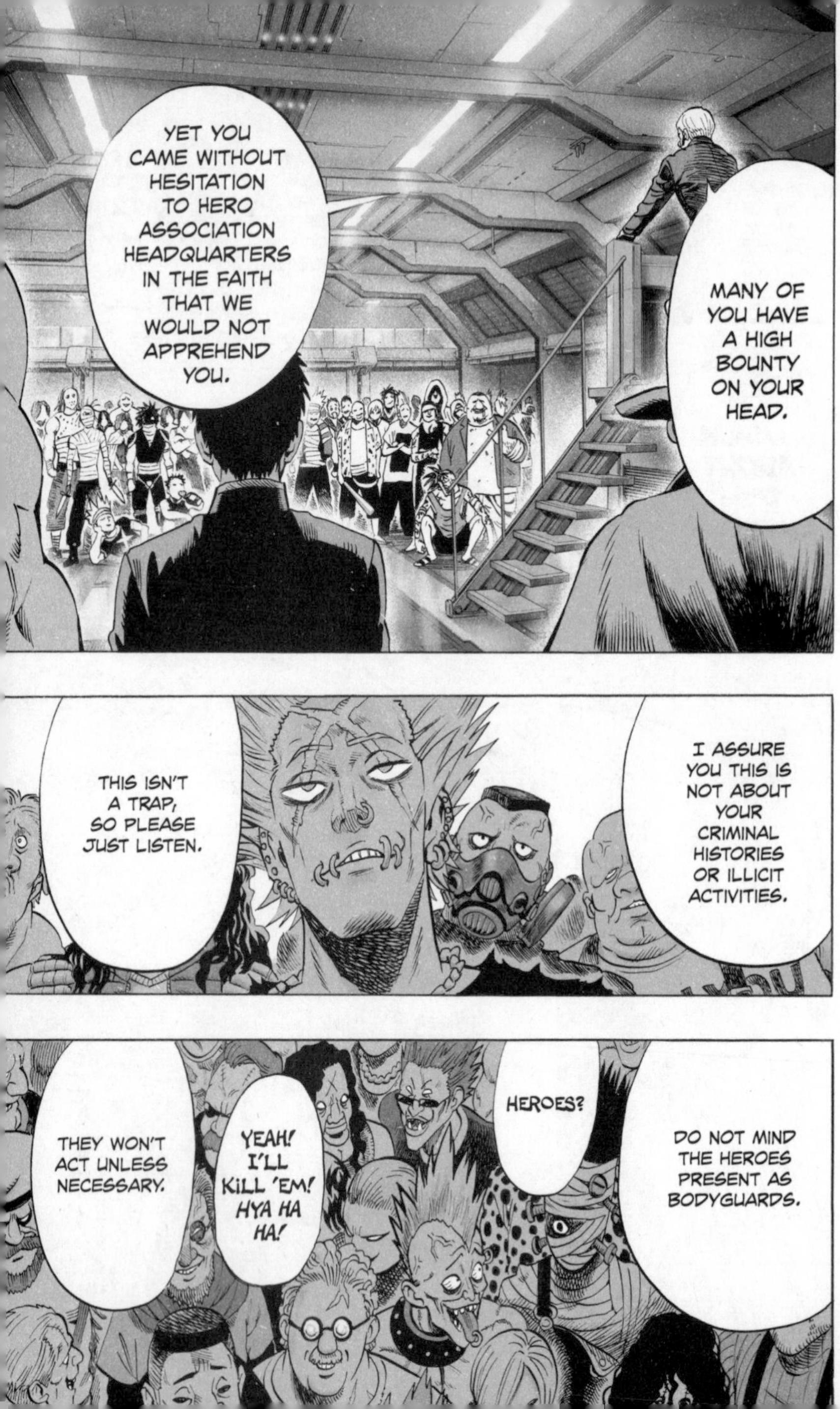
MANY OF YOU HAVE A HIGH BOUNTY ON YOUR HEAD.
YET YOU CAME WITHOUT HESITATION TO HERO ASSOCIATION HEADQUARTERS IN THE FAITH THAT WE WOULD NOT APPREHEND YOU.
I ASSURE YOU THIS IS NOT ABOUT YOUR CRIMINAL HISTORIES OR ILLICIT ACTIVITIES.
THIS ISN'T A TRAP, SO PLEASE JUST LISTEN.
DO NOT MIND THE HEROES PRESENT AS BODYGUARDS.
HEROES?
YEAH! I'LL KILL 'EM! HYA HA HA!
THEY WON'T ACT UNLESS NECESSARY.

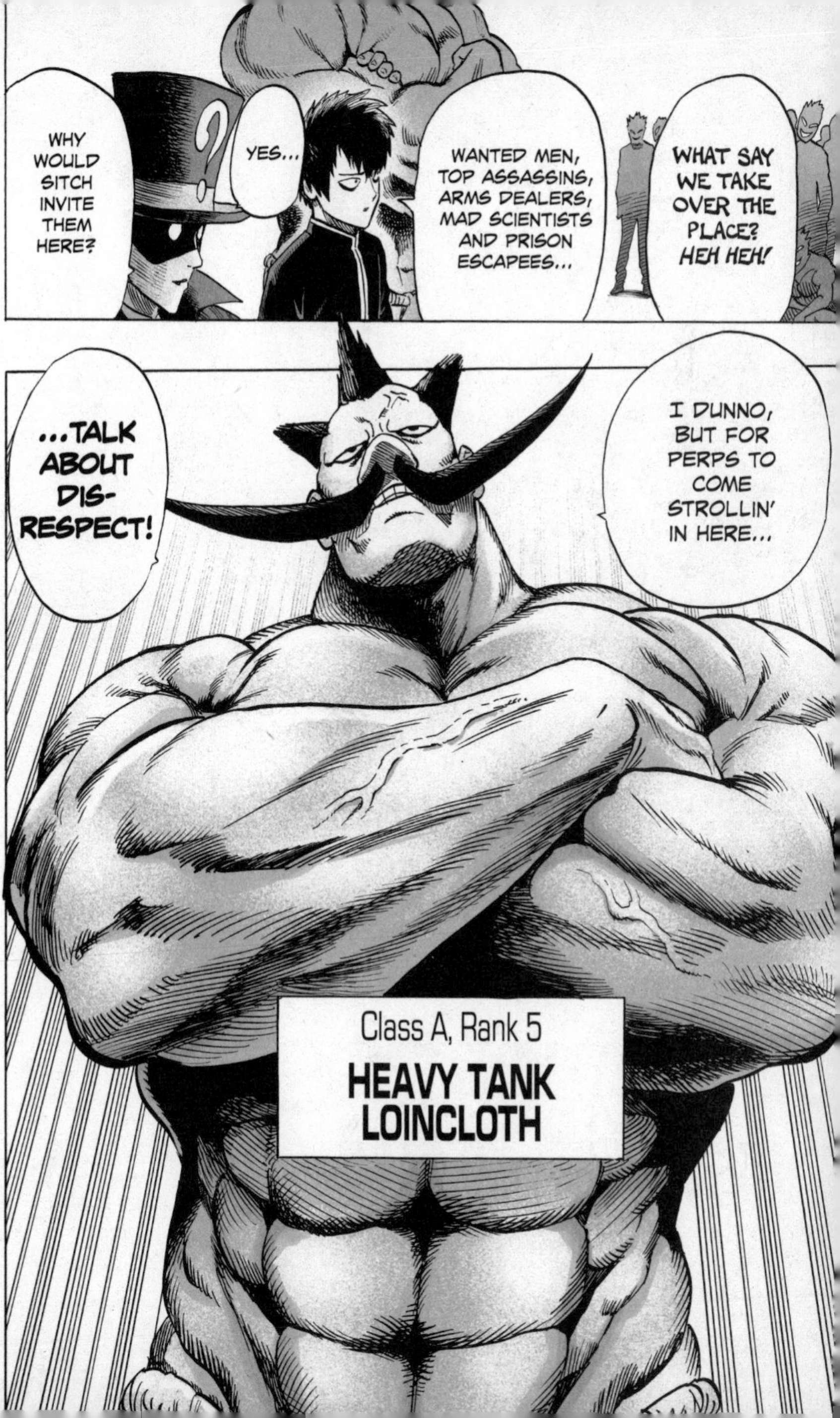
WHAT SAY WE TAKE OVER THE PLACE? HEH HEH!
WANTED MEN, TOP ASSASSINS, ARMS DEALERS, MAD SCIENTISTS AND PRISON ESCAPEES...
YES...
WHY WOULD SITCH INVITE THEM HERE?
I DUNNO, BUT FOR PERPS TO COME STROLLIN' IN HERE...
...TALK ABOUT DIS-RESPECT!
Class A, Rank 5
HEAVY TANK LOINCLOTH

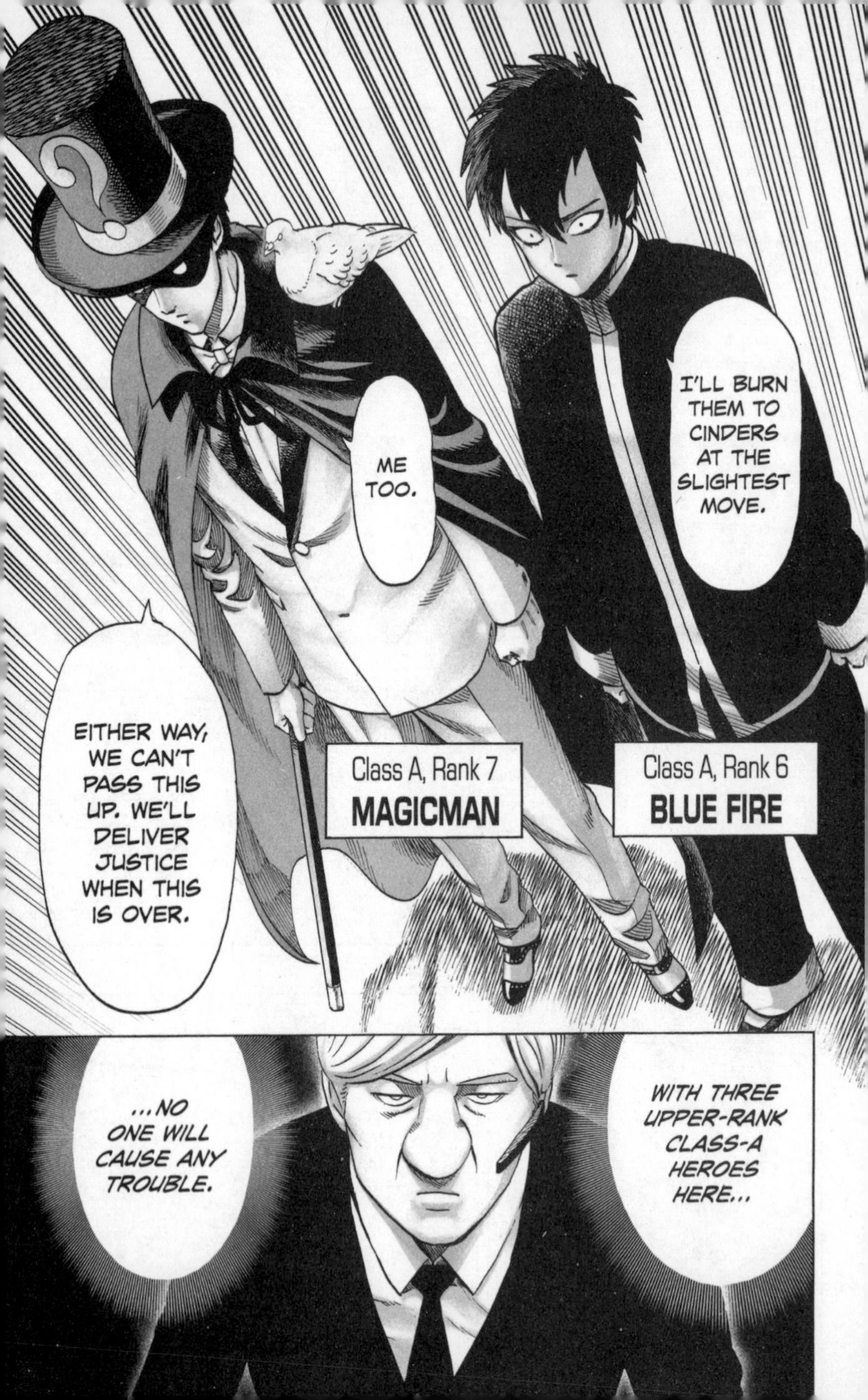
I'LL BURN THEM TO CINDERS AT THE SLIGHTEST MOVE.
ME TOO.
Class A, Rank 6 BLUE FIRE
Class A, Rank 7 MAGICMAN
EITHER WAY, WE CAN'T PASS THIS UP. WE'LL DELIVER JUSTICE WHEN THIS IS OVER.
WITH THREE UPPER-RANK CLASS-A HEROES HERE...
...NO ONE WILL CAUSE ANY TROUBLE.

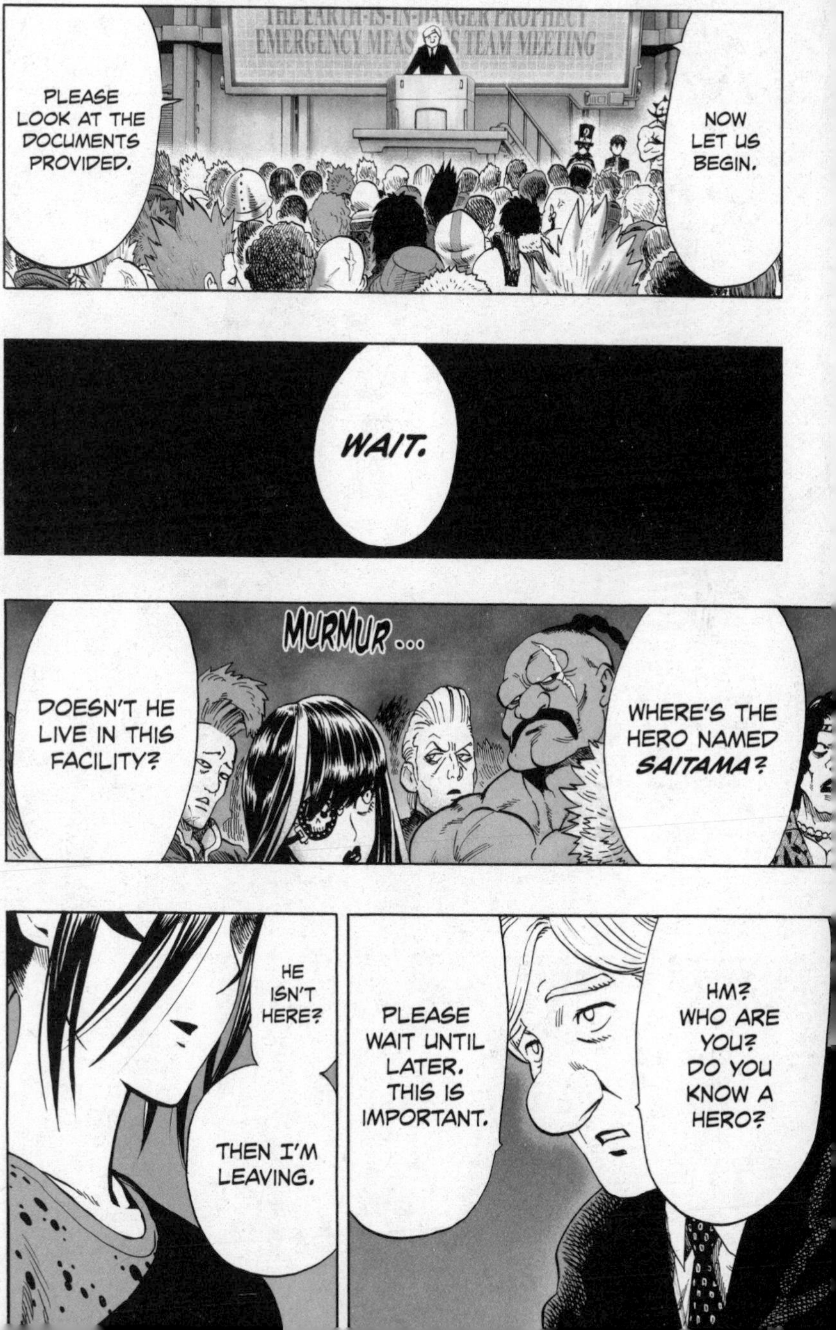
THE EARTH-IS-IN-DANGER PROPHECY
EMERGENCY MEAS S TEAM MEETING
NOW LET US BEGIN.
PLEASE LOOK AT THE DOCUMENTS PROVIDED.
WAIT.
MURMUR...
WHERE'S THE HERO NAMED *SAITAMA*?
DOESN'T HE LIVE IN THIS FACILITY?
HM? WHO ARE YOU? DO YOU KNOW A HERO?
PLEASE WAIT UNTIL LATER. THIS IS IMPORTANT.
HE ISN'T HERE?
THEN I'M LEAVING.

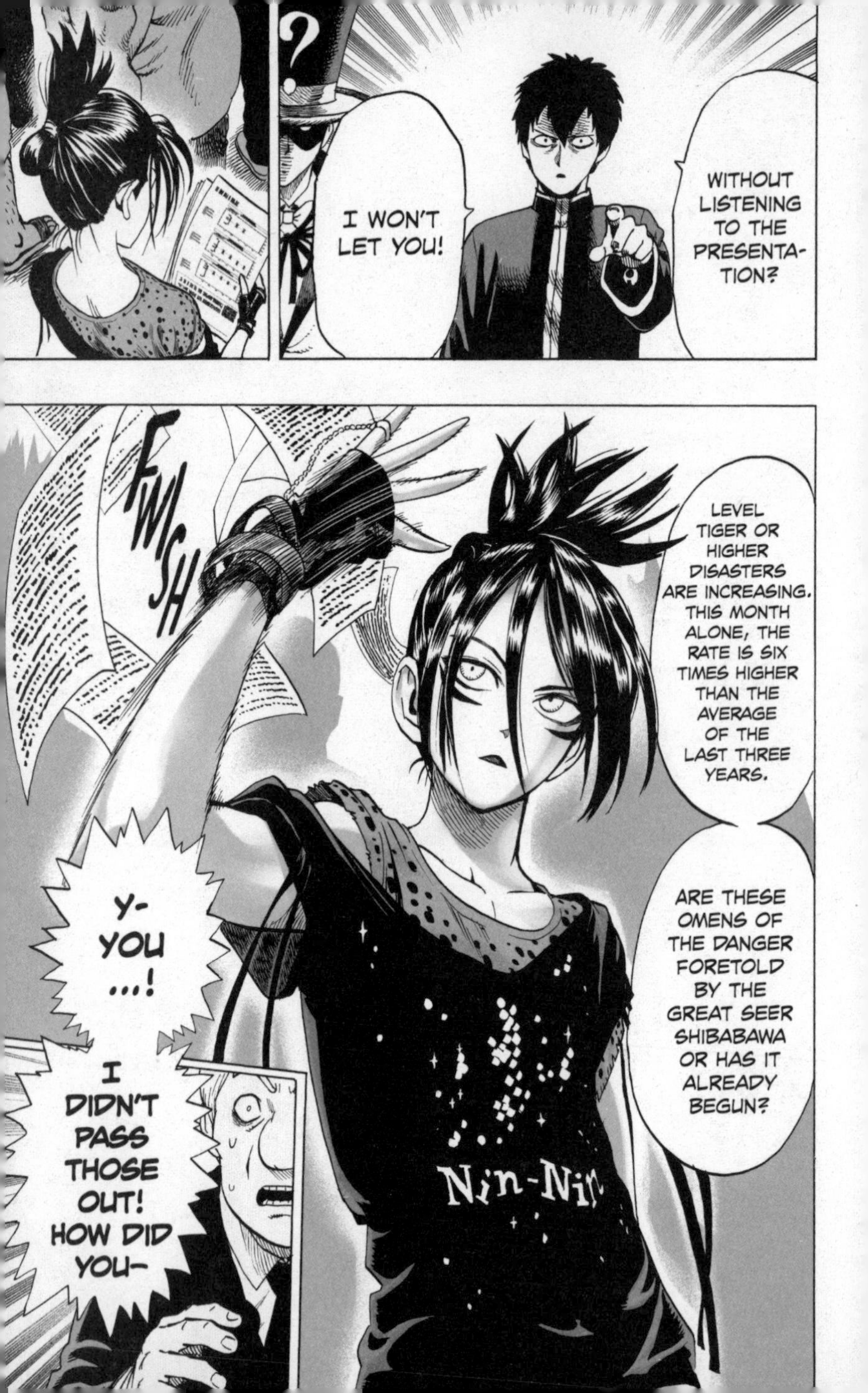
WITHOUT LISTENING TO THE PRESENTATION?
I WON'T LET YOU!
LEVEL TIGER OR HIGHER DISASTERS ARE INCREASING. THIS MONTH ALONE, THE RATE IS SIX TIMES HIGHER THAN THE AVERAGE OF THE LAST THREE YEARS.
FWISH
ARE THESE OMENS OF THE DANGER FORETOLD BY THE GREAT SEER SHIBABAWA OR HAS IT ALREADY BEGUN?
Nin-Nin
Y-YOU...!
I DIDN'T PASS THOSE OUT! HOW DID YOU-

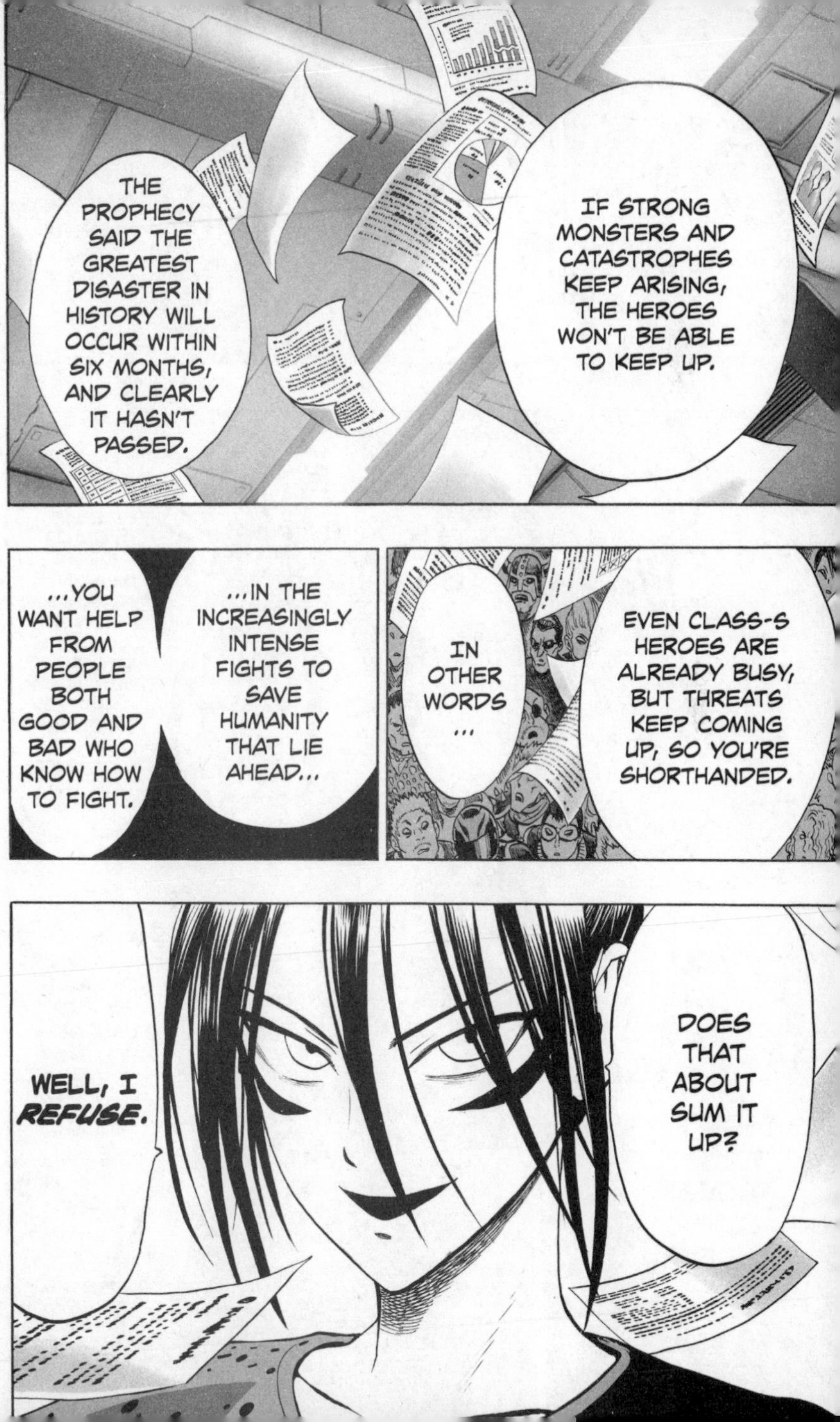
IF STRONG MONSTERS AND CATASTROPHES KEEP ARISING, THE HEROES WON'T BE ABLE TO KEEP UP.
THE PROPHECY SAID THE GREATEST DISASTER IN HISTORY WILL OCCUR WITHIN SIX MONTHS, AND CLEARLY IT HASN'T PASSED.
EVEN CLASS-S HEROES ARE ALREADY BUSY, BUT THREATS KEEP COMING UP, SO YOU'RE SHORTHANDED.
IN OTHER WORDS...
...IN THE INCREASINGLY INTENSE FIGHTS TO SAVE HUMANITY THAT LIE AHEAD...
...YOU WANT HELP FROM PEOPLE BOTH GOOD AND BAD WHO KNOW HOW TO FIGHT.
DOES THAT ABOUT SUM IT UP?
WELL, I *REFUSE*.

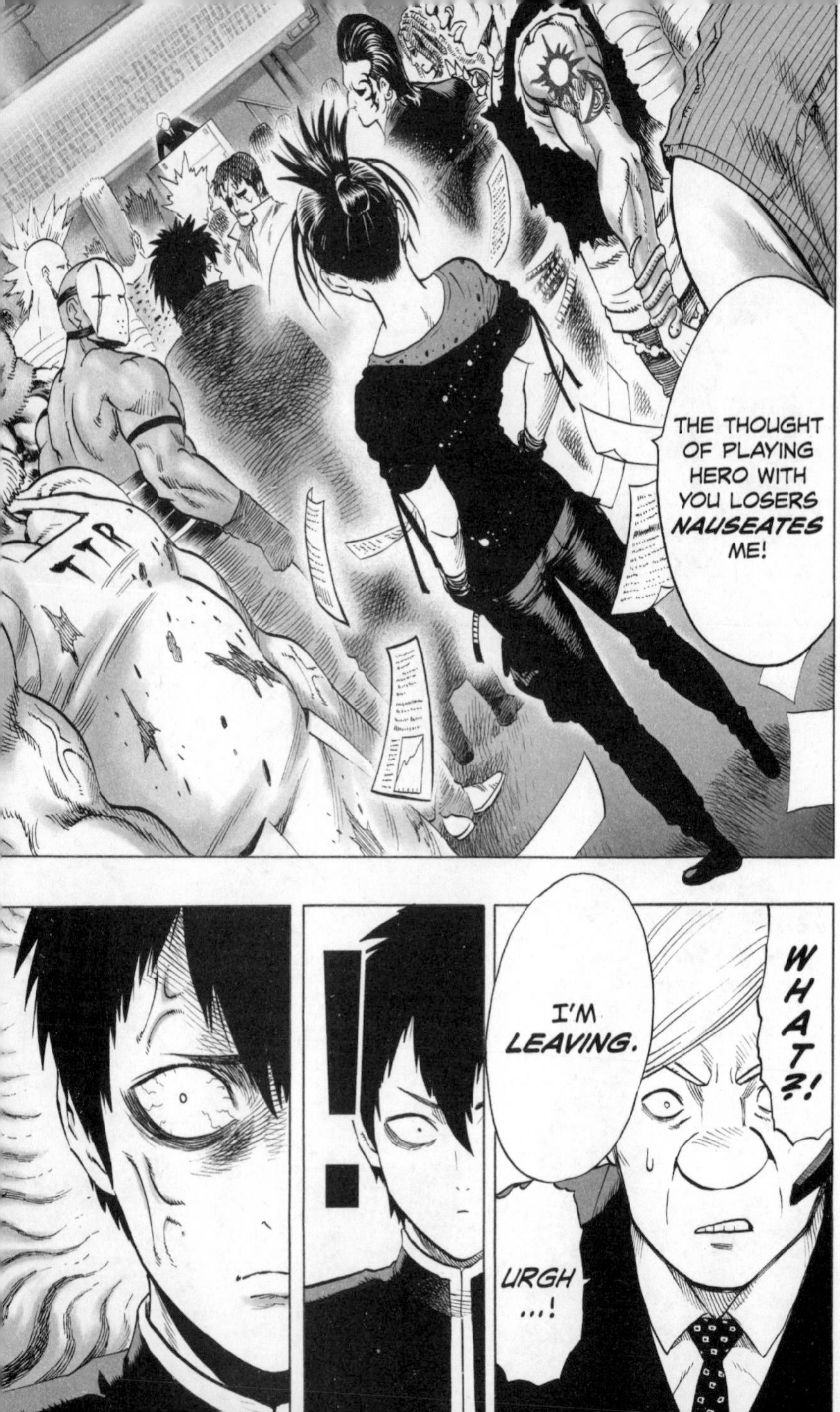
THE THOUGHT OF PLAYING HERO WITH YOU LOSERS *NAUSEATES* ME!
I'M *LEAVING.*
WHAT?!
URGH ...!
!

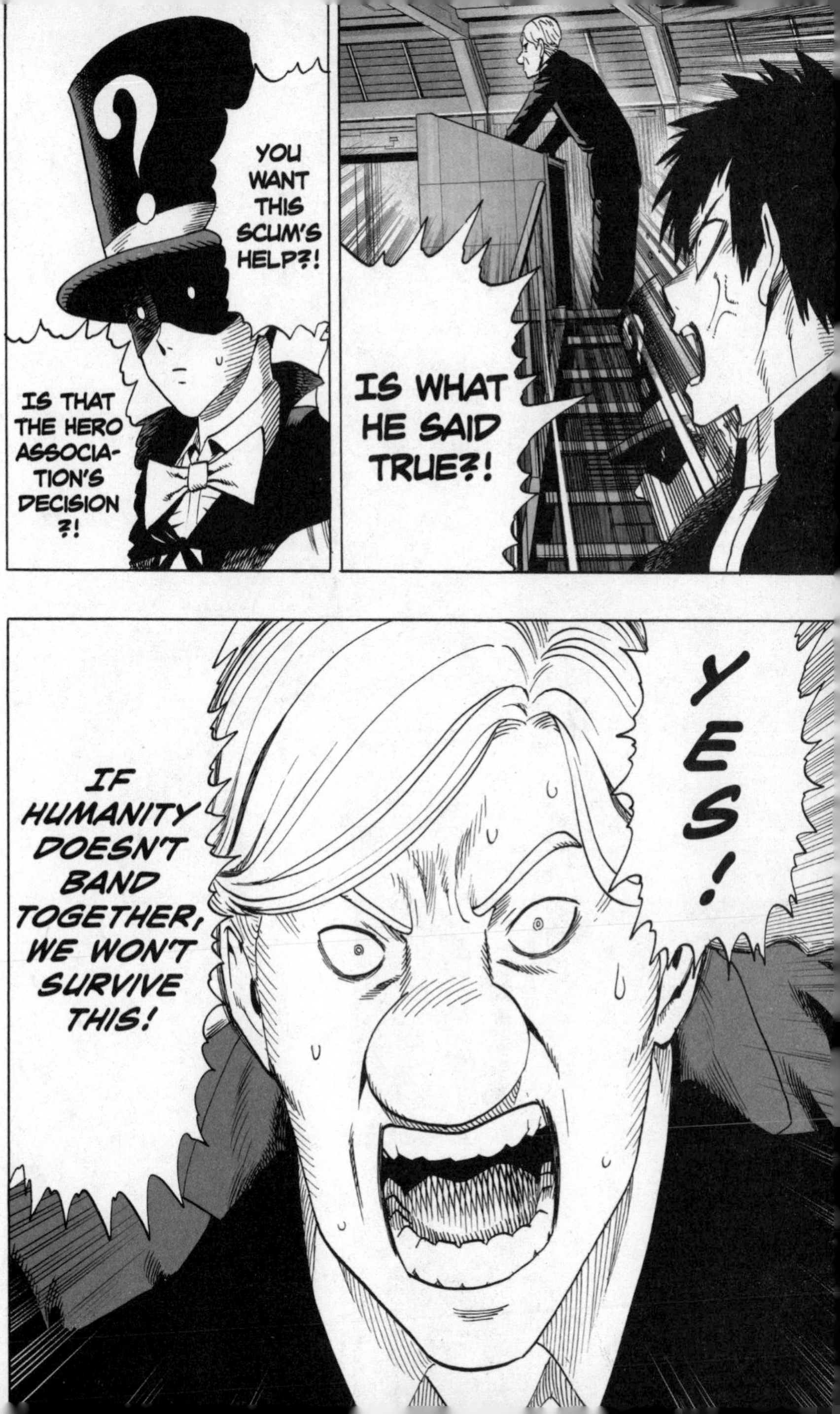
IS WHAT HE SAID TRUE?!
YOU WANT THIS SCUM'S HELP?!
IS THAT THE HERO ASSOCIATION'S DECISION?!
YES!
IF HUMANITY DOESN'T BAND TOGETHER, WE WON'T SURVIVE THIS!

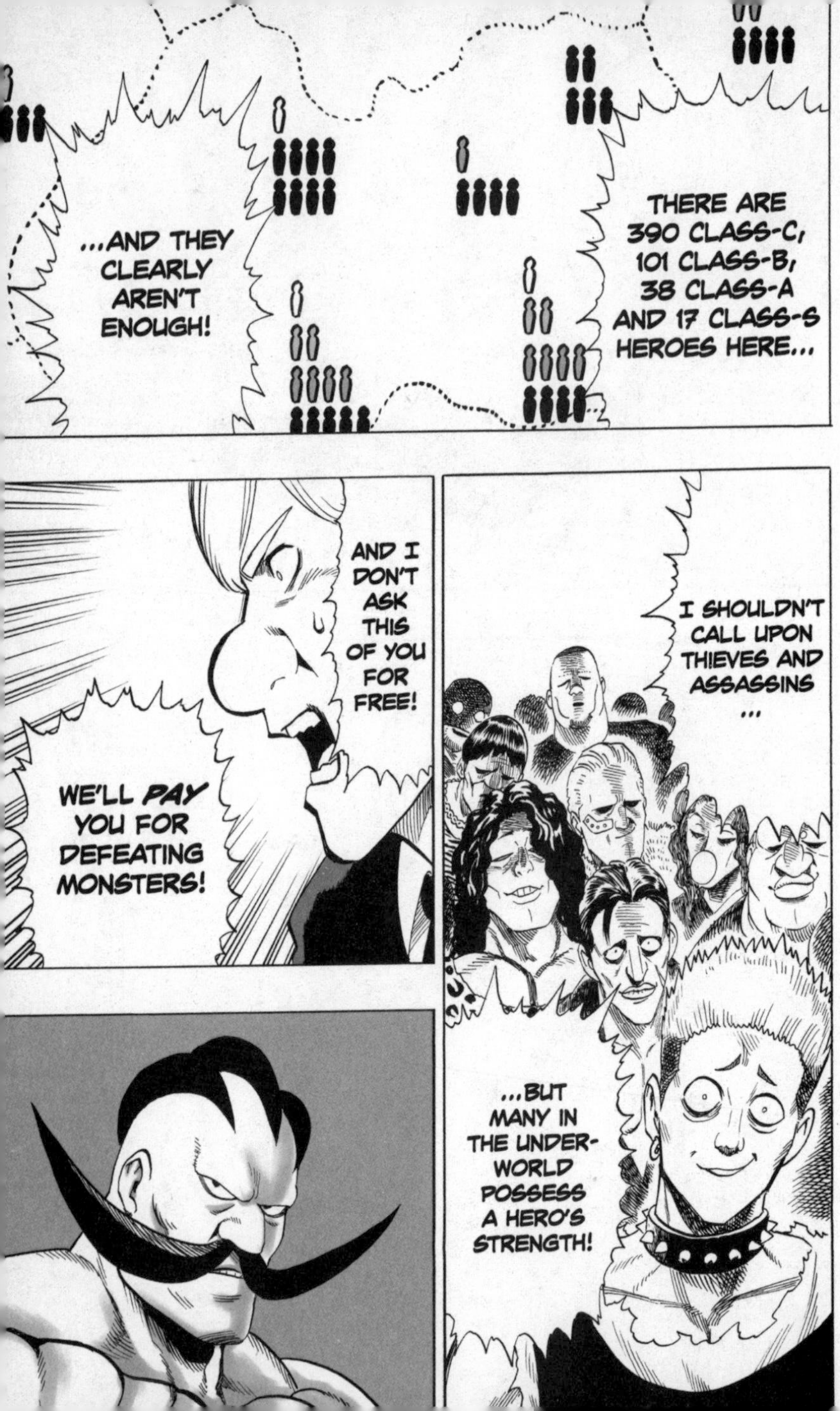
THERE ARE 390 CLASS-C, 101 CLASS-B, 38 CLASS-A AND 17 CLASS-S HEROES HERE...
...AND THEY CLEARLY AREN'T ENOUGH!
I SHOULDN'T CALL UPON THIEVES AND ASSASSINS...
...BUT MANY IN THE UNDER-WORLD POSSESS A HERO'S STRENGTH!
AND I DON'T ASK THIS OF YOU FOR FREE!
WE'LL *PAY* YOU FOR DEFEATING MONSTERS!

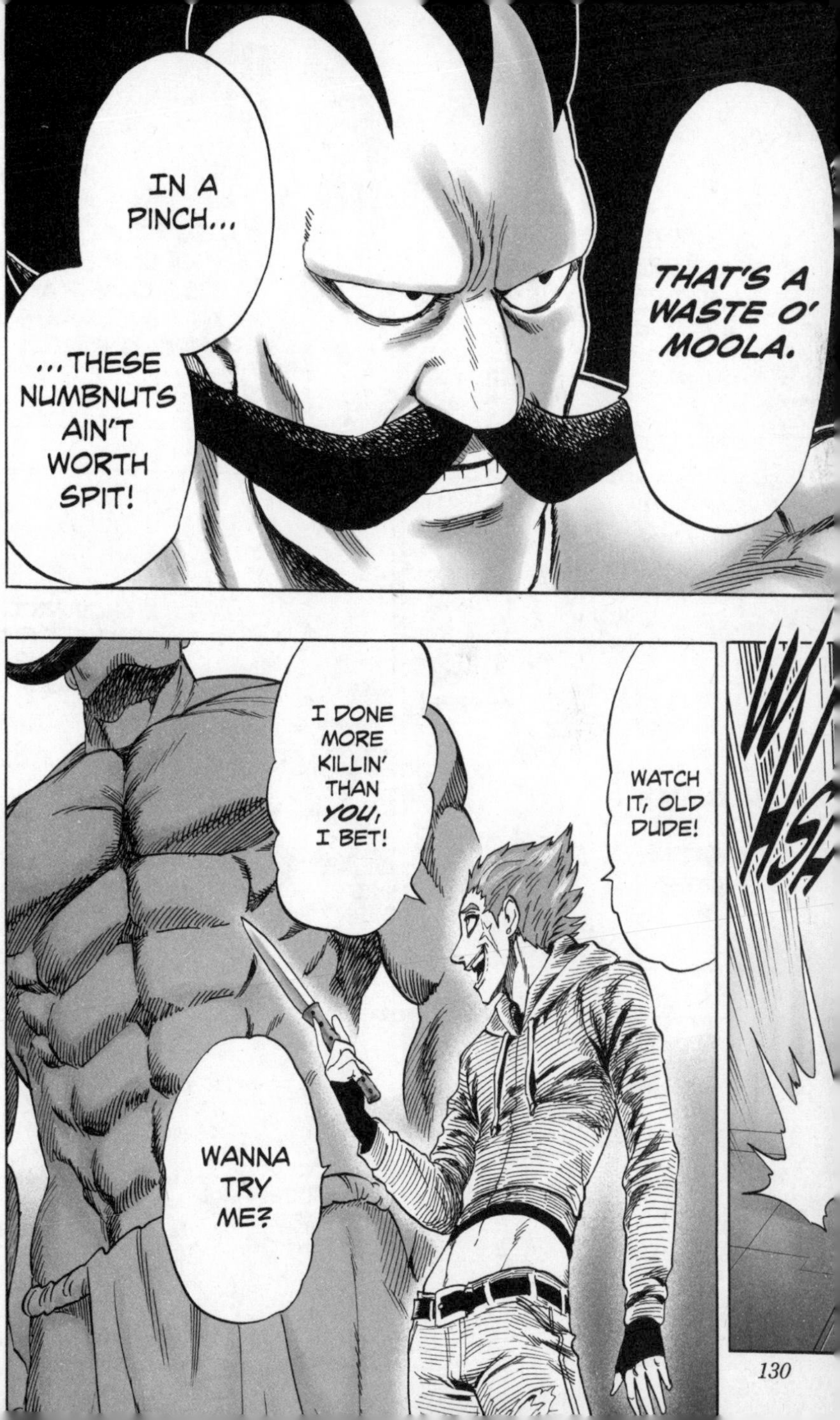
IN A PINCH...
...THESE NUMBNUTS AIN'T WORTH SPIT!
THAT'S A WASTE O' MOOLA.
WATCH IT, OLD DUDE!
I DONE MORE KILLIN' THAN *YOU*, I BET!
WANNA TRY ME?

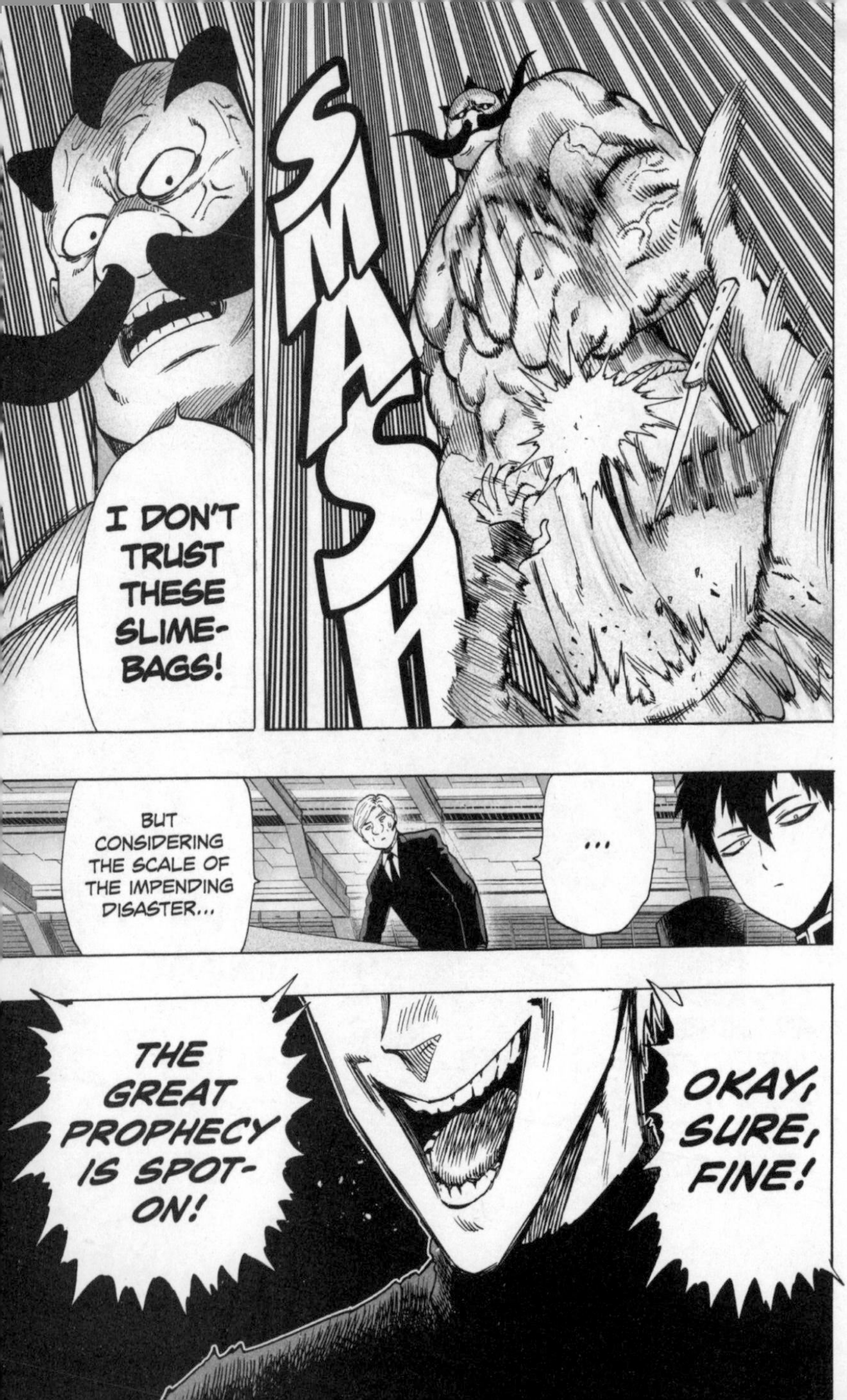
SMASH!
I DON'T TRUST THESE SLIME-BAGS!
...
BUT CONSIDERING THE SCALE OF THE IMPENDING DISASTER...
OKAY, SURE, FINE!
THE GREAT PROPHECY IS SPOT-ON!

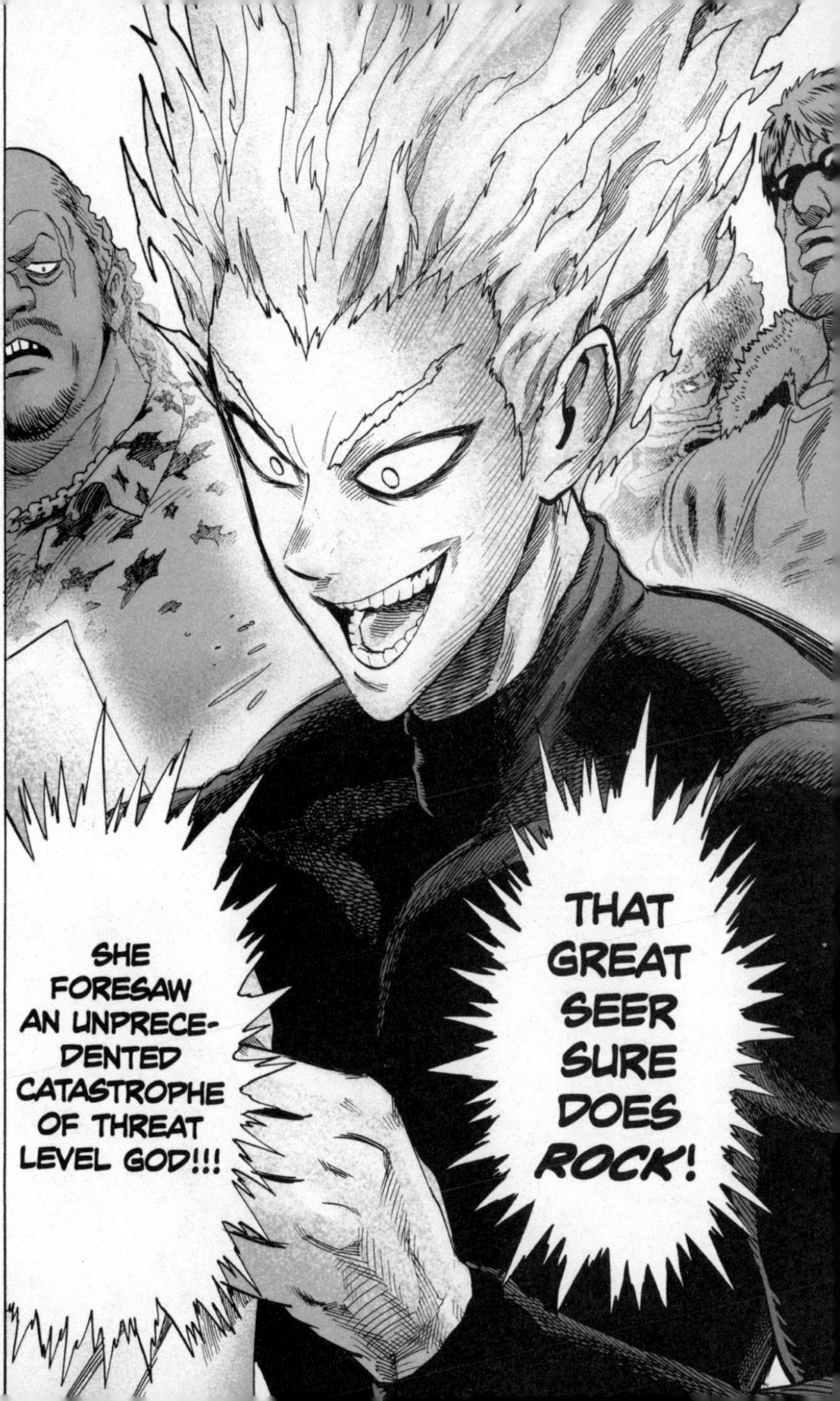
THAT GREAT SEER SURE DOES *ROCK*!
SHE FORESAW AN UNPRECE-DENTED CATASTROPHE OF THREAT LEVEL GOD!!!

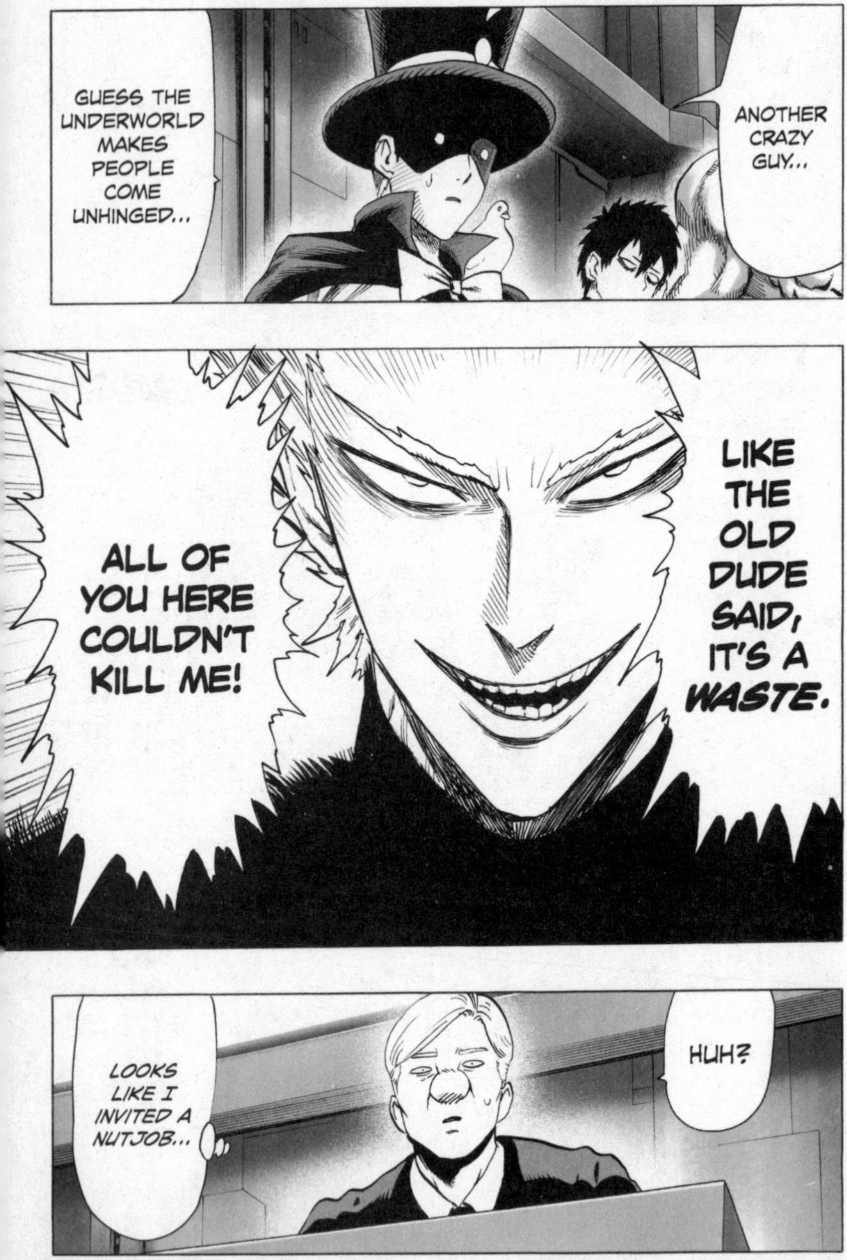
ANOTHER CRAZY GUY...
GUESS THE UNDERWORLD MAKES PEOPLE COME UNHINGED...
LIKE THE OLD DUDE SAID, IT'S A *WASTE*.
ALL OF YOU HERE COULDN'T KILL ME!
HUH?
LOOKS LIKE I INVITED A NUTJOB...

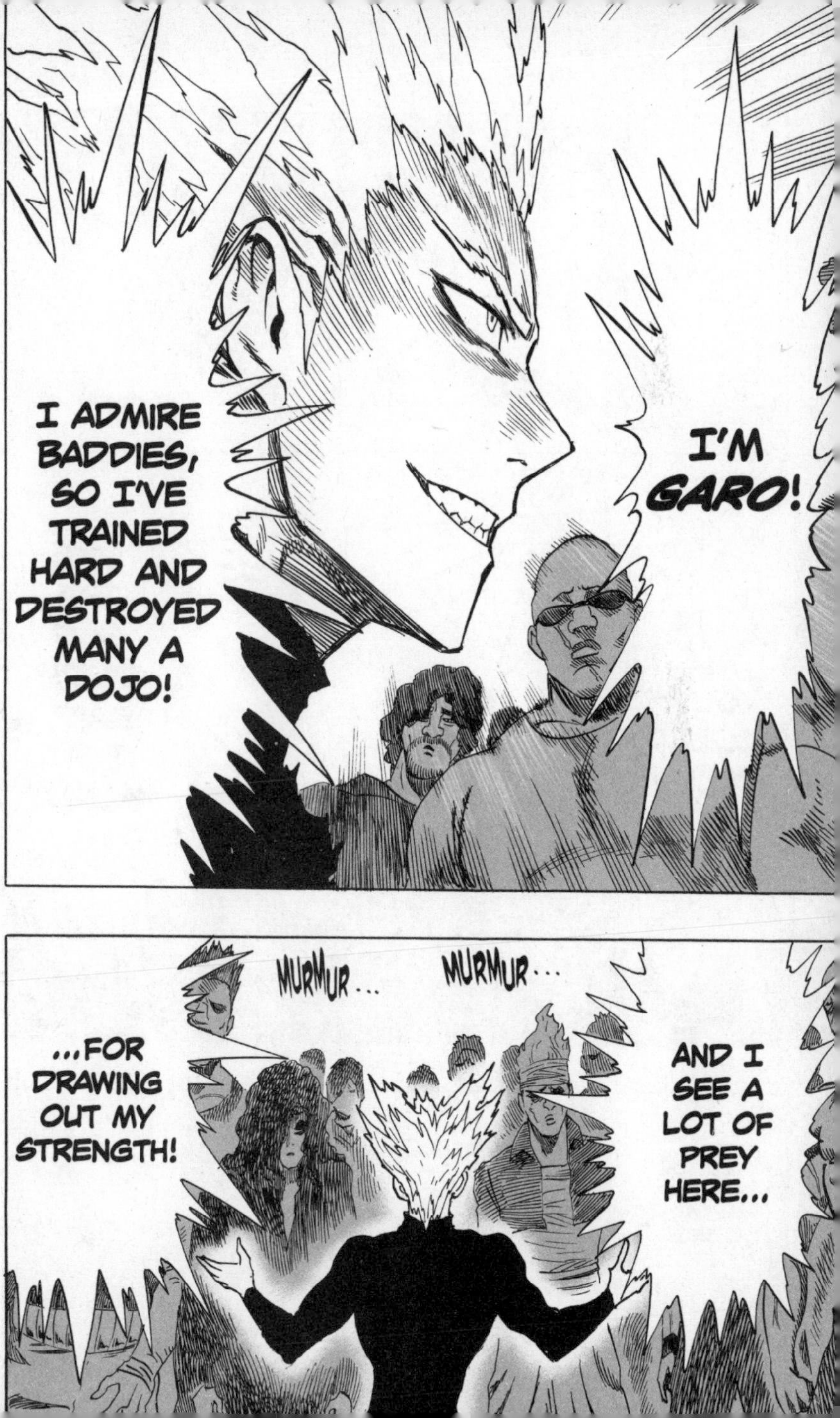
I'M GARO!
I ADMIRE BADDIES, SO I'VE TRAINED HARD AND DESTROYED MANY A DOJO!
AND I SEE A LOT OF PREY HERE...
MURMUR...
MURMUR...
...FOR DRAWING OUT MY STRENGTH!

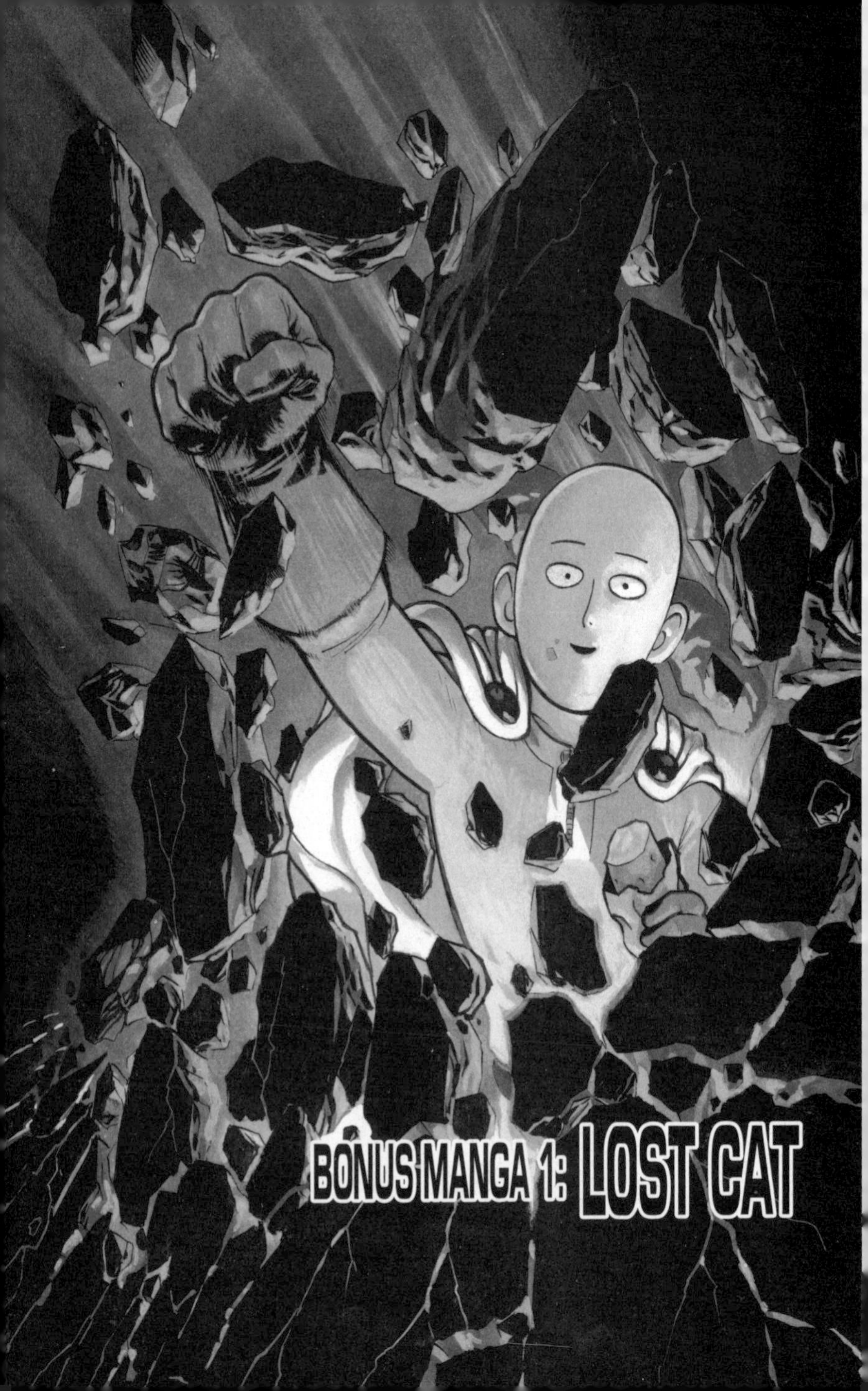
BONUS MANGA 1: LOST CAT

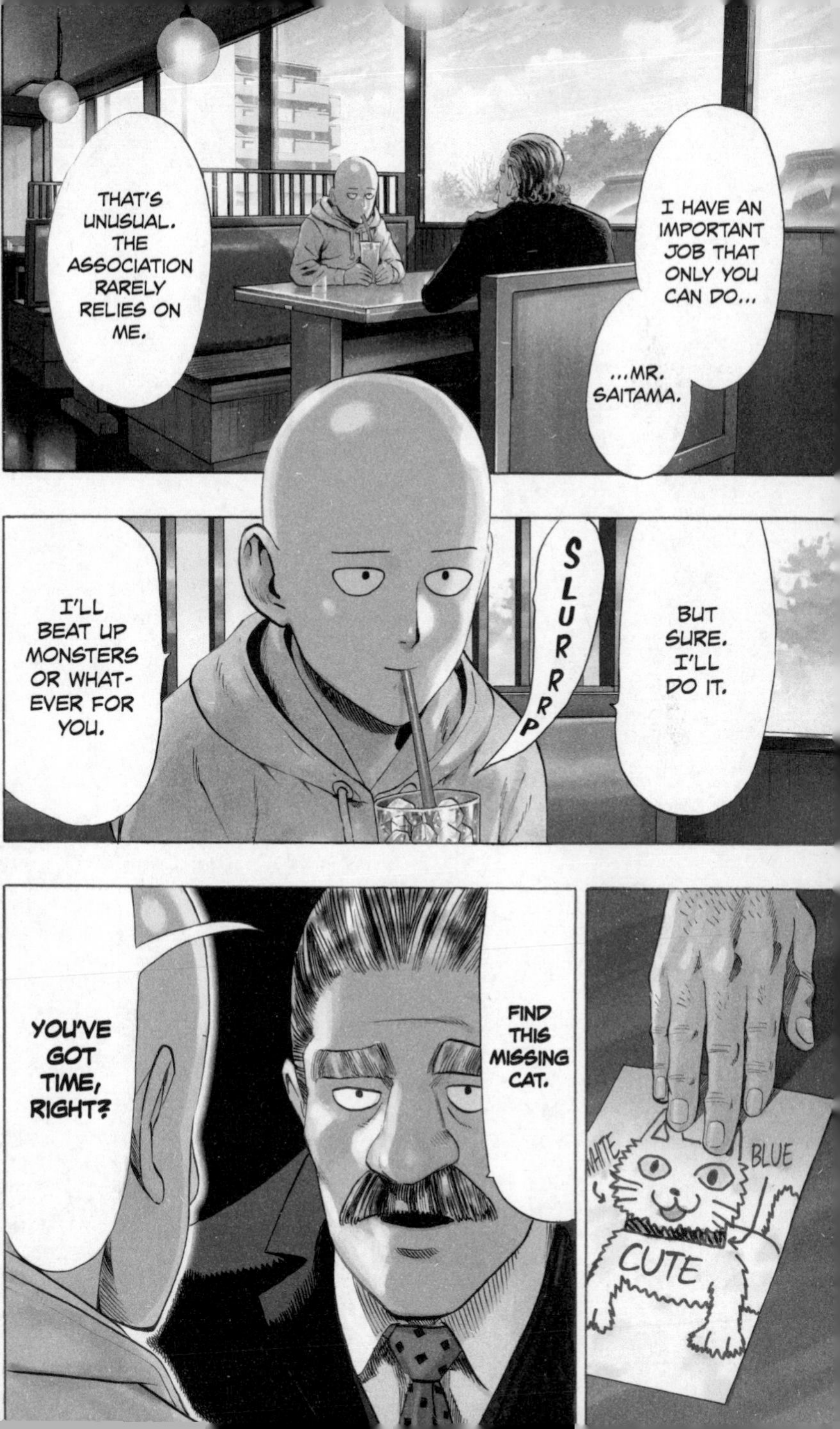
I HAVE AN IMPORTANT JOB THAT ONLY YOU CAN DO...
...MR. SAITAMA.
THAT'S UNUSUAL. THE ASSOCIATION RARELY RELIES ON ME.
BUT SURE. I'LL DO IT.
SLURRRP
I'LL BEAT UP MONSTERS OR WHATEVER FOR YOU.
WHITE
BLUE
CUTE
FIND THIS MISSING CAT.
YOU'VE GOT TIME, RIGHT?

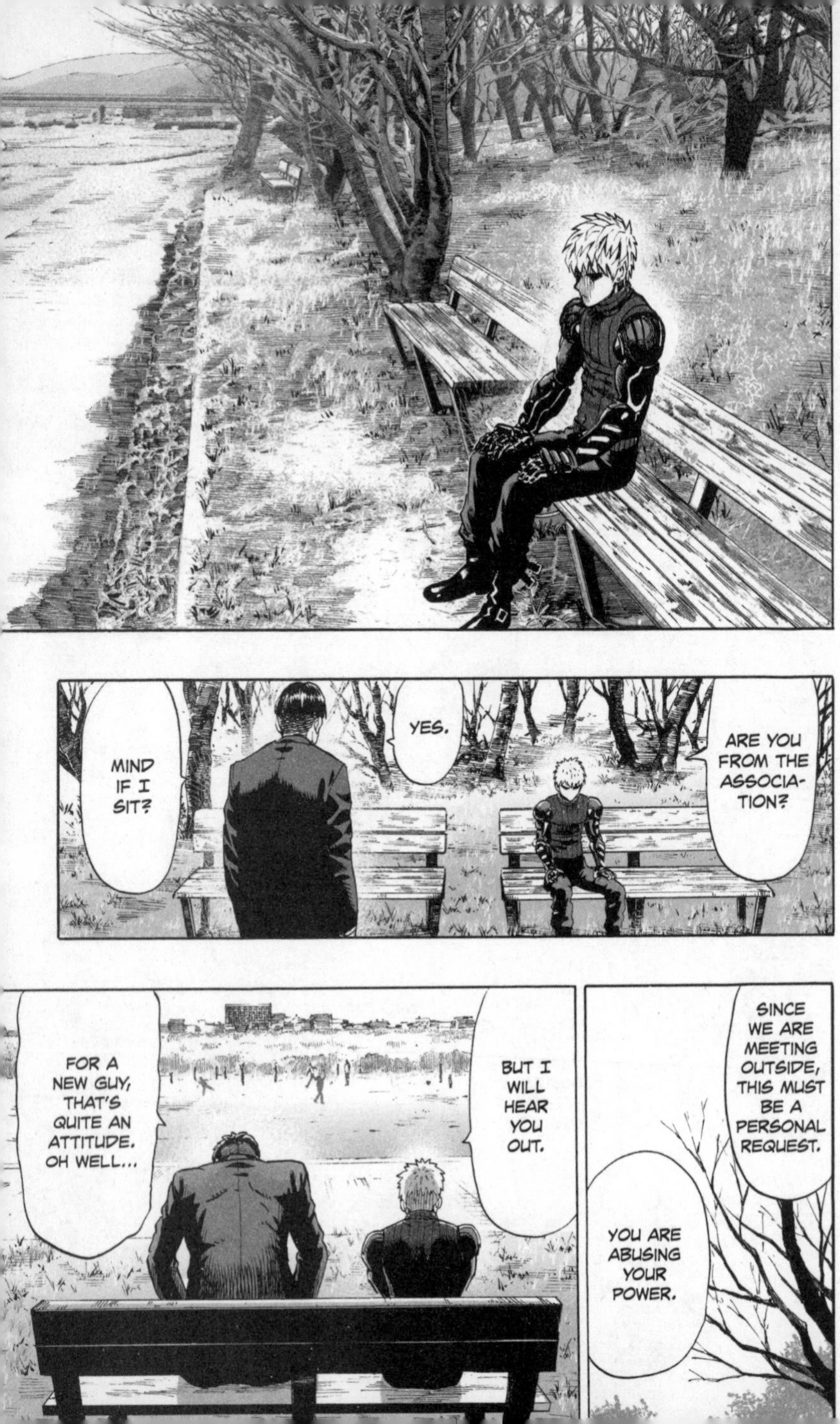
ARE YOU FROM THE ASSOCIATION?
YES.
MIND IF I SIT?
SINCE WE ARE MEETING OUTSIDE, THIS MUST BE A PERSONAL REQUEST.
YOU ARE ABUSING YOUR POWER.
BUT I WILL HEAR YOU OUT.
FOR A NEW GUY, THAT'S QUITE AN ATTITUDE. OH WELL...

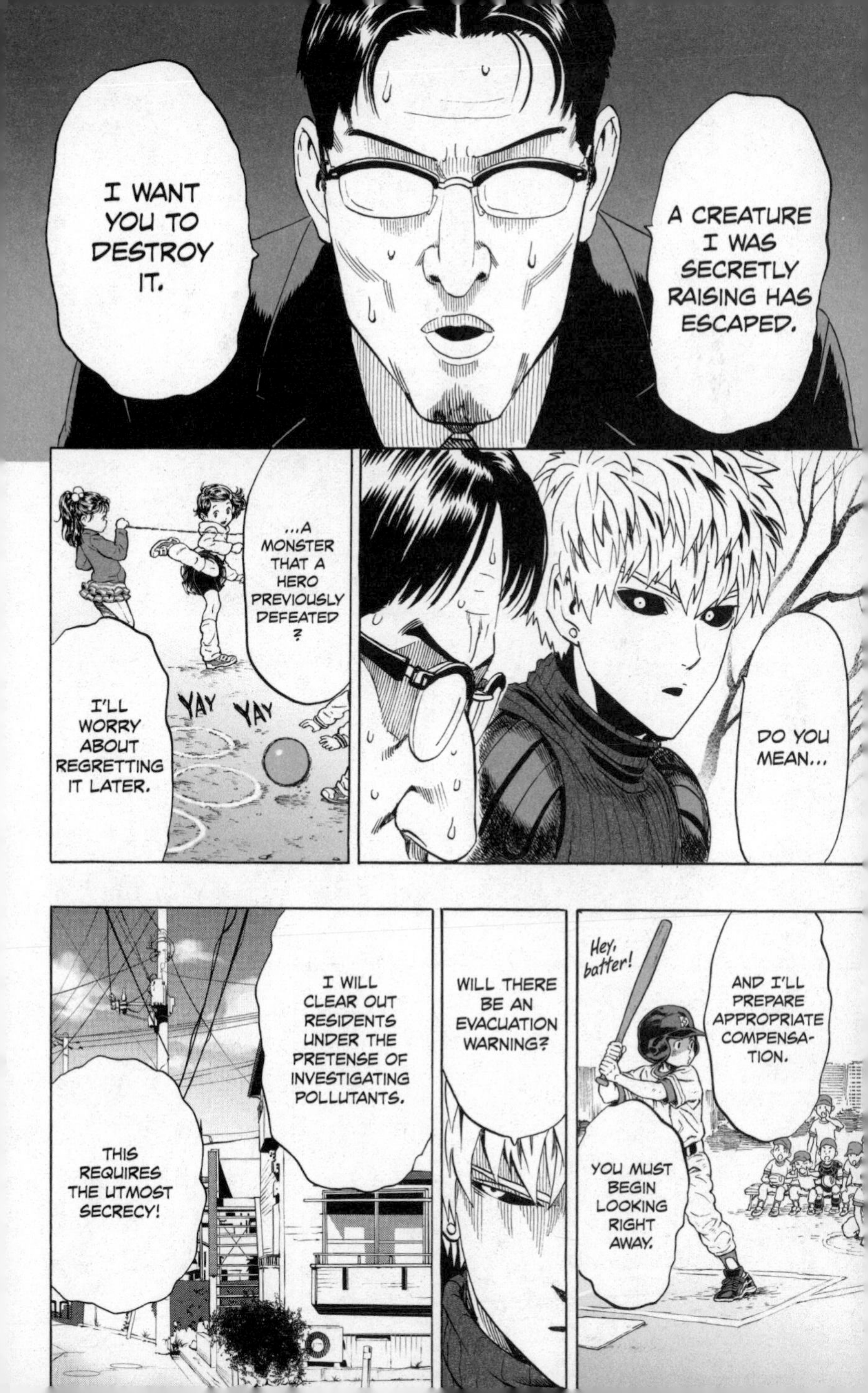
A CREATURE I WAS SECRETLY RAISING HAS ESCAPED.
I WANT YOU TO DESTROY IT.
DO YOU MEAN...
...A MONSTER THAT A HERO PREVIOUSLY DEFEATED?
YAY YAY
I'LL WORRY ABOUT REGRETTING IT LATER.
AND I'LL PREPARE APPROPRIATE COMPENSA-TION.
Hey, batter!
YOU MUST BEGIN LOOKING RIGHT AWAY.
WILL THERE BE AN EVACUATION WARNING?
I WILL CLEAR OUT RESIDENTS UNDER THE PRETENSE OF INVESTIGATING POLLUTANTS.
THIS REQUIRES THE UTMOST SECRECY!

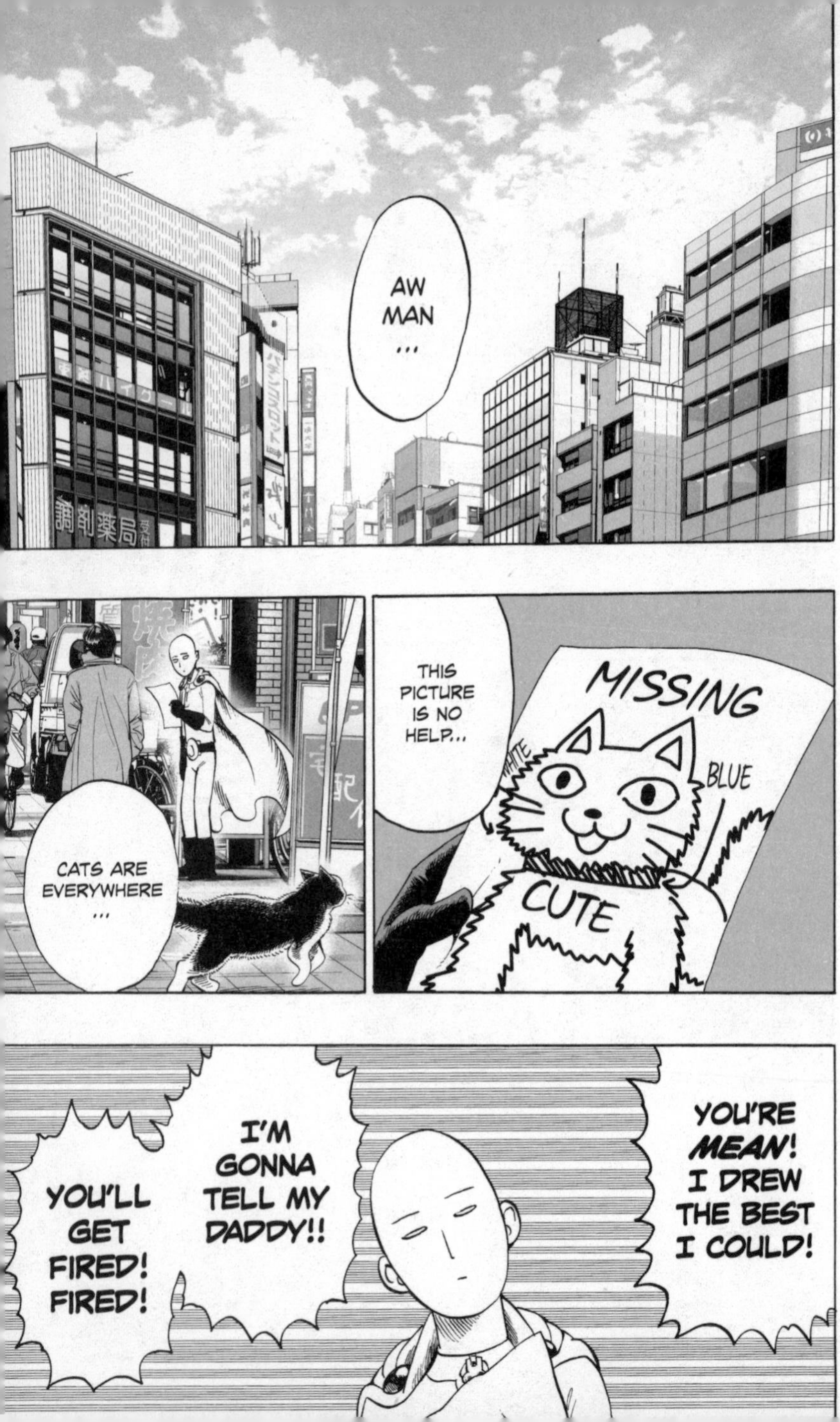
AW MAN ...
THIS PICTURE IS NO HELP...
MISSING
BLUE
CUTE
CATS ARE EVERYWHERE ...
YOU'RE *MEAN*! I DREW THE BEST I COULD!
I'M GONNA TELL MY DADDY!!
YOU'LL GET FIRED! FIRED!

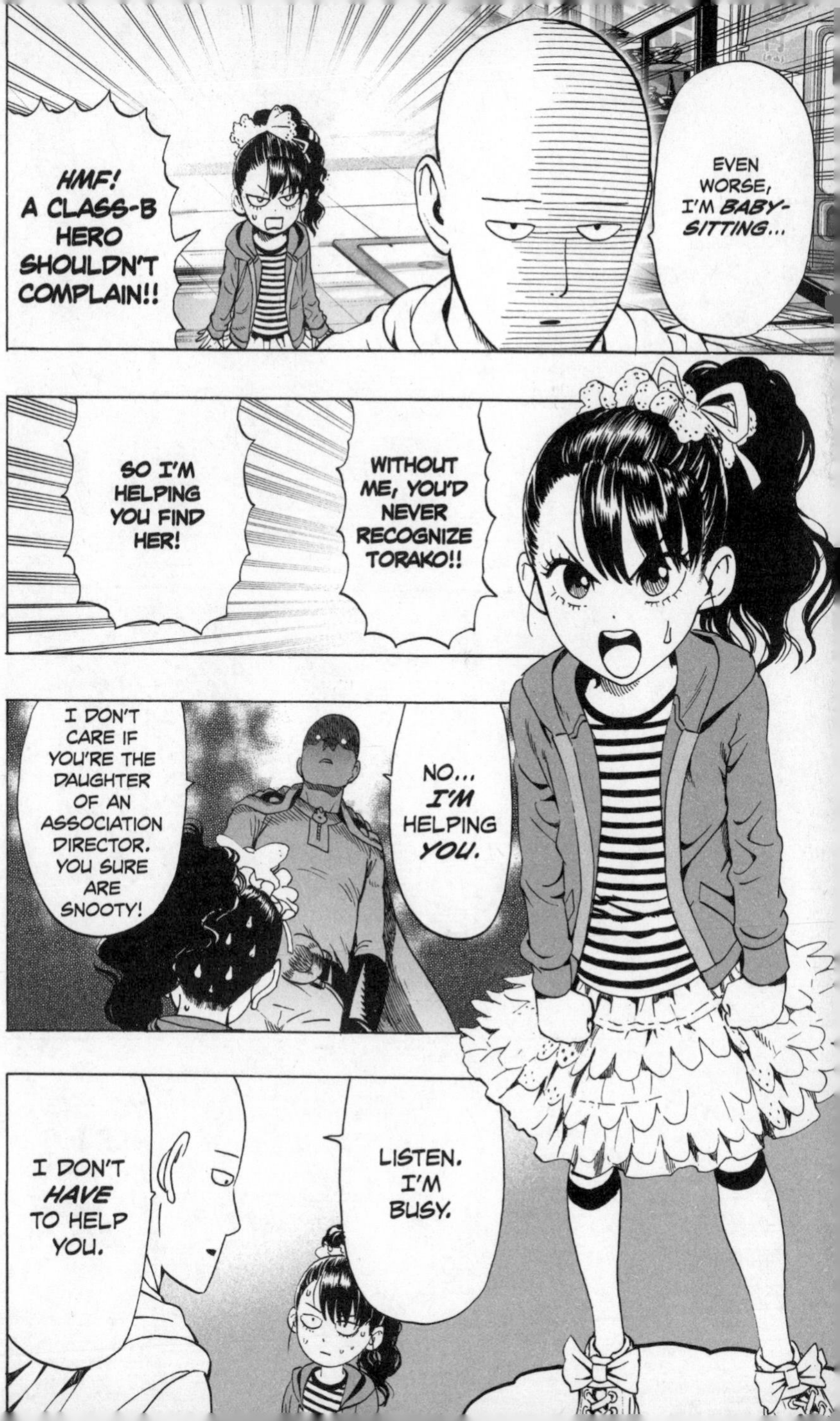
EVEN WORSE, I'M *BABY-SITTING*...
HMF! A CLASS-B HERO SHOULDN'T COMPLAIN!!
WITHOUT ME, YOU'D NEVER RECOGNIZE TORAKO!!
SO I'M HELPING YOU FIND HER!
NO... *I'M* HELPING *YOU*.
I DON'T CARE IF YOU'RE THE DAUGHTER OF AN ASSOCIATION DIRECTOR. YOU SURE ARE SNOOTY!
LISTEN. I'M BUSY.
I DON'T *HAVE* TO HELP YOU.

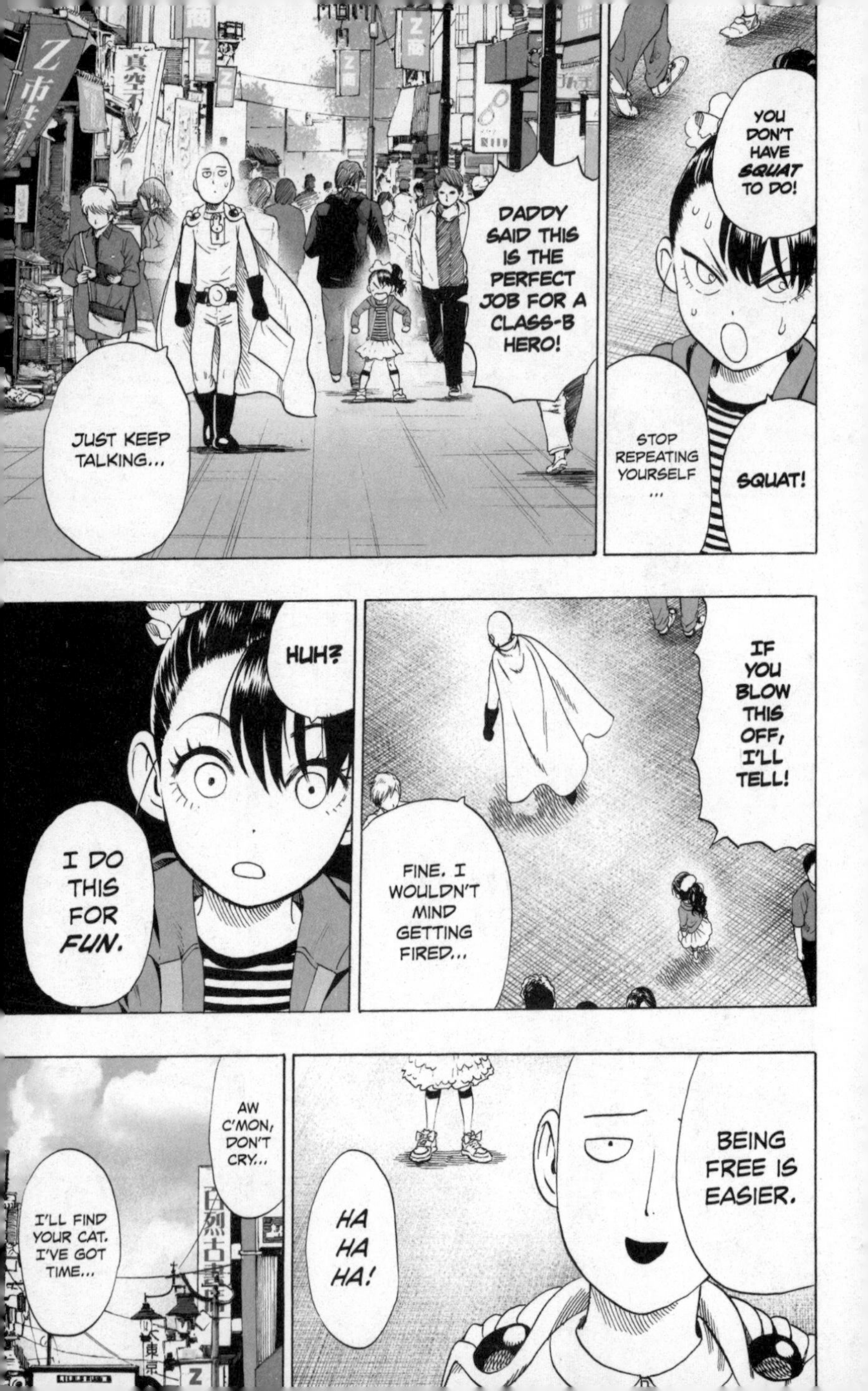
YOU DON'T HAVE SQUAT TO DO!
SQUAT!
STOP REPEATING YOURSELF ...
DADDY SAID THIS IS THE PERFECT JOB FOR A CLASS-B HERO!
JUST KEEP TALKING...
IF YOU BLOW THIS OFF, I'LL TELL!
FINE. I WOULDN'T MIND GETTING FIRED...
HUH?
I DO THIS FOR FUN.
BEING FREE IS EASIER.
HA HA HA!
AW C'MON, DON'T CRY...
I'LL FIND YOUR CAT. I'VE GOT TIME...

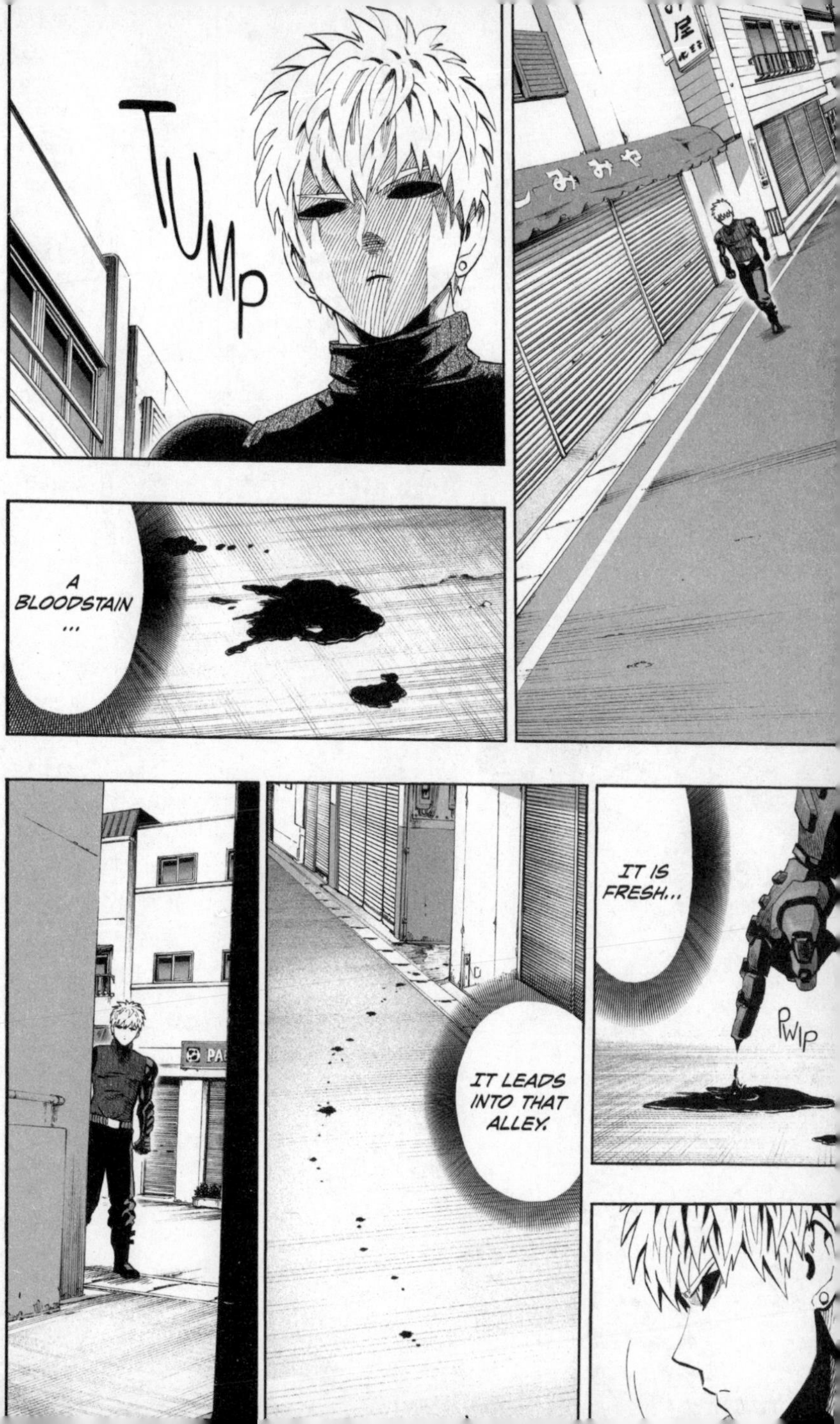
TUMP
A BLOODSTAIN ...
IT IS FRESH...
PWIP
IT LEADS INTO THAT ALLEY.

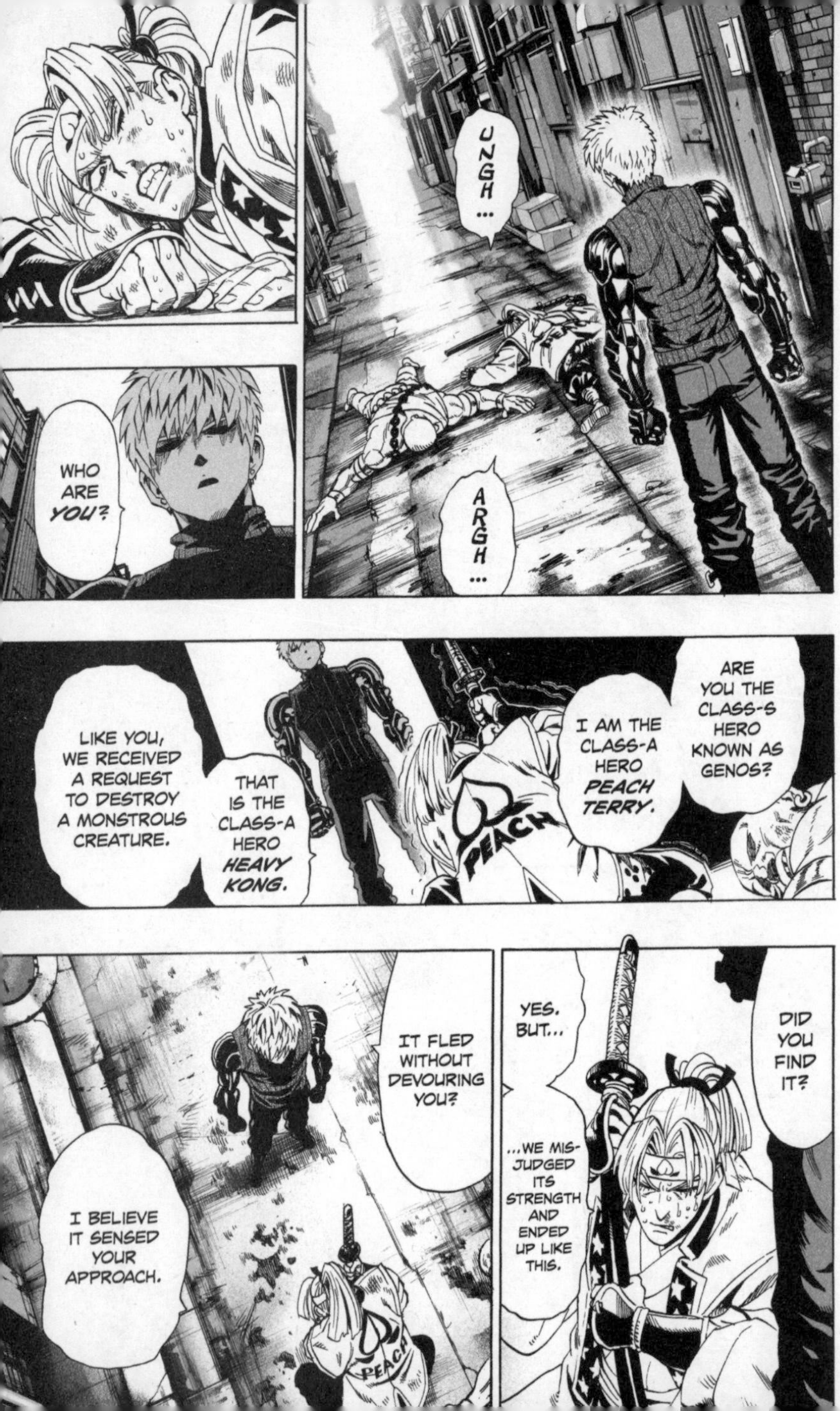
UNGH...
ARGH...
WHO ARE YOU?
ARE YOU THE CLASS-S HERO KNOWN AS GENOS?
I AM THE CLASS-A HERO PEACH TERRY.
PEACH
THAT IS THE CLASS-A HERO HEAVY KONG.
LIKE YOU, WE RECEIVED A REQUEST TO DESTROY A MONSTROUS CREATURE.
DID YOU FIND IT?
YES. BUT...
...WE MISJUDGED ITS STRENGTH AND ENDED UP LIKE THIS.
IT FLED WITHOUT DEVOURING YOU?
I BELIEVE IT SENSED YOUR APPROACH.
PEACH

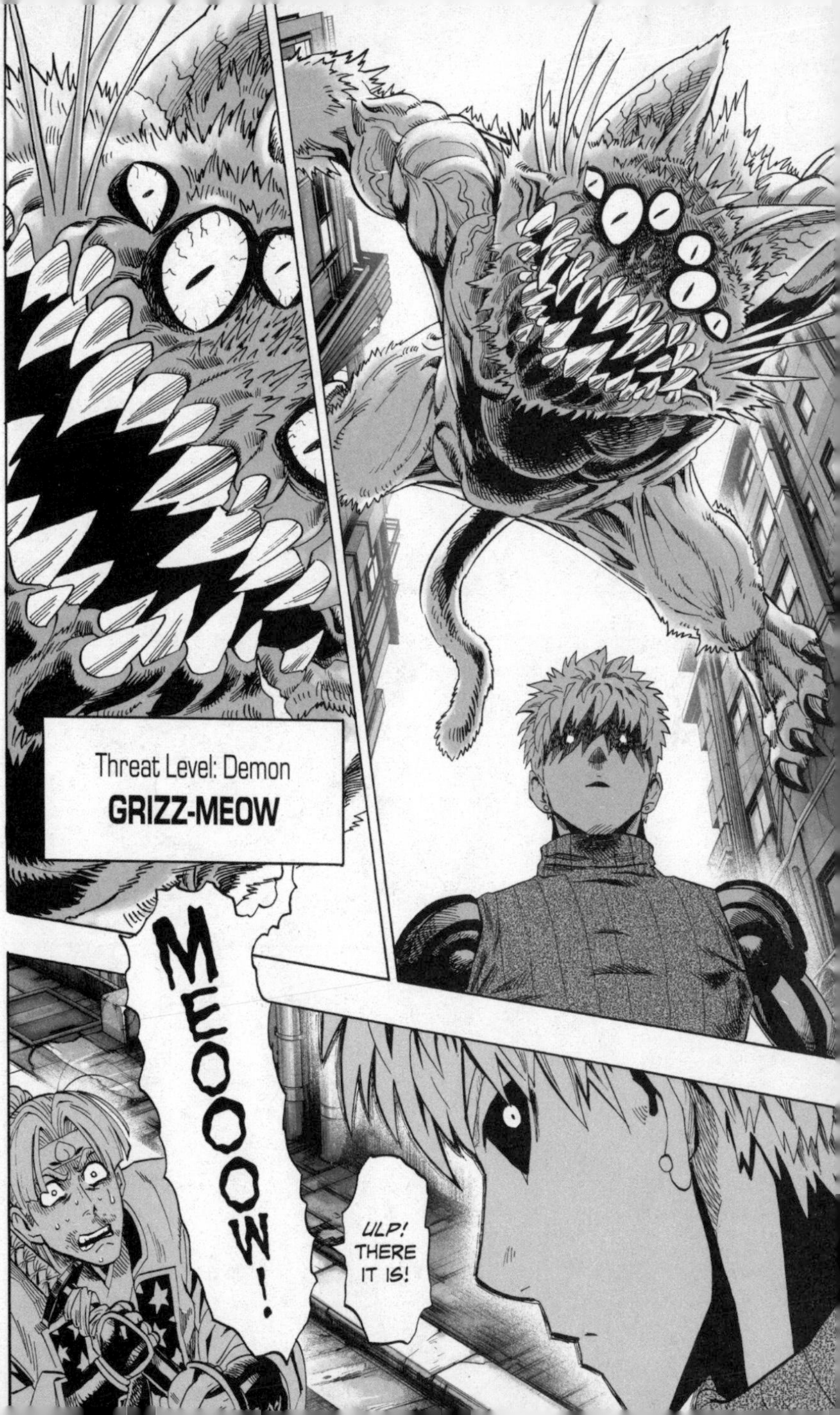
Threat Level: Demon
GRIZZ-MEOW
MEOOOOW!
ULP! THERE IT IS!

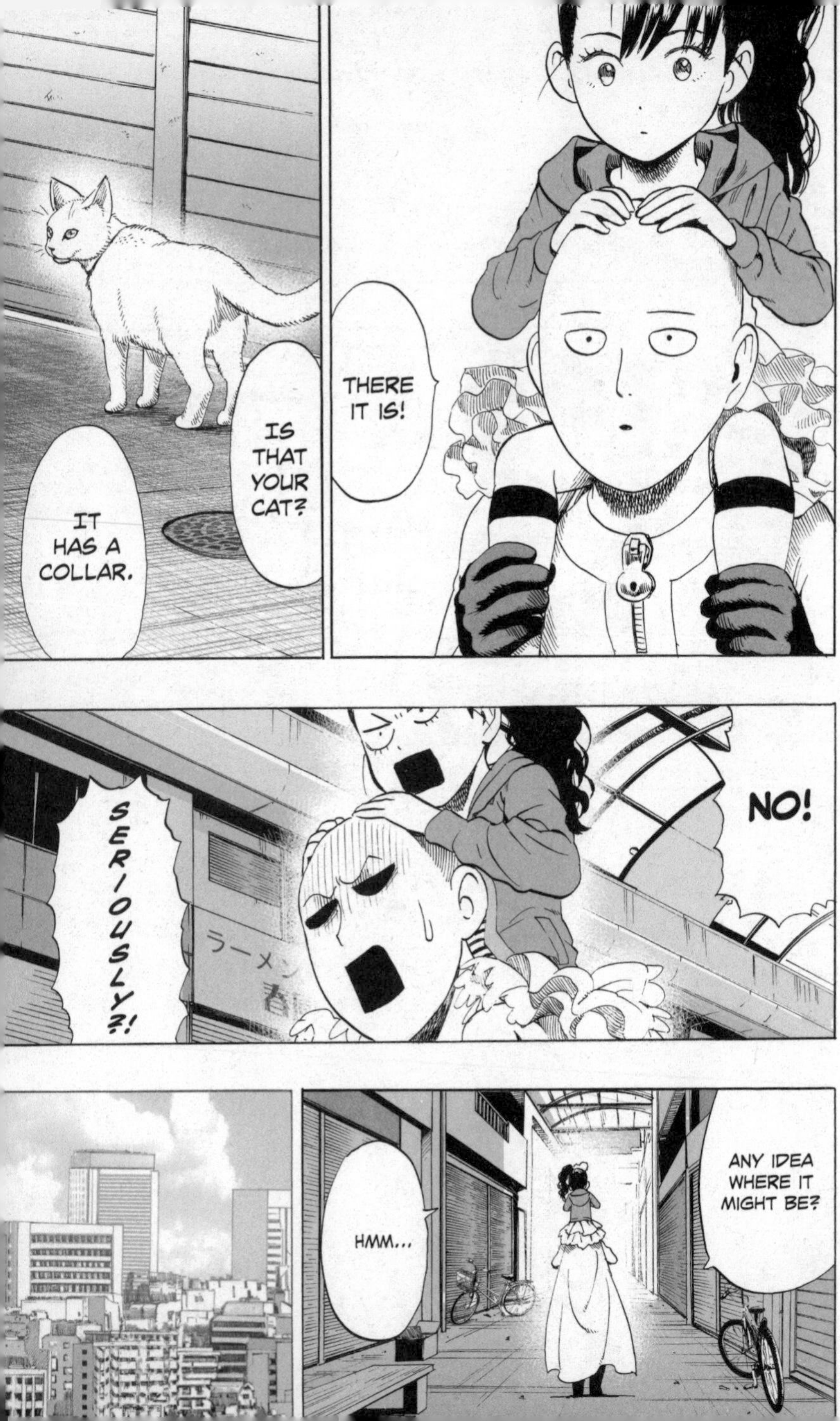
THERE IT IS!
IS THAT YOUR CAT?
IT HAS A COLLAR.
NO!
SERIOUSLY?!
ラーメン
ANY IDEA WHERE IT MIGHT BE?
HMM...

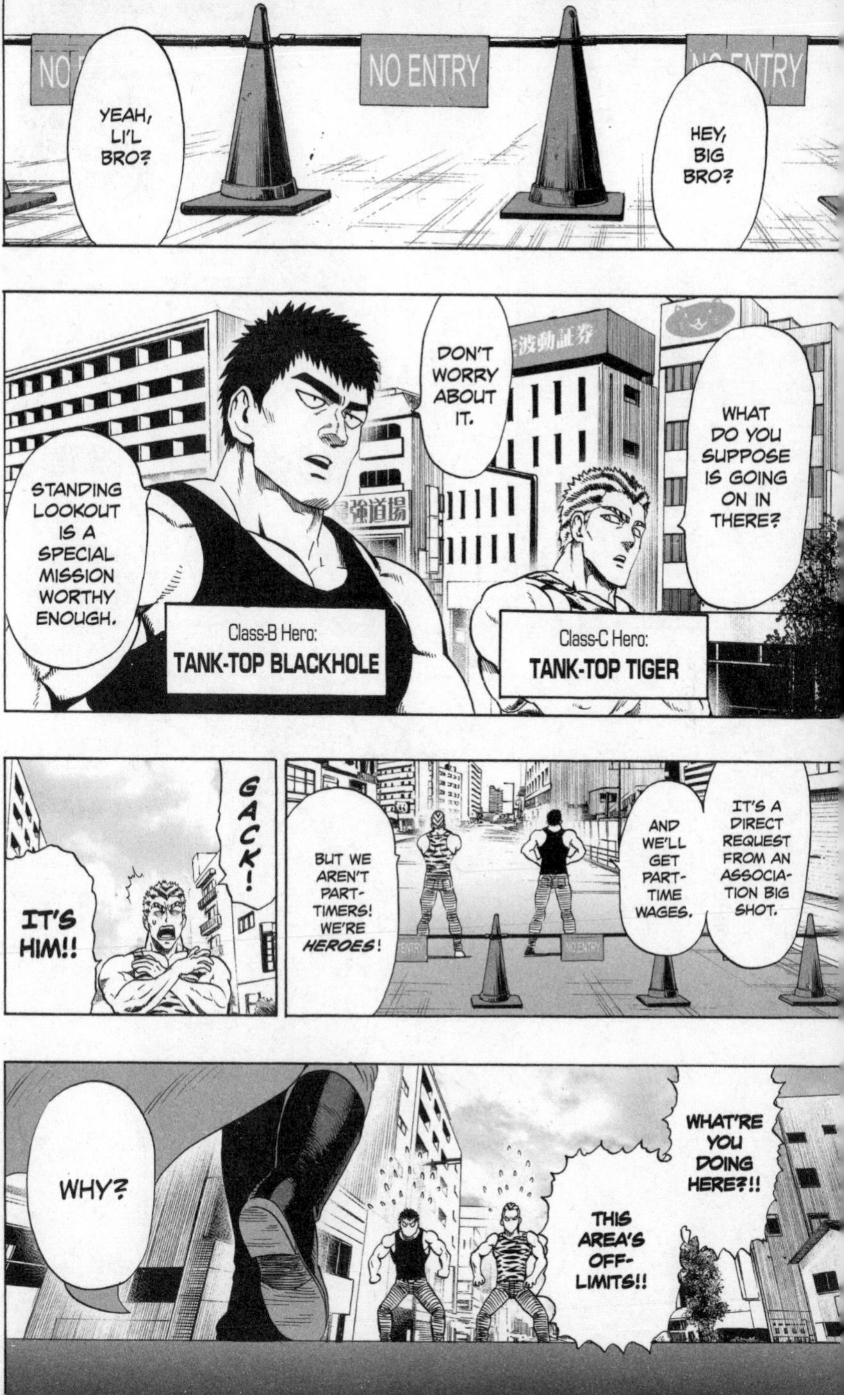
NO ENTRY
HEY, BIG BRO?
YEAH, LI'L BRO?
WHAT DO YOU SUPPOSE IS GOING ON IN THERE?
DON'T WORRY ABOUT IT.
STANDING LOOKOUT IS A SPECIAL MISSION WORTHY ENOUGH.
Class-C Hero: TANK-TOP TIGER
Class-B Hero: TANK-TOP BLACKHOLE
IT'S A DIRECT REQUEST FROM AN ASSOCIATION BIG SHOT.
AND WE'LL GET PART-TIME WAGES.
BUT WE AREN'T PART-TIMERS! WE'RE *HEROES*!
GACK!
IT'S HIM!!
WHAT'RE YOU DOING HERE?!!
THIS AREA'S OFF-LIMITS!!
WHY?

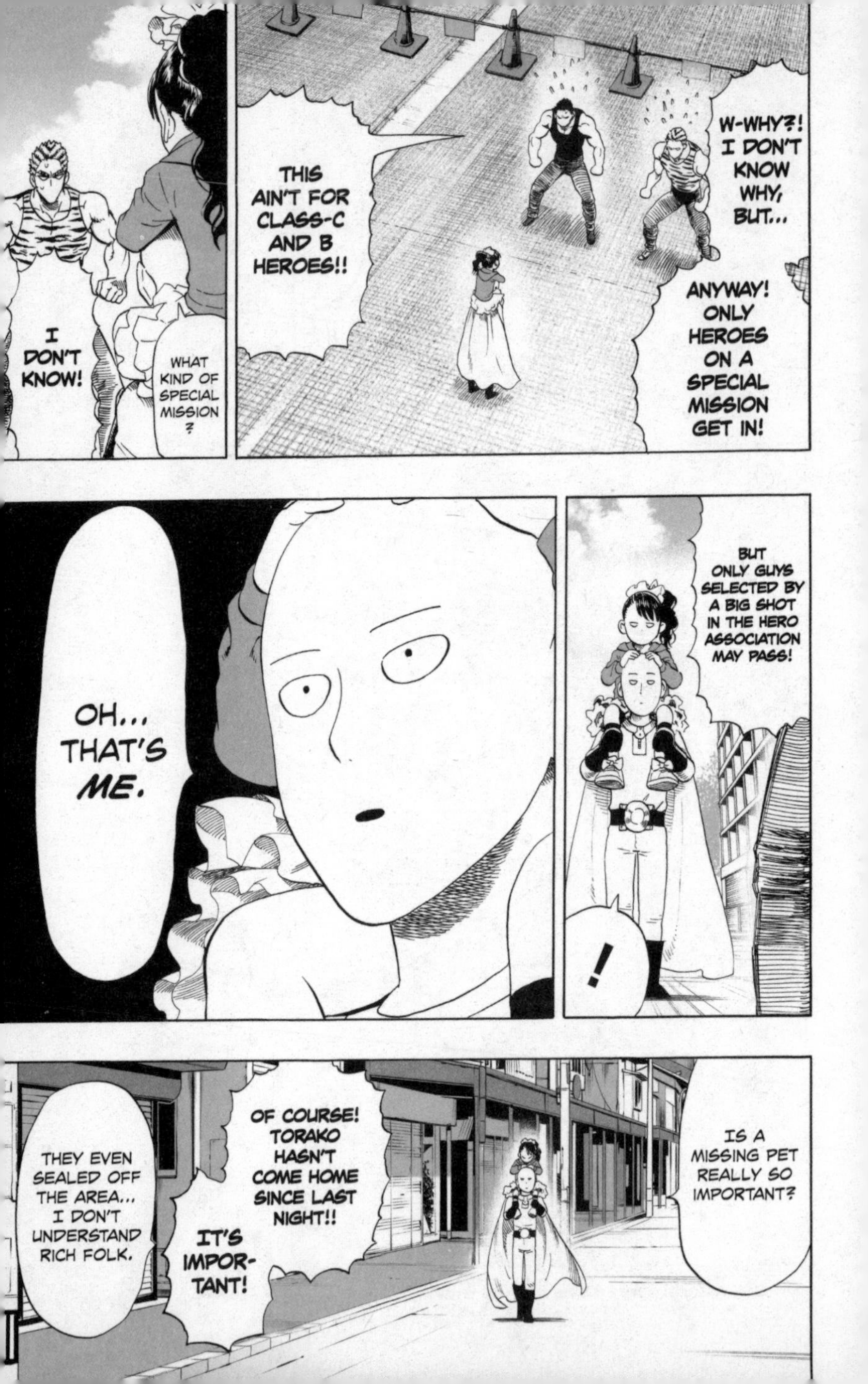
W-WHY?! I DON'T KNOW WHY, BUT...
THIS AIN'T FOR CLASS-C AND B HEROES!!
ANYWAY! ONLY HEROES ON A SPECIAL MISSION GET IN!
WHAT KIND OF SPECIAL MISSION?
I DON'T KNOW!
BUT ONLY GUYS SELECTED BY A BIG SHOT IN THE HERO ASSOCIATION MAY PASS!
!
OH... THAT'S ME.
IS A MISSING PET REALLY SO IMPORTANT?
OF COURSE! TORAKO HASN'T COME HOME SINCE LAST NIGHT!!
IT'S IMPOR-TANT!
THEY EVEN SEALED OFF THE AREA... I DON'T UNDERSTAND RICH FOLK.

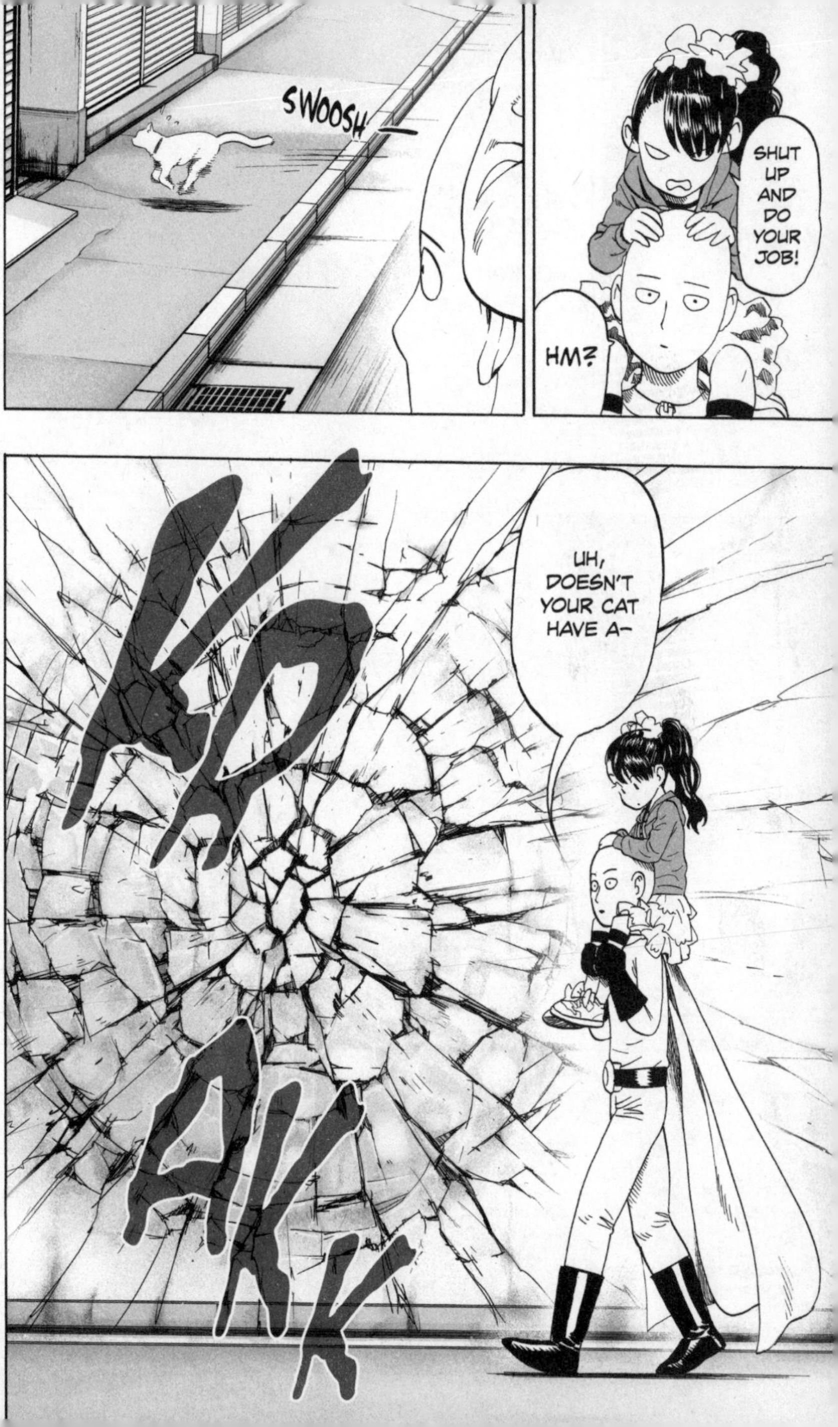
SHUT UP AND DO YOUR JOB!
HM?
SWOOSH
UH, DOESN'T YOUR CAT HAVE A-

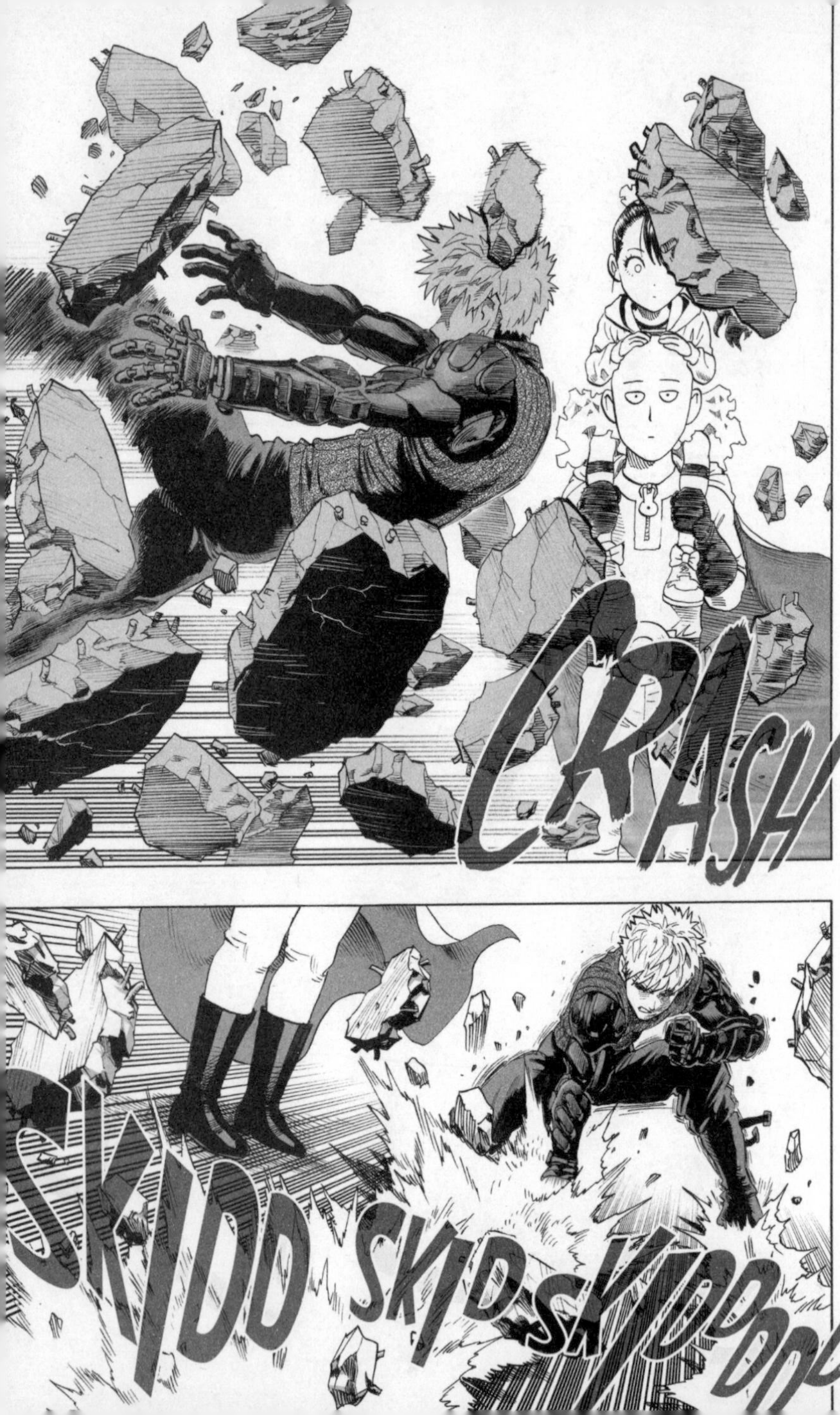
CRASH
SKIDD
SKIDSKIDDDDD

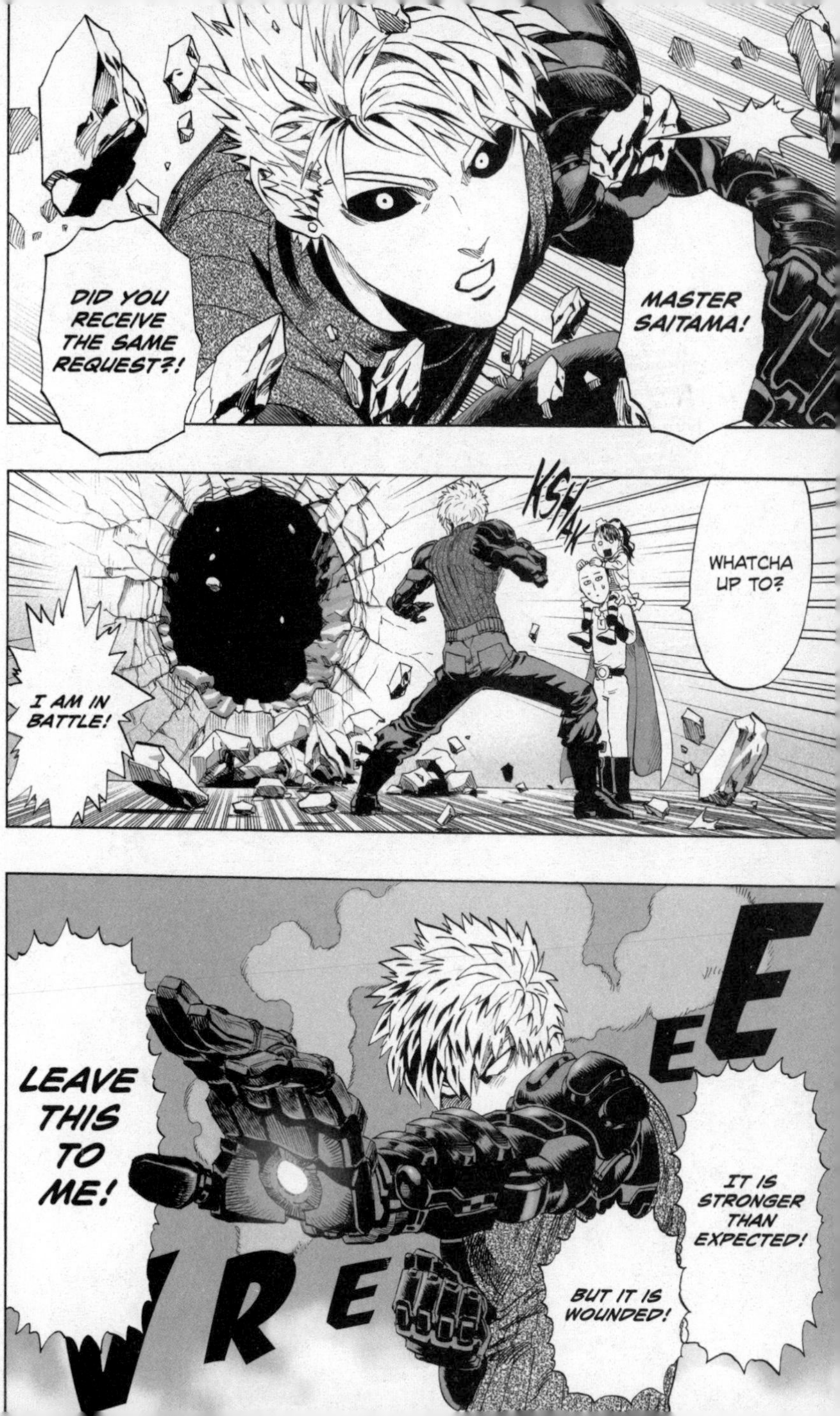
MASTER SAITAMA!
DID YOU RECEIVE THE SAME REQUEST?!
KSHAK
WHATCHA UP TO?
I AM IN BATTLE!
IT IS STRONGER THAN EXPECTED!
BUT IT IS WOUNDED!
LEAVE THIS TO ME!
EE
VRE

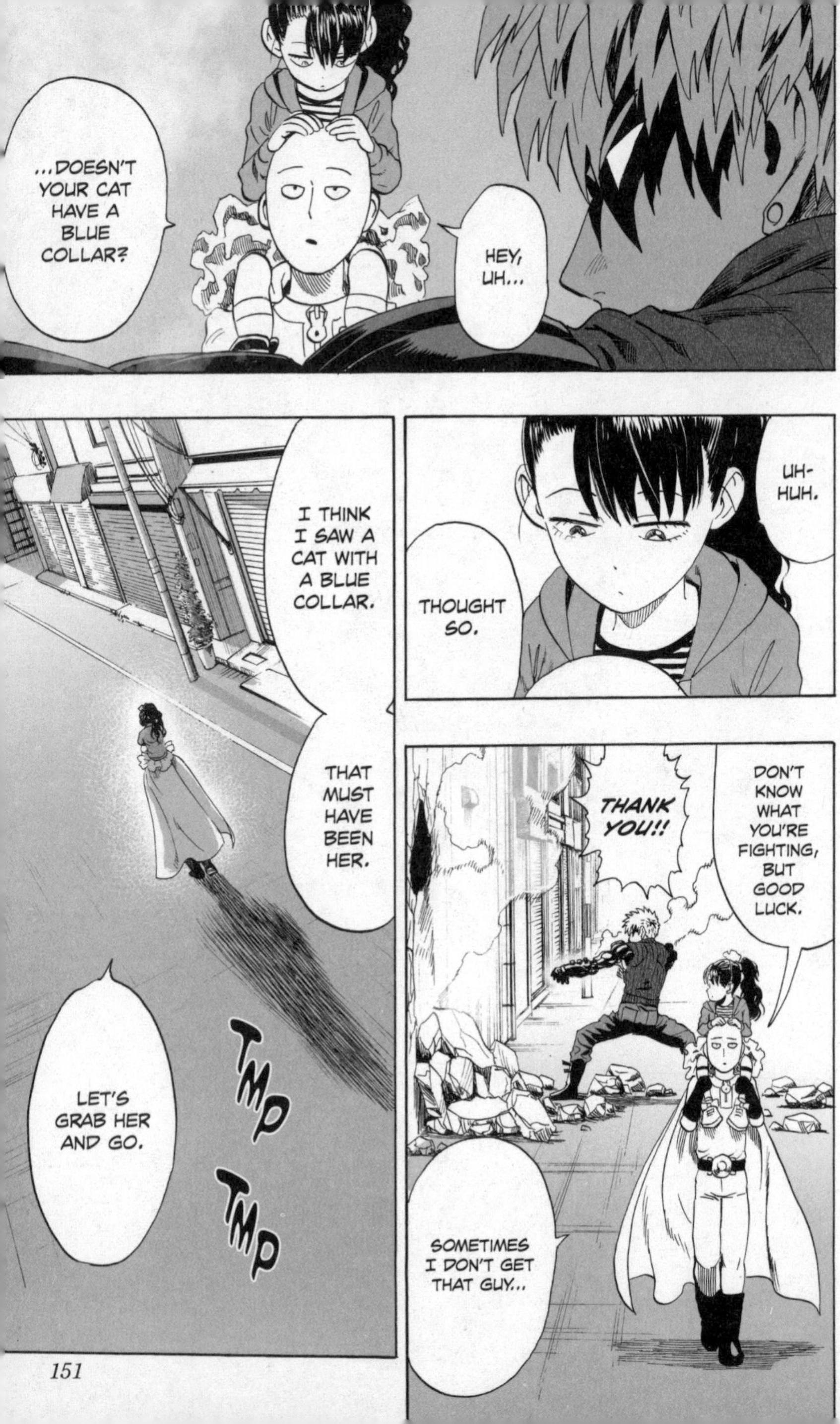
HEY, UH...
...DOESN'T YOUR CAT HAVE A BLUE COLLAR?
UH-HUH.
THOUGHT SO.
DON'T KNOW WHAT YOU'RE FIGHTING, BUT GOOD LUCK.
THANK YOU!!
SOMETIMES I DON'T GET THAT GUY...
I THINK I SAW A CAT WITH A BLUE COLLAR.
THAT MUST HAVE BEEN HER.
TMP
TMP
LET'S GRAB HER AND GO.

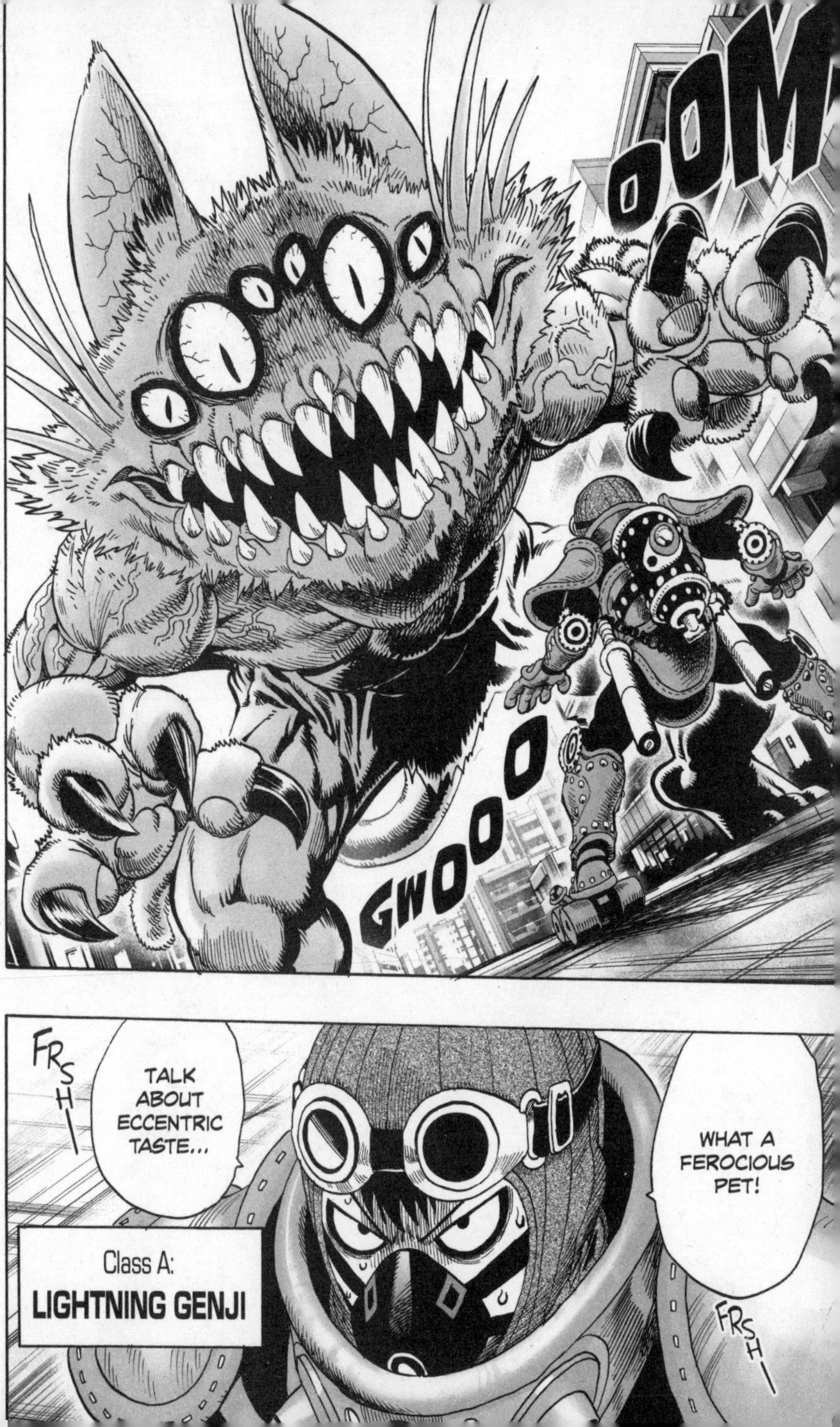
OOM
GWOOOO
WHAT A FEROCIOUS PET!
FRSHI
TALK ABOUT ECCENTRIC TASTE...
FRSHI
Class A:
LIGHTNING GENJI

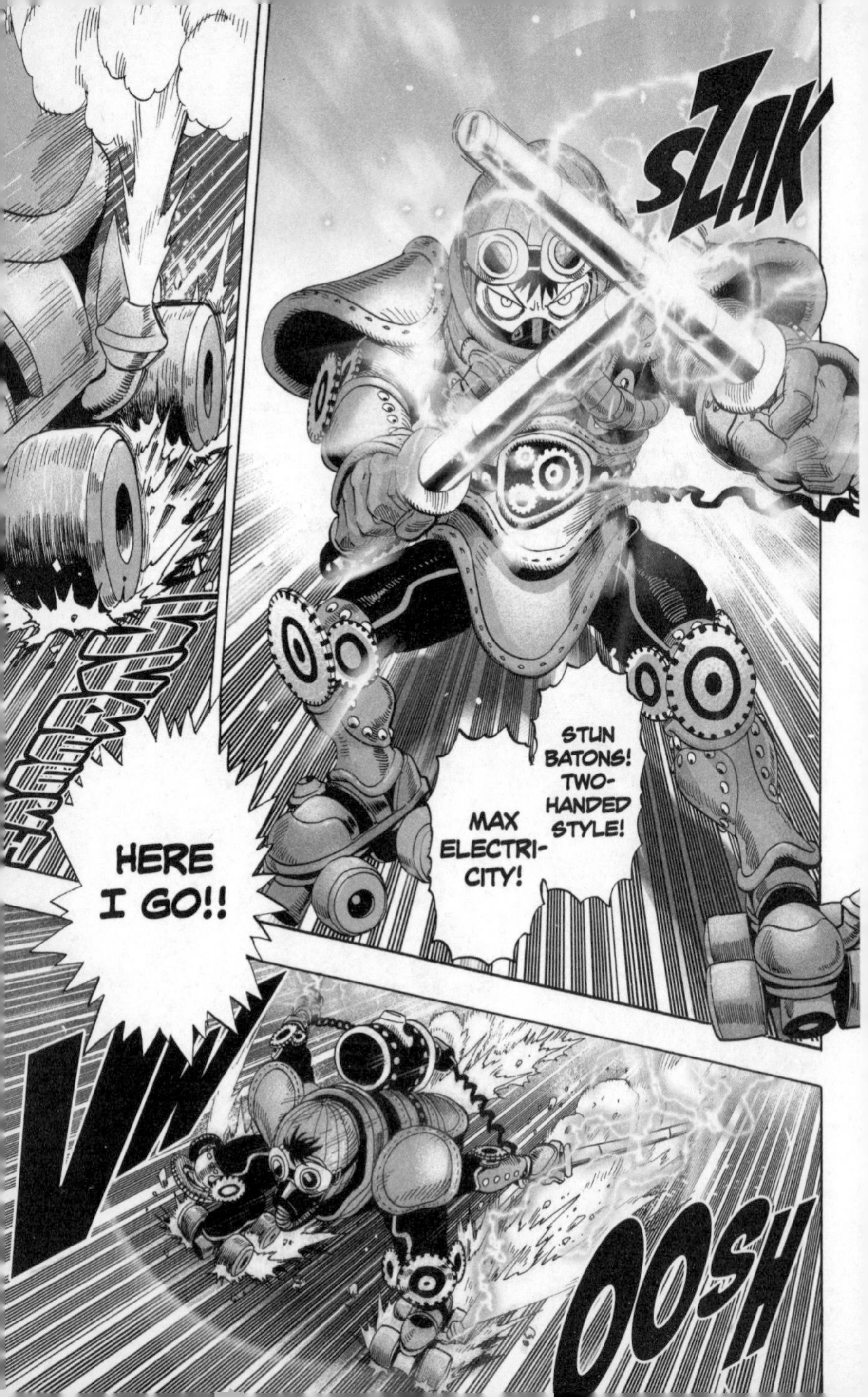
SLAK
STUN BATONS! TWO-HANDED STYLE!
MAX ELECTRI-CITY!
HERE I GO!!
VWOOSH

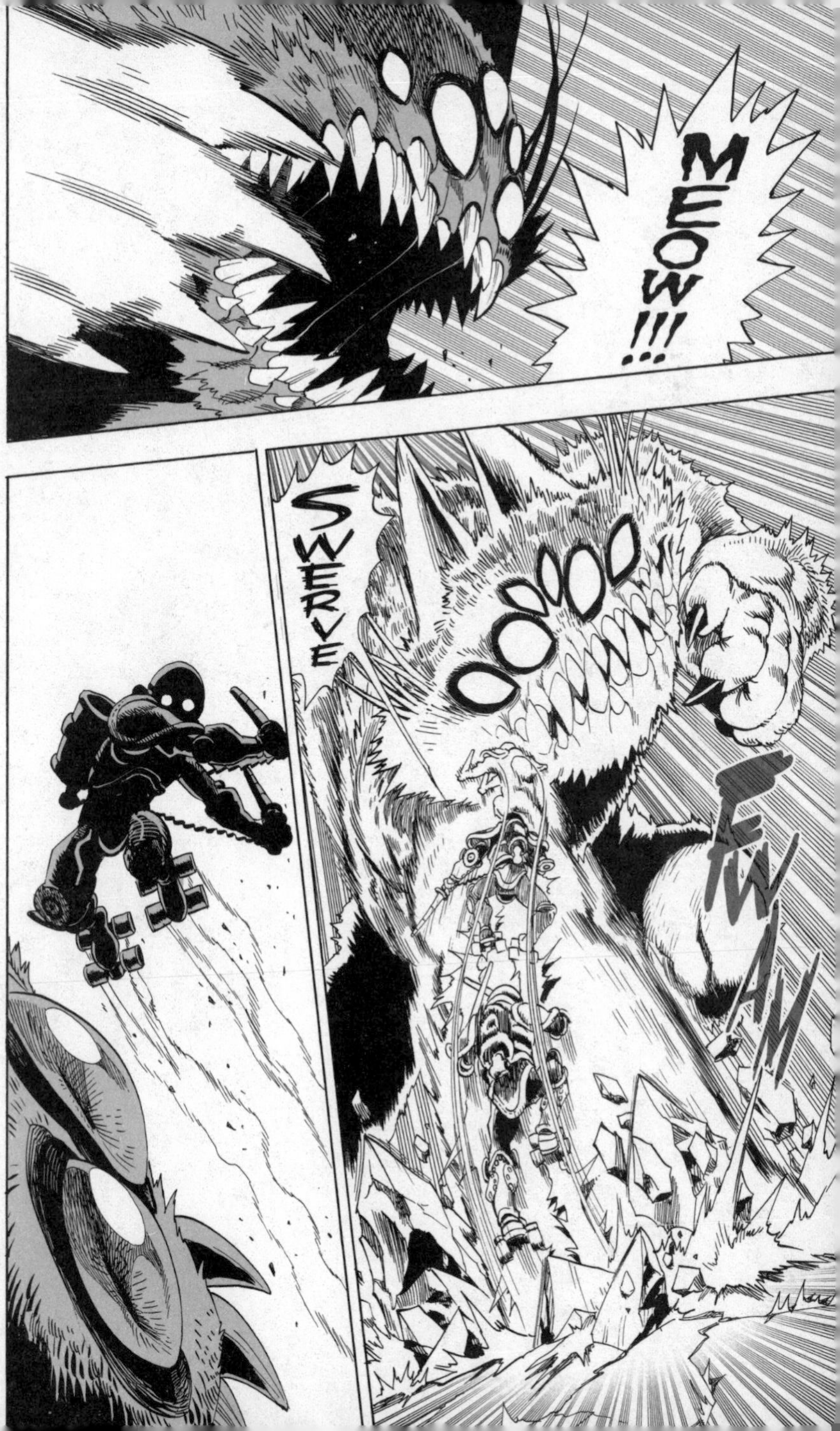
MEOW!!!
SWERVE
FWAM

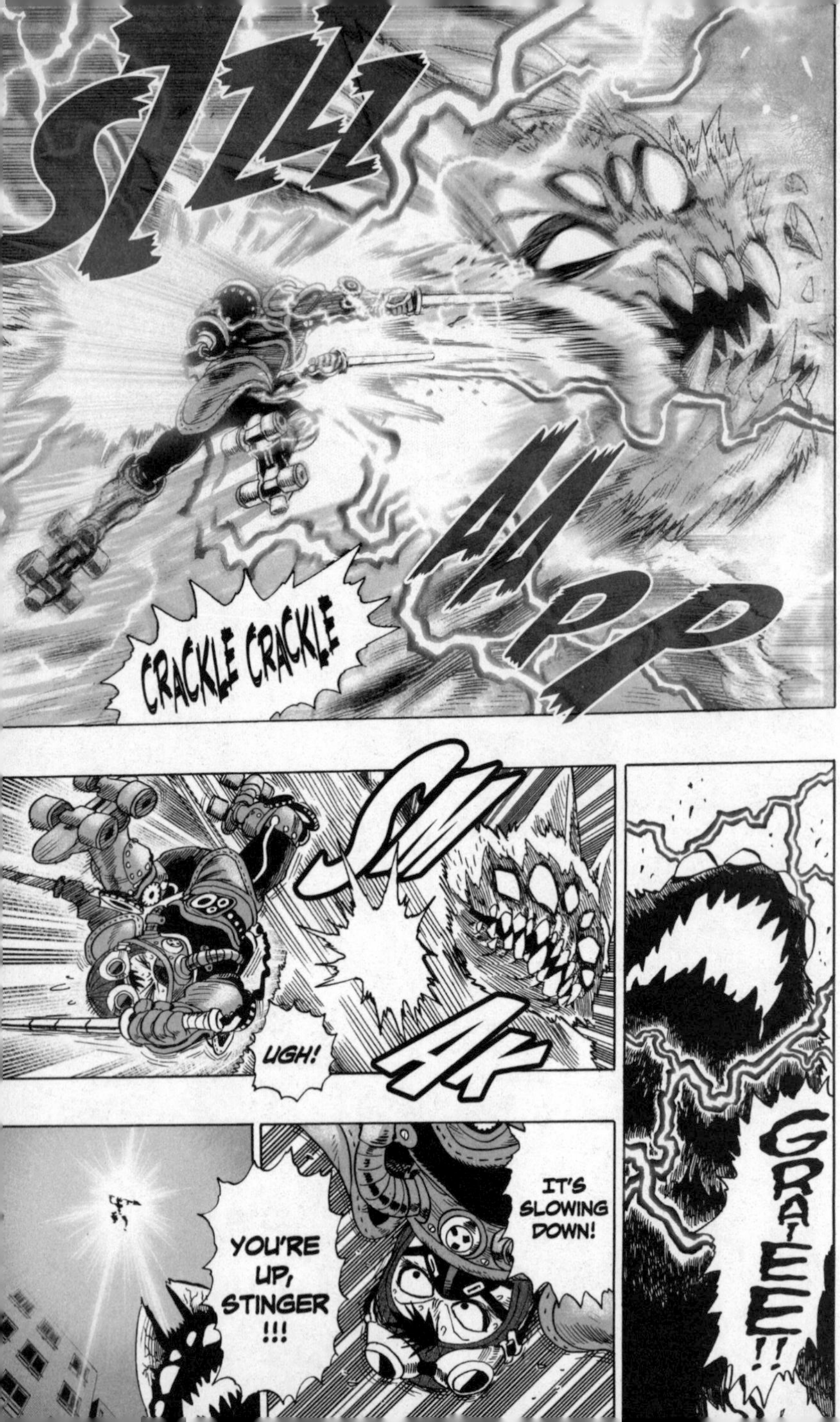
SIZZZ
ZAPP
CRACKLE CRACKLE
GRATEEE!!
CHAK
UGH!
IT'S SLOWING DOWN!
YOU'RE UP, STINGER !!!

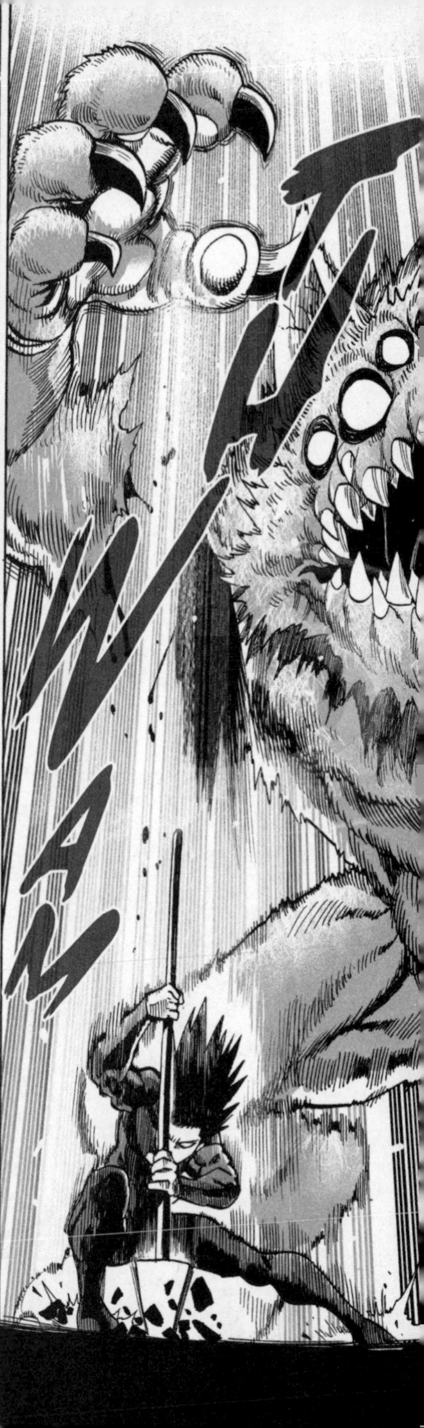

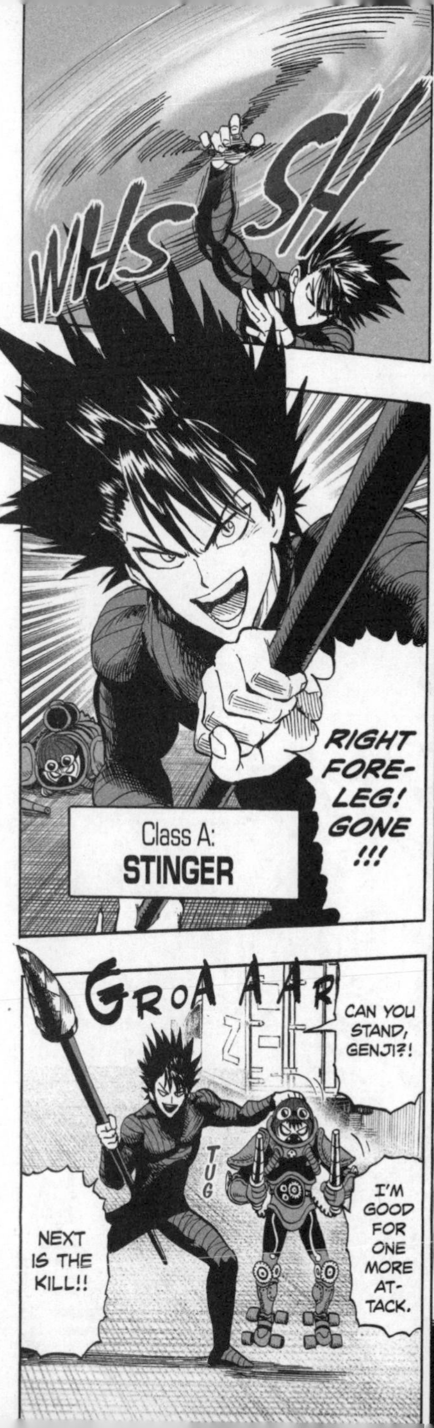
WHS SH
RIGHT FORE-LEG! GONE !!!
Class A:
STINGER
GROAAAR
CAN YOU STAND, GENJI?!
I'M GOOD FOR ONE MORE AT-TACK.
TUG
NEXT IS THE KILL!!

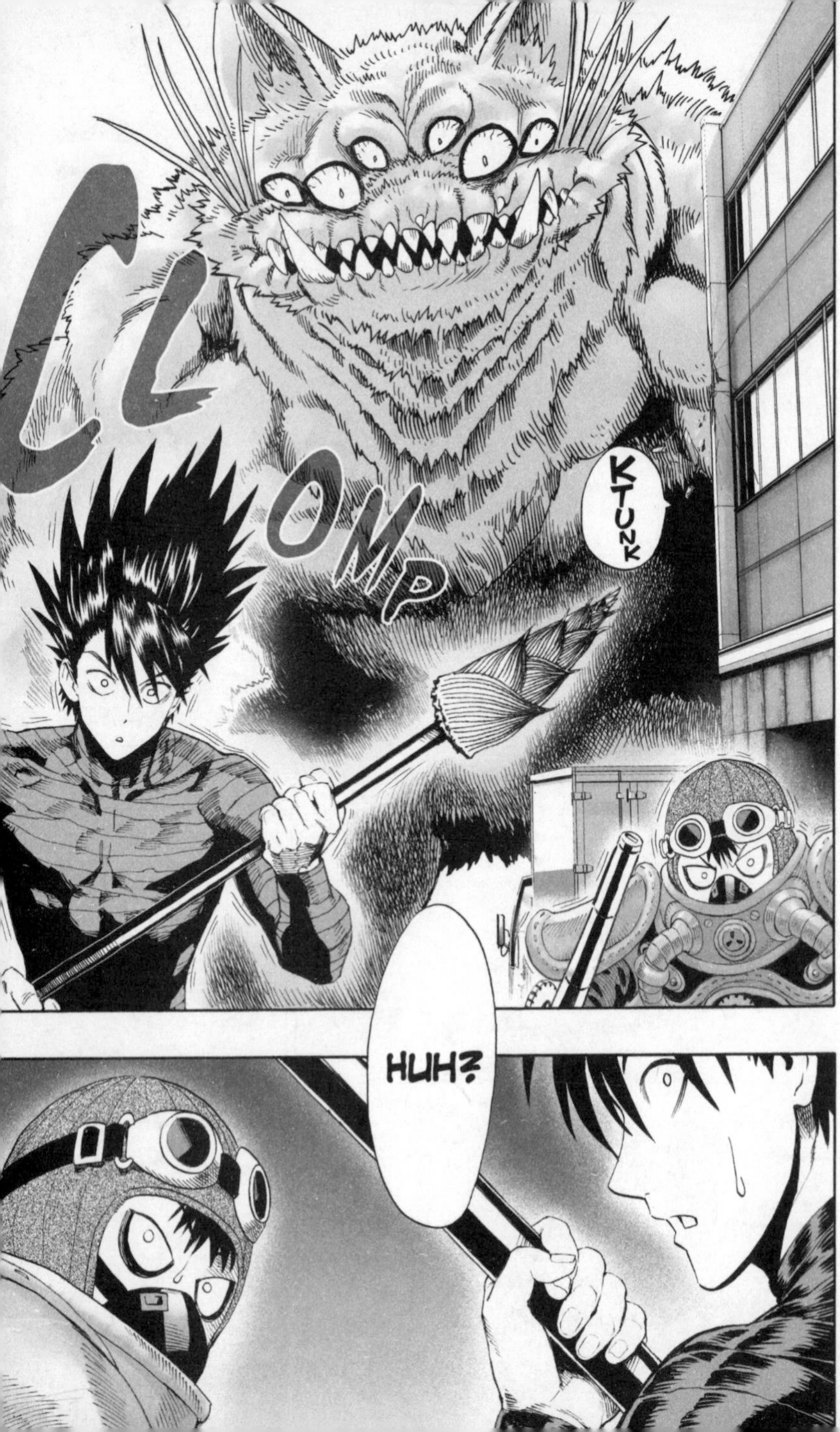
CLOMP
KTUNK
HUH?

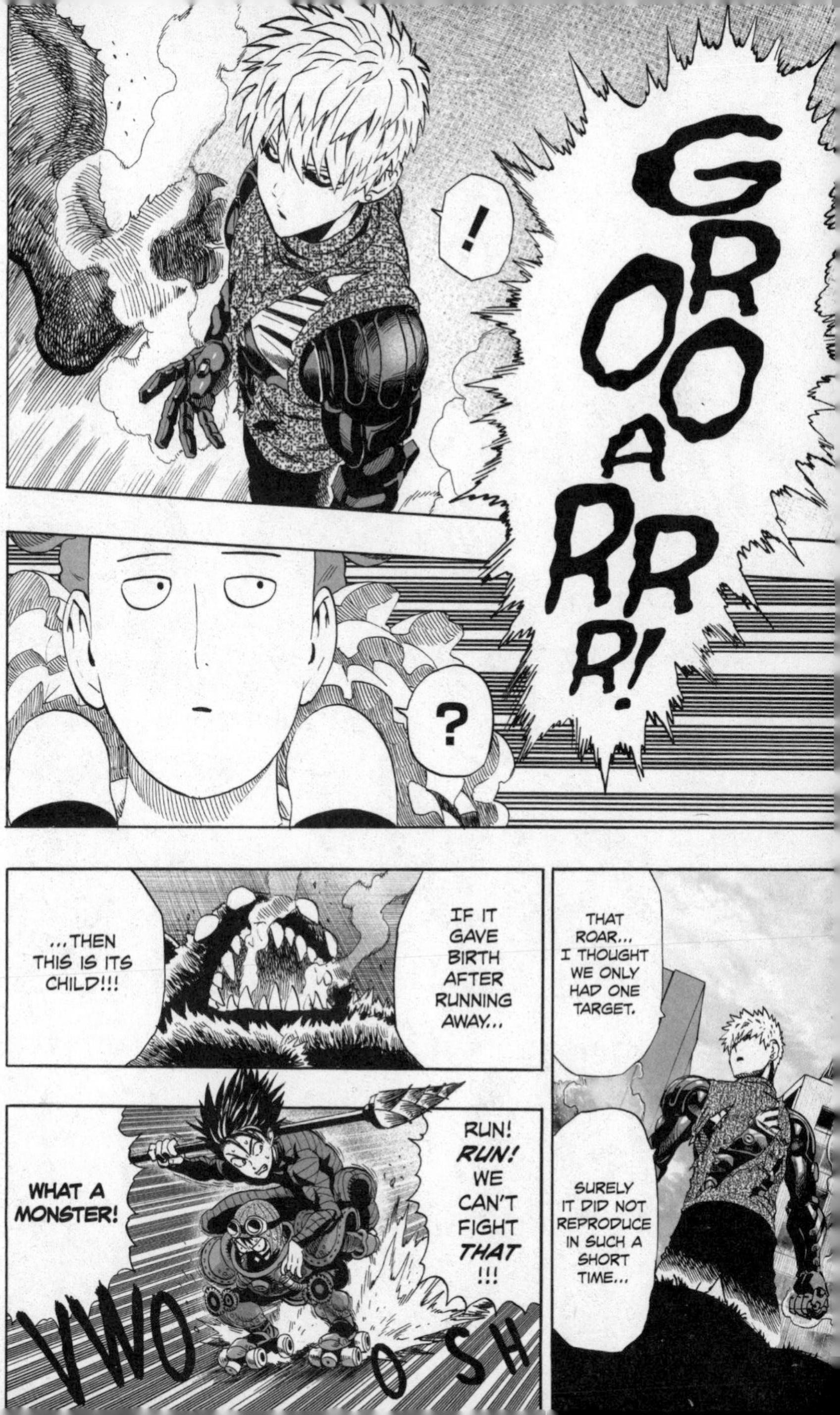
GROOARRRR!
!
?
THAT ROAR... I THOUGHT WE ONLY HAD ONE TARGET.
SURELY IT DID NOT REPRODUCE IN SUCH A SHORT TIME...
IF IT GAVE BIRTH AFTER RUNNING AWAY...
...THEN THIS IS ITS CHILD!!!
RUN! RUN! WE CAN'T FIGHT THAT!!!
WHAT A MONSTER!
VWOOSH

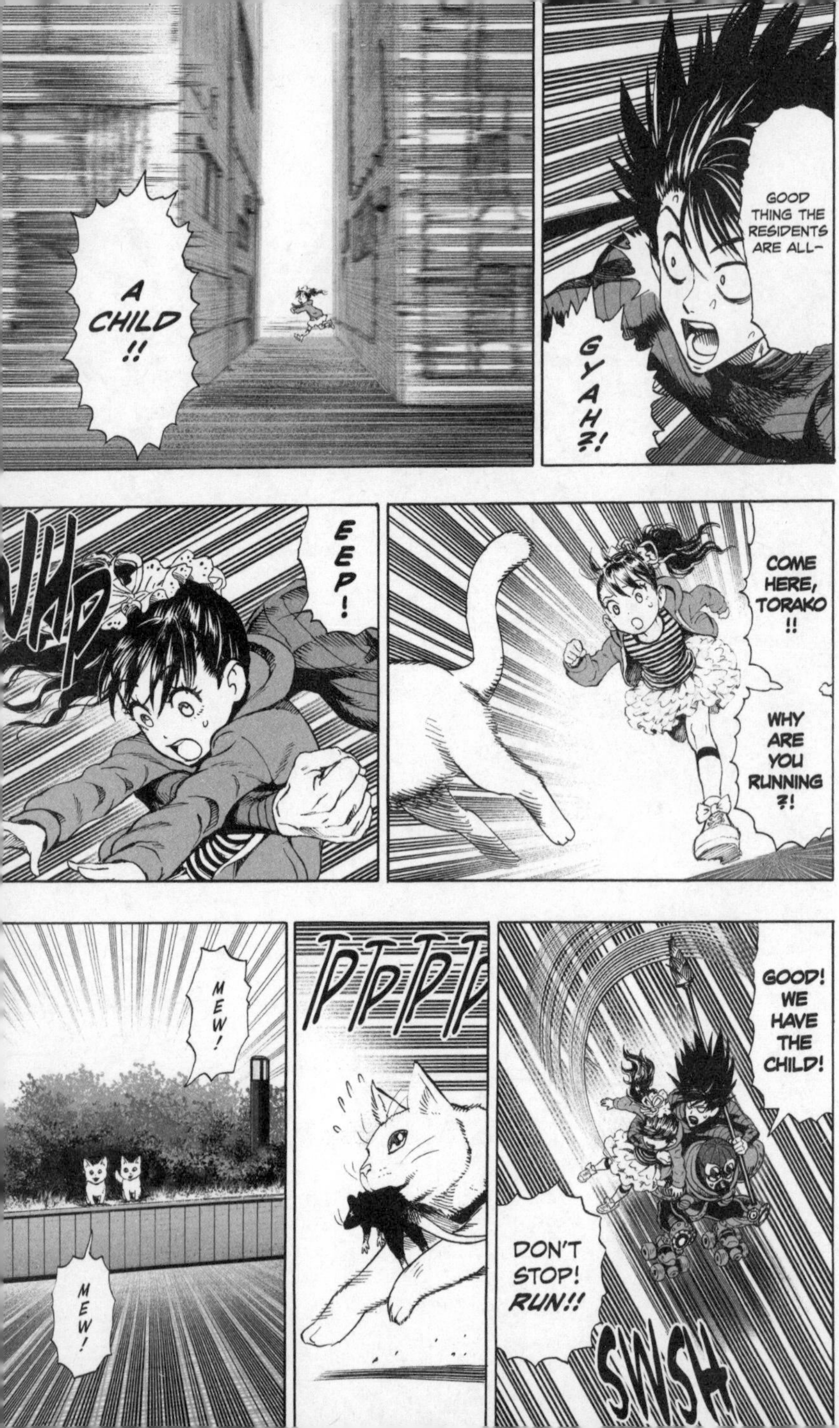
GOOD THING THE RESIDENTS ARE ALL—
GYAH?!
A CHILD!!
COME HERE, TORAKO!!
WHY ARE YOU RUNNING?!
EEP!
GOOD! WE HAVE THE CHILD!
DON'T STOP! RUN!!
SWISH
MEW!
MEW!

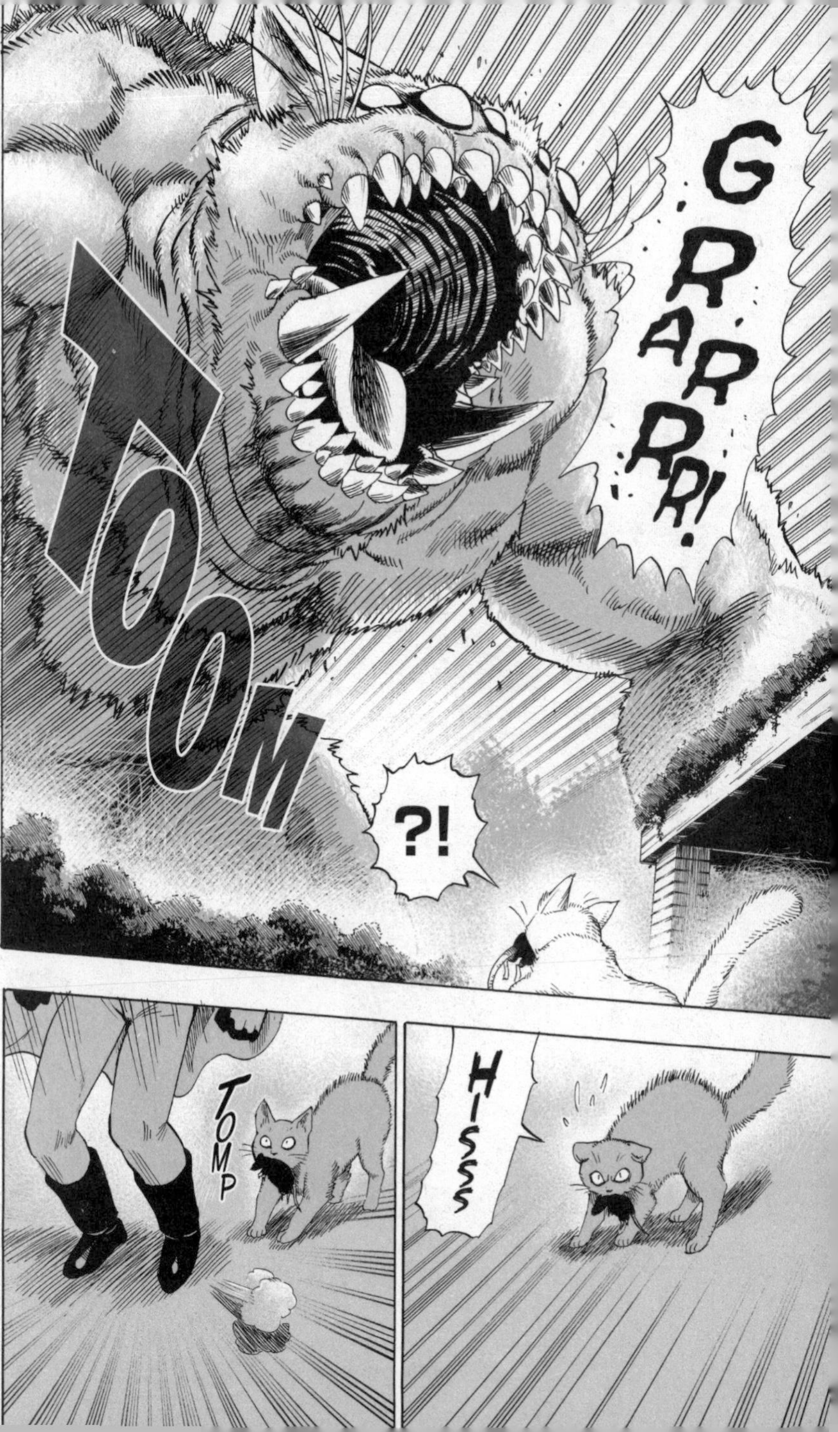
GRARRR!
TOOM
?!
HISSS
TOMP

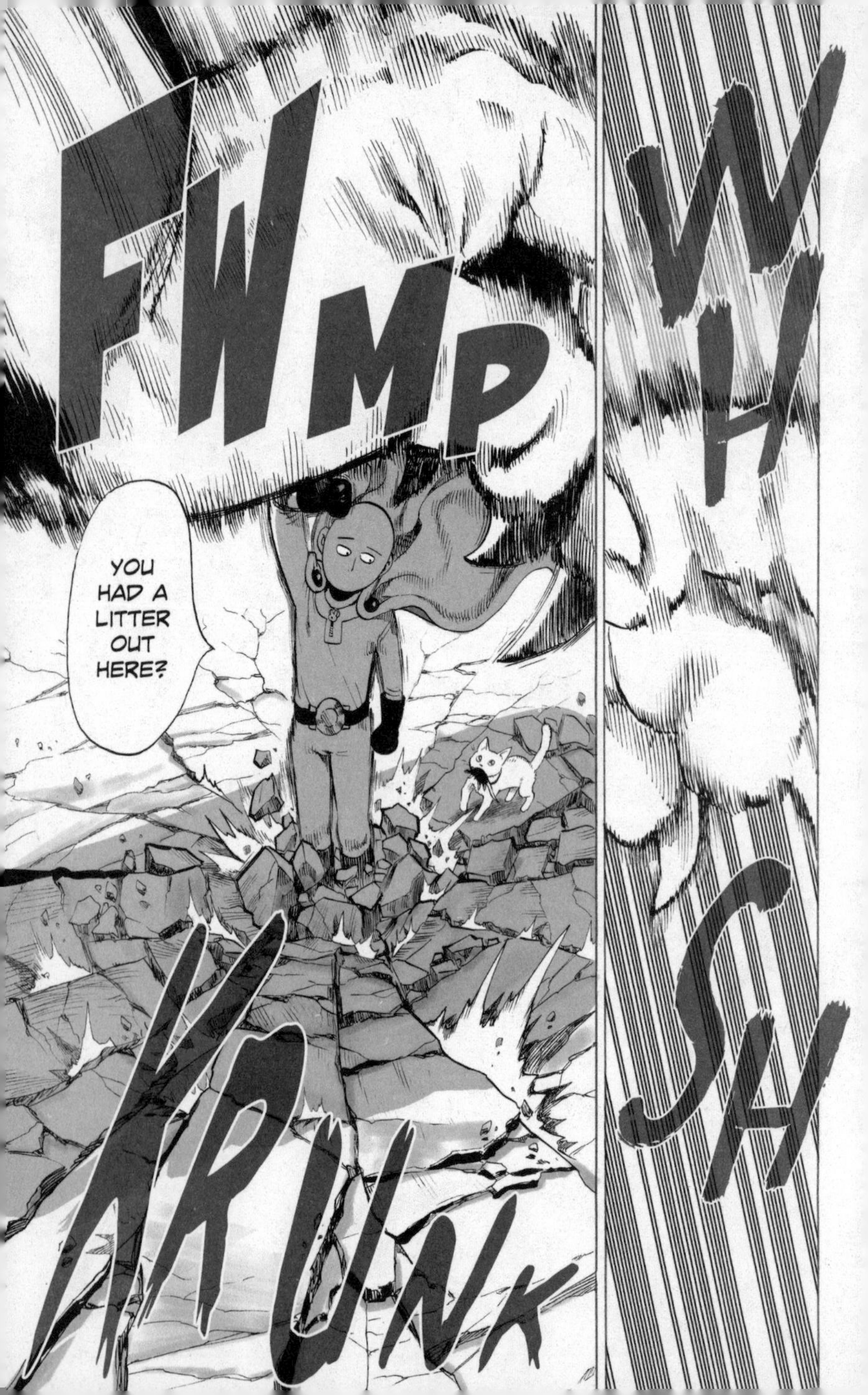
WHSH
FWMP
YOU HAD A LITTER OUT HERE?
KRUNK

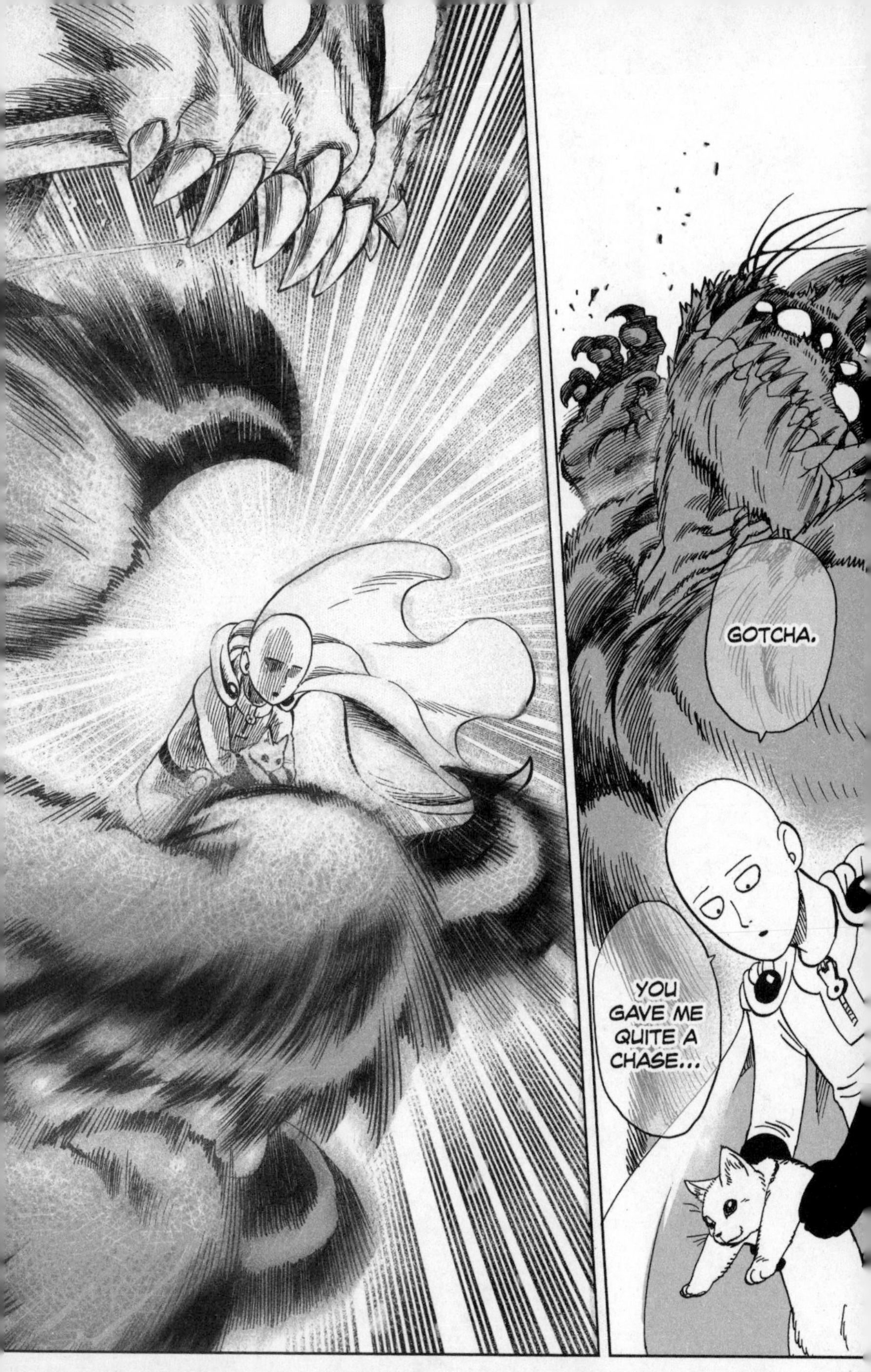
GOTCHA.
YOU GAVE ME QUITE A CHASE...

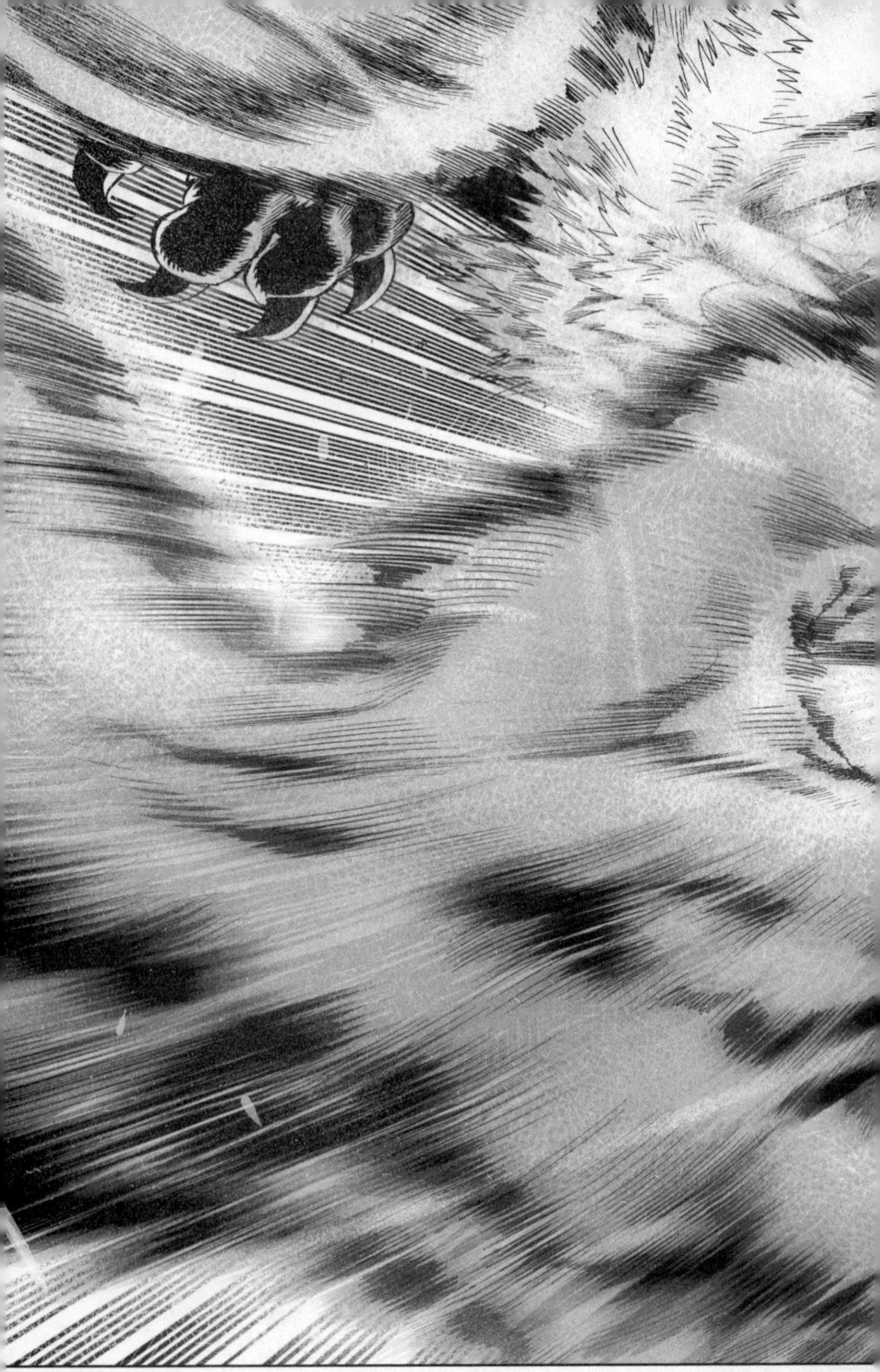

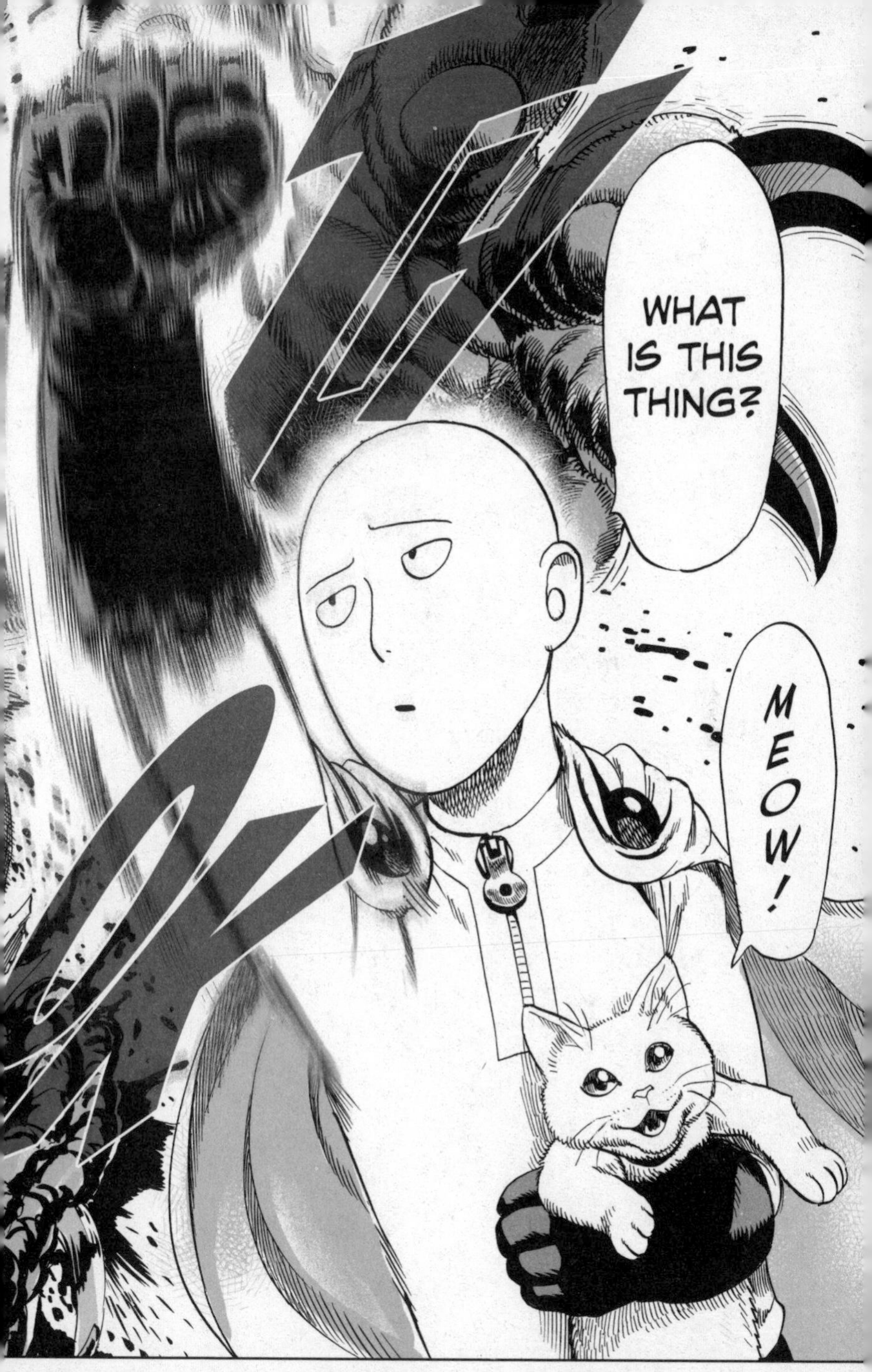
WHAT IS THIS THING?
MEOW!

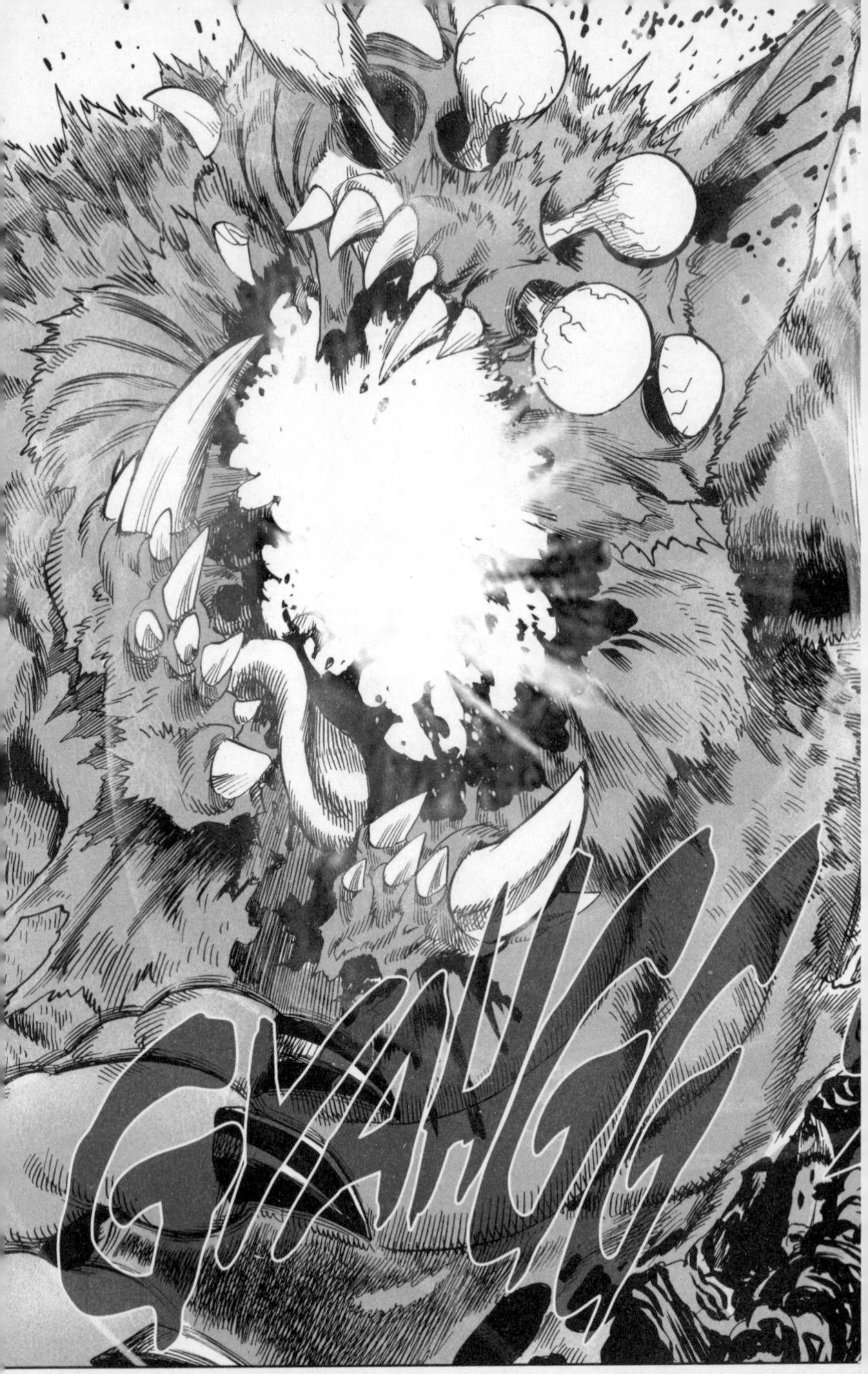

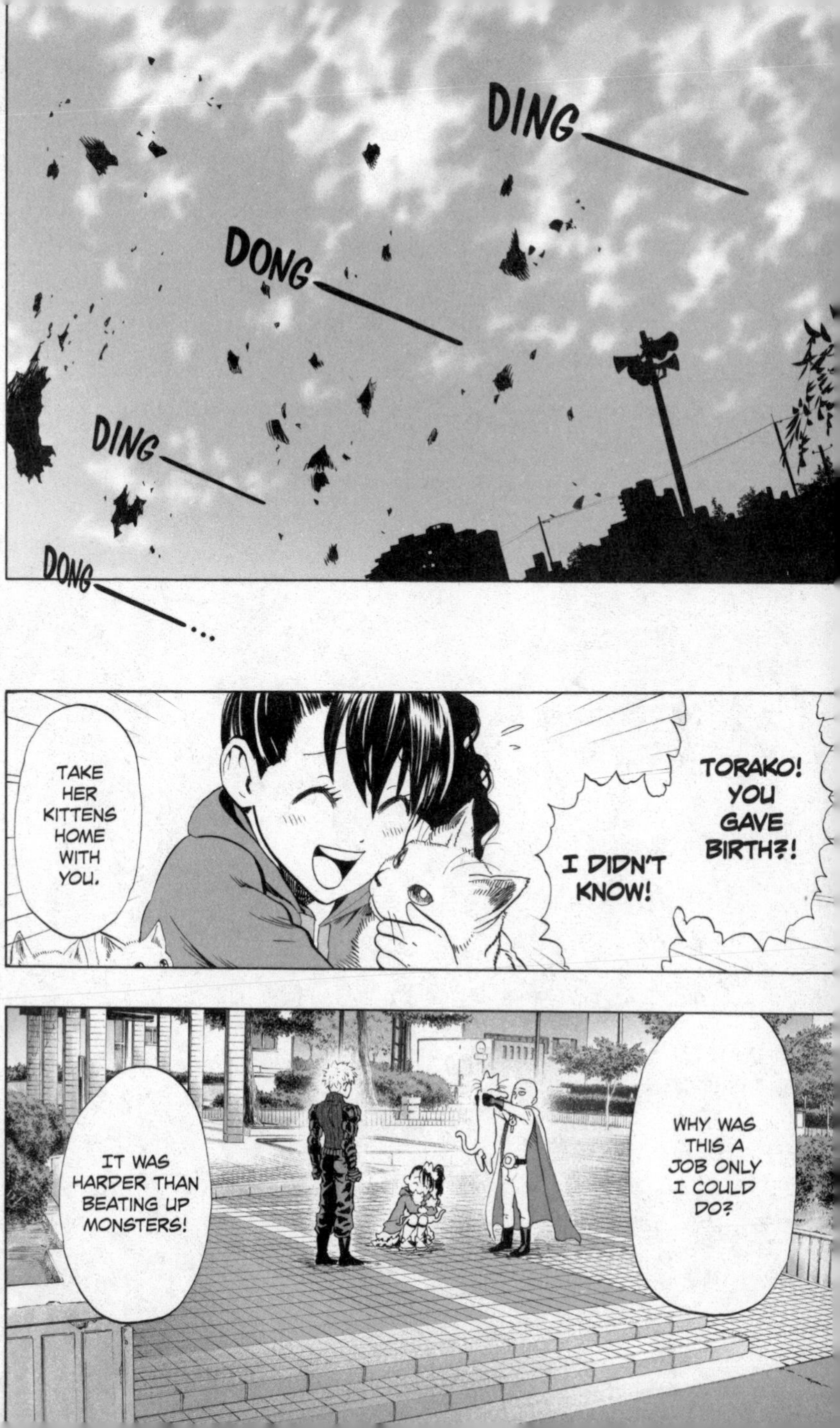
DING
DONG
DING
DONG...
TORAKO! YOU GAVE BIRTH?!
I DIDN'T KNOW!
TAKE HER KITTENS HOME WITH YOU.
WHY WAS THIS A JOB ONLY I COULD DO?
IT WAS HARDER THAN BEATING UP MONSTERS!

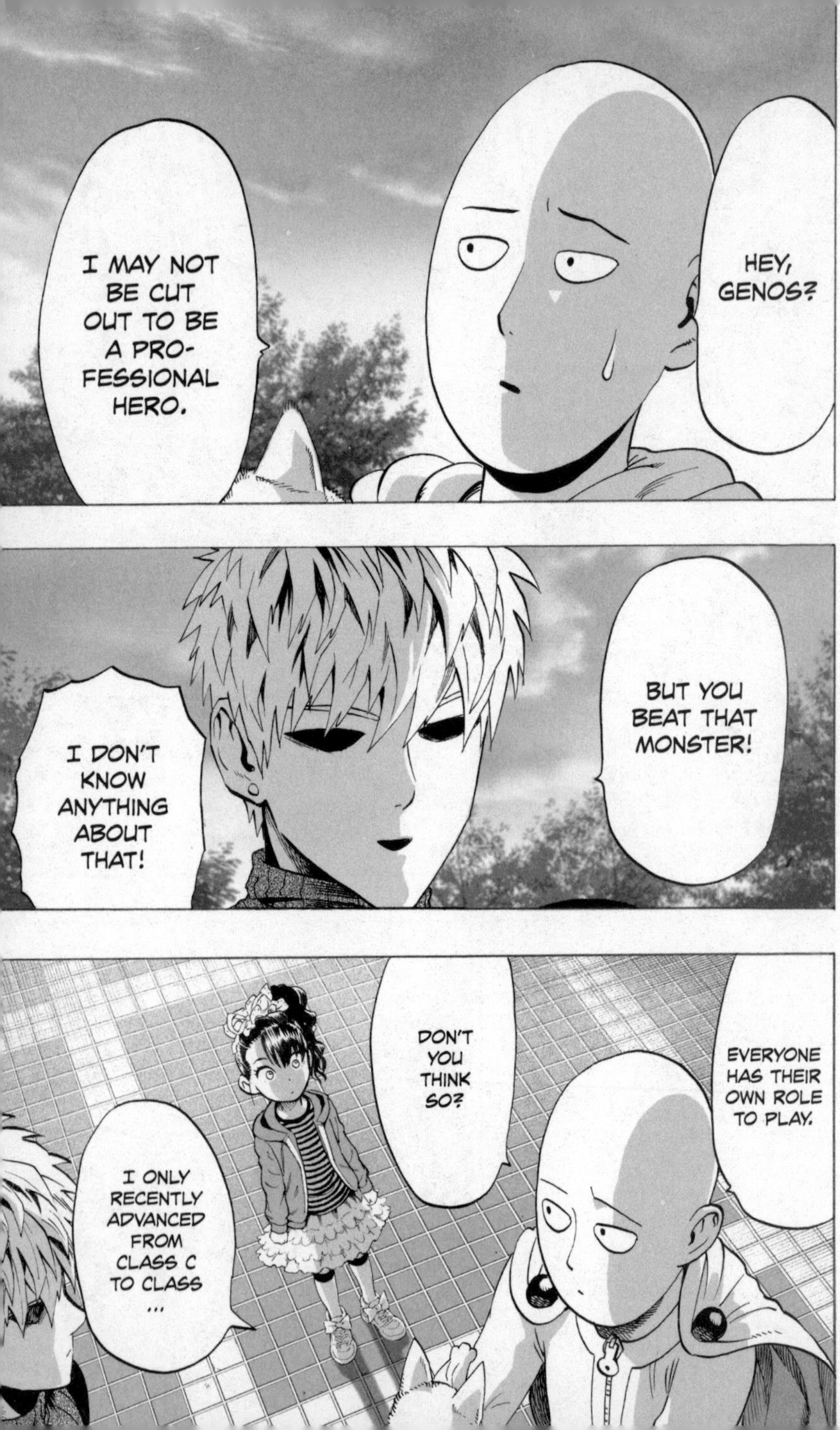
HEY, GENOS?
I MAY NOT BE CUT OUT TO BE A PROFESSIONAL HERO.
BUT YOU BEAT THAT MONSTER!
I DON'T KNOW ANYTHING ABOUT THAT!
EVERYONE HAS THEIR OWN ROLE TO PLAY.
DON'T YOU THINK SO?
I ONLY RECENTLY ADVANCED FROM CLASS C TO CLASS ...

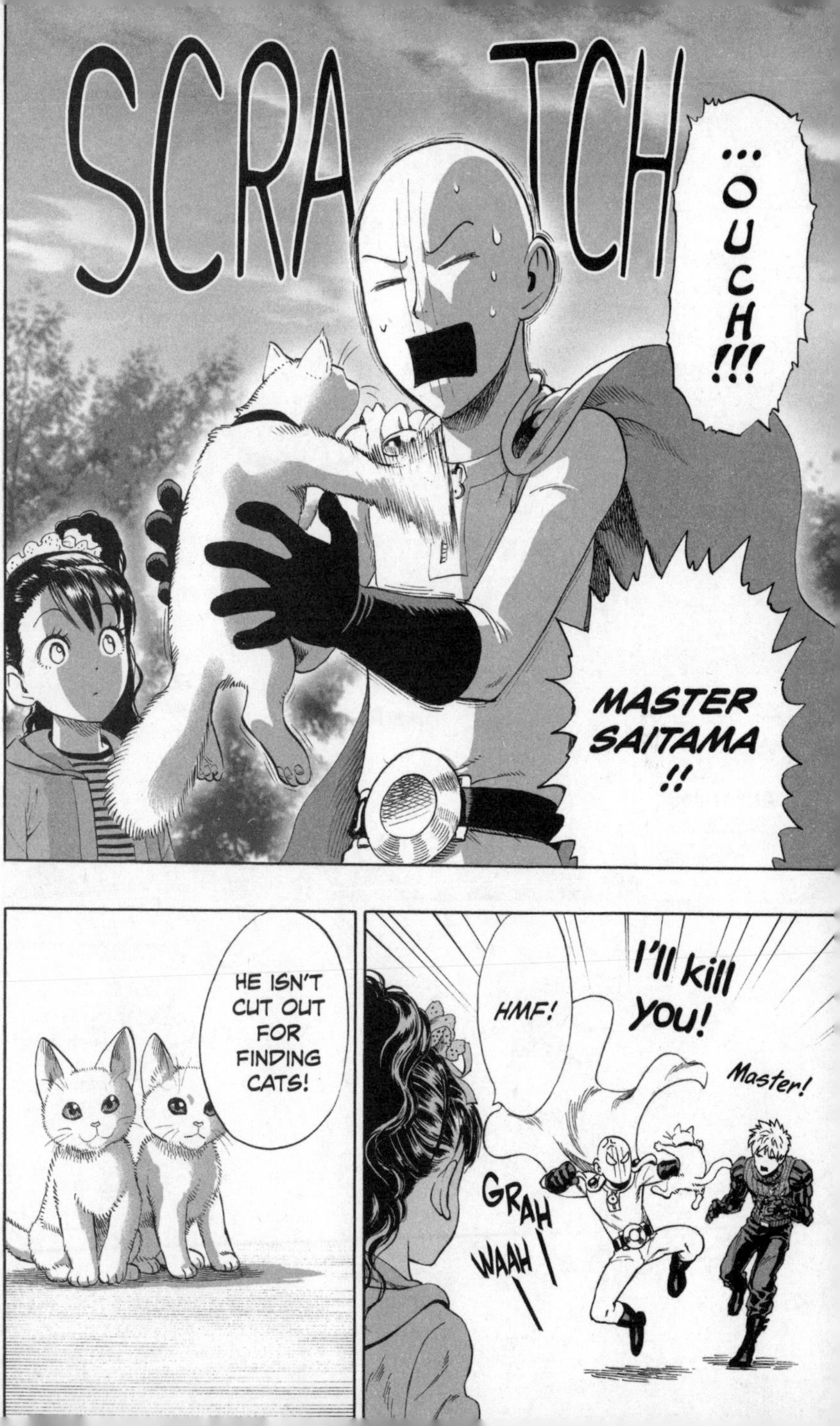
SCRATCH
...OUCH!!!
MASTER SAITAMA!!
I'll kill you!
HMF!
Master!
GRAH
WAAH
HE ISN'T CUT OUT FOR FINDING CATS!

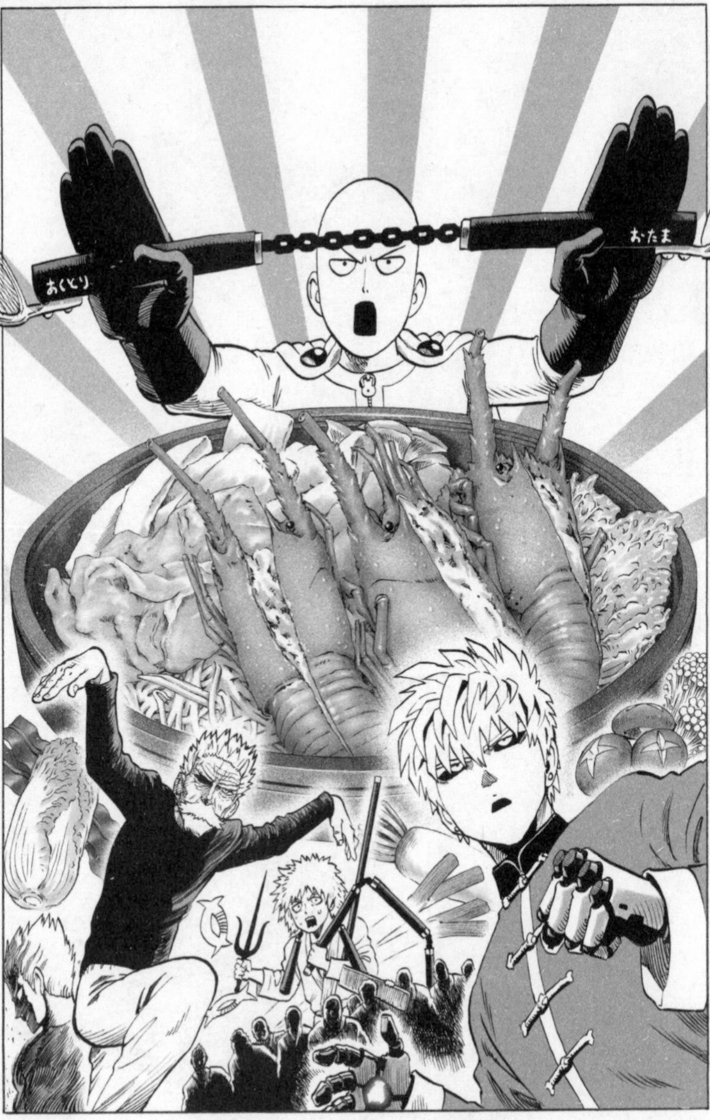
おたま
あくとり

BONUS MANGA 2: LOBSTER

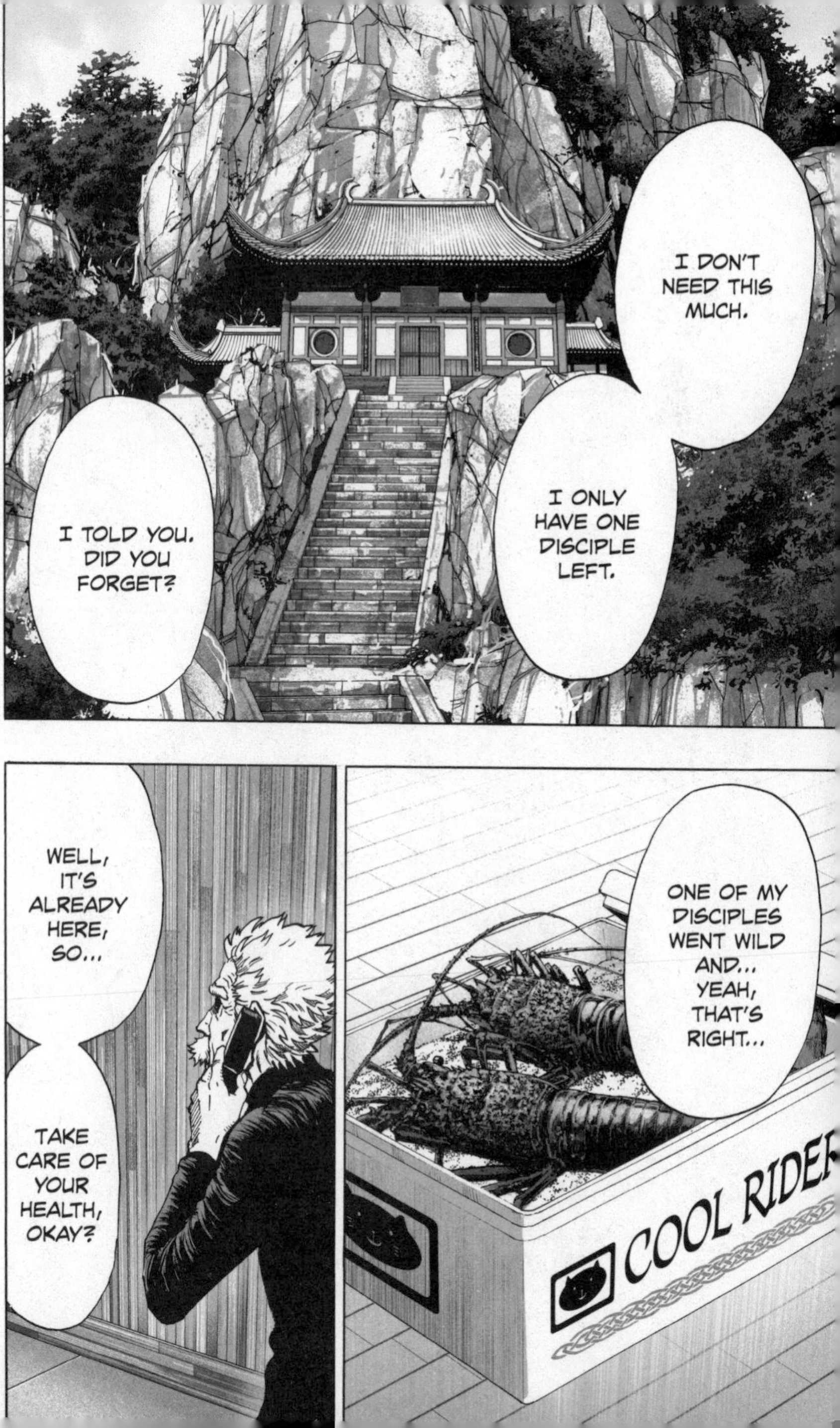
I DON'T NEED THIS MUCH.
I ONLY HAVE ONE DISCIPLE LEFT.
I TOLD YOU. DID YOU FORGET?
ONE OF MY DISCIPLES WENT WILD AND... YEAH, THAT'S RIGHT...
COOL RIDE
WELL, IT'S ALREADY HERE, SO...
TAKE CARE OF YOUR HEALTH, OKAY?

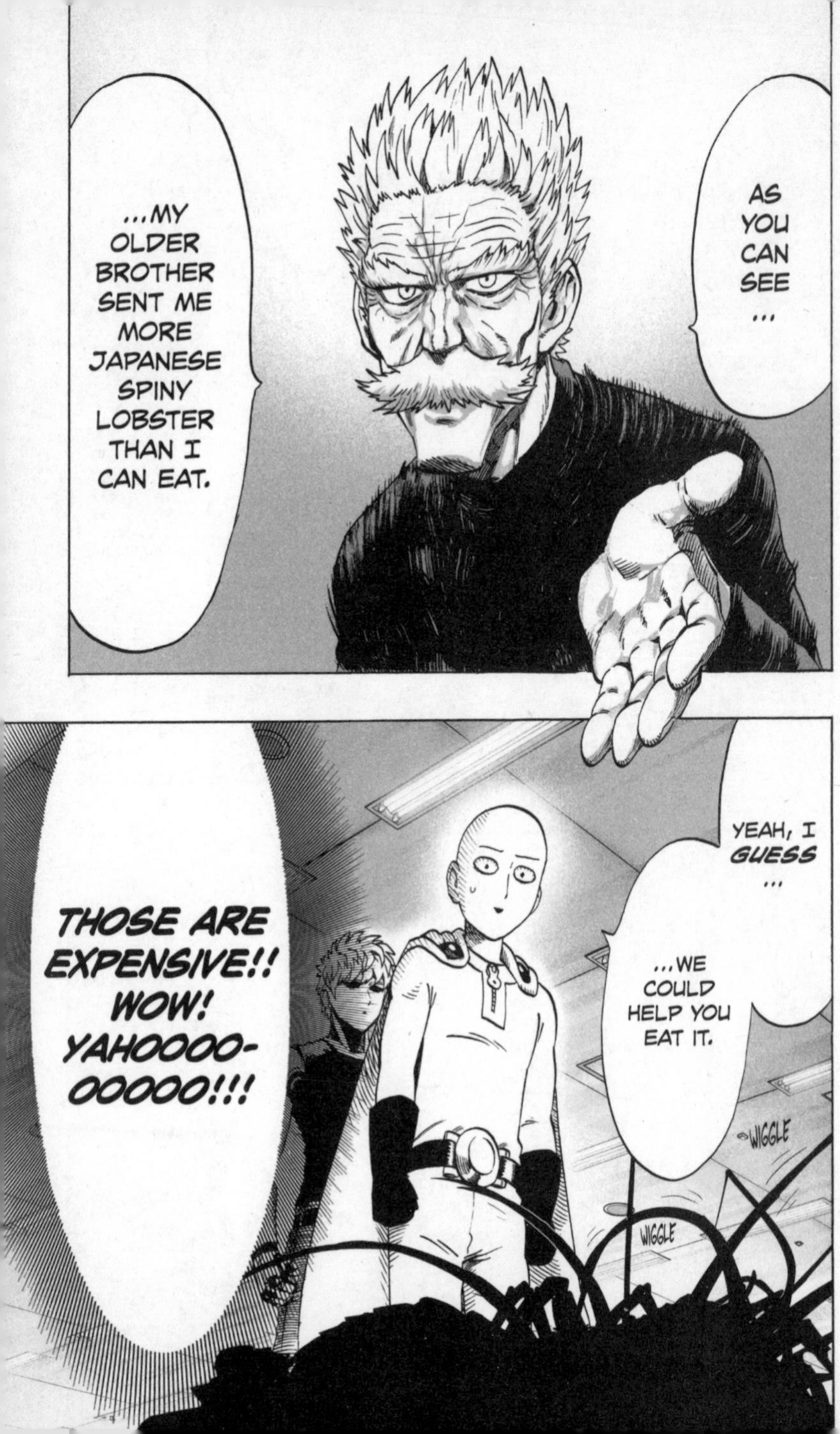
AS YOU CAN SEE...
...MY OLDER BROTHER SENT ME MORE JAPANESE SPINY LOBSTER THAN I CAN EAT.
YEAH, I GUESS...
...WE COULD HELP YOU EAT IT.
WIGGLE
WIGGLE
THOSE ARE EXPENSIVE!! WOW! YAHOOOO-OOOOO!!!

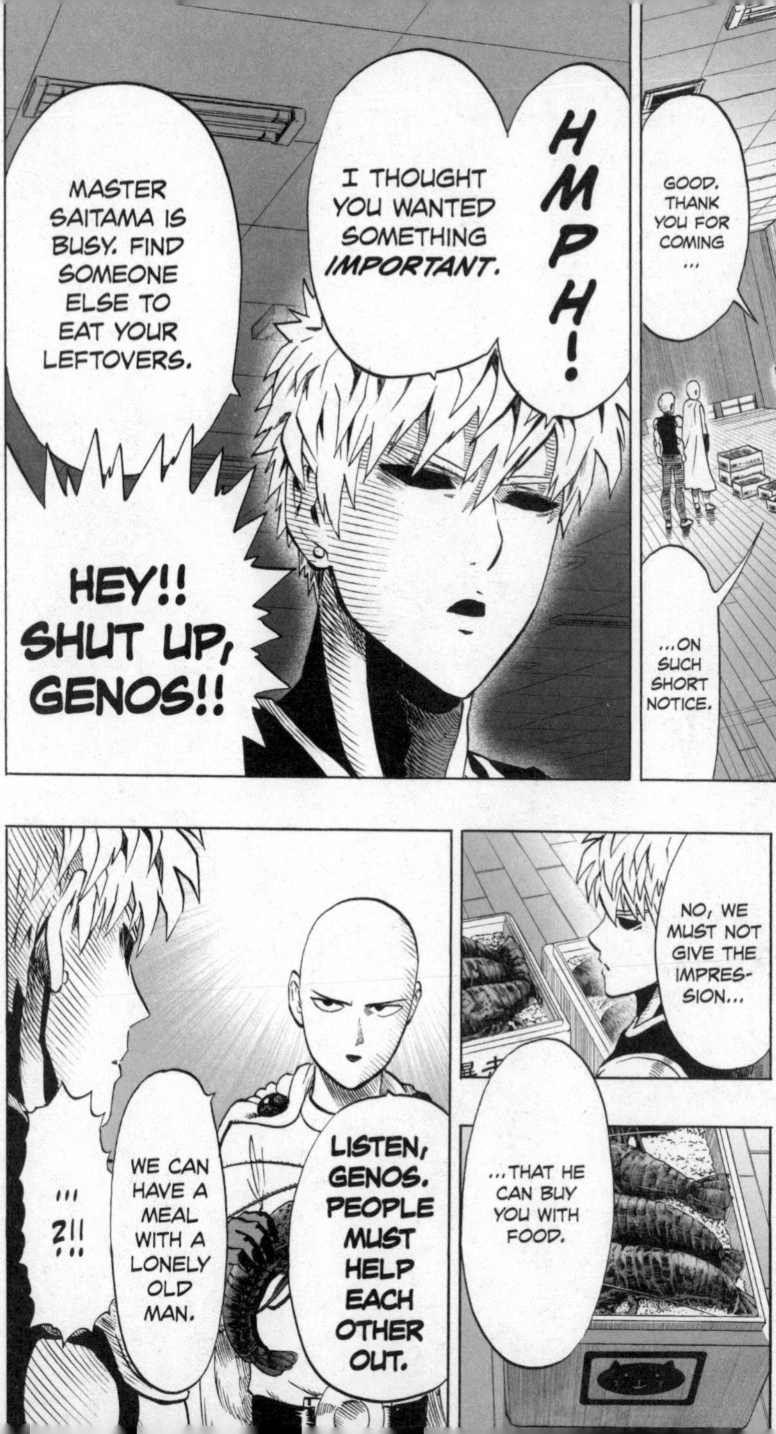
GOOD. THANK YOU FOR COMING ...
...ON SUCH SHORT NOTICE.
HMPH!
I THOUGHT YOU WANTED SOMETHING *IMPORTANT*.
MASTER SAITAMA IS BUSY. FIND SOMEONE ELSE TO EAT YOUR LEFTOVERS.
HEY!! SHUT UP, GENOS!!
NO, WE MUST NOT GIVE THE IMPRES-SION...
...THAT HE CAN BUY YOU WITH FOOD.
LISTEN, GENOS. PEOPLE MUST HELP EACH OTHER OUT.
WE CAN HAVE A MEAL WITH A LONELY OLD MAN.
!!! ?!!

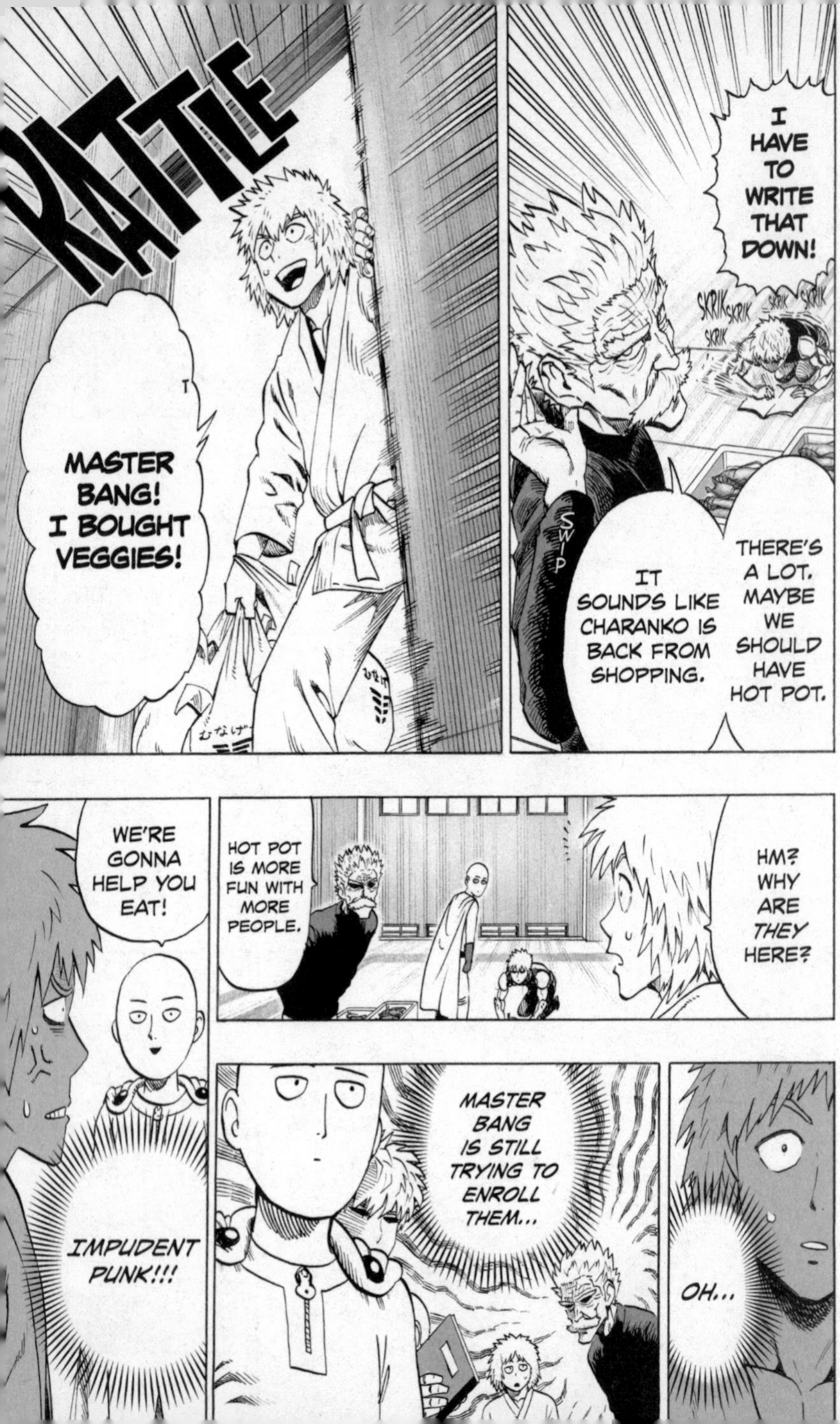
I HAVE TO WRITE THAT DOWN!
SKRIK SKRIK SKRIK SKRIK SKRIK
SWIP
THERE'S A LOT. MAYBE WE SHOULD HAVE HOT POT.
IT SOUNDS LIKE CHARANKO IS BACK FROM SHOPPING.
RATTLE
MASTER BANG! I BOUGHT VEGGIES!
HM? WHY ARE THEY HERE?
HOT POT IS MORE FUN WITH MORE PEOPLE.
OH...
MASTER BANG IS STILL TRYING TO ENROLL THEM...
WE'RE GONNA HELP YOU EAT!
IMPUDENT PUNK!!!

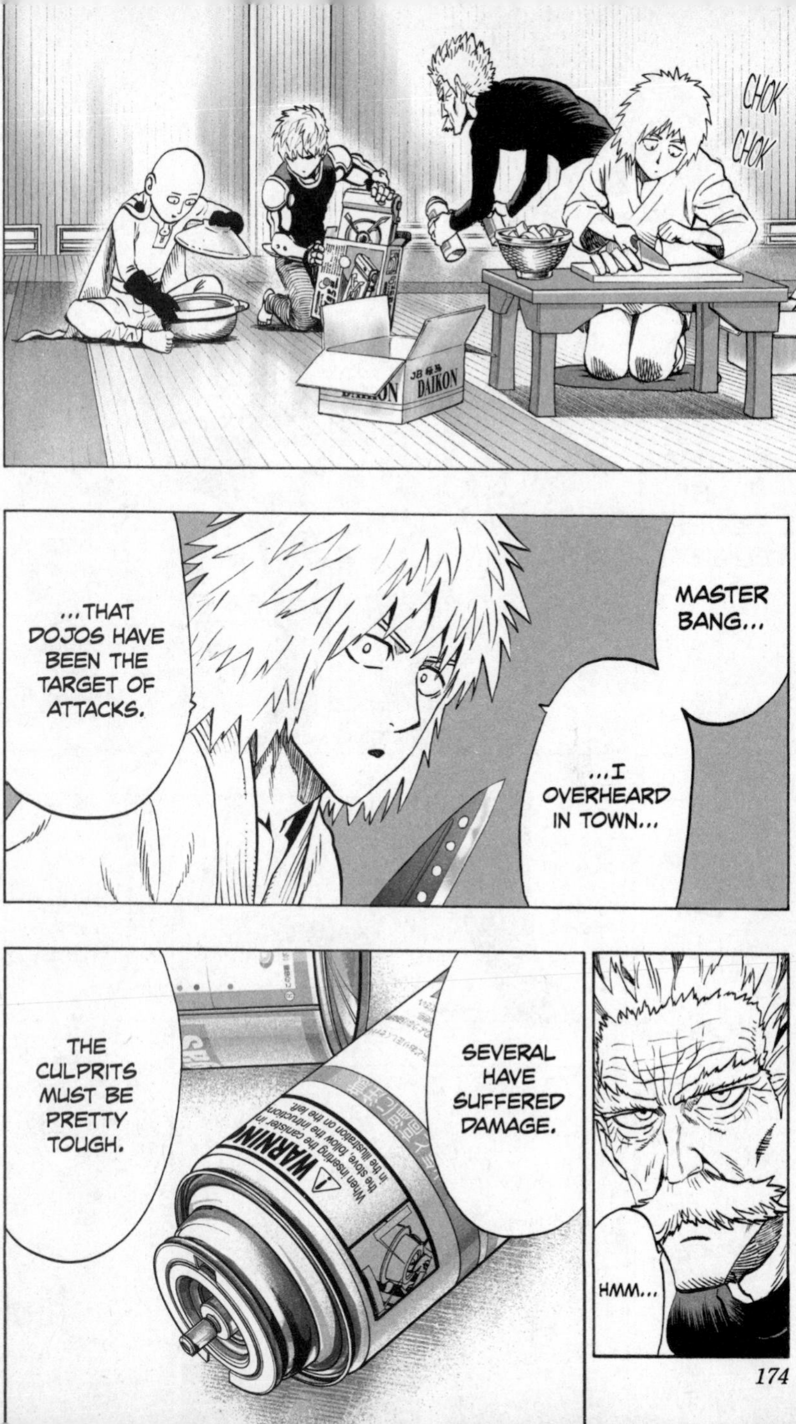
CHOK
CHOK
DAIKON
DAIKON
MASTER BANG...
...I OVERHEARD IN TOWN...
...THAT DOJOS HAVE BEEN THE TARGET OF ATTACKS.
HMM...
SEVERAL HAVE SUFFERED DAMAGE.
THE CULPRITS MUST BE PRETTY TOUGH.
WARNING
When inserting the canister in the stove, follow the infruction in the illustration on the left.

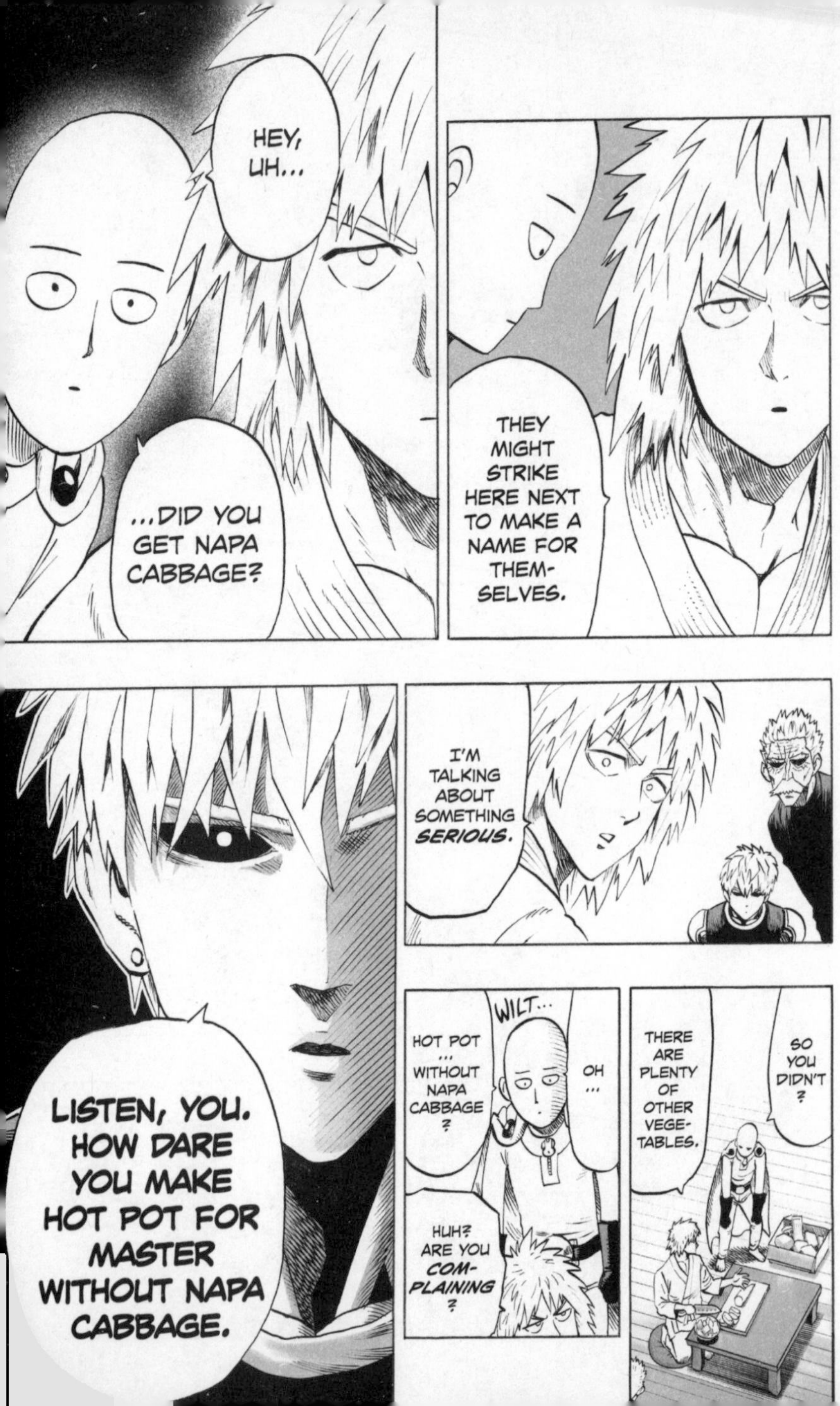
THEY MIGHT STRIKE HERE NEXT TO MAKE A NAME FOR THEM-SELVES.
HEY, UH...
...DID YOU GET NAPA CABBAGE?
I'M TALKING ABOUT SOMETHING *SERIOUS*.
SO YOU DIDN'T?
THERE ARE PLENTY OF OTHER VEGE-TABLES.
WILT...
OH ...
HOT POT ... WITHOUT NAPA CABBAGE?
HUH? ARE YOU *COM-PLAINING*?
LISTEN, YOU. HOW DARE YOU MAKE HOT POT FOR MASTER WITHOUT NAPA CABBAGE.

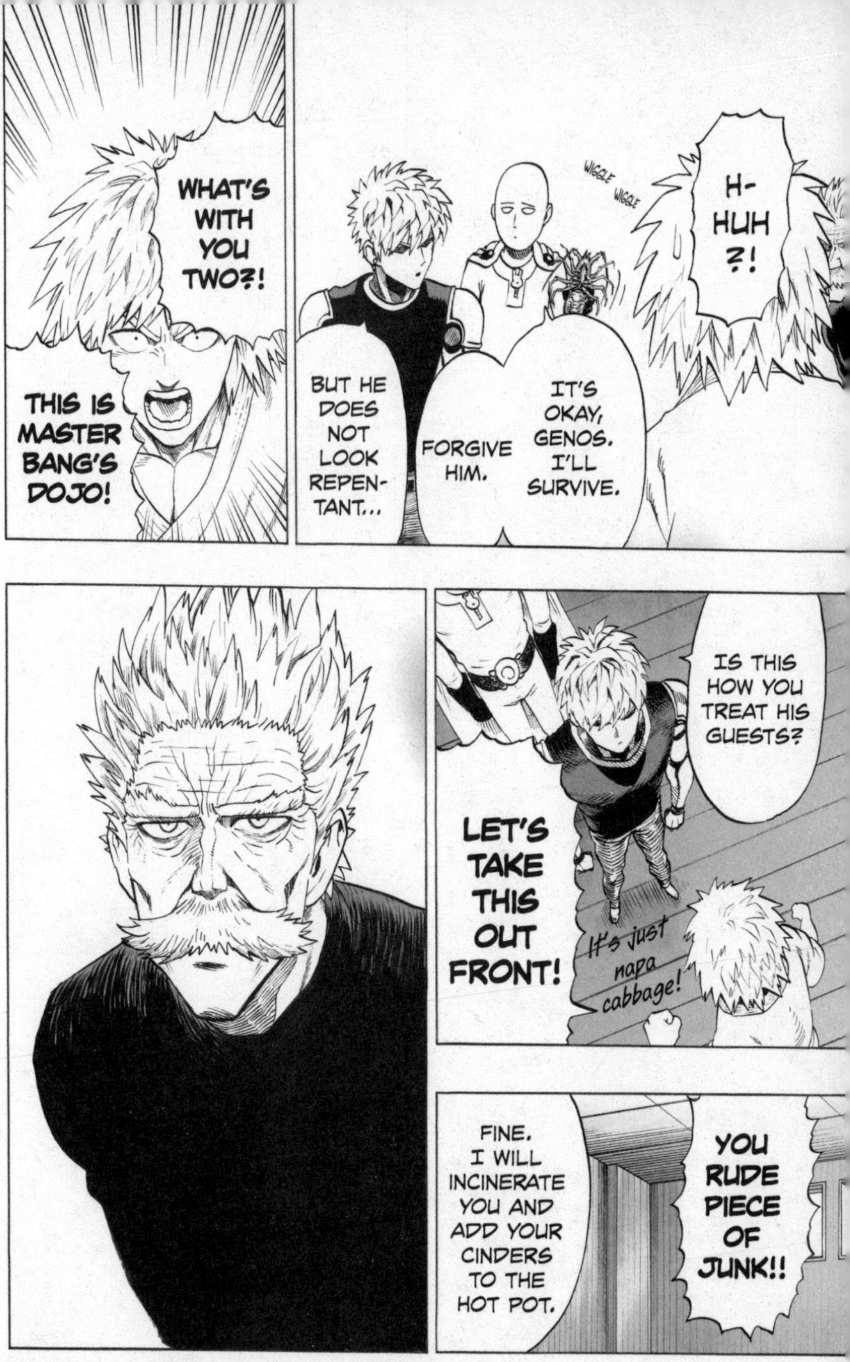
H-HUH?!
WIGGLE WIGGLE
IT'S OKAY, GENOS. I'LL SURVIVE.
FORGIVE HIM.
BUT HE DOES NOT LOOK REPENTANT...
WHAT'S WITH YOU TWO?!
THIS IS MASTER BANG'S DOJO!
IS THIS HOW YOU TREAT HIS GUESTS?
It's just napa cabbage!
LET'S TAKE THIS OUT FRONT!
YOU RUDE PIECE OF JUNK!!
FINE. I WILL INCINERATE YOU AND ADD YOUR CINDERS TO THE HOT POT.

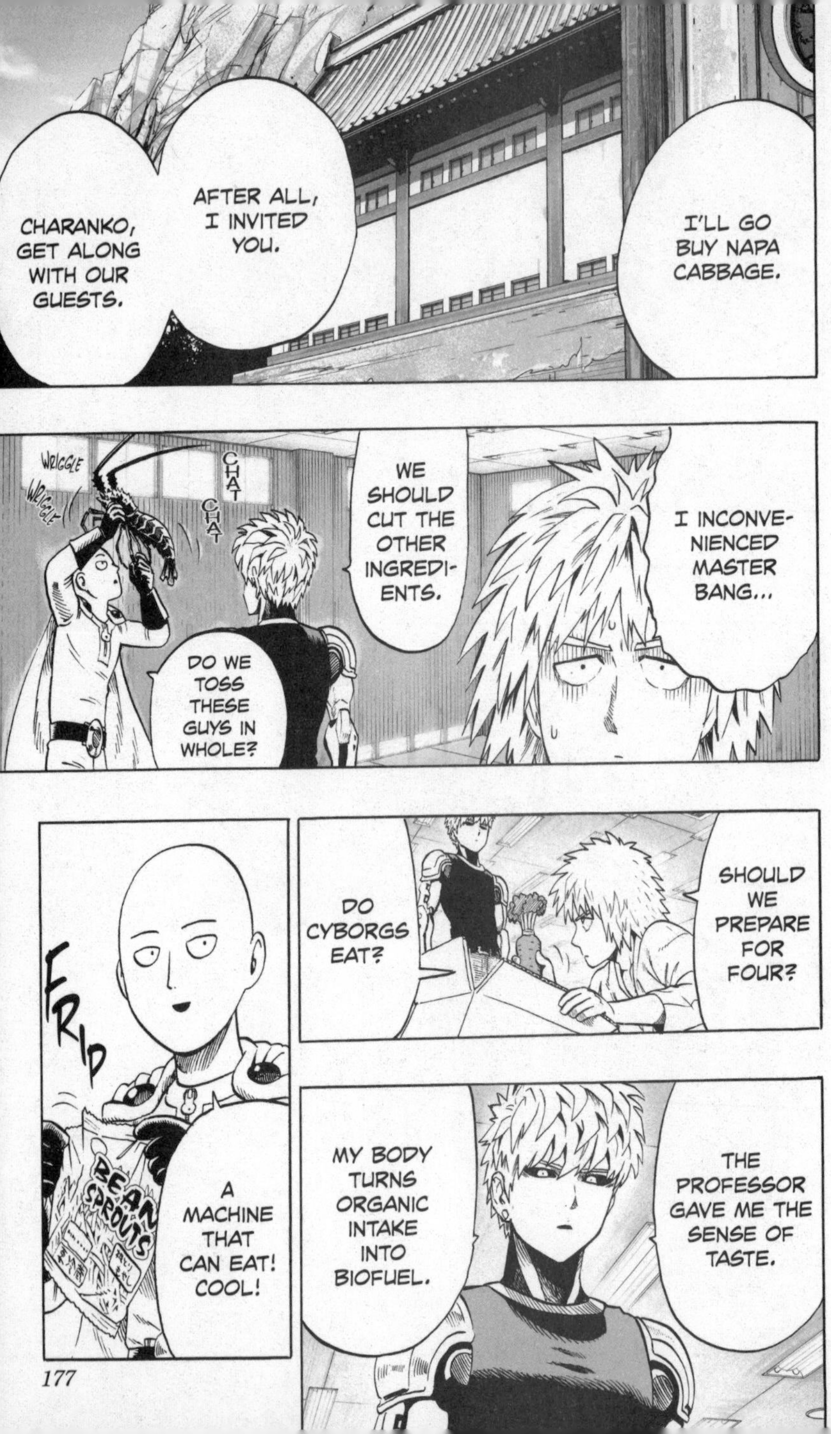
I'LL GO BUY NAPA CABBAGE.
AFTER ALL, I INVITED YOU.
CHARANKO, GET ALONG WITH OUR GUESTS.
I INCONVENIENCED MASTER BANG...
WE SHOULD CUT THE OTHER INGREDIENTS.
CHAT CHAT
DO WE TOSS THESE GUYS IN WHOLE?
WRIGGLE WRIGGLE
SHOULD WE PREPARE FOR FOUR?
DO CYBORGS EAT?
THE PROFESSOR GAVE ME THE SENSE OF TASTE.
MY BODY TURNS ORGANIC INTAKE INTO BIOFUEL.
A MACHINE THAT CAN EAT! COOL!
FRIP
BEAN SPROUTS

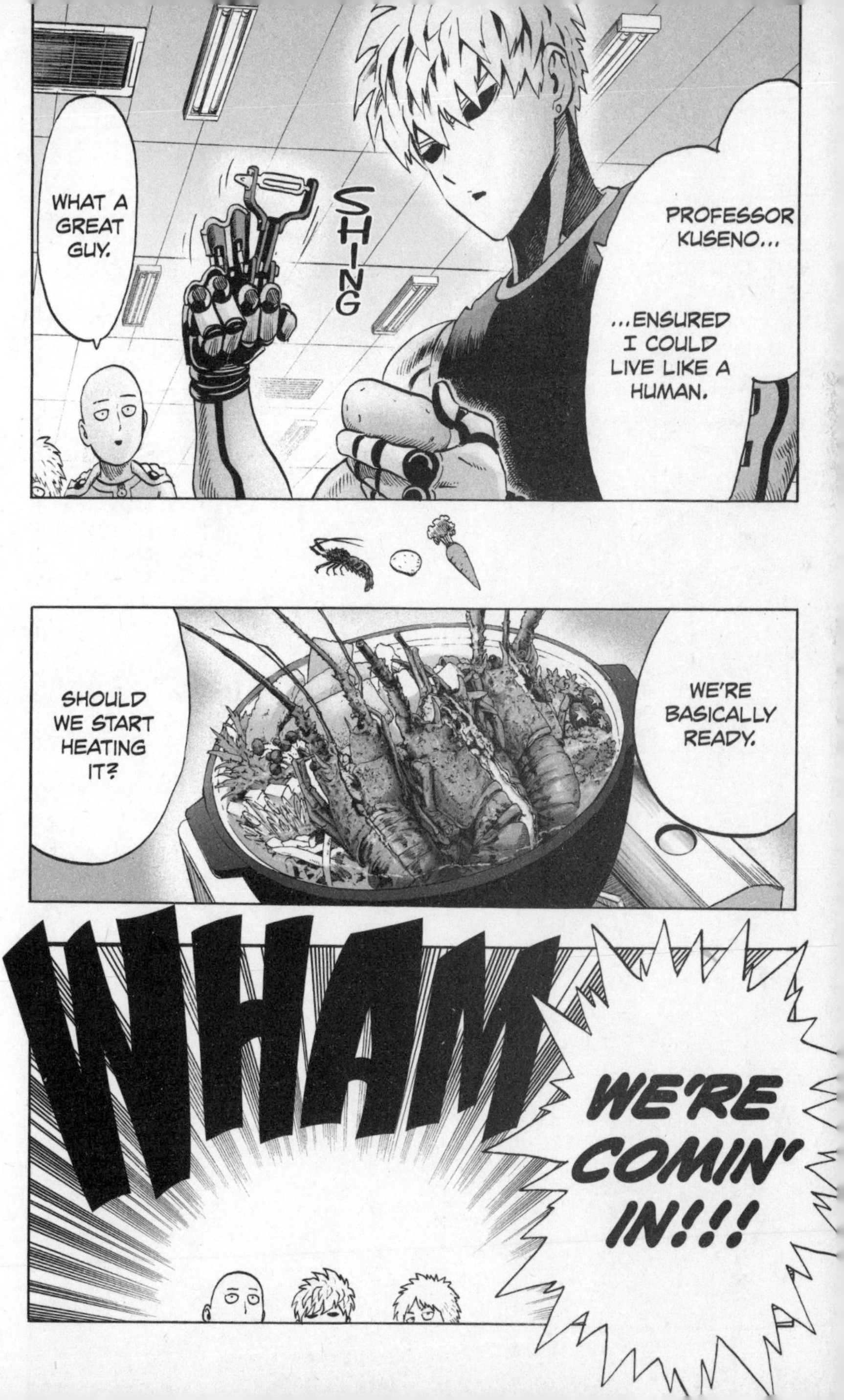
PROFESSOR KUSENO...
...ENSURED I COULD LIVE LIKE A HUMAN.
SHING
WHAT A GREAT GUY.
WE'RE BASICALLY READY.
SHOULD WE START HEATING IT?
WE'RE COMIN' IN!!!
WHAM

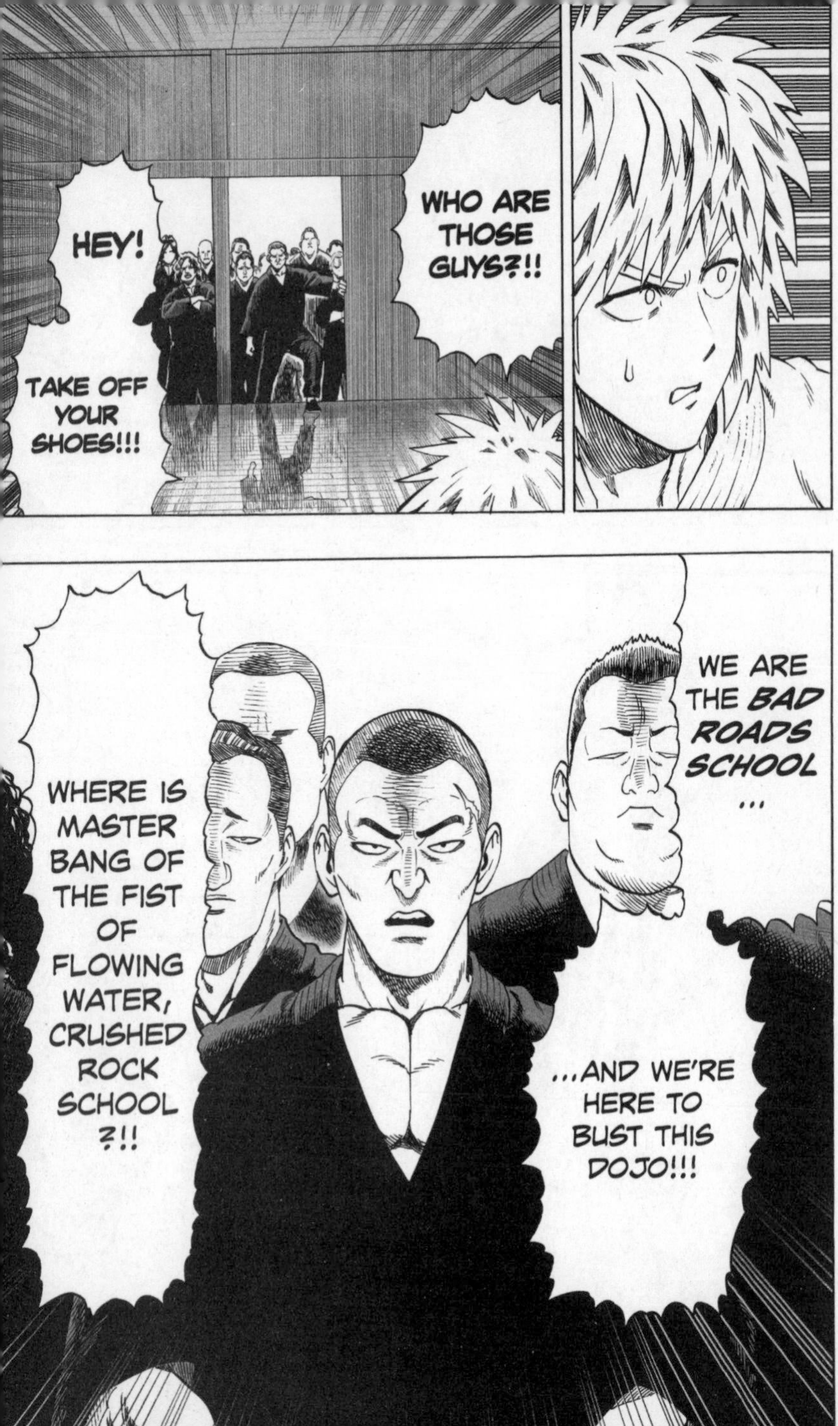
WHO ARE THOSE GUYS?!!
HEY!
TAKE OFF YOUR SHOES!!!
WE ARE THE *BAD ROADS SCHOOL* ...
WHERE IS MASTER BANG OF THE FIST OF FLOWING WATER, CRUSHED ROCK SCHOOL ?!!
...AND WE'RE HERE TO BUST THIS DOJO!!!

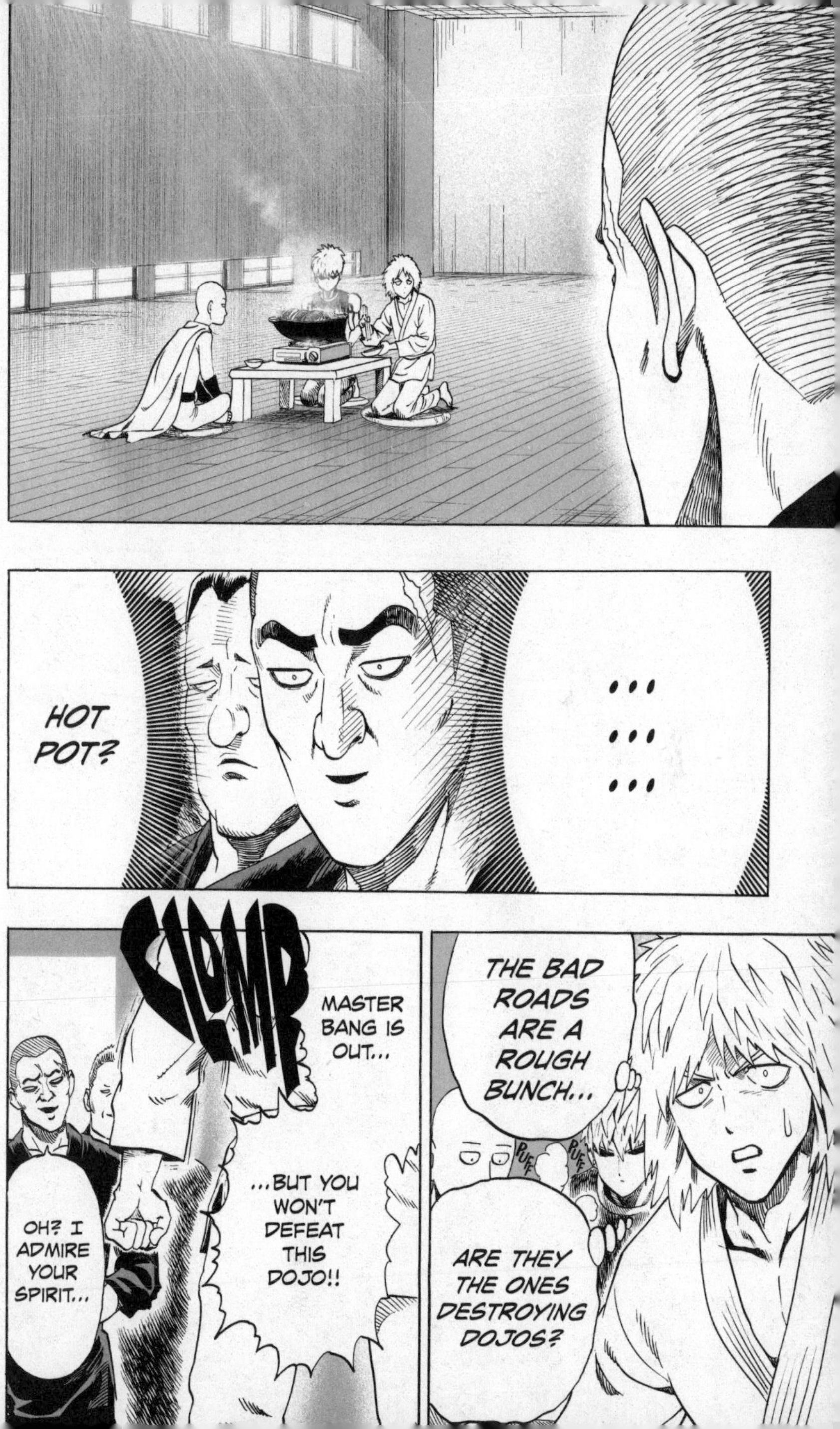
...
...
...
HOT POT?
THE BAD ROADS ARE A ROUGH BUNCH...
PUFF
PUFF
ARE THEY THE ONES DESTROYING DOJOS?
CLOMP
MASTER BANG IS OUT...
...BUT YOU WON'T DEFEAT THIS DOJO!!
OH? I ADMIRE YOUR SPIRIT...

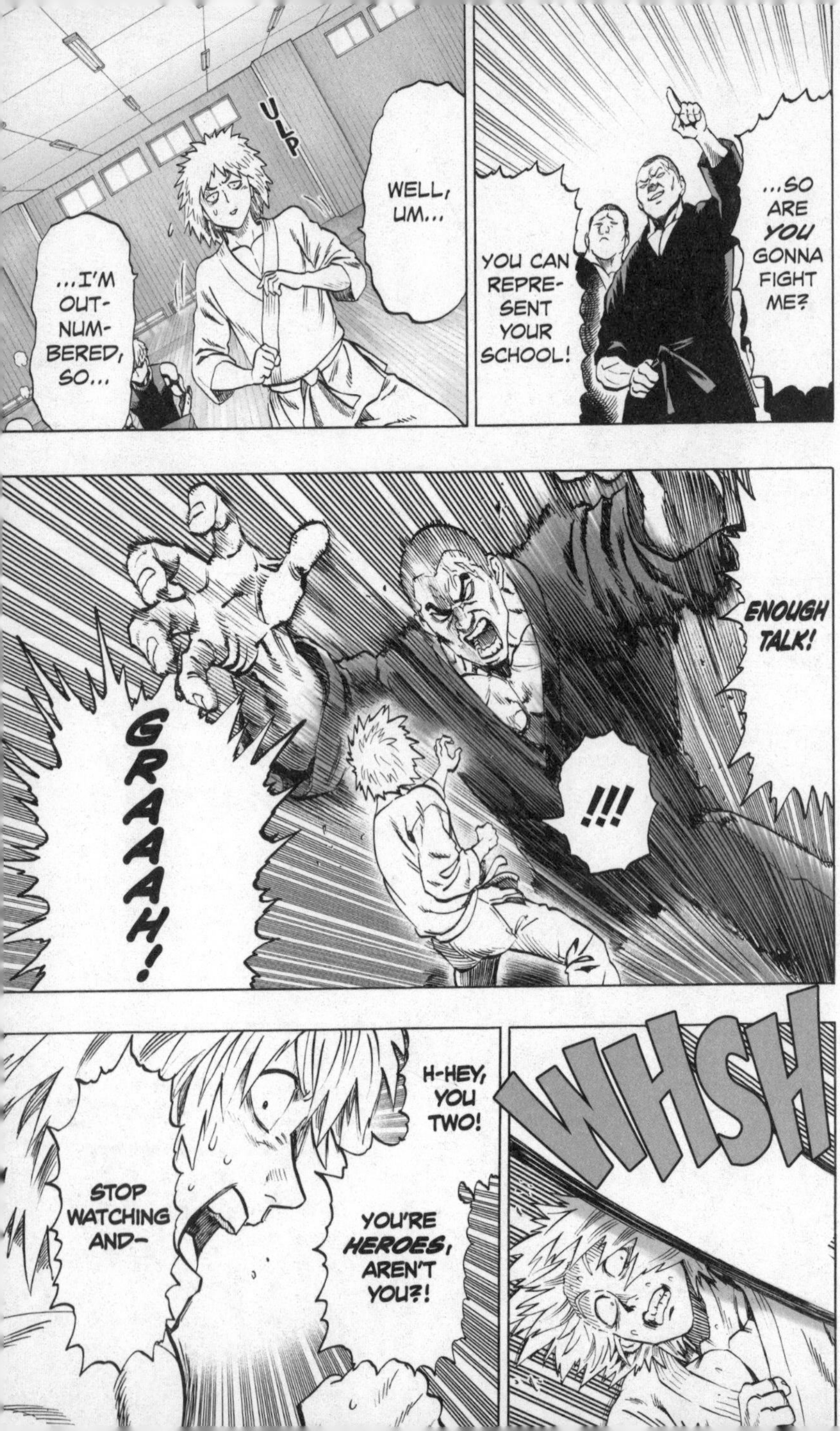
...SO ARE *YOU* GONNA FIGHT ME?
YOU CAN REPRE-SENT YOUR SCHOOL!
ULP
WELL, UM...
...I'M OUT-NUM-BERED, SO...
ENOUGH TALK!
!!!
GRAAAH!
WHSH
H-HEY, YOU TWO!
YOU'RE *HEROES*, AREN'T YOU?!
STOP WATCHING AND-

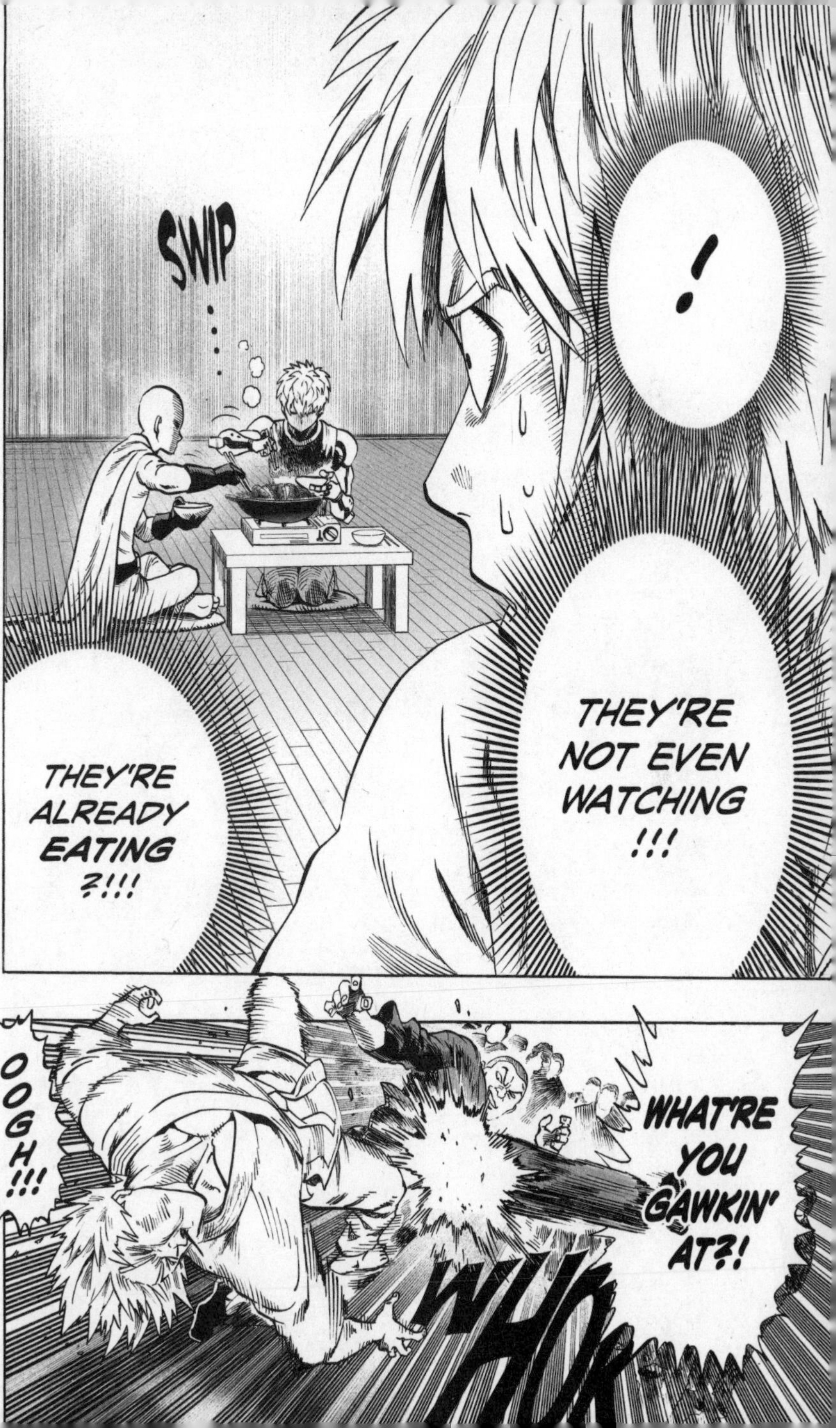
!
SWIP
THEY'RE NOT EVEN WATCHING !!!
THEY'RE ALREADY EATING ?!!!
WHAT'RE YOU GAWKIN' AT?!
OOGH!!!

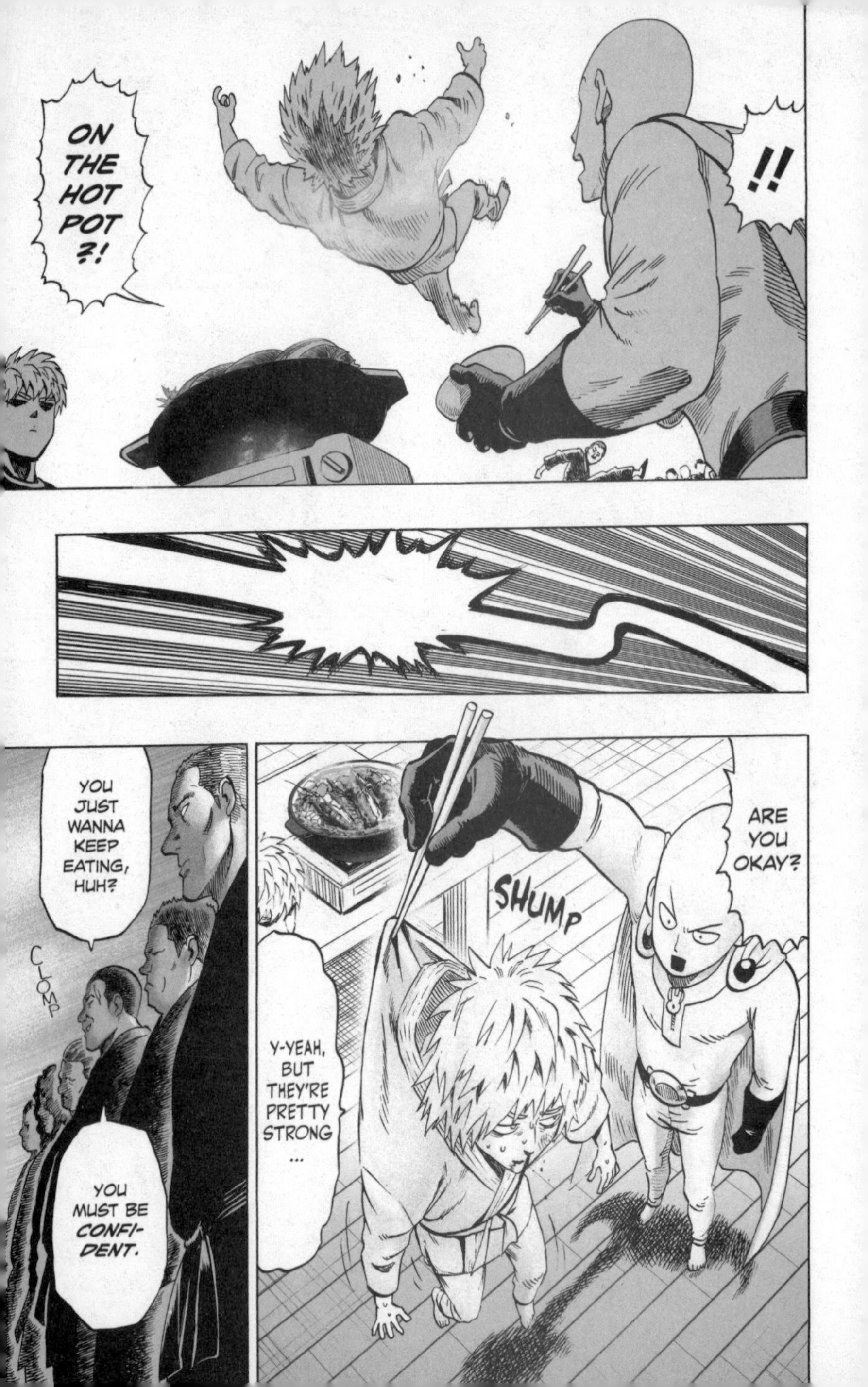
!!
ON THE HOT POT?!
ARE YOU OKAY?
SHUMP
Y-YEAH, BUT THEY'RE PRETTY STRONG...
YOU JUST WANNA KEEP EATING, HUH?
CLOMP
YOU MUST BE CONFIDENT.

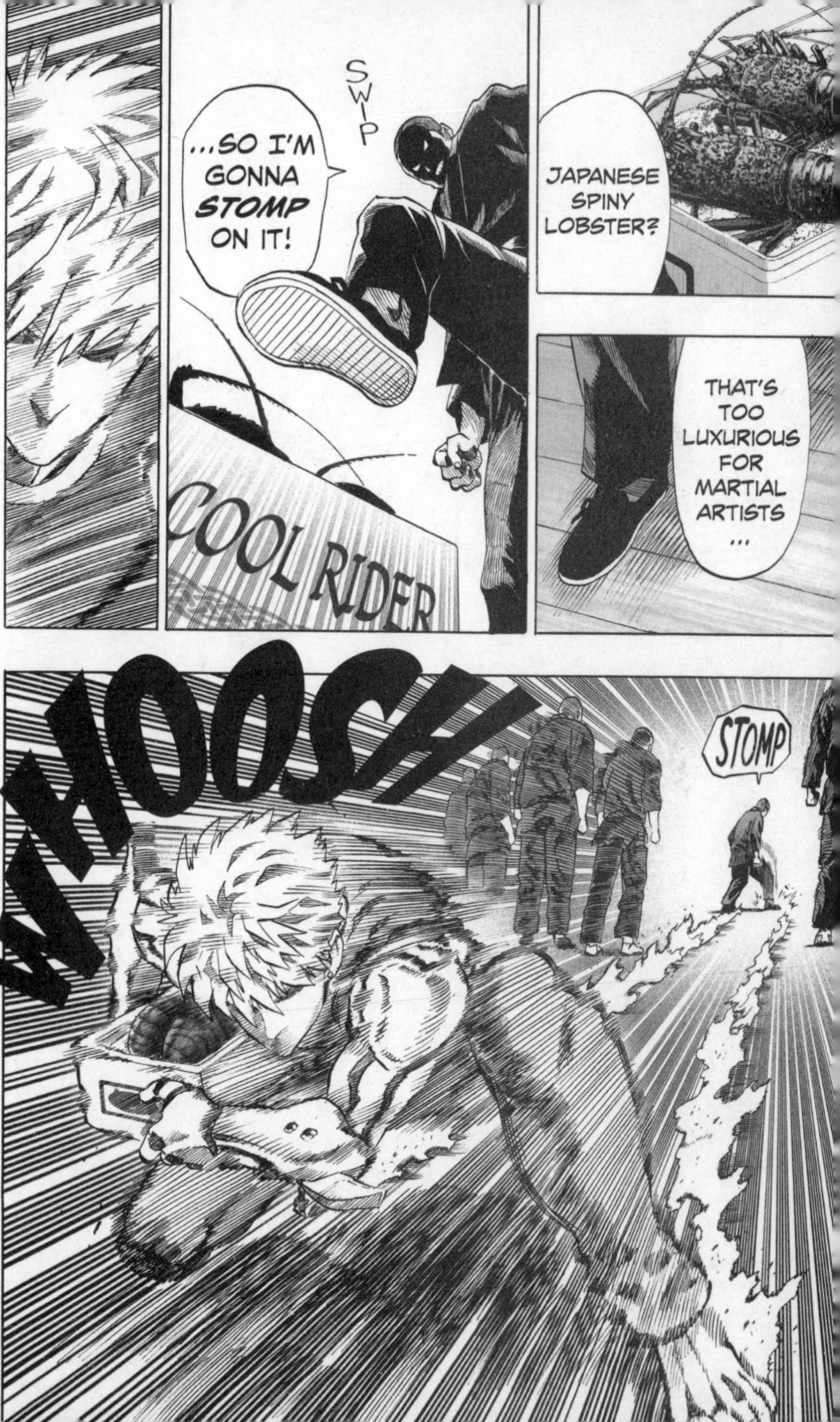
JAPANESE SPINY LOBSTER?
THAT'S TOO LUXURIOUS FOR MARTIAL ARTISTS ...
SWIP
...SO I'M GONNA STOMP ON IT!
COOL RIDER
STOMP
WHOOSH

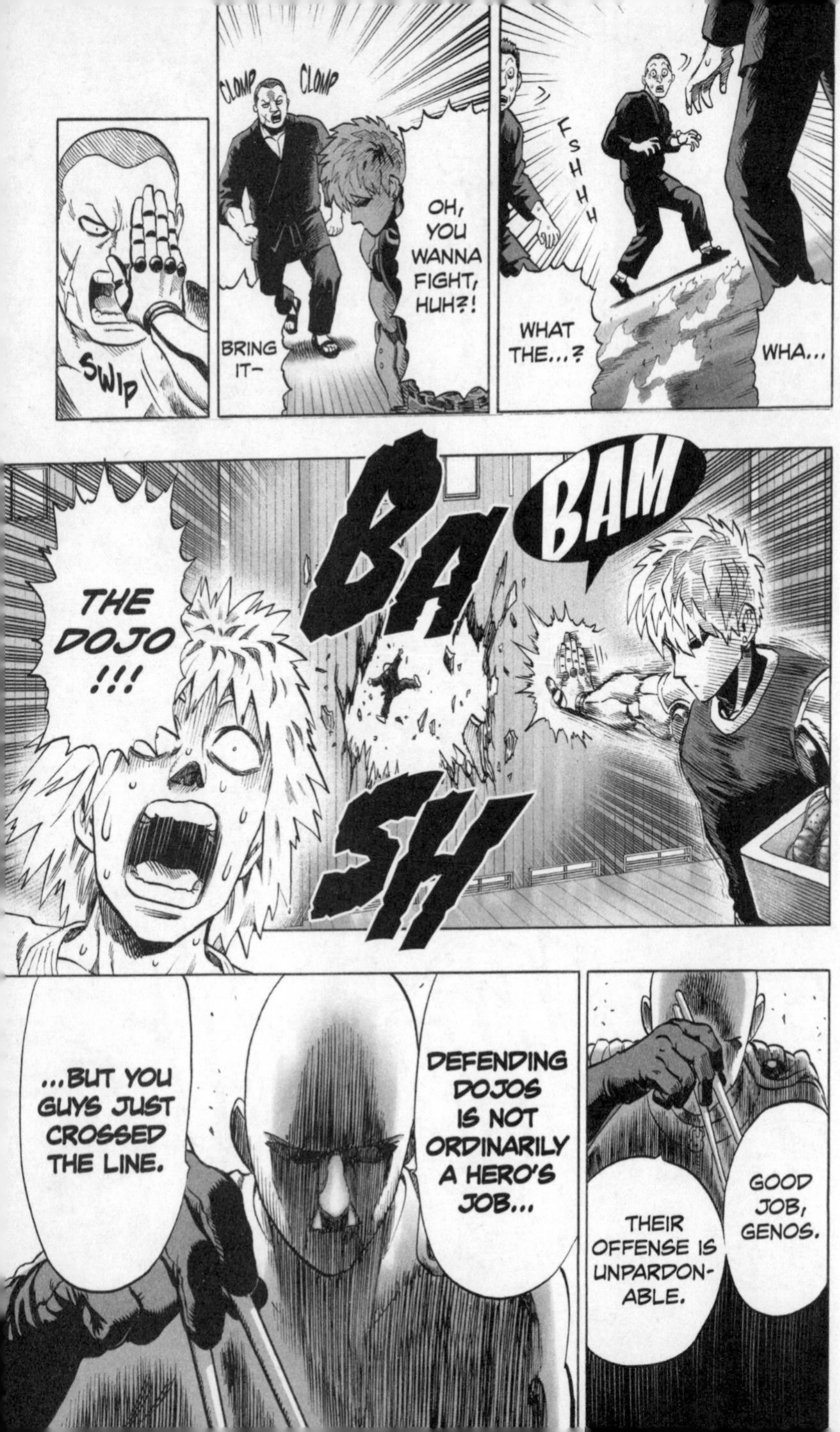

WHA...
FSHHH
WHAT THE...?
CLOMP
CLOMP
OH, YOU WANNA FIGHT, HUH?!
BRING IT-
SWIP
BAM
BASH
THE DOJO!!!
GOOD JOB, GENOS.
THEIR OFFENSE IS UNPARDONABLE.
DEFENDING DOJOS IS NOT ORDINARILY A HERO'S JOB...
...BUT YOU GUYS JUST CROSSED THE LINE.

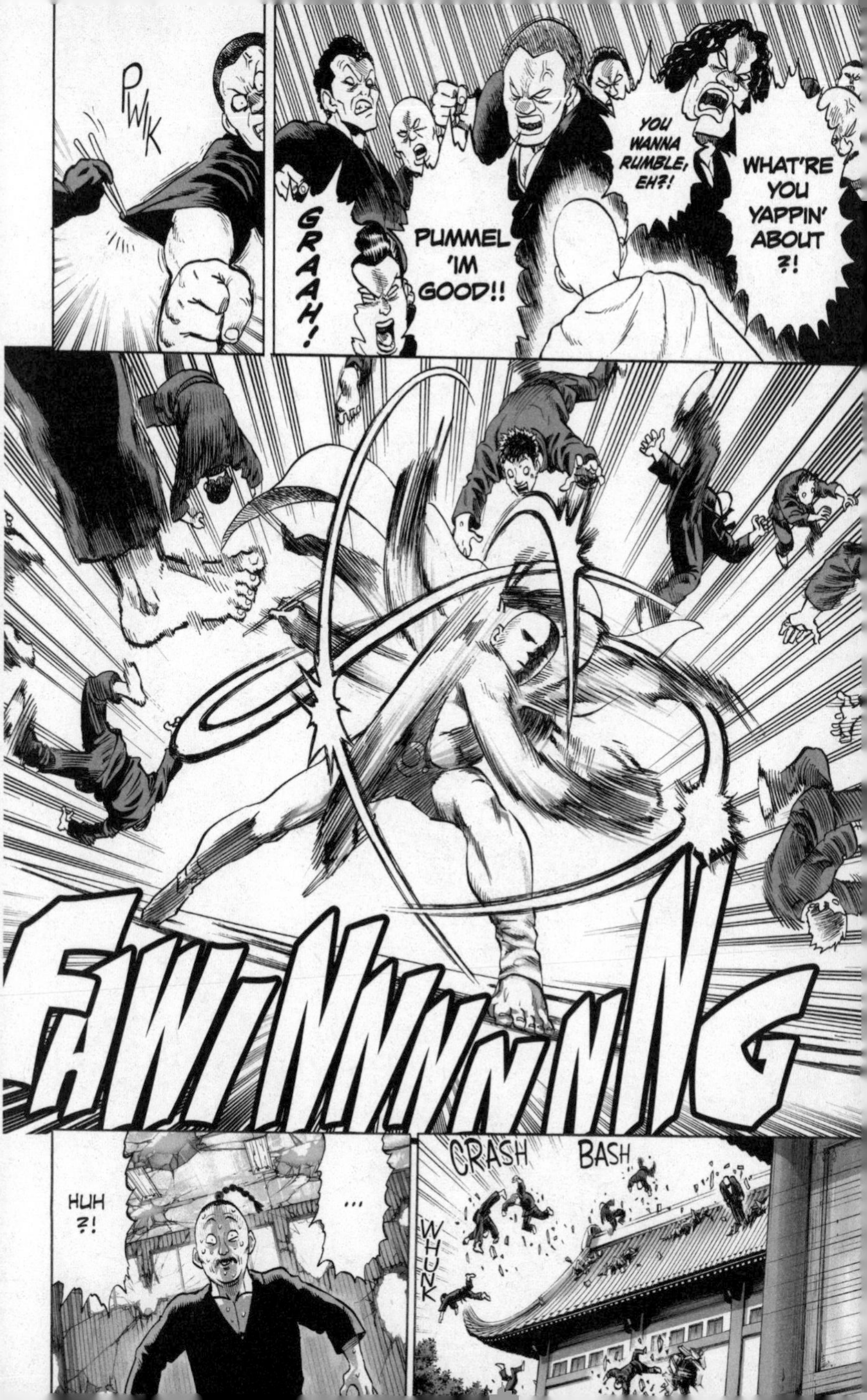
WHAT'RE YOU YAPPIN' ABOUT ?!
YOU WANNA RUMBLE, EH?!
PUMMEL 'IM GOOD!!
GRAAH!
PWIK
FWINNNNNNNNG
CRASH
BASH
WHUNK
...
HUH ?!

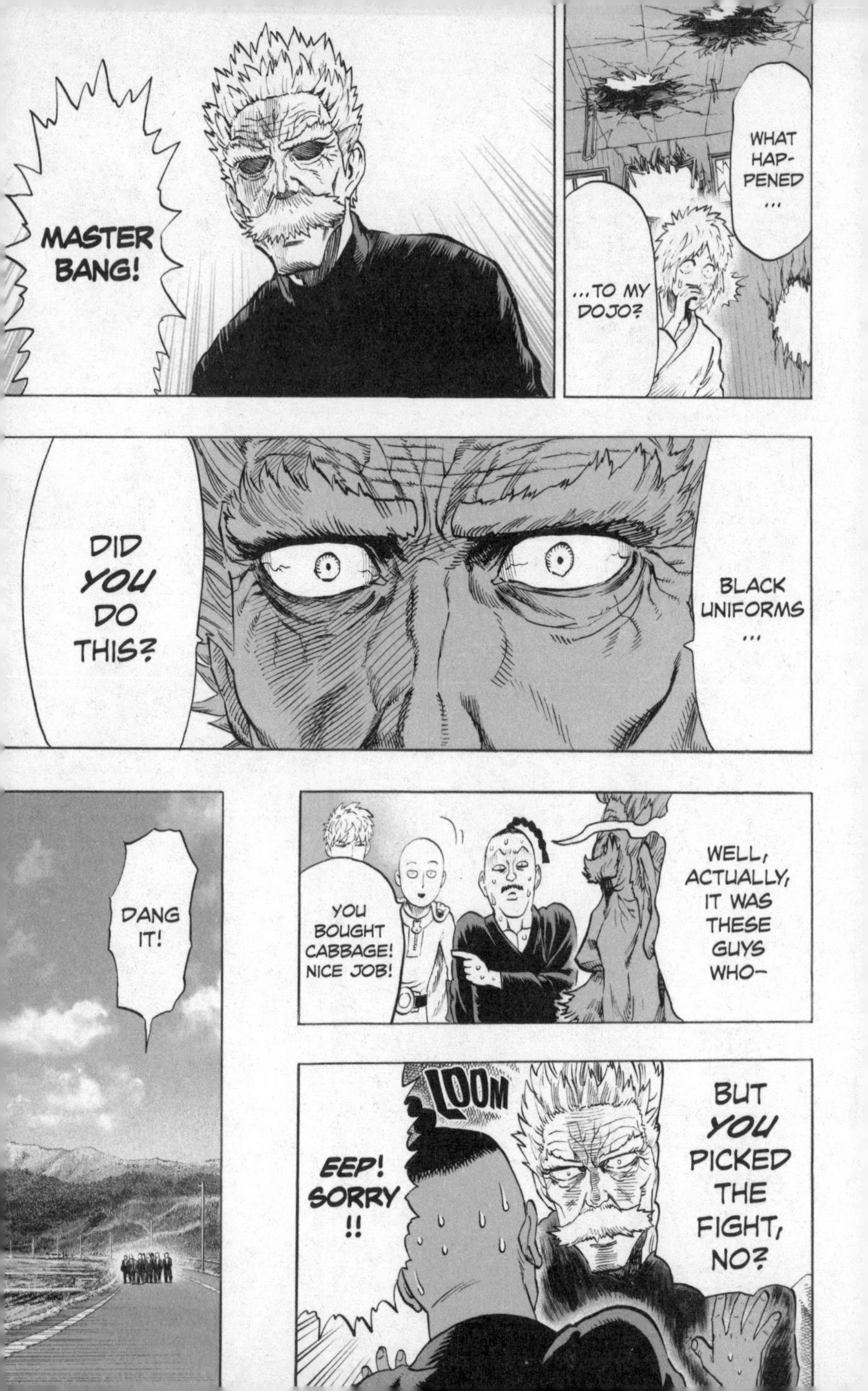
WHAT HAP-PENED ...
...TO MY DOJO?
MASTER BANG!
BLACK UNIFORMS ...
DID *YOU* DO THIS?
WELL, ACTUALLY, IT WAS THESE GUYS WHO-
YOU BOUGHT CABBAGE! NICE JOB!
LOOM
BUT *YOU* PICKED THE FIGHT, NO?
EEP! SORRY !!
DANG IT!

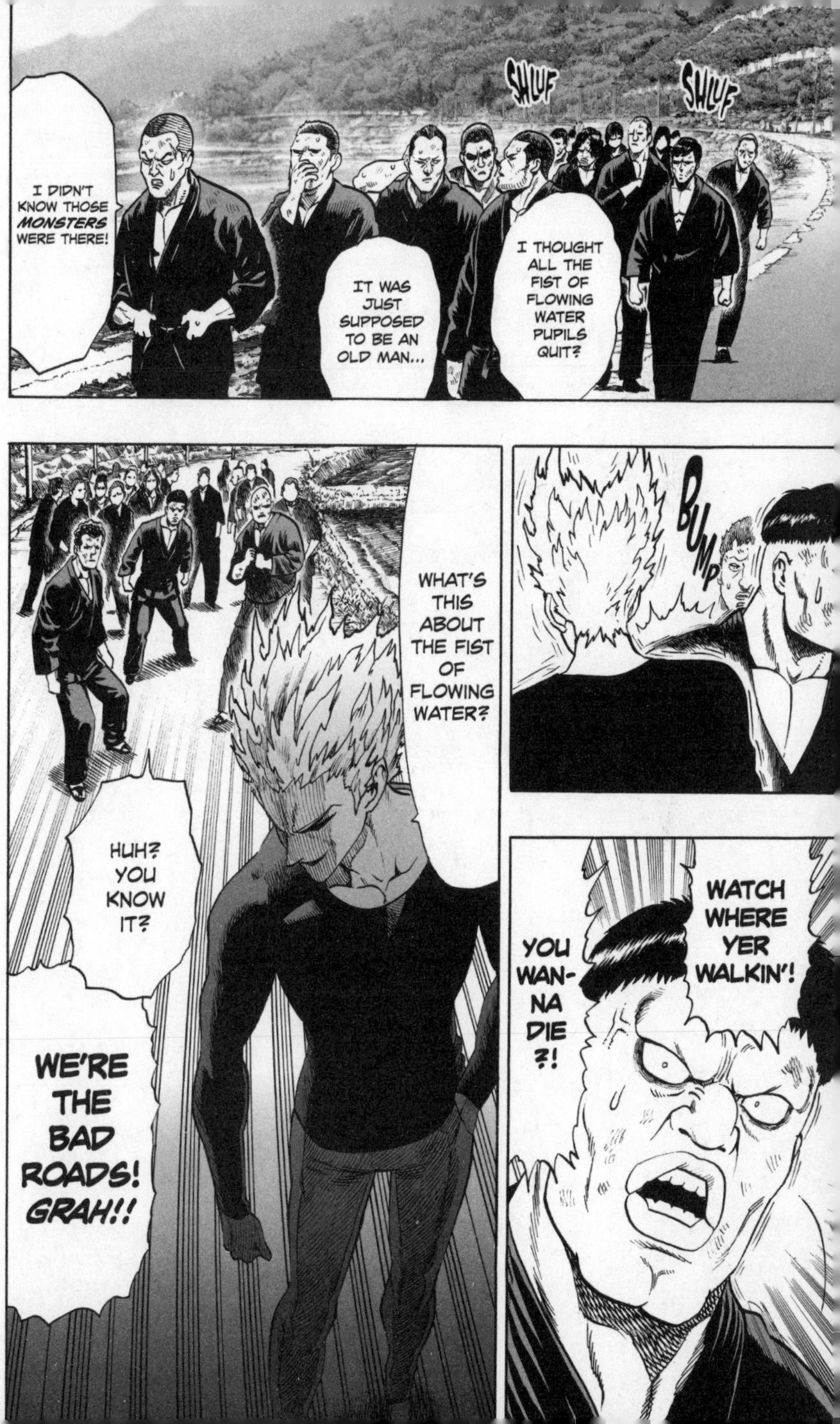
SHLUF
SHLUF
I THOUGHT ALL THE FIST OF FLOWING WATER PUPILS QUIT?
IT WAS JUST SUPPOSED TO BE AN OLD MAN...
I DIDN'T KNOW THOSE *MONSTERS* WERE THERE!
BUMP
WATCH WHERE YER WALKIN'!
YOU WAN-NA DIE?!
WHAT'S THIS ABOUT THE FIST OF FLOWING WATER?
HUH? YOU KNOW IT?
WE'RE THE BAD ROADS! *GRAH!!*

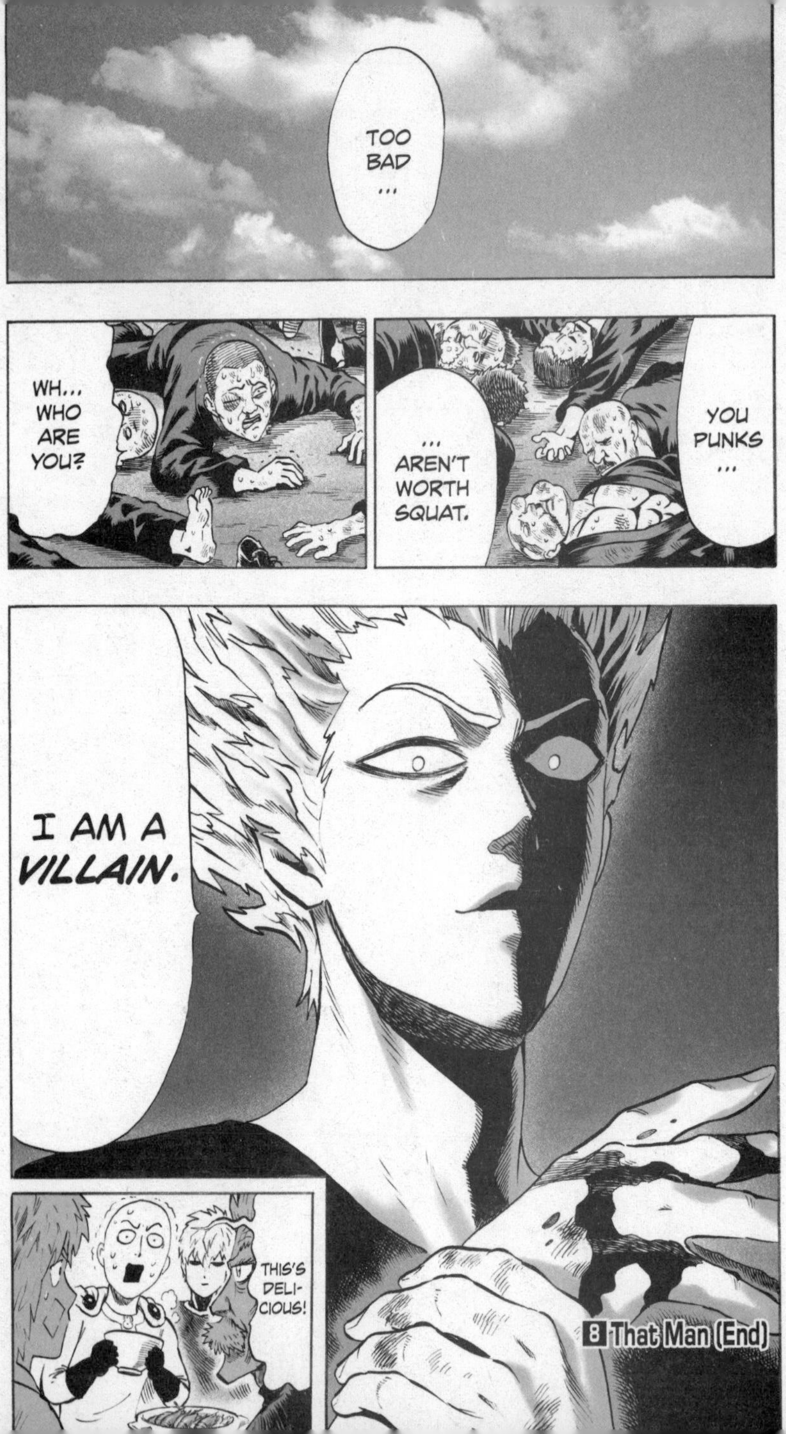
TOO BAD ...
YOU PUNKS ...
... AREN'T WORTH SQUAT.
WH... WHO ARE YOU?
I AM A *VILLAIN.*
THIS'S DELICIOUS!

8 That Man (End)

BONUS

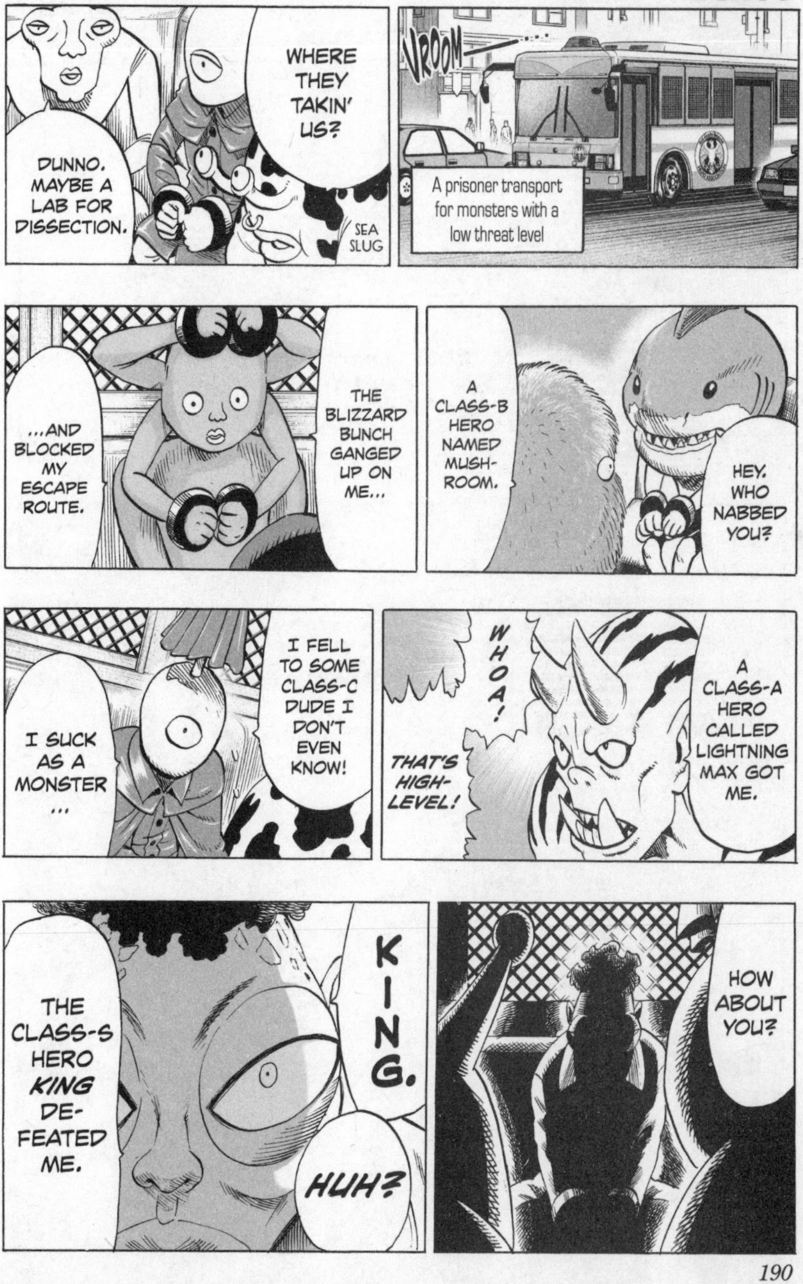
VROOM
A prisoner transport for monsters with a low threat level
WHERE THEY TAKIN' US?
DUNNO. MAYBE A LAB FOR DISSECTION.
SEA SLUG
HEY. WHO NABBED YOU?
A CLASS-B HERO NAMED MUSH-ROOM.
THE BLIZZARD BUNCH GANGED UP ON ME...
...AND BLOCKED MY ESCAPE ROUTE.
A CLASS-A HERO CALLED LIGHTNING MAX GOT ME.
WHOA!
THAT'S HIGH-LEVEL!
I FELL TO SOME CLASS-C DUDE I DON'T EVEN KNOW!
I SUCK AS A MONSTER...
HOW ABOUT YOU?
KING.
THE CLASS-S HERO *KING* DE-FEATED ME.
HUH?

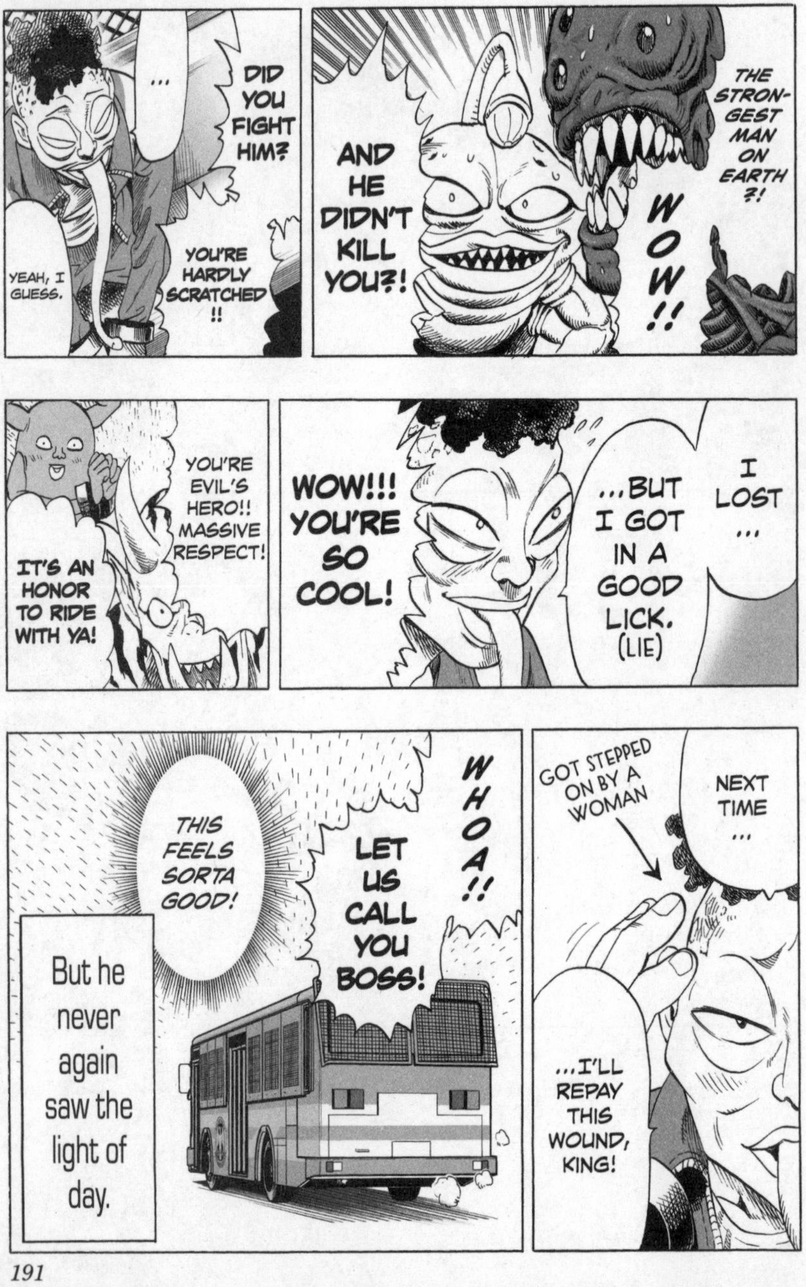
THE STRONGEST MAN ON EARTH?!
WOW!!
AND HE DIDN'T KILL YOU?!
DID YOU FIGHT HIM?
...
YOU'RE HARDLY SCRATCHED!!
YEAH, I GUESS.
I LOST...
...BUT I GOT IN A GOOD LICK. (LIE)
WOW!!! YOU'RE SO COOL!
YOU'RE EVIL'S HERO!! MASSIVE RESPECT!
IT'S AN HONOR TO RIDE WITH YA!
NEXT TIME...
GOT STEPPED ON BY A WOMAN
...I'LL REPAY THIS WOUND, KING!
WHOA!!
LET US CALL YOU BOSS!
THIS FEELS SORTA GOOD!
But he never again saw the light of day.

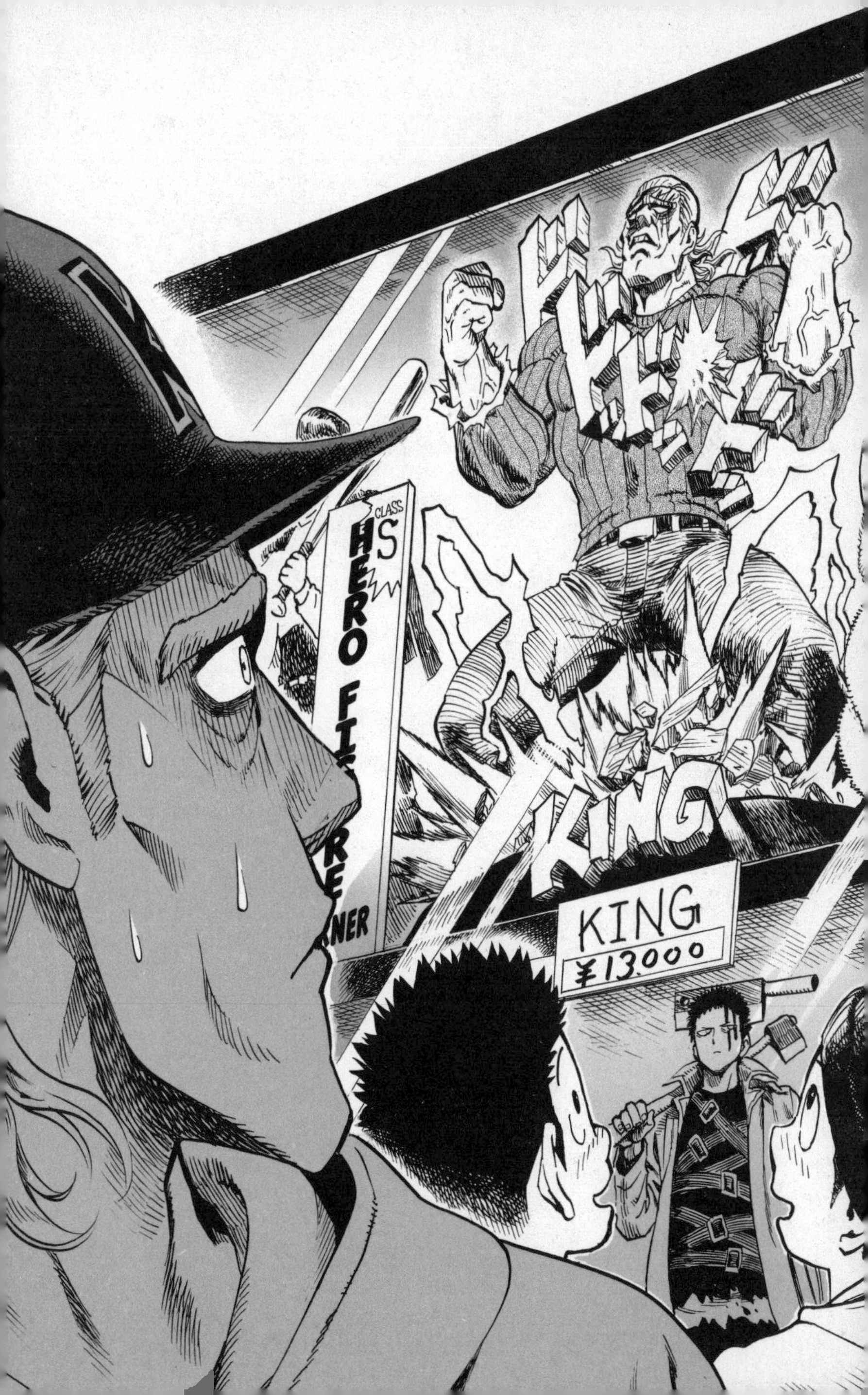
CLASS S
HERO
KING
KING
¥13,000

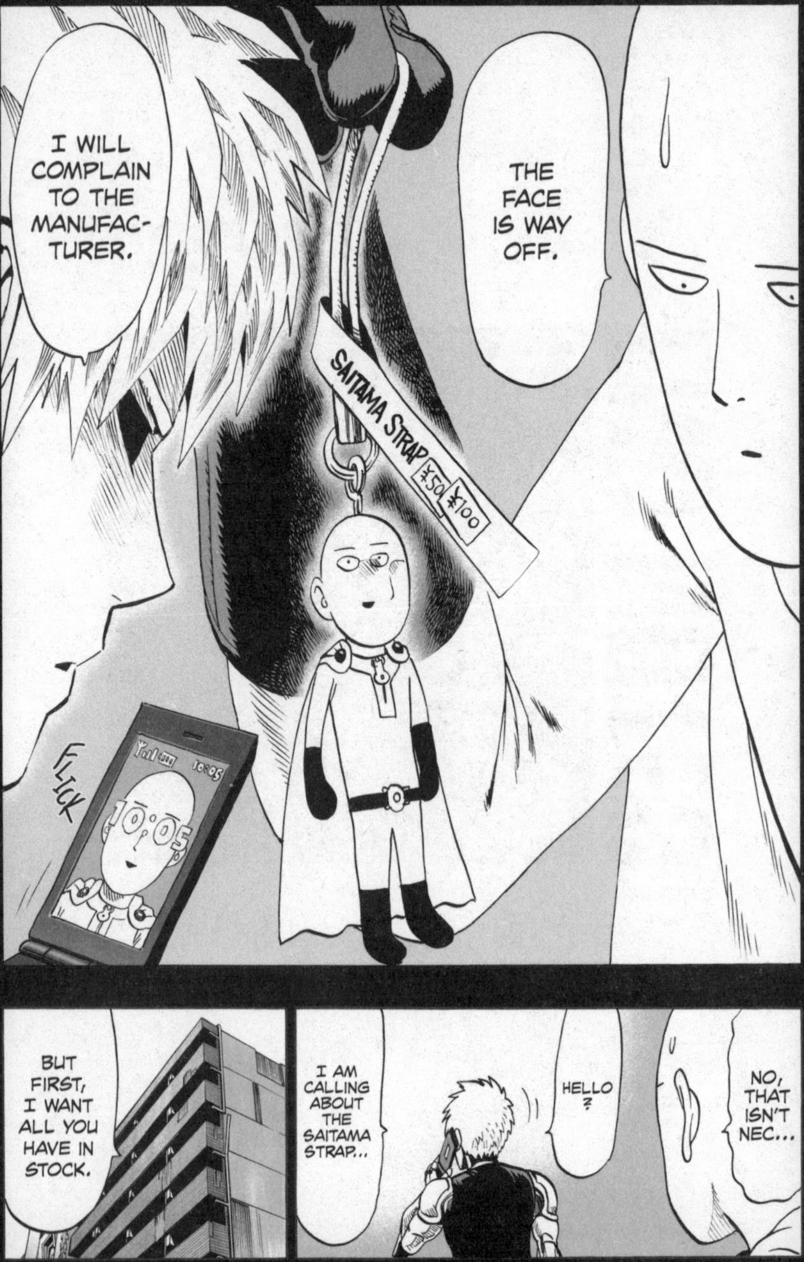
THE FACE IS WAY OFF.
I WILL COMPLAIN TO THE MANUFACTURER.
SAITAMA STRAP
¥50
¥100
FLICK
10:05
NO, THAT ISN'T NEC...
HELLO?
I AM CALLING ABOUT THE SAITAMA STRAP...
BUT FIRST, I WANT ALL YOU HAVE IN STOCK.

END NOTES

PAGE 21:

The meaning of the character printed
all over Saitama's shirt is "hair."

PAGE 172, PANEL 1:

The sign in the dojo says "To persevere."

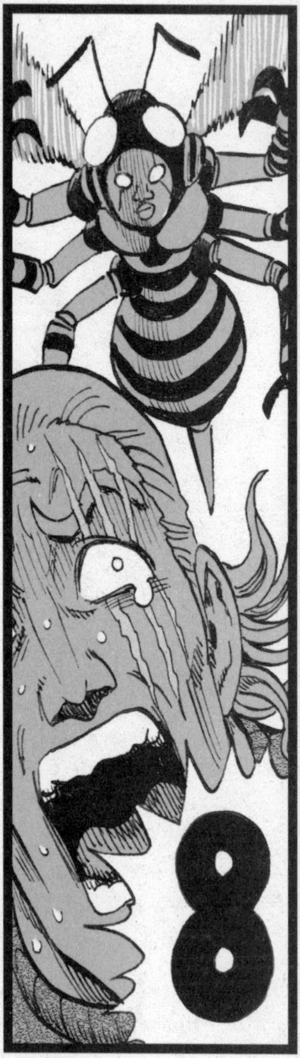
8

ONE-PUNCH MAN

VOLUME 8

SHONEN JUMP MANGA EDITION

STORY BY | ONE
ART BY | YUSUKE MURATA

TRANSLATION | JOHN WERRY
TOUCH-UP ART AND LETTERING | JAMES GAUBATZ
DESIGN | FAWN LAU
SHONEN JUMP SERIES EDITOR | JOHN BAE
GRAPHIC NOVEL EDITOR | JENNIFER LEBLANC

Printed in the U.S.A.

Published by VIZ Media, LLC
P.O. Box 77010
San Francisco, CA 94107

VIZ MEDIA
viz.com

SHONEN JUMP

10 9 8 7 6 5 4 3
First printing, September 2016
Third printing, January 2021

RATED T TEEN ratings.viz.com

PARENTAL ADVISORY
ONE-PUNCH MAN is rated T for Teen and is recommended for ages 13 and up. This volume contains realistic and fantasy violence.

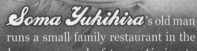
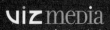

★EYESHIELD 21

STORY BY RIICHIRO INAGAKI
ART BY YUSUKE MURATA

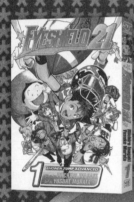

From the artist of *One-Punch Man!*

Wimpy Sena Kobayakawa has been running away from bullies all his life. But when the football gear comes on, things change—Sena's speed and uncanny ability to elude big bullies just might give him what it takes to become a great high school football hero! Catch all the bone-crushing action and slapstick comedy of Japan's hottest football manga!

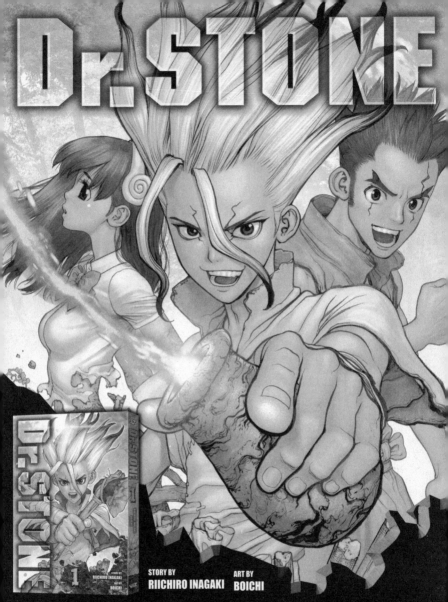

Dr. STONE

STORY BY
RIICHIRO INAGAKI

ART BY
BOICHI

One fateful day, all of humanity turned to stone. Many millennia later, Taiju frees himself from petrification and finds himself surrounded by statues. The situation looks grim—until he runs into his science-loving friend Senku! Together they plan to restart

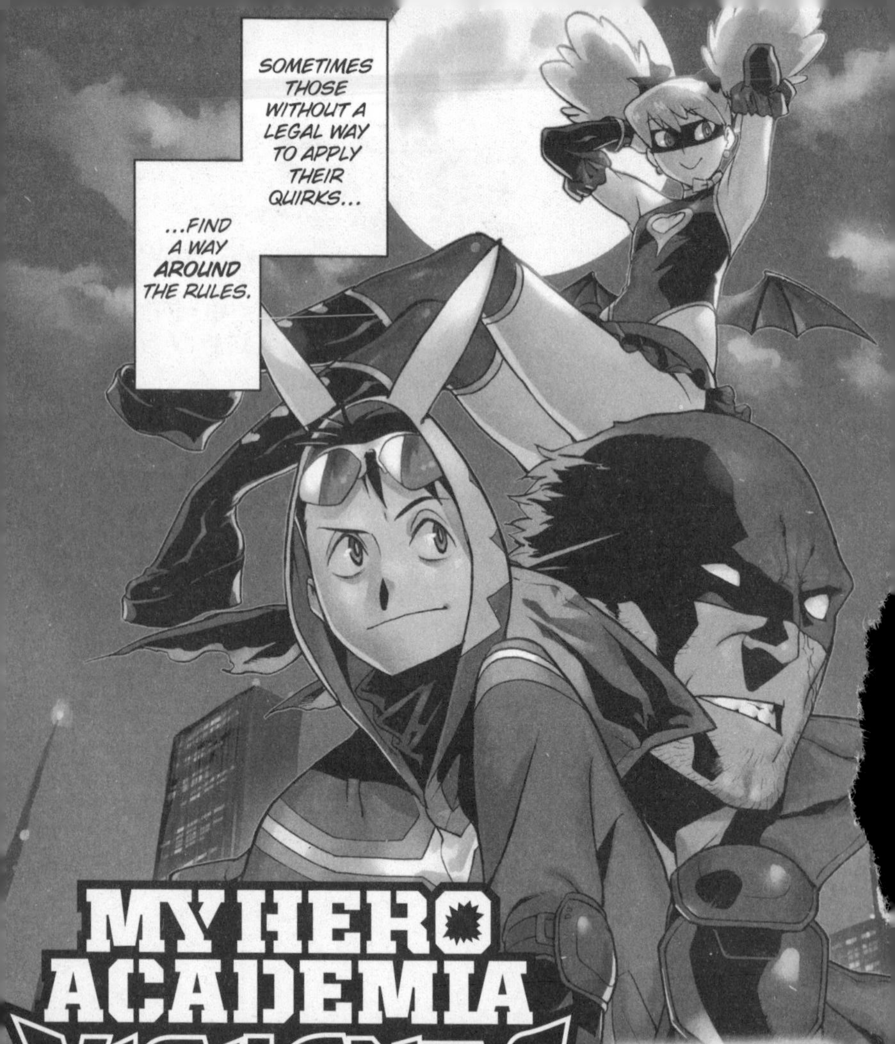
SOMETIMES THOSE WITHOUT A LEGAL WAY TO APPLY THEIR QUIRKS...
...FIND A WAY AROUND THE RULES.
MY HERO ACADEMIA
VIGILANTES

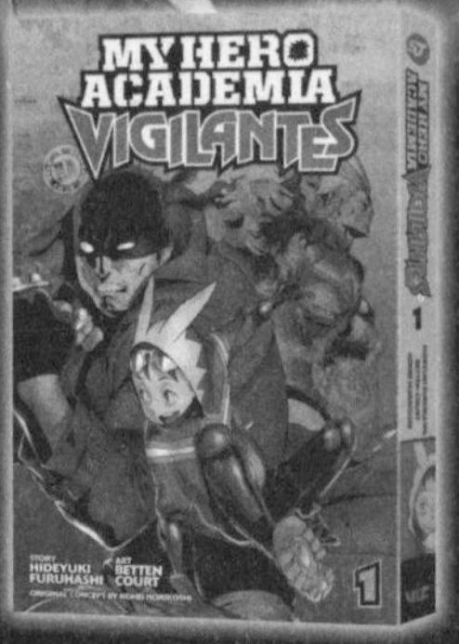
MY HERO ACADEMIA
VIGILANTES
1
STORY HIDEYUKI FURUHASHI
ART BETTEN COURT
1

STOP!

YOU'RE READING THE WRONG WAY!

★ ONE-PUNCH MAN READS FROM RIGHT TO LEFT, STARTING IN THE UPPER-RIGHT CORNER. JAPANESE IS READ FROM RIGHT TO LEFT, MEANING THAT ACTION, SOUND EFFECTS, AND WORD-BALLOON ORDER ARE COMPLETELY REVERSED FROM ENGLISH ORDER.

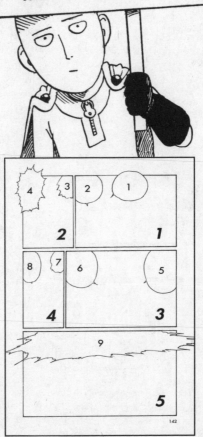